Total Relationship Marketing

This book is dedicated to the future of our daughters Charlotte and Madelene.

Total Relationship Marketing

Second edition

Evert Gummesson

Marketing strategy moving from the 4Ps – product, price, promotion, place – of traditional marketing management to the 30Rs – the thirty relationships – of a new marketing paradigm

OXFORD   AMSTERDAM   BOSTON   LONDON   NEW YORK   PARIS
SAN DIEGO   SAN FRANCISCO   SINGAPORE   SYDNEY   TOKYO

Butterworth-Heinemann
An imprint of Elsevier Science
Linacre House, Jordan Hill, Oxford OX2 8DP
225 Wildwood Avenue, Woburn MA 01801-2041

First published 1999
Reprinted 1999, 2000, 2001
Second edition 2002

British Library Cataloguing in Publication Data
Gummesson, Evert, 1936–
    Total relationship marketing. – 2nd ed.
    1. Relationship marketing   2. Marketing – management
    I. Title
    658.8

Library of Congress Cataloguing in Publication Data
Gummesson, Evert, 1936–
    Total relationship marketing: marketing strategy moving from the 4Ps – product, price,
    promotion, place – of traditional marketing management to the 30Rs – the thirty
    relationships – of a new marketing paradigm/Evert Gummesson. – 2nd ed.
    p. cm.
    Includes bibliographical references and index.
    ISBN 0 7506 5407 4
    1. Relationship marketing   I. Title
    HF5415.55.G86 2002
    658.8'12–dc21   2002074374

ISBN 0 7506 5407 4

For information on all Butterworth-Heinemann publications
visit our website at www.bh.com

Composition by Genesis Typesetting, Laser Quay, Rochester, Kent
Printed and bound in Great Britain by MPG Books Ltd, Bodmin, Cornwall

Contents

Tref — 601
Llwynpia 623

Figures and tables

Tables

Preface and acknowledgements

Relationship marketing (RM) has now become an accepted term in marketing, although it is unclear what its content is, what is mere rhetoric and what is hands-on action in a true relationship spirit. In this second, revised edition, cases, references and concepts have been updated. CRM and e-relationships have been given more space. In the hyped noise from media, consultants, companies – and university professors! – it is difficult to discern what is genuine and sustainable. The book presents my effort to sort this out, expressed as *total relationship marketing*, with the thirty relationships of marketing, the 30Rs, at its core. I do not hesitate to say that this is the most complete attempt so far to cover the topic of RM and CRM on a strategic level and offer the beginnings of a theory.

The seeds to the book started to grow in 1968, when I was hired by a large international management consulting firm. Reality made me brutally aware of the consultants' dependency on networks of long-term relationships. In 1982, I participated in the American Marketing Association (AMA) Conference on Services Marketing. Before flying back, a few restful days in the Everglades of Florida inspired me to see the resemblance between services marketing and the European network approach to business-to-business marketing. My first sketch of a new concept of marketing, based on relationships, networks and interaction, was born.

What I understood intuitively then has taken me decades to deepen and communicate – and I am still in a state of flux. I first presented the ideas at the EMAC (European Marketing Academy) annual conference in Grenoble, France, in 1983, and later at an AMA conference in the US. The audiences were not overly excited. The response from the First Nordic Meeting on Service Management in Helsinki, Finland, was better; I even remember one participant who was enthusiastic. But neither the time, nor my thoughts and my way of presenting them, felt sufficiently mature.

Many have contributed to the development of RM, and many have given me an opportunity to test and elaborate my RM concept. I would like to mention some people, organizations and events in particular; many more are found in the quotations and references of this book. Their reactions to my RM concept cover a wide range from almost embarrassing praise to warnings that I am way out of line. I have listened and tried to understand, but I have the responsibility – as well as the prerogative – to decide what to use and what to reject.

The tentative ideas were published in a report by the Marketing Technology Center (MTC, a Swedish Foundation for linking academe with the business world) and, in 1987, *The Journal of*

Long Range Planning and its Editor Bernard Taylor accepted a revised version of the report for publication. RM then consisted of nine relationships. In 1992, Management Centre Europe invited me to address business executives in Paris, and Christer Engléus of Informationskollegiet asked me to speak to a large audience in Stockholm. The relationships had expanded to twenty-two. Other important opportunities during the 1990s were: the series of International Colloquia in Relationship Marketing; the annual conferences of the EMAC and its recently born cousin ANZMAC (Australia and New Zealand Marketing Academy); the conferences at Humboldt-Universität, Berlin, and University College Dublin, Ireland. The ideas have been tried and developed in numerous presentations for students, academic researchers, business people and government representatives in Europe, North America, Australia and New Zealand.

In annual lectures at Stockholm University, meetings and correspondence, Philip Kotler has offered insightful views. I have had lively debates with George Fisk, Emory University, and Shelby Hunt, Texas Tech University. As RM has partly evolved from services marketing, service management and quality, many researchers from these areas have influenced me. Among them are: Christian Grönroos, Kaj Storbacka and Uolevi Lehtinen, and many other faculty members of the Swedish School of Economics and Business Administration and Tampere University, both in Finland; Bo Edvardsson and his staff at the Service Research Center (CTF), University of Karlstad, Sweden; Len Berry, Texas A&M University, and Parsu Parasuraman, University of Miami, who were early in emphasizing RM in services marketing; Eb Scheuing at St John's University, New York, and consultants and authors Pat Townsend and Joan Gebhardt, particularly through the bi-annual Quality in Services (QUIS) symposium and the International Service Quality Association (ISQA); and Johnny Lindström with his staff at the Swedish Institute for Quality (SIQ), and the Swedish Quality Award has helped to make business see the interdependency between quality and marketing.

Many others have generously given me the opportunity to speak and write about RM or through their dedicated work become sources of inspiration. Among those in the UK are: Martin Christopher, Adrian Payne and other faculty members of the Cranfield School of Management, and David Ballantyne, Monash University, Melbourne, themselves authors of successful books on RM; Bob Johnston, Warwick Business School, then Editor of the *International Journal of Service Industry Management*; Michael Baker, Michael Thomas, Andy Lowe, Mike Saren and Nikos Tzokas, University of Strathclyde; Douglas Brownlie, University of Stirling; Keith Blois, University of Oxford; Colin Armistead, University of Bournemouth; Richard Teare, Oxford Brookes University, Editor of the *International Journal of Contemporary Hospitality Management*; in Ireland, Tony Cunningham and the late Liam Glynn, University College Dublin; in Australia, Louise Young, UTS, Ian Wilkinson, UWS Nepean, and Jay Kandampully, University of Queensland; in New Zealand, Rod Brodie and Richard Brookes, University of Auckland, Brendan Gray, University of Otago; in Canada and Montreal, Ulrike de Brentani, Michèle Paulin and Ronald Ferguson, Concordia University, and at the University of Calgary, Nicole Coviello; in the US, Steve Brown and Mary Jo Bitner, Arizona State University, in connection with service research and an AMA Faculty Consortium; Jag Sheth and Atul Parvatiyar, Emory University, Atlanta; Roland Rust, University of Maryland; and David Bejou, Virginia State University. Others are: Latin American enthusiasts and crusaders Jackie Pels, Universidad Torcuato di Tella, Buenos Aires, Argentina, and Javier Reynoso, ITESM, Monterrey, Mexico; Johan Olaisen and Tor Wallin Andreassen, Norwegian School of Management (BI), Oslo; Willem Verbeke, Erasmus University, The Netherlands, who drew my attention to the conflict between RM and hypercompetition; and Anton Meyer, Ludwig-Maximilians-Universität, Munich, and Brigitte Pfeiffer, who gave me the privilege of addressing the German Marketing Association at its Marketing-Tag.

Among faculty and Ph.D. students at Stockholm University who provided me with material and comments and otherwise supported me, I would like to mention Tony Apéria, Karin Dahlström, Ola Feurst, Maria Frostling-Henningson, Bo Hedberg, Yvonne von Friedrichs-Grängsjö, Richard Gatarski, Bo Lennstrand and Henrik Uggla, and also students of its Marketing Academy; and the visiting researchers Kazimierz Rogozinski, Academia Ekonomiczna, Poznan, Poland, and Akiko Fujioka, Kyoto, Japan.

A large number of practitioners, particularly those who have engaged me in consulting and speaking assignments, have kept me in touch with the down to earth questions of marketing or contributed innovative ideas. In particular, I want to mention the support from Björn Wolrath, former CEO of Skandia, and his staff members Leif Edvinsson and Kjell Ängelid; Åke Ortmark, business reporter, author and TV personality; long-time friend and marketing strategist Carl-Gunnar Thor; and Caroline Monthelie, Loyalty Partners. The cooperation with MTC over the years and its current head Göran Liljegren has been important, in particular when we co-hosted the 8th International Colloquium in Relationship Marketing in 2000.

Through his intellect and friendship, Barney Glaser, together with Anselm Strauss, the originator of grounded theory, has enhanced my theoretical and methodological sensitivity, as well as given me courage to pursue my own research strategy. Within its spirit I consider all research a temporary stop – it is search and re-search and re-search in a never-ending journey. Knowledge development in practical work in learning organizations as well as scholarly research can only humbly report progress and should not boast about conclusive results. RM and CRM will not only be the object of development for the coming decades, but also of controversies and competition between professors, consultants and authors.

Evert Gummesson
Stockholm University, School of Business, SE-10691 Stockholm, Sweden
eg@fek.su.se; www.fek.su.se/home/eg/
February 2002

Introduction

The purpose of this book is to contribute to a more realistic approach to marketing management and current and future conditions. It addresses the question: 'What do you learn if you look at marketing as relationships, networks and interaction, and what can you do with this knowledge?' This way of approaching marketing is referred to as relationship marketing (RM), and within this concept the topical issues of CRM and one-to-one marketing belong.

The book has been written for all those who want to develop their knowledge of marketing – practitioners, students and academic researchers. As marketing management permeates every activity in today's business – and not only the marketing and sales departments – this book will be of particular interest to top executives and managers of all types of functions.

Chapter 1 is an introduction to RM and its thirty relationships, the 30Rs, prevalent in business. This is by far the broadest and most comprehensive framework of RM that has been designed; hence the reference to total relationship marketing. Each relationship is then covered in detail in Chapters 2–5. Chapter 6 is about return on relationships (ROR), that is, the financial effects of RM and the effects on relationship-oriented marketing and business planning. Chapter 7 deals with RM and new organizational formats, captured under the term network organization; the chapter also puts RM and its organization in the context of the market economy. Chapter 8 covers theories and experiences that were the foundation of RM, describes how RM and CRM have emerged from these, and how a new general marketing theory can be discerned. The book concludes with Chapter 9, a summary of the contributions from RM and CRM to a paradigm shift in marketing.

The structure of the book, particularly the presentation of the 30Rs, is, in a sense, encyclopaedic – a hypertext in modern terminology – which gives readers the option to look up what they are interested in without having to read every page in sequence from cover to cover.

Chapter

1

Rethinking marketing

What are RM, CRM and 1to1?

INTRODUCTION

In this chapter, the purpose and outline of the book are presented, and the concepts of relationship marketing (RM), customer relationship management (CRM) and one-to-one marketing (1to1) are introduced. Certain basics of marketing are treated, together with the significance of common sense, the ability to see marketing from different perspectives – through the 'relationship eye-glasses' – and to adjust to a paradigm shift in marketing. The chapter ends with an overview of general characteristics of relationships and a summary of the thirty relationships of RM, the 30Rs.

My definition of relationship marketing (RM) is as follows:

> Relationship marketing is marketing based on interaction within networks of relationships.

The concept of RM spread like wildfire during the 1990s. In its wake followed first 1to1, then CRM. The last two concepts represent the same basic thinking; together with less known designations they are brands for offerings from various consultants. Today, CRM is the most frequently used term, but as late as 1998 it was only one of several acronyms that fought for attention. RM is the broader, overriding concept. CRM and 1to1 do not deal with networks but focus on the customer–supplier interaction.[1]

My definition of CRM follows from the RM definition:

> CRM is the values and strategies of relationship marketing – with particular emphasis on customer relationships – turned into practical application.

Let's now look at the core concepts that constitute RM: relationships, networks and interaction.

Relationships require at least two parties who are in contact with each other. The basic relationship of marketing is that between a supplier and a customer (Figure 1.1).

---

[1] Peppers and Rogers launched 1to1 in 1993 and have since, with a great ardour, built a publishing and consulting business around the concept; see Peppers, Rogers and Dorf (1998) and Peppers and Rogers (1999). For more on 1to1 and CRM, see Newell (2000); and specifically CRM, see Pricewaterhouse-Coopers (1999) and Ryals and Payne (2001).

Figure 1.1 The basic marketing relationship

Figure 1.2 A network of relationships

A *network* is a set of relationships which can grow into enormously complex patterns. The graphic pattern of a network is shown in Figure 1.2. In the relationships, the simple dyad as well as the complex networks, the parties enter into active contact with each other. This is called *interaction*.

Two experiences in particular drew my attention to the importance of relationships in marketing.

The first dates back to 1968. Just hired by a large international management consulting firm, one of my tasks, besides doing consulting assigments, was to sell the services of a group of consultants. My knowledge of marketing was based on textbooks used in business school education and practical experience as a marketing manager of consumer goods. I was taken by surprise when realizing that the consulting company did little or nothing that the books prescribed. No explicit marketing strategy, no marketing organization, no marketing planning, no marketing research, no specialized sales force, no advertising, no public relations.

Should the fresh consultant tell the CEO the bad news – that they were doing everything wrong – followed by the good news: I'm here to set it right? There was a disturbing fact, though. The company was making a profit and expanding. It must be doing something right.

Through observation and advice from senior colleagues – one had worked for fourteen years as consultant to the same large corporation – I learnt that one thing in particular mattered beside the professional knowledge: the network of relationships that the individual consultants belonged to through professional achievements, birth or membership. And furthermore, relationships were equally important internally when consultants were selected by their colleagues to staff new assignments.

> Creating and maintaining a network of relationships – outside as well as inside the company – constituted the core marketing of the consulting firm. Advertising, public relations, image-building and other marketing activities could be supportive, but they could not be the core activities.

Another significant experience occurred twelve years later while working for Ericsson. The then CEO, Björn Svedberg, commissioned an assignment with the following words: 'Evert, explain to us what we are actually doing in our marketing and selling!' A supplier of telecom equipment and systems worldwide, Ericsson is currently best known for market leadership in mobile telephone systems and an alliance with Sony. Each sale was large, complex, high tech and long term. A major marketing strategy – although it was not officially perceived as such – was the creation and maintenance of long-term relationships with a few large telecom operating companies, as well as the cultivation of relationships with research institutions, own suppliers, government agencies, politicians, banks, investors, the media and others. The relationships concerned many people in several tiers and functions within the customers' organizations and also within Ericsson's own organization.

> Ericsson's success was based on a combination of state-of-the-art technology and a well-developed network of relationships.

These two experiences taught me a very obvious and common sense lesson: when your current real world experience clashes with your previous experience and received theories, rethink! Simply put:

| INSIGHT | When – after careful scrutiny – you find that the terrain differs from your map, trust the terrain and your own judgement! |

A management consulting company is a service operation, involved in business-to-business marketing (B-to-B), but not in business-to-consumer marketing (B-to-C). Ericsson is a combination of manufacturing and services in B-to-B, but indirectly dependent on the purchasing behaviour of its customers' customers, eventually the consumer. Although the frameworks presented in marketing books claimed to be universally valid, they dealt with consumer goods marketing: cola drinks, painkillers, cookies and cars. Contrary to common belief, consumer goods marketing is the smallest part of all marketing; services marketing and B-to-B account for the major share. The books did not include services, and only marginally included B-to-B. There was not a word about relationships – and there still is very little! The textbooks diverted the mind from substantive and significant issues.

Today, RM and CRM are beginning to provide a framework for such marketing situations as described by the two experiences. But their applicability has also invaded B-to-C. RM is becoming a general marketing approach. It offers a paradigm shift in marketing. Here are some more examples of the variety of marketing situations in which relationships are crucial:

- Christer, who runs the locally well-known and highly esteemed Ulla Winbladh Inn, Stockholm, Sweden, is always present and has an apartment above the restaurant. He keeps a close watch on guests and employees and senses the atmosphere, making sure that everything runs smoothly. He knows many of the guests and makes them personally welcome. 'You must like your guests,' he says. 'If you don't, the job is impossible.'
- In a few years Amazon.com became one of the world's largest bookstores. Founder Jeff Bezos used the opportunities inherent in the new infrastructural network of the Internet to reach out globally, create an individual relationship with each customer, and effectively interact with customers. As a customer you can not only order books but also read book reviews from other readers and write your own reviews. Amazon is a learning network which registers which type of books you order and offers you new books within your profile.
- Instead of letting a large number of suppliers fight for contracts at lowest price, companies increasingly choose to develop intimate relationships with a limited number of suppliers. In the 1990s, Motorola cut the number of suppliers by 70 per cent, 3M by 64 per cent and Ford by 45 per cent. Information technology (IT) can facilitate the creation of close customer–supplier networks. An extreme example is Procter & Gamble, the world's largest producer of packaged consumer goods, who has joined forces with Wal-Mart, the world's largest retailer. They have set up an information system which coordinates online the production and delivery of the goods with the sales in the stores.
- Resources are increasingly being built through networks of cooperating companies. In the early 1990s, IBM had formed alliances with several of its major customers, competitors and suppliers. Some of the most important were Toshiba (joint factory in Japan for colour screens), Mitsubishi (selling IBM mainframes in Japan under its own name), Intel (joint development of

chips), Apple (joint development of operative systems and technology for the integration of sound, data, graphics and video), Lotus (IBM being an agent for Lotus software), Sears (joint ownership of Prodigy, software for home shopping) and Siemens (joint development of chips). Furthermore, IBM North America cooperated with some 4000 companies.[2]

- Denmark's grand industrialist, the now 87-year-old Maersk McKinney Møller, mixes with kings and queens, presidents, government members and the world's most powerful business leaders. As a personal friend of Thomas Watson – the man who turned IBM into the world's largest computer company – he served for many years as the only non-American on the board of directors of IBM. His personal and social relationships on a mega level – his 'non-market network' – make it possible for him to direct conditions in the market in his favour. These people are socially empowered to influence regulations, provide financial assistance, bypass gatekeepers and expedite bureaucratic procedures. They also have access to privileged information.

These examples give glimpses of the significance of relationships, networks and interaction, through personal contact and IT, at grass roots and government level, in small local businesses and global giants, and in diverse types of countries and cultures.

In the first two examples individual relationships are in focus. It is important that the guests enjoy the Ulla Winbladh and keep coming back. Long-term customer relationships are created with loyal consumers who speak well of the inn to friends and acquaintances. Whereas the success of an inn is based on human relationships (h-relationships), the second example, Amazon, brings us into the new economy and its most holy chamber, that of the World Wide Web and the Internet. Here, the focus is on electronic relationships (e-relationships). These two examples epitomize customer retention, customer loyalty, referrals and word of mouth, that is, what CRM and 1to1 are mainly about.

But RM reaches further than that. The third example shows that it can be efficient for companies to have few or even a single supplier and to have few customers. Collaboration becomes a key marketing strategy. By linking their order and delivery systems, they cement sustaining relationships; the relationships become part of their organizations' structural capital. Transaction costs are kept down as selling, purchasing and invoicing become streamlined.

The fourth example shows that not even global giants like American IBM, Japanese Toshiba and German Siemens can develop, manufacture and market their products and services on their own. They enter into alliances with customers, competitors, distributors and others to gain time and cost advantages and to access markets. The corporations add to each other's resources for the benefit of all stakeholders.

---

[2] Based on a *Fortune* article (Kirkpatrick, 1992, p. 120).

In the last example, relationships are formed on a level above the market proper. Certain conditions have to be fulfilled to allow presence in the market. Royalty, politicians, ambassadors, government officials and others are engaged to create these conditions. It happens on a mega level where friendship and political support play a decisive role for marketing success.

The book is about these and other relationships. The relationships will be listed, described, analysed, illustrated and discussed. RM is not just another bag of tricks to capture customers, it offers a wide range of conditions for more efficient management and marketing – and opportunities of making money. This will be elaborated on throughout the book.

In the late 1990s, half of the large US corporations ('the *Fortune* 500') had Relationship Managers and the number is probably growing.[3] Key Account Managers (KAMs) who are in charge of large B-to-B customers, as well as CRM managers to handle the transition to CRM-systems, have grown in numbers. These positions, however, are only the beginning; RM and CRM have to permeate the whole organization and its culture to become effective.

The concept of *The New Economy* became a household term at the turn of the millennium. But what was it actually? The question is relevant, but there is no good answer. As has happened to many of the recent terms and concepts, its glory has faded. However, the phenomena it attempted to represent have not disappeared, even though the dotcom hype has cooled down. We have a host of other concepts. The post-industrial society tells us what we are running away from but not where we are heading. The service society, the knowledge society and the information age all centre around a resource or a product.

I prefer to talk about society in two complementary dimensions. One is *the value society*, stressing value creation as the desirable outcome of economic activity and consumption. As consumers and citizens, we are not specifically looking for goods, services, knowledge or information. We want something of value. Value is commercially offered on the market by suppliers. Especially in services and often in B-to-B, customers are co-producers. Much of the value is our own creation; what we do for family and friends, and do-it-yourself, now moving from painting our own house to self-service on the Internet.

The other dimension is *the network society*, stressing the overriding structure of organizations and society. Companies and markets are networks of relationships within which we interact, completely in accordance with the definition of RM. Manuel Castells describes the network society in three thick volumes, which have received global accolade. He speaks about the corporation as 'the network enterprise': 'Networks are the fundamental stuff of which new organizations are and will be made.'[4]

---

[3] Whiting (1998).
[4] Castells (1996; quotation from p. 168).

RM and CRM operate within the spirit of the value and network societies. It does not mean throwing the Old Economy overboard. It simply means that some things disappear and new things arrive. We are dealing with elusive phenomena such as everything goes faster and faster; globalization with ever-growing transnational corporations and alliances; the European Union (EU), and most recently the euro replacing Deutschmarks, Finnish marks, guilders, lire, Irish pounds and other currencies (whoever understands what all this will mean in practice until it is too late); the aftermath of the often clumsy efforts to deregulate and privatize; the ever-increasing importance of intangible values such as knowledge and brands; and the whole of the IT evolution. Networks with blurred boundaries between a company, its market and society display the whole of management and business in a new light.

Society is a network of relationships – and so is business!

Relationships are at the core of human behaviour. If we dissolve the social networks of relationships, we dissolve society and the earth is left with a bunch of hermits. In that case no marketing is needed, for two reasons. The short-term reason is that hermits live alone. They breed their own sheep for wool, cheese and meat, they grow their own vegetables, and they tailor their own clothes, if any. They do not need mobile phones because there is no one to call. No market for Nokia.

The long-term reason is that the human race will be extinct after one generation. But if it is true that nature has a genetic urge for multiplication, couples and families will spring up and the atomistic world of individuals will turn into a growing network of relationships.

As citizens and family members we are surrounded by relationships in our daily lives. We have relationships at work, with neighbours, with stores and other providers. Driving a car is a complex social interaction with other drivers in a network of roads.

People have girlfriends and boyfriends, go steady, marry, have an affair, divorce. Many have used matrimony as a metaphor for commercial relationships: to enter into marriage with a customer or to divorce a supplier. 'Business dancing' has been suggested as another metaphor.[5] Dancing is a dynamic relationship. You can invite somebody to dance with you. It can be a smooth waltz, but you can also step on your partner's toes. Peters[6] makes it even more dramatic: 'Today's global economic dance is no Strauss waltz. It's break dancing accompanied by street rap. The effective firm is much more like carnival in Rio than a pyramid along the Nile.'

Relationships are central for business people. Craftsmen exchange services with other craftsmen whom they know and trust. The first thing I heard about business was that you need

---

[5] Wilkinson and Young (1994).
[6] Peters (1992, p. 17).

to be well connected, and that it helps to have relatives in high places and to belong to the right clubs. People who knew each other did business and then the seller wined and dined the buyer. As individuals, we voluntarily enter formal relationships through associations. Rotary, for example, brings people together from different trades and professions. The Rotarians get to know each other and business relationships are facilitated by the long-term friendship that develops among them.

Marketing and business are subsets or properties of society. In practice, relationships, networks and interaction have been at the core of business since time immemorial.

Relationships have certainly not gone unnoticed by business people.[7] For example, Ericsson has expanded and remodelled its network for 125 years. The sad story is that relationships have too long gone unnoticed in research and education. Does the current interest in RM and CRM imply that marketing theorists are getting closer to marketing reality? Are we beginning to discern the marketing content of Japanese keiretsus, Chinese guanxies, global ethnic networks, the British school tie, trade between friends, loyalty to the local pub, and so on? Marketing theory has not invented these phenomena, practice has. Some practitioners have lived them, others have not. A book can draw your attention to relationships by adding them to the map, making them visible.

Relationships between customers and suppliers are the ground for all marketing. Within the current marketing management mode of thinking, much of marketing is reduced to impersonal exchange through mass promotion and mass distribution. The manufacturer offers products and services via an intermediary and the consumer offers money. The manufacturer and even the retailer are no more than trademarks, they may even be totally anonymous to the consumer, who in turn is just a statistic. This approach to marketing does not comply with the reality of society.

In contrast, the prime focus of RM and CRM is on the *individual*, on the *segment of one*. It's 1to1 marketing. But focus is also on groups of like-minded people, *affinity groups*. The group members share a common interest, they want a relationship with the supplier, its products and services, and even with each other. Golfers, environmentalists, computer freaks and Harley-Davidson owners belong here. They form *communities*.

The roots of RM

During the industrial era, mass manufacturing of standardized goods gave birth to mass marketing and mass distribution. During this brief period of our history, marketing theory and education evolved around consumer goods marketing. Services marketing and B-to-B – where

---

[7] One of the early academic proponents for a network view of the market was Thorelli (1986).

relationships were also central during the industrial era – were blank spots in research and education.

Research and practice in marketing during the past thirty years points particularly to the significance of relationships, networks and interaction. Literature on RM and CRM is emerging at an exponential rate in many languages. With certain exceptions, the literature is narrow, characterized by treating single issues in RM such as consumer loyalty, databases for smarter direct marketing, call centres, customer clubs or CRM software systems. These are all valuable bits and pieces, but they lack a coherent framework, an overriding theory.

The more radical theories that have contributed to RM and CRM are *services marketing* and *the network approach to B-to-B*. A first effort to merge these two schools was made by Gummesson in 1983. Relationships, networks and interaction play a certain but subdued role in traditional *marketing management*, popularly referred to as *marketing mix* or the *4Ps* (product, price, promotion, place). It has hegemony over marketing education throughout the world, but refers first and foremost to the mass marketing of standardized consumer goods. Despite its limitations it is erroneously presented as a general marketing theory.[8] In the *sales management* literature, relationships are emphasized but usually limited to the salesperson's interaction with the buyer.

These three approaches, services marketing, B-to-B as networks and traditional marketing management, are central in the RM root system, but the roots have been extended during the past decades. One of the new branches is *total quality management* (TQM). The core of the TQM concept is customer perceived quality and customer satisfaction – which is also the core of the marketing concept. TQM has inspired the concept of *relationship quality*, that is, the efforts to improve quality of relationships, and not just the quality of goods and services. Relationship quality emerged in the large quality programme of Ericsson in the early 1980s. The purpose was to make explicit the fact that relationships are part of customer perceived quality. This is far from the traditional engineer's production-centric quality concept. Often the human aspect, the h-relationship, 'to be liked', sorts out the winner from the loser.[9]

RM is also a result of – or possibly a cause of – new organizational structures and processes where the roles of customer and supplier are not as clear-cut as in Figure 1.1. The fuzziness stands out better in Figure 1.2, where suppliers and customers interact in a network together with competitors, own suppliers, intermediaries and others. RM is not happening in a vacuum, it is mirroring other events in business and society. When organization is discussed in the following chapters, it is treated as a network of relationships and referred to as the *network organization*.[10]

---

[8] For a critical discussion of marketing management theory, see Gummesson (2002).
[9] Gummesson (1987b, 1993); Holmlund (1997).
[10] Other terms with a similar meaning are *virtual* or *imaginary organizations*. See also Davidow and Malone (1992); and Hedberg et al. (1997).

Accounting has often stood out as a nightmare for marketers and salespeople, and been felt as a bureaucratic obstacle to relationship building. Investors, stock market analysts, top management and controllers have, however, gradually begun to question the role of traditional accounting: Do we really measure what matters? Modern accounting goes beyond the mere financial numbers. Accountants who are by training historians acknowledge the impact of customers, employees, services, knowledge, IT readiness, environmental effects and innovation as antecedents to future profit. The current efforts to design accounting for today's and tomorrow's business life are found under the concepts of the *balanced scorecard* and *intellectual capital*. Both concepts help to give a framework to the measurement of *return on relationships* (ROR). Chapter 6 is dedicated to these issues.

IT is the latest branch of the RM root system. I have felt uneasy about how IT, primarily the Internet, the Web and the growing mobility, should be integrated with RM. It is easy to get enthralled by the media hype and the trendy praise for all the blessings of technology. Dotcoms and quick startups with young people, their ability to use the media as image builders to create celebrity status, the naivety of reporters, and the stock markets approaching the outer space of wealth, turned dotcom shares into sweepstakes and casinos. The roller-coaster ride of the stock markets gave birth to enchanted winners and queasy losers, the latter group in the majority after 2000. What in this daily hullabaloo will exert sustainable influence and what is just a short-lived, albeit colourful, butterfly. We begin to discern some answers, to see IT in a context, as part of marketing theory. IT has a lot in common with RM. The Internet, email and mobile telephony form new networks within which we can interact. IT has not fathered RM and CRM as is sometimes claimed, only changed it. The IT influence is covered specifically in R12, the e-relationship, but is also an integral part of the whole book.

Contributions to RM also come from other directions, both from theory and practice. As theory and scientific literature only cover fragments of reality, it is crucial to add knowledge from the *reflective practitioner*. Business leaders, marketers, consultants and others disseminate their experience in action by running corporations as well as through lectures, interviews, articles, handbooks and memoirs. Sometimes professors of business schools have practical experience of business or government. Furthermore, we shall not forget our lifelong and daily experience of being buyers and consumers, perhaps *reflective customers*. All this knowledge can be integrated in research and contribute to more dynamic and rich progress beneficial to both education and practice. Knowledge, experience, compassion and reflection – the *pre-understanding* of the individual – are grounds for enhancing the *understanding* of marketing. The personal experience and the practitioner's gut feeling are not always welcomed in the parlours of science. There is, however, a growing tendency to take better care of *tacit knowledge* or *knowledge by acquaintance*. This kind of knowledge has not found a language and a theory, but is used by the insightful both in practice and research.[11]

Marketing offers no fully-fledged theory, but the word theory will be used here in a broad sense. The most complete theory that has a link to marketing is the neoclassical micro-economic theory, also called price theory. To reach the self-imposed desire for rigour and theoretical completeness, a series of limiting assumptions have to be made, such as all customers being the same, all suppliers being the same and all products being the same. It disregards differentiated offerings and brands, services, quality and relationships. Thus, micro-economic theory distances itself from the variety and complexity of real life, and the validity of the theory becomes weak, even non-existent.[12]

Furthermore, the borderline between theory and practice is thin. To design theory, researchers interview and observe marketers and customers. Activities and decsisions in companies form empirical evidence for theory. Thus there is no *a priori* conflict between theory and practice; they are two sides of the same coin. There often is, however, animosity between representatives of theory and practice who claim that their side of the coin shines brighter. Such pseudo-conflicts do not contribute to knowledge development and are left aside here. If international research in marketing was less obsessed with techniques and less committed to received theory, we would have more *reflective researchers* who contribute more valid knowledge and therefore make more good.

Basic values of marketing

The 'new' IBM says it will reap greater rewards from long-lasting relationships with customers, Sony Thailand says that it is going from excessive mass marketing to RM, and banks everywhere claim that they pursue strategies to strengthen the relationships with customers.

Management thinker Peter Drucker said somewhere that 'the problem with good ideas is that they quickly degenerate into hard work'. There is invariably a gap between ideas and action, between RM philosophy and CRM application. The gap can be caused by lack of implementation skills and stamina, but also by difficulties in grasping the essentials. There may be a lack of data, or inability to put data together in a meaningful pattern or map – 'theories' – which facilitate decisions and actions. The difficulties are caused by at least four

---

[11] The reflective practitioner is discussed by Schön (1983); understanding and pre-understanding are central in hermeneutics (see Gummesson, 2000, pp. 57–82); tacit knowledge is treated by Polanyi (1962); and knowledge by acquaintance by Russell (1948).

[12] Hunt and Morgan (1995).

'random variables': customers, competitors, the general economy and technology change. None of these and their interdependence can be predicted with accuracy.

The gap is also caused by marketers who have not internalized marketing values. Drucker was an early proponent of the *marketing concept*. In his classic management book from 1954, he says: 'Marketing . . . is the whole business seen from the point of view of its final result, that is, from the customer's point of view.'[13] The essence of the marketing concept is understanding customer needs and wants. If a company offers goods and services that satisfy needs and create value for the customer, customer satisfaction and the right customer perceived quality, the company stands the best chance of success. This *marketing-oriented and customer-centric approach* is in opposition to *production orientation*, according to which the customer is obliged to buy what is available or not buy at all. Production orientation is typical of markets with a shortage of goods and services, and markets of centrally planned economies, but also of complacent industries in wealthy market economies such as in Europe and the USA.

The marketing concept is popularly expressed as *customer in focus*. This has become a widespread slogan, understood and implemented only by a few of those who express it. They may just perceive it as a fad which it is timely to confess to, or yet another smart trick to trap the consumer. The customer in focus values have not killed the old values, just pushed them into a corner from which they make recurring and successful efforts to break out.

| INSIGHT | I propose that inadequate basic values and their accompanying procedures – the wrong paradigm – is the biggest obstacle to success in marketing. If marketers and top management do not understand and accept relationship values as a natural vantage point, there will be no positive effect of RM, nor of the installation of computerized CRM systems (eCRM). |

The most fundamental values of RM are:

1 *Marketing management should be broadened into marketing-oriented company management.* Since the early 1970s, I have made a distinction between the marketing and sales department and the *marketing and sales function* in order to emphasize that marketing and sales are more than just the activities of specialized departments. They are functions that must permeate every corner of an organization, not least the minds and actions of management. This is an old thought which has turned out to be enormously difficult to convey and implement. In companies I successfully use the terms *full-time marketers* (FTMs) and *part-time marketers*

---

[13] Drucker (1954, p. 36). For a discussion on the past and future of marketing, see Baker (1999a, b).

(PTMs) to stress that everybody, irrespective of task and expertise, influences customer relationships either full-time or part-time. Marketing management in this sense requires marketing orientation of the whole of the company, that is, marketing-oriented management.

2 *Long-term collaboration and win–win.* The core values of RM are found in its emphasis on *collaboration and the creation of mutual value.* It includes viewing suppliers, customers and others as *partners* rather than *opposite parties.* In 1976, Michael Baker in the UK suggested that marketing be defined as 'mutually satisfying exchange relationships'. RM should be more of *win–win* than *win–lose,* more of a *plus sum game* than a *zero sum game.* In a plus sum game, the parties increase value for each other; in a zero sum game, what one gains is the loss of another. A constructive attitude is expected by all those involved and all should find the relationship meaningful. If these conditions are fulfilled, the relationships may become sustaining. For a supplier, it is important to retain existing customers, a fact which is increasingly being stressed. Extending the *duration* of the relationship becomes a major marketing goal. Too much emphasis has been put on the acquisition of new customers and too little on caring for existing customers. RM and CRM encourage *customer retention* and discourage *customer defection*; they encourage *retention marketing* first and *attraction marketing* – getting new customers – second.

3 *All parties should be active and take responsibility.* RM should not be mixed up with traditional selling, which represents the supplier perspective and does not put the customer and an interactive relationship in focus. In relationship selling, the initiative comes from the salesperson and depends on ' . . . how well the relationship is managed by the seller'.[14] In this sense, relationship quality and a long-term relationship become the consumer's trust in the salesperson based on the salesperson's present and past performance.[15] But the initiative to action cannot be left to a supplier or a single party of a network; everyone in a network can, and should, be active. Contrary to the mythology of marketing, the supplier is not necessarily the active party. In B-to-B, customers initiate innovation and force suppliers to change their products or services. Consumers suggest improvements but have a tough time getting lethargic and complacent suppliers and legislators to listen. Chat groups on the Internet empower customers to reach out at no cost but time; it makes customer-to-customer interaction (C-to-C) possible. Customers can exert pressure on suppliers and it may even go so far that hate sites are created. At the same time, the supplier has more and better information available to act on. In services marketing consumers are often both producers and 'project leaders', whereas the role of the provider is limited to offering an arena.

---

[14] Levitt (1983, p. 111).
[15] Crosby, Evans and Cowles (1990).

4 *Relationship and service values instead of bureaucratic–legal values.* Bureaucratic–legal values are characterized by: rigidity; legal jargon; application of dysfunctional laws and regulations; a focus on internal routines; more interest in rituals than in results; belief in the supplier as the expert and the customer as ignorant; the customer being a cost and a residual of the system; customers as masses and statistical averages; and the importance of winning over the customer in a dispute. These values historically dominate governments and their agencies. Its representatives have previously disclaimed marketing, but the international wave of privatization, deregulation and demand for competition, as well as the failure of the command economies, has forced a change. RM is a valid concept for public organizations as well, and an understanding of how marketing could be applied to public bodies to the benefit of the consumer/citizen is growing. Unfortunately, bureaucratic–legal values are also common in private companies. RM requires different values based on relationships and services to the customer. These values establish that all customers are individuals and different in certain respects; that the outcome is the only thing that counts; that customers are the source of revenue and should be in focus; and that the supplier's task is to create value for the customer.[16]

With these values, RM may stand out as a naively idyllic and benign agenda. RM requires more ethical behaviour than traditional marketing. But all business people do not base their activities on RM values as presented here. Competition means winning over somebody, even destroying others, showing who is the biggest, the best and the wealthiest. Short-term greed often overrules long-term survival. For some, this fight has a value in itself. One of the strategies in *hypercompetition* is called 'simultaneous and sequential strategic thrusts', defined as ' ... a series of actions designed to stun or confuse competitors, disrupting the status quo to create new advantages and erode those of the competitors'. Furthermore, these thrusts ' ... are used by hypercompetitive firms to harass, paralyse, induce error, or block competitors'.[17] The values of hypercompetition run contrary to RM values.

Although collaboration is the core property of RM, my RM concept holds that *both competition and collaboration are essential in a functioning market economy.* Traditional marketing is prejudiced in favour of the benefits of competition. It sees collaboration as inhibiting the forces of the market. The misunderstanding is obvious among those politicians and business leaders who advocate competition as a cure-all for society's problems, a counter-reaction to the socialistic advocacy for central planning and regulations.

---

[16] See Gummesson (1993, pp. 40–2).
[17] D'Aveni (1994, p. 34).

RM versus transaction marketing

RM is often presented as the opposite to *transaction marketing*, the one-shot deal.[18] In transaction marketing, the fact that a customer has bought a product does not forecast the probability for a new purchase, not even if a series of purchases have been made. A customer may repeatedly use the same supplier because of high switching costs, but without feeling committed to the supplier or wanting to enter a closer relationship. Transactions lack history and memory and they don't get sentimental.

In RM, loyalty – especially customer loyalty – is emphasized. In the 'loyalty ladder',[19] the lowest rung is the contact with a *prospect* who hopefully turns into a *customer* and a first purchase. Recurrent customers are *clients*; those who have come back and a long-term relationship is in the making. In the next stages the client becomes a *supporter* and finally an *advocate* for the supplier.

Transaction marketing has no ambition to climb the loyalty ladder. Still, it is often a realistic and functional option. A purchase can concern standardized goods at lowest price within a specified delivery time and grade of quality. Such deals are made, for example, on metals exchanges. A consumer may only buy a home on a single or a few occasions in a lifetime and rarely has surgery on the appendix more than once. IT offers new alternatives and can facilitate the consumer's search for the lowest price of a branded product, or even bidding in an international auction, a service offered by eBay.[20] Through the deregulation of telecom services, the customer can choose the operator with the lowest rate at a specific hour to a specific destination.

But even a one-shot deal can mean deep interactive relationships. If a company builds a new office, the interaction with the builder and a network of providers may be intense for a year or two. The company may not build another office for the next few decades. If you have surgery and stay in a hospital, the interaction will be intense and painfully intimate, but both parties hope that the relationship will be superfluous as the wound heals.

In order to conceptually incorporate transaction marketing in RM, it can be seen as the zero point of the *RM scale*.[21] The scope of the relationships can then be enhanced until a customer and a supplier are practically the same organization. The *zero relationship* of RM has a *price component* within which the lowest price connects the buyer and the seller. Micro-economic theory advocates that price be the sole determinant of a purchase. This limitation makes the theory a blind guide to marketing management, as it only represents one extreme point on the

---

[18] See Jackson (1985a, b), who treats marketing and RM in the B-to-B context.
[19] Christopher, Payne and Ballantyne (1991, p. 22).
[20] Bunnell and Luecke (2000).
[21] See also Grönroos' 'marketing strategy continuum' (2000, pp. 252–3), and a further elaboration of this scale in Lehtinen, Hankimaa and Mittilä (1994).

relationship scale. The zero relationship also has a *convenience component* which implies that the customer often buys where it is simplest and most convenient on a certain occasion. On such occasions price is almost immaterial.

The fact that this book is about RM and advocates relationships as essential in marketing does not imply a religious belief in relationships as a magic panacea. On the contrary, we know that human relationships can be a source of insurmountable hassle as well as of unlimited joy. But we cannot live without them. The larger share of world literature and entertainment deal with relationships between adults, parent and child, police and crook, and not least between the players in a business venture. The oil tycoon JR of the classic soap opera *Dallas* stood out as an international role model for greed-driven manipulation of all types of relationships, be it oil contracts, politics or family matters.

A relationship should not be retained if it works badly. Long-term relationships and customer care are not the same as admitting customers to the geriatric ward of the supplier, attaching them to the bed and keeping them on life support. Relationships should not necessarily be broken just because there is a conflict, however. They can often be restored and improved or they may be the best option for the parties despite a conflict. The beginning of a relationship is often romantic and passionate. It is when the passion phase fades that the real work of building a relationship starts.

Jackson[22] succinctly states a common-sense RM strategy: 'Relationship marketing . . . can be extremely successful where it is appropriate – but it can also be costly and ineffective if it is not. Conversely, transaction marketing . . . can be profitable and successful where it is appropriate but a serious mistake where it is not.'

Common sense, intuition and experience

Running a company revolves around two eternal themes: *make sure you have something to offer* and *make sure you sell it at a price that is higher than your costs.*

It is a matter of common sense. The issue is how to make it happen. Common sense, sound judgement, instinct, intuition, insights and wisdom are stressed in the handbook-type marketing literature; in the scholarly literature they are often treated with contempt. I feel inspired by the way common sense is defined in *Brewer's Dictionary of Phrase & Fable* from 1870:

> Common sense does not mean that good sense which is common . . .
> but the point where all five senses meet, supposed to be the seat of the
> soul, where it judges what is presented by the senses and decides the
> mode of action.

---

[22] Jackson (1985a, p. xi). See also Dwyer, Shurr and Oh (1987); Anderson and Narus (1991); and Paulin, Perrien and Ferguson (1997).

Let us widen the five senses to include experience, intelligence, emotions (today even referred to as 'emotional intelligence'[23]), masculine and feminine instincts, and extrasensory perception if we have it. The complexity of today's markets and organizations, the advanced technology, and the differentiation of goods and services conceal the obvious and we get lost in a maze. Companies grow and employees cannot overview the meaning of their job. We need to go 'back to basics' – or rather, 'forward to basics' – as it is not a matter of regressing to a past society but of adapting to the present and the future. When Scandinavian Airlines (SAS) commenced its turnaround in the early 1980s, one of the instruments was 'smile courses'.[24] Among other things, people were taught that it is important to smile to customers; they will then like you more than if you look gloomy and disinterested. Common sense and sound judgement had to be reinstated. They had got lost in the red tape and standardized mass production of the industrial society. Nordstrom, an exceptionally successful US chain of department stores, says in its *Employee Handbook* under the heading 'Nordstrom Rules': 'Rule No. 1: Use your good judgement in all situations', and adds: 'There will be no additional rules.'

Many have stressed 'management by walking around', leadership through presence where and when it happens. The concept 'rapid reconnaissance' is used in science and refers to the scientist's need to quickly assess a situation or a problem.[25]

This is not the kiss of death of research and science. It only means that we must enhance our ability to utilize *both* systematic analysis *and* personal experience and insights.

The rules of the marketing game are rewritten through political events and changes in values, consumption patterns and technology. Marketing reality requires living with complexity, paradoxes, uncertainty, ambiguity and instability. Many markets are perceived as chaotic, but chaos holds opportunities for those who can see them and use them better than the competition. Chaos is not chaotic *per se*, there is order in chaos,[26] but we fail to see the underlying pattern. It was an uncertain venture when, more than a century ago, European companies took their new products to South America. Many of these ventures succeeded and spawned today's global corporations. Currently, the former Soviet Union nations are chaotic markets having gigantic potential; Hong Kong – the epitome of capitalism – has become part of communist China; Asian economies are shattered; and membership of the North American Free Trade Agreement (NAFTA) or the EU offers new conditions. We may wish to reduce uncertainty, but the market economy is built on dynamic change, which is only partially predictable.

---

[23] Goleman (1995).
[24] Carlzon (1987).
[25] Patton (1990, p. 134) mentions this as a research strategy in social sciences when a qualitative, inductive approach is deployed.
[26] Prigogene and Stengers (1985).

What do we see through the relationship eye-glasses?

We need new approaches that reflect today's markets and help us find our way in these markets. There is no general marketing theory that makes us see everything at the same time. New categories, concepts, models and theories work as lenses through which we perceive the world. If the lenses are wrongly curved, the world will look blurry. If they are tinted, it may look sunny when in fact it is cloudy. Certain lenses improve our vision at close range, others at a distance. As marketing is a complex field, a single pair of glasses is not sufficent. There are bifocals that allow two perspectives, but we need more than two. This book offers the *relationship eye-glasses*. If we look through these glasses we can only see relationships, networks and interaction. RM is about what you see through these glasses.

New concepts, models and theories can very well be the emperor's new clothes and only the innocent child dares say the obvious: 'But he doesn't have anything on!' I have, however, come to the conclusion that RM and CRM provide a new costume which is both visible and tangible. RM offers more common sense in marketing, and it makes important phenomena visible in the confusing world in which marketers search for meaning. CRM offers systems to implement RM strategies. It is then up to the readers to try RM and CRM on their own reality and draw their own conclusions. If marketing executives or salespeople either get a feeling of *déjà vu*, or are made aware of something they might already have sensed or even used but were unable to articulate, it means that the text is close to reality and has validity.

My conclusion is that a radically new thinking in marketing – a paradigm shift – is necessary.[27] But it is not enough to think in new ways to claim a paradigm shift; it must also materialize in action.[28] Research and experience have contributed with general properties of relationships which can help us understand and evaluate individual aspects of relationships and networks. These properties are presented in the next section. An overview of the thirty specific relationships which I have found applicable in marketing-oriented management follows.

General properties of relationships, networks and interaction

In studies of relationships, networks and interaction, a series of general properties have emerged. In the network approach of B-to-B, a distinction is made between three types of connections which together form a relationship between buyers and sellers:[29]

---

[27] For criticism against RM, see Blois (1996); Bliemel and Eggert (1997); Mattsson (1997); Fournier, Dobscha and Mick (1998); Snehota and Söderlund (1998); Brown (2000); and Möller and Halinen (2000).

[28] RM as a tool for implementation is treated by Gummesson (1998b).

[29] Håkansson and Snehota (1995).

1 *Activity links* embrace activities of a technical, administrative and marketing kind.
2 *Resource ties* include exchanging and sharing resources which are both tangible, such as machines, and intangible, such as knowledge.
3 *Actor bonds* are created by people who interact and exert influence on each other and form opinions about each other.

The interaction can also be approached as a hierarchy where *activities* (lowest level) together form *episodes* which form *sequences* which form *relationships*. The relationships constitute the *partner base*, the organization's total network.[30] *Relationscapes* has been suggested as a designation for all the relationships that are included in a network.[31] These relationships may be active and visible; they could also be invisibly embedded in the network by being passive and unobtrusive, yet still be influential.

It is also feasible to list the properties or dimensions which a party may perceive in a relationship. In a study of service consumers, as many as forty-five properties were identified.[32]

The general classifications and properties of relationships can be useful in RM for decision-making and planning. In the next four chapters, where thirty relationships, the 30Rs, are presented, applications of these properties will be continuously examined.

The following sections will summarize important general properties of commercial relationships. The properties are somewhat overlapping; they do not readily lend themselves to clear-cut definitions.[33]

Collaboration

Collaboration has already been claimed to be the fundamental property of relationships between suppliers and customers, competitors, consultants, government agencies and others. The collaboration can be linked to a single deal or be continuous. The degree of collaboration could be combined with the degree of competition.[34] A situation with little competition and little collaboration between two or more companies can be a good start for expanded collaboration. A high degree of collaboration and a low degree of competition provide a base

---

[30] Holmlund (1997).
[31] Strandvik and Törnroos (1997).
[32] Ward, Frew and Caldow (1997).
[33] This section is a synthesis from research within the B-to-B network approach; studies within sociology and psychology (see Granovetter, 1973, 1985; Boissevein, 1976; Scott, 1991); practical business experience; plus some specific references in the text.
[34] According to Wilkinson and Young (1994).

for a long-term and harmonious relationship. Relationships can also thrive in a situation of both extensive collaboration and competition. If the collaborative part is insignificant and competition takes over, it becomes imperative to either divest in the relationship or to consciously work for a reinforced relationship.

Longevity

It has been stressed that the long-term relationship is a pillar of RM. This is in opposition to transaction marketing, which is characterized by single deals and customer promiscuity. The concepts of duration, retention and defection have been defined above. A long-term relationship can be more effective for all parties, especially if it takes a long time to build the relationships, a common case in B-to-B. Switching costs may be high and no relationship should be broken because of negligence or lack of interest. The parties learn how to handle the relationship and utilize it to their benefit. Sometimes it is rational to break a relationship. It may have become obsolete or lost its zest. For example, it is reasonable to change advertising agency at times in order to stimulate creativity.

Commitment, dependency and importance

If a relationship is important, we are dependent on it and we must then commit ourselves to making it work. If a delivery is delayed, a whole factory or construction site may stop, particularly if they are part of a just-in-time (JIT) production system. Dependency is dramatically obvious when emergencies occur, for example when an ambulance or fire-fighters are needed. There are also daily and trivial dependencies on the telephone, the newspaper, and public transport to and from work. In services marketing, three levels of dependency and commitment have been proposed.[35] On Level 1, customers are primarily attracted by low prices. The effect of this attraction quickly fades away if the competition also lowers its prices. Level 1 is often easy to copy. On Level 2, the relationship has deepened. There is no longer just a price relationship, but also a communication with the customer that may consist of face-to-face contact or personally addressed direct mail. Level 3 adds a structural dimension which means that the parties have pooled resources and are therefore highly committed to making the relationship work. The Procter & Gamble and Wal-Mart production–sales–delivery system is such an example.

---

[35] Berry and Parasuraman (1991, pp. 136–42).

Trust, risk and uncertainty

The success of closer collaboration between customer and supplier is often credited to trust. Consumers can trust an airline, a plumber or a doctor, but also a certain brand. A company can have a trusting relationship with a bank which facilitates credit decisions. Management consultants live on their clients' trust for them; to 'objectively' measure their performance is usually not feasible or meaningful. Individual lawyers and accountants can be important to a person and they must be available when needed; the client may not want to turn to other professionals, even if they work in the same firm. Often we only know partially what we are buying – we do it on trust – for example, when our dentist performs root canal surgery. We only know the value of an insurance policy when a claim is made; we have probably not quite understood the fine print and legal conditions of our home insurance or retirement plan. This ignorance creates uncertainty. Alliances represent a great risk; there may be arguments, one party may pick the other party's brain without giving anything in return. The degree and significance of trust varies widely between cultures and nations, which has been analysed by Fukuyama (1995). He points out that the mom and pop business, embracing the next of kin and friends, has its own rules and a tight social control, whereas large-scale operations require trust in the socitey as such. He makes a distinction between high-trust societies and low-trust societies.

Power

Power is an undervalued concept in the marketing literature. The formation of gigantic global groups today is a matter of power. Brands give power. The Internet as a medium for information and interactivity gives the customer more power. Power in a relationship is only rarely symmetrical, meaning that each party has the same amount of power. An asymmetrical relationship means that one party is weaker and may feel used, but the relationship can still be functional if there is no better alternative for the weaker party. It can also be perceived as unfair and at the first opportunity the weaker party exits. Patients with toothache are left to the discretion of dentists and their willingness to serve them; they may be left at the mercy of an emergency clinic where patients must wait long hours. The symmetry of power can change. A company in a booming market may be short of components and the supplier has the power, but when the market turns downward the customer can negotiate cuts in prices and delivery times. To use one's position to the extreme is detrimental to sustaining a relationship; a certain amount of goodwill and helpfulness is demanded from all parties.

Frequency, regularity and intensity

Certain relationships are frequently and regularly active, such as travel to and from work or bank transactions. Following a fixed timetable, which is part of a long-term contract, the Swedish railways transport rolls of paper from Sweden to newspaper printers in London every day according to a strict timetable. Other relationships are rare, such as engaging a funeral parlour or estate agent, but loyalty to a specific provider can still be strong. Education can require an intense relationship during several years, heart surgery an intense relationship during a few days. The relationship to a convenience store can be sustaining and frequent, but not particularly intense.

Adaptation[36]

In long-term relationships the parties must adapt to one another. In B-to-B this adaptation can be far reaching as the years pass by and termination of the relationship can be very costly for one or all of the parties. Adaptation can mean large investment which is customized to the needs of other parties and that cannot necessarily be used for anything else. It can concern manufacturing, finance, information systems and knowledge, but it can also be mental and social. Also, in B-to-C consumers adapt to a system and procedures. For example, most consumers want paying bills to be an effortless routine. When payment systems are changed, as currently banks force customers to transfer to Internet banking, it requires you to invest in a computer, an Internet subscription and installation of software. The system requires you to learn the job of a bank teller and to comply with inconvenient, yet non-robust, security procedures. For some this may be a positive adaptation; it may offer more flexibility and the customer may save time. For others, such as the elderly, adaptation may not even be an option.

Attraction

In the marriage metaphor of long-term relationships, attraction between the parties is a dominant factor. The predecessors of the EU were alliances and mergers between countries, and matrimony between princes and princesses were a major instrument of securing sustainability and peace. When, in 2001, Norwegian Crown Prince Haakon married Mette-Marit, a girl of the people with a past, it was not because of political, economic or social

---

[36] See also Hallén, Johanson and Seyed-Mohamed (1993).

convenience, rather the contrary. Attraction – love – took over. In a similar vein, studies have shown that attraction between companies may require a combination of rational financial motives and psychological factors.[37] Even in business, a partner should be cool and sexy. This also applies for the image that companies convey through their brands (see R13 on parasocial relationships). The importance of attraction for establishing relationships both within industries and to customers is perhaps nowhere more protruding than in entertainment, sports, tourism and politics.

Closeness and remoteness

Closeness can be physical, mental or emotional. The physical proximity facilitates mental and emotional contact. Companies that want to do business in a foreign country often have to be continuously present in order to obtain credibility. Cultural differences exist between countries, and ethnic and religious groups may build mental distance despite physical closeness. Certain relationships become truly personal, especially if you meet often and even associate privately. Others are remote in the sense that the conduits are machines, such as ATMs. The Internet and email create a virtual closeness, but there is still a physical distance. Closeness strengthens the feeling of security. The majority of relationships thrive on tacit understanding between parties and only a minority are regulated in contracts. Consumers are often far away from manufacturers who must rely on distance information through intermediaries, such as reports from market research institutes.

Formality, informality and transparency

Commercial relationships are usually more informal than formal. As consumers we rarely have a contract or any other written obligation, but there are exceptions. As members of a golf club we have consented to abide to strict rules and we cannot usually just move to another club; to be effective a retirement plan may force us to stick to the same insurance or finance company, and the payments and contracts are formal and regulated. If we break the rules we may be punished or even be dropped as customers. The better we know the people in a small store, the more informal the relationship may be. They may let us in after opening hours or give us credit if we have left our purse at home. In B-to-B, informality is an absolute necessity as a supplement to formal agreements. Problems are solved over the telephone and the parties trust each other. Negotiations and exchange of information may occur at the golf course or in a hotel

---

[37] Halinen (1997, p. 270f).

bar, sometimes leading to major deals with long-term effects. The formal aspects must be heeded, however. One such aspect is the degree of transparency. For example, how much are we obliged to reveal to the other parties concerning our own cost and revenue?

Routinization

A common complaint in marriages is the lack of romance and excitement; after a period of passion the relationship turns into routine. Although it sounds dull, routine procedures may be conditional for efficiency and cost effectiveness, both in commercial and marital relationships. Banking today is routinized through computers and telephones, and the days when you went to your local branch office and were greeted by a bank teller, with whom you had a chat, may be numbered. Even if you think you telephone your local bank branch, a digital switch will select a free line to a call centre, which can be located anywhere in a country, even abroad. In B-to-B, routines are established for deliveries, and both the customer and the supplier follow rituals and standard procedures. Increasingly, these routines are handled by machine-to-machine interaction (M-to-M). However, customers also abandon suppliers who show no interest in them. So there is a trade-off between routines and standard procedures for speed and low cost, and the feeling that the relationships develop and live.

Content

The content of a business relationship is traditionally described as economic exchange. One party provides goods and services and the other provides money; streams of goods or services go in one direction and financial streams go in the other. In this sense marketing is exchange. In new marketing and management theory, the relationship is increasingly seen as interaction and joint value creation. The content of a relationship is often knowledge and information. This is a rationale for alliances, for example for product development or for a hotel to join a room reservation network. This way a company 'can become bigger without growing'. Coordination and utilization of resources for manufacturing and distribution can be important, for example competing newspapers who share a printing plant and the distribution to subscribers in order to slash costs.

Personal and social properties

These are age, sex, profession, education, ethnicity, personality type, geographical and social mobility, as well as personal traits such as lust for power, or an ability to create trust and confidence. Charm, charisma, personal vibrations and chemistry belong here, all phenomena that are difficult to analyse but which we recognize when we encounter them. In social network analysis, efforts are made to identify patterns of relationships: cliques, clusters, blocks. The analysis offers matrices and descriptions of structures of personal relationships. The sociogram is a graphical technique to show patterns of relationships between individuals. Relationships can be of the first degree concerning friends, of the second degree concerning friends of friends, of the third degree, etc. The relationships can be direct or can be arranged through a mediator.

It is often asked which properties are the most important. The idea then is to be Pareto optimal and to zoom in on the properties that account for the lion's share of the benefits of RM. Collaboration must always be in the core of a relationship. Some claim that power is always decisive, others that commitment and trust are the key.[38] Most of the properties are fuzzy entities which overlap in several respects. Rankings are misleading, as the importance of a property is relative to a specific situation. For example, if trust is taken for granted in a specific business culture, it is only when trust is abused that the property stands out as pivotal. Something else is needed, such as superior social contact or a formal contract.

The general properties of relationships can contribute to the evaluation of a relationship and its development or liquidation. But they cannot alone serve as a basis for marketing decision-making, planning and execution. Even if each of them highlights an interesting phenomenon, they must be put into context. I have therefore chosen to define types of relationships which are composed of many properties and which can be recognized in the management of marketing.

The 30Rs of RM – introductory specification of thirty relationships

The philosophy of RM and the examples have to be converted into tangible relationships that can become part of a company's marketing and business planning. This has been done by defining thirty relationships – the 30Rs. These are listed and briefly characterized in Table 1.1. With the exception of the first relationship, R1, the relationship between a supplier and a customer – which is the foundation of marketing – the Rs are not in ranking order. Their significance varies between companies and markets. In reading the text, keep the vantage points of RM in mind by posing the question: If we view marketing through the relationship eye-glasses, what do we see and how can we use what we see?

The relationships are grouped in the following way. The first two types are *market relationships*. These are relationships between suppliers, customers, competitors and others

---

[38] About power, see Thorelli (1986, p. 38); about commitment and trust, see Morgan and Hunt (1994).

Table 1.1 The thirty relationships of RM – the 30Rs

Classic market relationships (Chapter 2)

R1   The classic dyad – the relationship between the supplier and the customer
      This is the parent relationship of marketing, the ultimate exchange of value which constitutes the basis of business.

R2   The classic triad – the drama of the customer–supplier–competitor triangle
      Competition is a central ingredient of the market economy. In competition there are relationships between three parties: between the customer and the current supplier, between the customer and the supplier's competitors, and between competitors.

R3   The classic network – distribution channels
      The traditional physical distribution and the modern channel management, including goods, services, people and information, consists of a network of relationships.

Special market relationships (Chapter 3)

R4   Relationships via full-time marketers (FTMs) and part-time marketers (PTMs)
      Those who work in marketing and sales departments – the FTMs – are professional relationship makers. All others, who perform other main functions but yet influence customer relationships directly or indirectly, are PTMs. There are also contributing FTMs and PTMs outside the organization.

R5   The service encounter – interaction between customers and service providers
      Production and delivery of services involve the customer in an interactive relationship with the service provider, often referred to as the moment of truth.

R6   The many-headed customer and the many-headed supplier
      Marketing to other organizations – industrial marketing or business marketing – often means contacts between many individuals from the supplier's and the customer's organization.

R7   The relationship to the customer's customer
      A condition for success is often the understanding of the customer's customer, and what suppliers can do to help their customers become successful.

R8   The close versus the distant relationship
      In mass marketing, the closeness to the customer is lost and the relationship becomes distant, based on surveys, statistics and written reports.

R9   The relationship to the dissatisfied customer
      The dissatisfied customer perceives a special type of relationship, more intense than the normal situation, and often badly managed by the provider. The way of handling a complaint – the recovery – can determine the quality of the future relationship.

R10   The monopoly relationship: the customer or supplier as prisoners
      When competition is inhibited, the customer may be at the mercy of the supplier – or the other way around. One of them becomes prisoner.

R11   The customer as 'member'
      In order to create a long-term sustaining relationship, it has become increasingly common to enlist customers as members of various loyalty programmes.

R12   The e-relationship
      The electronic relationship, the e-relationship, represented by the Internet, email and mobile telephony, is set against the h-relationship, the human relationship. The concept of high tech–high touch becomes increasingly more crucial to watch in RM and CRM.

R13   Parasocial relationships – relationships to brands and objects
      Relationships do not only exist with people and objects, but also in the form of mental images and symbols such as brands and corporate identities.

R14   The non-commercial relationship
      This is a relationship between the public sector and citizens/customers, but it also includes voluntary organizations and other activities outside of the profit-based and monetarized economy, such as those performed in families.

necessary conditions for market relationships. The metaphor points to connections and dependencies that must be considered when a company organizes its marketing. The doll becomes a symbol of the network organization where the borderline between organization, market and society is not as clear as in traditional organization theory and economics.

The definitions and content are controlled by current practical and theoretical relevance as I have interpreted it. Behind the 30Rs is a strong influence of *grounded theory*, and the openness and sensitivity required by this inductive approach to science. As long as you keep searching for a type of phenomenon – in this case relationship marketing – persistent search will make patterns, categories and systems emerge. Glaser says: 'The researcher must have patience and not force the data out of anxiety and impatience . . . *He must trust that emergence will occur and it does* [italics added].'[39] That the relationships became thirty is an outcome of a grounded theory approach. It does not mean that the Rs need to be 30. Anyone who can motivate more or different categories or condense them into fewer is welcome to do so. The outcome of successful theory construction is to conceptualize a field, generalize beyond the mere description of events, and make it more intelligible and manageable.

IN BRIEF

The 30Rs will be further presented and explained in Chapters 2–5. The principal idea of each relationship is treated and practical examples are given. The purpose of the classification into 30Rs is to make RM operative, that is, useful for planning and implementation of marketing activities. All Rs are not applicable to each company and each situation; it is a matter of selecting a specific relationship portfolio for the marketing plan.

In reading the book it is essential to recall its vantage points. You have to wear the relationship eye-glasses and pose the question: If we look at marketing as relationships, networks and interaction, what do we see and what can we do with it? The relationships need not necessarily be read in chronological order, but the reading should rather be guided by relevance for the reader's interests and situation.

---

[39] Glaser (1992, p. 4) and Glaser (2001).

Chapter

2

Classic market relationships

In this chapter

The first three relationships are marketing classics, although here they are observed through the relationship eye-glasses. The relationship between the customer and the supplier (R1) – the classic dyad – constitutes the foundation for commercial exchange and interaction; it is the parent relationship of marketing. It is supplemented by a third force, competition, which is a necessary element of a market economy; the relationship between a customer, its present supplier and the supplier's competitors constitute the classic triad (R2). Physical distribution has always been central in marketing. It has broadened into channel management and here it is viewed as a network of relationships, the classic network of marketing (R3).

RELATIONSHIP 1

The classic dyad – the relationship between the supplier and the customer

The relationship between the one who sells something and the one who buys something forms the *classic dyad of marketing, a two-party relationship. This is the parent relationship of marketing.*

The two interacting parties are a *supplier* and a *customer*. Customer usually means *external customer*. The notion of the *internal customer* has become widely accepted and is defined as one of the nano relationships (R25).

The supplier is the *seller*, and the seller can be represented by a salesperson, whose task is personal selling. In the latter meaning there is a face-to-face relationship or a relationship via letter, telephone, email, the Internet or other media.

In individual market relationships a customer interacts with another individual who is a *salesperson*, or another employee of the selling organization. Market relationships also exist between companies, industries, regions, countries and groups of countries. When the selling situation is more extensive and complex, the selling activity turns into negotiations. The salesperson becomes a negotiator and the negotiations are often handled by a team from either side.

Caring for existing customers used to be second to *attracting new customers*. The salesperson who acquired new customers was dynamic, while the guy who 'just' took care of old customers was considered old and tired and frightened of the new. Today, keeping, caring for and developing existing relationships is given priority. The strategy is: court your own customers before you start courting somebody else's customers.

A rationale for investing in existing customers is that customers are increasingly being perceived as the scarce resource of a business; another is that getting new customers is costly. Consequently, long-term and stable relationships come into focus. Most RM definitions emphasize the establishment, maintenance and sometimes termination of customer relation-ships. The first stage, to acquire a customer and establish a relationship, is of course always of importance, but the second stage, to maintain a sustaining business relationship, is the more demanding part of marketing.

The terms *retention marketing* and *zero defection*[1] emphasize the relationship to existing customers. The latter term is paraphrasing the 'zero defects' quality strategy. This strategy says that a company should continuously improve its quality and deliver defect-free goods and services. Zero defection means a defect-free relationship, reducing the loss of customers to zero. This strategy does not imply that customers should be kept at all costs. If a customer has no need for our offering or the customer will remain unprofitable, defection should be encouraged. There should be an ongoing *customer migration*; customers immigrate to us, or emigrate from us to other suppliers. This is a freedom factor in a market economy. What the zero defection strategy really says is that customers should not leave because of disinterest from the supplier, late delivery, sloppy service or wrong pricing.

A key question is: To what extent is it profitable to keep a relationship, and when should we accept that a purchase is just a one-shot deal? Among marketers we often hear that it is five to ten times as expensive to make a new customer than to keep an old customer. I do not know how well this is proven, but it has become a buzz axiom.

A salesperson adage says that 'real selling isn't making sales but making customers'. This strategy has been taught at sales courses as a practical experience. It is more uncertain how many understand and live the strategy. Carl Sewell in Dallas, the world's most successful Cadillac dealer, has understood and follows the advice. To him, selling cars is creating a lifelong relationship to each individual customer. He estimated that each customer was worth US $332 000. That was what a Cadillac customer was expected to spend on purchasing and servicing cars during a lifetime. As one measure to strengthen the relationship, Sewell keeps the auto repair shops open on Saturdays and evenings. He explains his relationship credo as follows:[2]

- If you're good to your customers, they'll keep coming back because they like you.
- If they like you, they'll spend more money.
- If they spend more money, you want to treat them better.
- If you treat them better, they'll keep coming back and the circle starts again.

It is hard to argue with this credo, it is common sense.

---

[1] The term 'zero defection' is taken from Reichheld and Sasser (1990).
[2] Sewell (1990, p. xviii).

A major question is whether it is possible to create a relationship if you have thousands or even millions of customers as can be the case, particularly in B-to-C. Is not mass marketing through advertising and supermarket distribution the only possibility? In mass marketing, the customer is anonymous. The contact through 'mass communication' is *indirect*, *impersonal* and *one-way*. In fact, it is deceptive to call it communication, which should be a two-way street.[3] At best it is *information*, at worst it is barely *noise*.

In the rationalistic mode of the Western industrialized world, the cost of keeping personal relationships is too high, especially if the product or service is cheap or exposed to price competition. Therefore, relationships are made mechanical, which is possible by means of large-scale mass marketing, supermarkets and self-service. Personal relationships are substituted for packages which carry product and price information, and the consumers themselves fill trolleys and bags with goods. The same impersonal concept also has its virtual application on the Web.

The transfer from an individual relationship to a mass relationship offers many intermediary forms. The notion of *customized mass marketing* may appear to be an oxymoron, but is an increasingly viable marketing strategy where modern technology can be helpful.

Marketing attempts to create an impression of a personal relationship to customers even if the supplier does not know the customers or even meet them. It is a *pseudo-personal relationship*, but, all the same, it could be an efficient one. There are, however, quality differences in the personal relationships between a family doctor and a patient, or a restaurant keeper and a regular dinner guest, and the relationship between a consumer and a newspaper advertisement or a poster in the subway.

| CASE STUDY | **Slater Menswear** |

Slater Menswear, in Glasgow, is an example of customized mass marketing. It is the world's largest men's store and the entrance displays a diploma from the *Guinness Book of Records* to prove this. The store guarantees at least 12 000 suits in stock (including well-known fashion brands) and a price level 25–50 per cent lower than in the average store. As a customer you are quickly attended to by a sales assistant who is helpful but leaves you alone if you prefer to look around on your own. You can turn to any sales assistant, they do not seem to protect you against their colleagues. They advise you on colour and fit. Measurements for changes are taken immediately, are offered without extra cost and are ready the next day, or if you are

---

[3] Edfeldt (1992, p. 100).

pressed for time, within an hour or less. If you are from overseas, they complete the documents for a sales tax refund and they do it without you even asking for it. The documents must be signed by Customs when you leave the country and then sent to an address, but Slater has already given you an addressed envelope with a stamp. If you wish, the refund goes onto your credit card so you do not have to bother about foreign cheques and excessive bank fees in your home country. Everything is smooth, quick and easy. It is large scale, but the personal service is high. It is difficult to leave Slater without buying. According to owner Paul Slater, one explanation for the low prices is the purchasing and payment policy:[4] 'We buy large amounts from the manufacturers and pay them within three to five days of delivery, allowing us to pass on discounts to our customers. Experience has shown that we are very easy to deal with and we have succeeded in building up very successful relationships with some of the large fashion houses over the years. Slater creates a positive relationship to vendors as they are not spoilt with speedy payment. This in turn makes Slater more competitive to consumers. However, low price is not enough; the staff also quickly establish a relationship with the customer.'

Direct marketing has long worked with personally addressed letters to enhance the impression of a close relationship.[5] Computers can repeat the name of the customer in the text of the letter and the order card. The tone can be personal: 'Dear Mr Smith: You have been selected . . . '. *Reader's Digest* was early in deploying this technique in a large-scale international operation for individualized direct mail.[6] In the middle of the 1960s this was a sensation, but was frowned upon by many companies and advertising agencies. Even if most consumers intellectually understood that the letter was not genuinely personal, the individualized letter increased the response rate dramatically.

| CASE STUDY | *Reader's Digest* |

Reader's Digest established advanced relationships with the subscribers of the magazine at its start in 1922 by using the customer base for direct mail. Eighty years later, the monthly magazine is printed in seventeen languages and has

---

[4] The quotation is from an advertisement for Slater Menswear.
[5] Blomqvist, Dahl and Haeger (1993) particularly stress the usefulness of direct marketing for RM.
[6] For the history of the *Reader's Digest*, see Heidenry (1993).

twenty-eight million subscribers. When the operations were broadened to books and music, its address list – the customer base – became their most valuable asset. The new products were sold to existing magazine subscribers through personally addressed letters. The mailing lists were divided into segments: subscriber, subscriber and buyer of one (two . . .) books, subscriber and buyer of one (two . . .) music albums, and other combinations. It turned out that the more products a consumer had bought, the higher the probability that he or she would buy yet another product. The long-term relationship between *Reader's Digest* and the consumer determined future sales. It was clearly established in sophisticated statistical tests that socio-demographic variables for segmentation, such as age, sex and income – which are routinely recommended in marketing textbooks – added no value whatsoever.

Hanna Andersson is a mail-order children's clothing business in Portland, Oregon. One way to keep in touch with customers and make loyalty rewarding is their Hannadowns concept. According to their mail-order catalogue: 'When your kids outgrow their Hanna clothes, send them back to me in good used condition, and I'll reserve your credit for 20 per cent of the purchase price. That's a real head start on your next order! Meanwhile we'll donate your clothes to kids in need, where they'll become favorites all over again.' Other mail-order operations such as L.L. Bean and Land's End are now showing that individual relationships to consumers are possible not only all over the American continent, but also to European and Japanese consumers.

Direct marketing is increasingly using the telephone and media other than mail;[7] that is the reason for changing the name from direct mail. *Telemarketing* has become a major industry. For example, Teleperformance, an international telemarketing service, claims that 70 per cent of marketing and sales communication is handled by telephone, that a telephone contact is five to ten times as efficient as mail contact, and is often as effective as a face-to-face visit but costs five times less.

Now it is CRM that counts. It has already been defined as a systematic way of applying RM in practice, particularly when it comes to customer relationships. CRM means active work to handle customer relationships on a large scale with long-term profitability and survival in mind. The steps in 1to1 summarize well what it takes:[8]

- *Identify individual customers* and *establish how they can be reached*.
- *Differentiate* customers by their values and needs.

---

[7] See Rapp and Collins (1995).
[8] Rogers, in Newell (2000, p. xiv).

- Interact with customers, establish a *dialogue*.
- Customize, treat every customer as an *individual* through personal contact or an automated process.
- Make the relationship a continuously *learning relationship*.

There is an addendum: 'These steps are tough.' They may sound simple, even trivial, but they require persistence.

In a narrow sense, the supplier only zooms in on the customer relationship and the application of IT. To make CRM a winner, however, two things are needed:

1 To set the customer–supplier relationship in the context of the company's whole network of relationships, such as the relationships to competitors, governments, media and internal customers, that is, both market, mega and nano relationships. If not, the customer–supplier relationships will just hover among the clouds and never touch the ground of reality.
2 To balance IT with human contact. IT plays a prominent part in CRM, but did so in direct mail and direct marketing as well. CRM is not just the Internet, websites and email, it has a human side too. Today, we talk about electronic CRM (eCRM), to which I would like to add hCRM, 'h' meaning human. We will recurrently meet 'e and h' in the text.[9]

The foundation of CRM is the RM philosophy and to develop goals and strategies within its spirit. To execute the strategies, system and IT support are needed. As always in times of change there is resistance. The real job is to unlearn, to fight obsolete knowledge and behaviour, and generate a truly learning organization. It is then tempting to follow the ostrich strategy and put your head in the sand, not face reality and install systems, software and consulting packages, hoping that these will clear up everything.

But this is myopic, naive, and costly. New technologies, least of all the Internet, cannot solve any problems automatically. *Problems are solved by people who understand the new, have incentives to implement the new and have resources to do the new.* Only then can the CRM arsenal of techniques and consultants be effective.

When companies have many customers, especially in B-to-C but also in many cases of B-to-B, CRM is dependent on *data warehousing*, a process to search, store and integrate data from all available sources, systems and organizational units. The data warehouse is a more advanced form of database, often supplemented by mini-bases, *data marts*. It is not so easy to execute the RM ideas and integrate everything, particularly not during a pioneering phase. In the era of mass marketing, new sales were often solicited among old and prospective customers in a mess. Large companies had, and most still have, tens, sometimes even hundreds or thousands,

---

[9] See also Gummessson (2001a).

of databases without contact between each other. Insurance companies had several databases on the production side (registering policies, invoicing, settling claims) and others on the sales and marketing side (different product lines, different regions). The waste with resources became gargantuan, in sales calls, mail and advertising. In the old times, insurance was often sold by part-time agents as an extra source of income. The agents operated in a local market, a part of their home town or in their workplace, and they knew their customers and prospects. A successful agent handled his database through personal relationships, a box of cards, curiosity, local gossip, daily observations, charm and a nose for business. Good agents saw the use of good customer relationships. That was hCRM, the practice of CRM of its time, but the agents did not know it in those terms; it was their use of common sense, experience and a desire to add income.

The thought behind *permission marketing* is that customers have scarce time and do not want to be disturbed unnecessarily. Therefore, customers are asked for permission, something that an interactive relationship makes possible. Surely the number of prospects goes down, but each prospect holds a better potential.[10] Permission marketing is preventive and constructive as compared to the negative messages on letterboxes: 'No advertising, thank you!' Or even: 'No junk mail!'

In a technical sense, data warehousing can now integrate information about customers and other stakeholders in our networks of relationships. Data become accessible and can be used in more advanced combinations. If the goldmine of the new economy is a rich database, the gold has to be extracted and refined. This occurs in *data mining*, a systematic process which may use advanced models and techniques. The mining process can be statistical and automated as the computer searches for patterns and pools data on customers and their purchasing behaviour, and develops hypotheses and suggestions for strategies. Data mining offers an opportunity to see structures and links that might be converted into implementable knowledge. With this knowledge, a company can better customize and target its messages, goods and services, boost its competitive power and increase customer retention.

Conditions for *up-selling* and *cross-selling* – not new but always hard to implement in large organizations – are improved. Up-selling means, for example, that consumers expand their current retirement plan to a higher level of annual savings and thus increase their pension, or sign for a more advanced type of policy. Cross-selling means that those who have pensions plans in the insurance company are also offered other insurance, such as house and car insurance.

Now that everything can be done by computers, what then is left for the marketer to do? In fact, the most important is still there. Decisions need to be taken on what data to store, how to store it, and what models and software to use, which proposals from the data mining process to execute, and how the outcome shall be monitored. The proposals shall be assessed in

---

[10] Godin (1999).

relation to business missions, objectives, experience, common sense, intuition, instinct, social and emotional intelligence – all easily concealed behind the facade of IT tinsel. The demands on the person grow as more advanced technology is used.

The new includes *call centres*. They have taken over more of customer service and customer contact, especially in enterprises with many customers in both B-to-C and B-to-B. A call centre is a specialized unit where the employees talk to their customers over the phone or email to provide assistance and information, and handle complaints and suggestions from customers. What's new is the specialized role and that mass customization has been brought one step forward. Although the toll-free 800 number was opened in the United States in 1967 it took until the 1980s for companies to realize its potential for a dialogue with consumers. In most other countries similar telephone services are quite recent.

It is also new that the call centre employee has access to information about the caller on his or her computer screen; that customers – within the spirit of RM – are encouraged to call; that self-service has been made possible through the digital push-button phone; that the telephone system can be optimally utilized through automatic direction of a call to a free line; and that the call centre is not predestined to be in a certain physical location.

The call centre business is now a major industry comparable in size to many of the pillars of the industrial economy, such as textile or shipping. Unfortunately, statistics lag behind, still with their feet in the industrial era more than in the value and network society.

However, there are snakes in the technological paradise. To make the quality of automatic phone calls and call centres certain, there must be an option to speak to a real person if the customer needs it. For example, when an issue goes beyond the knowledge and power of the employee, the call must be quickly transferred to someone else. It is not satisfactory when companies and governments still today – in the spirit of the Russian commissar – put the caller on hold: 'Right now many people are calling but . . . '. It does not help to design a website which is loaded with banners, advertising, peripheral information and on top of this is hard to interpret. There will be growing pressure on call centres and their staff when they come more in use and serve many needs, all the way from standardized matters to advice on how to order on the provider's website, to smooth complaints handling.

In Europe, the leading Norwegian insurance company Storebrand has implemented a comprehensive CRM programme to establish a correct and complete customer database. The programme began around 1990, far ahead of the now widespread CRM software and CRM consultants. 'Had we known the hardships we had in front of us we would never have dared to begin,' says Alfred Bakken, senior vice president and in charge of Storebrand's 'dialogue concept'. For an insurance company it is a production necessity to keep records. The novelty is that the database is now actively used for marketing and the maintenance of closer and long-term relationships; marketing and production have entered wedlock. Through the database, the company can identify each individual's needs for insurance and target customized offerings to each of its 900 000 customers. Getting the customer database in order was found to be a mammoth undertaking. The base contained a high error rate, including people who died long ago. The oldest 'customer' who still received mail died the same year as Napoleon Bonaparte, which was in 1821. Talk about caring for old customers!

The establishment of an accurate and useful database has been made possible through IT. But eCRM takes you nowhere unless you adapt your efforts to RM values and manage them properly. At the Ritz-Carlton hotels, each employee is trained to note a guest's likes and dislikes. The data are entered into a computer database which includes the guest history of Ritz-Carlton's 240 000 repeat customers: credit card number, corporate rates, previous hotel visits, non-smoker, etc. It is a practical measure that creates a bond with the guest. It smooths the interaction between the customer and hotel staff at reservations, check-in and check-out, and it helps to make each visit a memorable visit. The disadvantage of impersonal treatment caused by large-scale operations is partly offset, and IT, in combination with personal customer contact, makes relationship maintenance efficient.

In a market economy, a company must make a profit to survive. An excellent relationship with customers is no goal in itself; productivity in marketing must be kept up. Sales staff and others who negotiate deals must know how to close a deal within a reasonable time and with reasonable prices. The customers must offer a reasonable profit potential. For example, Storebrand found that 100 000 of its customers were not reasonably profitable. Some qualities of the horse salesmen and the poker player are needed, but must be weighed against the ability to cement long-term, professional and trusting relationships with customers. Short-term greed is not a viable RM strategy.

Even if they breathe a certain manipulative attitude, there are classic books that advocate much of what RM stands for – long-term relationships, win–win and personal contact. The number one bestseller in this field is probably Dale Carnegie's *How to Win Friends and Influence People* from 1936. It is reputed to have sold thirty million copies since then. What it says is generic; there has not been any need to revise it except for some references that are not known by today's readers. Heinz Goldman's *How to Win Customers* from 1958 has sold 2.5 million copies. Both books are translated into most languages and are reprinted continuously. The old type salesman especially followed the same guidelines as CRM but without IT support. Even if selling and sales management have been part of marketing textbooks, they have usually been treated just as a subgroup of the third of the 4Ps: promotion. But there is also literature on consultative selling (the salesperson investigating needs, informing and giving advice rather than trying hard pressure sales techniques), team-selling and negotiation techniques.

The supplier gives *promises* to the customer.[11] The customer reciprocates by promising to pay. Promises create expectations which must be met for the relationship to be sustained; it

---

[11] See also Calonius (1987).

is a part of business ethics which makes both parties trust one another. A trusting relationship is rational as it reduces red tape and the risk for litigation. A European businessman, long settled in Japan, has portrayed the Japanese business relationship as follows:[12] 'The Japanese customer demands personal contact with his suppliers. He does not buy on the basis of sales letters, catalogues, brochures and the like. He wants to speak to the seller ... These personal promises must of course later be confirmed in a written document, but this is usually very brief. It is of primary importance that the buyer has contact with one particular person at the selling company, one who feels totally responsible for the contract ... The human being plays the lead role – not long and complicated contracts on paper.'

For small businesses – and most of them do not want to grow – the relationships can be a goal *per se* for the owners. In a study of small hotels in Scotland, it turned out that the 'familial unit' – the nuclear family, relatives, friends, regular customers, employees, suppliers – came first and the hotel second. The same pattern was found among small businesses in a ski resort in Sweden.[13] The network and the interaction was a personal goal, a lifestyle which was beyond financial goals. This attitude and behaviour is poorly considered in economic theory, where the supplier is expected to rationally pursue economic self-interest, usually meaning growth and maximization of net income.

Person-to-person contact with consumers is common, especially when selling expensive and complex products like cars, homes and retirement plans. In other service-producing operations like small stores, hotels, restaurants and schools, the personal interaction can also be extensive. Sales to households via the telephone or door-to-door has decreased in many countries but is important in others. The milkman is an institution in the UK; in The Netherlands the retailer brings a whole store in his van. From its start, Electrolux based its success on selling vacuum cleaners door-to-door. Their most successful salesman sold 14 000 cleaners during his career. He made an average of five per day; three is enough to bring the salesperson into the star class.[14] He points to the importance of the minute details in the interaction with the customer:

- You have twenty seconds to develop a positive contact.
- Do not ring one long demanding signal but two short, merry signals.
- Stand back five feet from the door and a little to the side so that the customer must open the door completely.
- Shake hands with the customer to improve contact.

---

[12] Delaryd (1989, p. 25).
[13] The study from Scotland is by Lowe (1988); the Swedish study is by von Friedrichs-Grängsjö (2001).
[14] From an interview with Ove Sjögren (Ohlson, 1994).

Systematic work with these and other details, together with continuous learning and testing, have a decisive influence in situations where the salesperson must quickly establish a relationship.

The transition from person-to-person contact to person-to-machine contact has reduced the personal relationships in areas where they used to be ubiquitous. Banking is a current example where the dealings with a bank teller are replaced by an automated teller machine (ATM), a telephone or a computer. The social interaction has transformed into e-interaction, which involves a radical shift in the bank–customer relationships (see R5, the service encounter, and R12, the e-relationship).

Production and marketing have moved through several stages during the past century and developed more options:

1 Everything was *customized* in the crafts society, both goods and services. The technical quality of the products was usually high; they were expensive but lasted a long time, sometimes a lifetime. Every customer was a segment of one – it was 1to1 – and marketing was thus individual and personalized. The choice was often limited, however.

2 *Mass manufacturing* in the industrial society lowered prices but offered the same product to everyone with ensuing misfit between the product and individual needs. All individuals belonged to the same segment and were exposed to heavy advertising, that is, *impersonal mass marketing of standarized goods.*

3 *Crude segmentation* through the mass marketing of mass manufactured products by means of socio-demographic variables such as age, sex and income, and sometimes previous buyer behaviour, allowed a limited number of product variants.

4 *Refined segmentation* and more subtly defined *niches* of lifestyles and previous buying behaviour catering for specific, individual needs.

5 *Customized mass production* of both goods and services unites large-scale advantages with individual needs. We are not back to square one of the crafts society, but we have recoverd 1to1 treatment. It becomes *surgical marketing,*[15] which requires a diagnosis of the current market and precision in our efforts to reach the right customers with the right offering. *Economies of scale* have also become *economies of scope.*

The circle is closed. The stages take us 'forward to basics', to the individually and community customized offering. We have broadened the scope of options through new production, distribution and promotion techniques. These stages are not mutually exclusive, rather coexisting supplements. We will still need craftspeople, and Pepsi Cola will be produced in

---

[15] Frankelius (1997).

mass quantities and be partly mass marketed. But the dominance of the industrial mass manufacturing and mass marketing society is broken.

Identifying marketing's parent relationship is not enough and R1 can be divided into several special types of market relationships. R1 only shows the tip of the iceberg, whereas the 30R approach attempts to show the whole iceberg. Marketing is also dependent on the supporting nano and mega relationships. The following relationships highlight interaction between parties in networks of relationships and different facets of the interaction process.

The classic triad – the drama of the customer–supplier–competitor triangle

A cornerstone of the market economy is the presence of several suppliers in each market. Competition arises, consisting of a triad of players: *the customer, the customer's present supplier* and *competing suppliers*.

The treatment of competition in this section assumes an RM perspective; it is not an orthodox overview. There is extensive literature on competition.[16] At the same time as the interest for RM and collaboration is growing, the interest in competition is growing. The well-established recommendation to create a sustainable competitive advantage through product differentiation, lowest cost or niche marketing is being challenged. Competition increasingly seems to turn into *hypercompetition*, a state of flux and warfare. Hypercompetition is intense, fast and thrives on continuous disruption of competitive advantages, both one's own and those of competitors. A strong player in the market is one with superior ability to manoeuvre in constant turmoil.[17] The mega mergers of the past decade in various industries such as media and financial services and the large global companies such as Coca-Cola, Wal-Mart and McDonald's only accept total dominance of markets; all else is failure.[18]

In market economies, competition is hailed as the driver of economic evolution and a necessary condition for wealth. This is a traditional view advocated by the business community, and also by governments in countries where deregulation and privatization have become forceful strategies.

However, the 'capitalist' societies are *mixed economies* in which market forces and regulations have entered into wedlock. In totally unregulated markets many destructive forces set in: only a few may be able to obtain the necessities of life; price competition may become cut-throat with streams of bankruptcies; quality may be impaired and dangerous products will be sold

---

[16] Porter (1980, 1985, 1990). See also Hamel and Prahalad (1994); Hunt and Morgan (1995); and Moore (1996).

[17] See D'Aveni (1994); and Verbeke and Peelen (1996).

[18] See Klein (2000); Quinn (2000); and Hertz (2001).

freely; powerful corporations offset competition; and criminal networks will flourish. The opposite extreme – total regulation – leads to rigidity. There is no general formula that tells us in what proportions freedom and regulation should be mixed. Every market and period have to search for their own specific solution.

Competition is desirable whenever it is efficient, but it is certainly no panacea. Through competition, relationships are formed between customers and many possible suppliers. It gives rise to types of relationships other than a monopoly (see R10). The customer is given a choice, and a supplier can never be sure to have the customer in its pocket. Nor can a customer be sure to have a supplier in his or her pocket.

In its idealized and theoretical form, the market functions through the 'invisible hand' provided by supply and demand and refereed by competition and price. Every moment millions of purchasing and selling decisions are made, and millions of activities are performed by individuals, and, today, also by computers. These decisions and activities are accumulated and – according to neoclassical economics – strive in the direction of a *long-term market equilibrium*. It is a continuous process aiming at a moving target.

I propose a pendant to market equilibrium, namely *marketing equilibrium*, composed of three forces: *competition*, *collaboration* and *regulations/institutions*. My thesis is that:

INSIGHT	The focus on collaboration is the most important contribution from RM, with an impact on both marketing management and economics, and that collaboration in a market economy needs to be treated with the same attention and respect as competition.

But collaboration will not be efficient without the other two forces. In order for regulations, through government resolutions, laws and rules, to operate in practice, institutions are needed. Institutions inform, facilitate execution and check obedience. They can range from very formal institutions like the courts and the tax authorities to religious creed, family values, accepted practice, moral codes, professional ethics, and a shared, tacit understanding of good manners. Although both collaboration and regulations/institutions are mentioned in the marketing literature, they are not in its core and they are often treated as impediments to competition.

Even if RM puts emphasis on collaboration, I would like to see RM as the synthesis between competition, collaboration and regulations/institutions (Figure 2.1). The issue is which combination of these three forces will best contribute to an optimal and dynamic balance – a marketing equilibrium – in each specific situation?

Figure 2.1 The three forces of the market economy which together can create marketing equilibrium

The global wave of privatization and deregulation is a reaction to markets that have become stifled. The bureaucratic–legal values led to a misguided interference by politicians and an unreal belief in centralized control of society. Inadequate and obsolete formal regulations/institutions were allowed to rule.

Deregulation does not mean abandoning all regulations. It is a search for more adequate laws and institutions which are supportive to constructive forces of society and hold back destructive forces. *In fact, it is not deregulation but re-regulation.* Since the beginning of the 1980s, this has been a leading strategy around the world.

Collaboration, hypercompetition, privatization and re-regulation create new relationships between customers, their current suppliers, competitors and other parts of society. How these relationships should be handled we only know to a limited degree today. For example, the re-regulation of the financial sector caused chaos in many countries.

The extreme belief in the automatic blessings of competition is just as naive as the dream of the total, planned economy where 'experts' with the 'right' knowledge and armed with regulations and institutions survey a country's economy and through 'facts' and 'analysis' engineer an equilibrium in a completely integrated system. There is no known market that has functioned without regulations and institutions, nor one that functions without competition and collaboration. In the former Soviet Union and its colonies, where the socialist extreme – the total regulation of the market – was replaced by the capitalist extreme – completely free competition – the outcome is chaos, poverty, injustice, bribery and violence. 'Good institutions' that support economic activity are required, both the formal ones and those inherent in the informal, collective consciousness of a people.

There are necessary elements of the market economy that competition and the free market forces do not master. They can be worded in two paradoxes. The *first paradox* says: *Regulations are needed to secure that free competition will not be curbed.* In spite of all the sweet talk about competition, every individual company or industry prefers to be spared the hazards of competition; on the other hand, they consider it essential for other companies and industries. The *second paradox* says: *The goal of competition is to get rid of competition.* Being competitive means that a company attempts to reduce the influence of other suppliers through various activities, among them barriers to entry and disruptive hustle and bustle.

Regulations therefore are not the same as restrictions. They can also be dynamic influences by forcing slow companies to take action, for example to declare the content of their products, and to make environmental considerations. The EU is designing institutions and regulations, among others courts to handle discrimination and contract disputes. It is a formidable task as both differences in national politics, tradition, language, culture, ethics and legal premises are being thrown into a melting pot. Whether a dinosaurian bureaucracy – big, with a small brain and in reality extinct – is being born in the EU 'capital' Brussels, Belgium, or whether the EU is succeeding in constructing institutions that make markets more functional, is yet to be seen.

One of the winners of the 1993 Nobel Prize in the Economic Sciences, Douglass C. North, has studied the significance of institutions and regulations in a market economy. In his Nobel Lecture, North (1993) proposed that the study of economic development 'ignored the incentive structure embodied in institutions [and] it contained two erroneous assumptions: one that institutions do not matter and two that time does not matter'.

North continued: 'Institutions form the incentive structure of the society and are the underlying determinant of economic performance.' Being an economic historian with a longer time perspective than marketers, he claims that it takes 500–600 years to implant a functioning institutional framework in a society; it is the outcome of the collective consciousness of a people. The possibilities of creating 'instant capitalism' are consequently no more than daydreams which many African countries and Russia have verified.

There are signs that the interest in collaboration is gaining ground not only in real business life but also in marketing theory. Alderson[19] long ago complained about the economists' lack of interest in cooperation: 'Cooperation is as prevalent in economic activity as competition. Marketing cries out for a theory of cooperation to match the theory of competition.' Solomon[20] says that 'business life, unlike life in the mythological jungle, is first of all fundamentally cooperative'. According to Mattsson and Lundgren,[21] 'competition and collaboration are not

---

[19] Alderson (1965, p. 239).
[20] Solomon (1992, p. 26).
[21] Mattsson and Lundgren (1992–93, p. 9).

antipodes but two different dimensions, one being a condition for the other'. Brandenburger and Nalebuff (1996) introduce the term 'co-opetition', a combination of cooperation and competition; Doz and Hamel (1998) use the term 'co-option' for turning competitors into allies. Gray points to collaboration as a solution to the multi-party problem and says: 'Despite powerful incentives to collaborate, our capacity to do so is underdeveloped.'[22]

In the same spirit Senge, in his treatise on learning organizations and the need for dialogue, says:[23] 'Interestingly, the practice of dialogue has been preserved in many "primitive" cultures . . . but it has been almost completely lost to modern society. Today, the principles and practices of dialogue are being rediscovered and put into a contemporary context.' The word dialogue comes from the Greek and literally means 'thinking together'.

A company's result and behaviour may be more dependent on its partners in long-term relationships than how it is positioned to competitors or mass markets. Viewing the company and its market as part of a network is central in RM. Consequently, the classic triad of a buyer, a supplier and a few competitors is naive and too simplistic. An important general conclusion for competition is that *competition occurs between networks of firms rather than between individual firms.*[24]

Neoclassical economics is based on the existence of anonymous mass markets, while in reality these markets are far from anonymous. In B-to-B each customer and each competitor are often personally known. This is often true in B-to-C as well; for example, restaurant owners' relationships to loyal guests, and the dentists' relationships with their patients. Consumer goods can be bought and sold on a scale ranging from total anonymity to the consumer and the retailer being buddies. Retail outlets may be small and intimate or be huge 'hypermarkets' that resemble the impersonal and standardized assembly line of a factory.

Competition usually refers to rivalry between suppliers. In times of shortage there is also competition between buyers, and buyers have to court sellers by queuing, appealing to personal relationships, exerting pressure and power, or paying under the table. In many countries housing, higher education, legal services, day care and health care are in short supply – and for some strange reason these shortages are accepted as inevitable. In a similar vein, the offical institutions of the Soviet Union accepted that soap, bread and cars were scarce commodities. In the former East Germany, the waiting time for the Trabant car was twelve years before the Berlin wall was knocked down. And the Trabant was obsolete and expensive, was reputed to cause throat and breathing disorders, and had a highly variable manufacturing quality.

If networks of relationships become completely stable over the long term, true competition ceases to exist. A new supplier stands little chance of entering the market, the door is locked.

---

[22] Gray (1989, p. 54).
[23] Senge (1990, p. 10).
[24] Thorelli (1986).

This is not new but it still seems to come as a surprise to marketing theory and it is not acknowledged in economic theory except as an anomaly. Arndt wrote about locked and domesticated markets: 'To an increasing degree, transactions are occurring in "internal" markets within the framework of long-term relationships, not on an ad hoc basis.'[25] Collaboration sometimes knocks out competition, and marketing becomes a political game.[26]

In Japan – where long-term relationships are institutionalized in the culture – it happens that a new supplier gets an order from a customer and the regular supplier may perceive this as a failure in his relationships with the old customer. It is not necessarily a failure, the customer just wants to stimulate competition and make sure the regular supplier stays alert: don't take me for granted! Japanese companies use more than one bank to secure excellence in service and to create an incentive for banks to be continuously interested in their customers.[27]

TQM does not specifically consider competition, but the vantage point is to be 'world class' or 'best in class' in order to survive. *Benchmarking* refers to a comparison with the very best – not the average or the mediocre. It requires comparison, not only with competitors but with best practice in whatever company or industry it can be found.

Competitive bidding is demanded by law in certain instances, above all when government agencies purchase goods and services. A purpose of the bidding procedure is to make markets mechanical and impersonal. Tenders must be delivered before a specified hour and competitors are expected to submit their bids independently. This does not always work in practice. The building and construction industry lives with continuous bidding contests. From time to time, however, secret cartels are uncovered where competitors have split the market and design bids to help an elected 'colleague' win a contract. Industrial espionage in order to learn about competitor bids is not uncommon. Bribes exist: pleasure trips; parties with 'hostesses'; help to build a summer house; and lots of other ingenious variants. However, bids are not always rational. They tend to get stuck on price comparisons as price is the easiest variable to measure. Service, quality, and not least security, trust, commitment, joint development and flexibility – which are in the core of long-term relationships – are difficult to pinpoint in simple short-term indicators.

At the same time, it is common that a supplier gets a first order in competition and if this order is successful, new orders will follow through negotiations without a bidding procedure. The first order is often not profitable but a precursor to future profits. Competition in its entirely free and price-based version may cause excessive *switching costs* (costs to change to another supplier) as well as excessive *transaction costs* (costs of handling the purchase and the sale).

---

[25] Arndt (1979, p. 69).
[26] See Arndt (1983); and Stern and Reve (1980).
[27] Based on Delaryd (1989, pp. 30 and 98ff).

Blumberg has pointed out that the strength of the market economy – competition and the profit incentive – encourages fraud.[28] It pays to cheat! He calls this *the paradox of the market economy*. Everybody is familiar with this from jobs and private consumption, but it is swept under the carpet in marketing theory. The official image is idealized: competition as the driver to create customer satisfaction and in its wake profitability and long-term success. Customers are asked about the quality they get, but their knowledge is limited. In 1271, St Thomas Aquinas stated that it takes great knowledge to assess quality and that most consumers lack this knowledge. This is just as true today, maybe even more true as the complexity of society and its offerings has grown. A cynic is reputed to have said: 'Customers are not as stupid as you think. They are much more stupid.' Maybe this is not just a cynicism but is sometimes true and is explored by suppliers. For example, prices are sometimes raised before a sale and then reduced – '25 per cent off!' – meaning the same price as before the raise; some taxi-drivers tamper with meters; and some suppliers exploit customer stress, confusion and helplessness.

Can good customer relationships emerge in spite of such behaviour? Yes, it seems so to a degree as customers, especially consumers, must buy on trust. If the consumers believe they have been given the right product or the correct service they feel satisfied. Or they lower their expectations and accept the imperfections of life; they become 'happy slaves'.

Markets show ongoing efforts to find a marketing equilibrium. When telecoms experience restrictions from regulations, they attempt to (legally) circumvent these by creating new networks through alliances or utilizing new technology. Competition thus takes new forms and the effects of existing regulations are nullified; re-regulations become imperative, and so forth.

Could it be that hypercompetition is the real driver of the upsurging interest in RM, that there is a need to neutralize the effects of increasingly faster, more fierce and ruthless rivalry? When competition becomes hypercompetition, perhaps collaboration must become *hypercollaboration*?

The classic network – distribution channels

Physical distribution is the most obvious network in marketing; it constitutes a classic network. The common designations today are *supply chain, channel management* and *logistics*, but in RM a network view is preferable to sequential and linear thinking that the words chain

---

[28] Blumberg's (1989) study is based on 700 essays written by sociology students who had worked in different industries. From their job experience, they have told about systematic methods to swindle their customers.

and channel indicate. Distribution networks are numerous, complex and interwoven. Sometimes they are efficient and fast, following the shortest route to market. Sometimes they are slow, inefficient and replete with detours and broken chains. As consumers we are surrounded by them. We are unpaid workers in the distribution networks when we shop for food, walk to the postbox with a letter or drive our car to work.

When traditional marketing literature deals with distribution, its domain is physical distribution of consumer goods, although a major share of distribution concerns industrial goods as part of B-to-B.[29]

However, the networks of the distribution channels distribute not only goods but also *services, information, people and other living organisms*, often in combination.

The distribution system for consumer retailing is a service network. Its core mission is to make goods conveniently available. The system is supported by services other than the actual goods distribution, such as location and parking facilities. These goods distribution channels are well developed in most countries and industries, but there are exceptions. At the time of the dissolution of the Soviet Union, the state was unable to organize the distribution of a loaf of bread. Waiting lines were part of daily life in Moscow and eventually you needed an ID to be allowed to buy bread. It was not the lack of grain that prevented the supply of bread, but the lack of functioning networks.

The relationships between the parties in the distribution network vary for many reasons. If a store is part of a chain, the producer often sells to central buyers. The goods are sent to a central warehouse or regional warehouses, or direct to the store. Many intermediaries can influence the deals in the supply chain. The goods are eventually bought by consumers. If a household consists of several individuals, it becomes an organization and the family members play different roles in a similar way as in organizational buying. All actors in the distribution chain – except the last one, the consumer – are both buyers and sellers.

If a few chains in the daily goods distribution are big and powerful, the relationships between the producer and the central buyers become predominant. The producers risk having no relationship with consumers and cannot monitor the changes that take place in attitudes and buying and consumption behaviour. The producers try to compensate for this through market surveys and visits to stores, whereas retailers link consumers to the stores through cards and membership (see R11).

Producers can circumvent the traditional wholesaler–retailer networks through tele-marketing, mail order, and the opportunities that are increasingly offered by TV, personal computers, modems, the Internet and World Wide Web. Companies can set up chains of

---

[29] An overview of distribution channels is found in Stern, El-Ansary and Coughlan (1996). On distribution in business marketing, see Gadde (1994). There is an emerging interest to view distribution from an RM perspective: see, for example, Weitz and Jap (1995); and Pelton, Strutton and Lumpkin (1997).

one-product shops. Factory outlets – each selling their own brand at substantially reduced prices – began to gather in outlet villages during the 1990s. In 1997, the Great Western Designer Outlet Village with some hundred stores was opened in Swindon, UK, including global brands such as Laura Ashley, Levi's, Nike, Tie Rack and Timberland. Network marketing is a system for marketing goods and services which is usually based on contacts with friends and friends-of-friends. Multi-level marketing (MLM) offers a network of collaborating one-man firms who support each other: 'You are in business for yourself, but not by yourself.'[30] Often these firms are operated out of the owner's home at minimal overhead and investment.[31] Tupperware is an example of successful party selling of household goods. Every two and a half seconds a new Tupperware party is set up. You cannot really get closer to your customer. When recruiting new salespeople, Tupperware says: 'More than Just Parties. The location is never a problem. Perhaps you would prefer a demonstration during a lunch hour or after work. Maybe you'd like to invite a few friends for coffee at a nearby restaurant.'

Distribution of goods is *per se* a service – which may seem confusing – but services as the focal point for distribution are put on hold in the literature. In reality, services are the core of a great part of today's distribution systems. Examples are the services provided by restaurants, insurance companies, hairdressers, consultants, electric power companies, water suppliers, telecoms and stock exchanges. Important, but often badly managed, consumer services are repair and maintenance of homes and household equipment. Internal services in organizations are not treated.

If services are viewed as activities, often interactive between customer and provider, it is the availability of these potential activities – the service distribution infrastructure – which makes marketing possible. Such examples are the network of post offices, postboxes and the postal deliveries. Post offices were early global network builders. Through bureaucracy and monopoly, they long lagged in adjusting to contemporary society. Under pressure from deregulation and competition, mail services have undergone changes. Two examples of innovators are FedEx and DHL, both started by students around 1970. FedEx has a hub and spokes system which means that all mail is flown to Memphis, Tennessee, where it is sorted during the night and delivered the next morning. DHL uses Brussels, Belgium, as its main hub in Europe. Both have aircraft of their own, and pick up and deliver with their own vans. The mail is marked with a bar code and can be traced quickly. Time of delivery is guaranteed and many ancillary services have been developed to facilitate distribution from the perspective of the two customer groups, the senders and the receivers.

---

[30] Hawkins (1991, p. 8).

[31] Serious MLM should not be mixed up with the type of pyramid selling where a company persuades independent salespeople to buy big parcels of goods which they in turn sell to others who sell to others and so forth, in each instance at a cost plus price. These pyramids have sometimes just become a gamble with most of the participants as losers.

Distributions of people and information are also services, for example being able to travel by train but also to call Amtrak for information on train departure, arrival and fares. The role of a forwarder is to direct goods through a transport network. Whereas goods must be lifted and stored, people usually walk themselves or drive their own cars. Consumers are feeders to an institutionalized system, like when they walk endless concourses at airports, carrying heavy luggage. Transportation is seldom associated with do-it-yourself but it may be the largest do-it-yourself system in existence. Travelling – including tourism, conventions, business travel, hotels and other facilities – is among the fastest growing industries. Travelling consists of fragmented components, centred around a transportation technique such as aviation. Gradually, the understanding for more integrated systems has emerged – the seamless service – where the customer is in focus and not the technique or tradition. As SAS advertised: 'We used to fly aircraft. We now fly people.' Packaged vacation tours have assembled the pieces of the trip and the stay in order to make holidays hassle-free.

Different means of transportation are increasingly being perceived as complementary rather than competitive. Fast railroads connect city centres with airports. In Sweden, the domestic and international airline redesigned malfunctioning ground transportation to and from airports, and implemented a functioning system despite the disinterest from local transport companies; the fight for the air passenger at one stage was not in the air but on the ground. The reconstructed Union Station in Washington, DC, which was ready in 1988, is an example of how different transport techniques meet in symbiosis: train, bus, taxi, rental car and closeness to the national airport via the 'metro'. The station is also a service centre with restaurants, shops and movie theatres; I have even participated in a banquet held on the main station floor. Travellers are still inconvenienced by transfers from one means of transportation to another.

Other living organisms are also the object of transportation and quite extensively so. In recent years weird and cruel animal transport has been exposed, that is, large B-to-B distribution networks from farms to butcheries to consumers. Studs are flown from Ireland to Australia and after completion of their task they fly back; race horses are being transported regularly; hearts and kidneys are transported express to hospitals for transplants, involving several types of vehicles and strict handling procedures. Fresh food such as fish, newly shot deer and moose, flowers and vegetables are distributed locally through personal contacts, but sometimes pass a multitude of actors from where they were caught or grown to towns and cities. These examples reinforce the lack of realism of the distribution literature, still too focused on a limited number of types of distribution.

Excellence in after-sales services in B-to-B is an antecedent to future sales and is often a matter of distribution of people. On the world market, exporting companies often have difficulties in the distribution of service people; keeping them on the spot is often judged to be too costly. To fly out personnel for troubleshooting can work in certain markets but not in others. In Japan it is considered unsatisfactory; it is too slow and the personal relationships become shallow.[32]

Distribution of speech and data via electronic media are not part of the distribution systems as they are presented in marketing theory. The e-relationship has many unique properties and is treated as a separate relationship (R12). Physical and electronic distribution supplement each other. By converting physical transportation into electronic transportation, the speed can be accelerated, for example a letter being replaced by fax or Internet transmission. On the other hand, it will probably not be feasible to fax parcels or people unless the IT-based virtual reality and cyberspace machinery can act as a surrogate for actual physical presence.

The concept of *logistics* concerns the flow of goods, all the way from the extraction of raw material, manufacturing of components and assembly, to finished goods in the store and their arrival at households. The goods flow is accompanied by an information flow via documents and computer transmissions. Logistics cuts across functional and hierarchical borders. The idea of logistics is in tune with the efforts to organize along processes instead of functions. The consumers' transport of goods to their homes and their treatment of the goods is also part of the logistics flow. Increasingly, environmental laws require recycling, which is why logistics are stretched even further (see R15).

Logistics requires a holistic understanding of a business operation. It is a matter of making processes more effective, so that manufacturing and delivery are performed straighter and faster and on time, keeping costs and capital employed down. The slower the logistic process, the more capital is tied up and the longer the time before the customer pays. Logistics is also a marketing strategy. One strategic decision concerns the scope of the suppliers' offerings: Should the supplier offer a complete systems solution or a partial solution, or enter into alliance with other companies who provide elements of the system?

Kiichiro Toyoda, founder of Toyota Motor Company, coined the concept *just-in-time* (JIT) as early as in the 1930s. 'Just' and 'time' are equally important; only what was absolutely necessary should be delivered, and this should be done at the very minute when it was needed.[33] The Toyota factory stops after thirty minutes if scheduled deliveries of components do not arrive. In comparison, the traditional auto factory strategy was to order large quantities of components and store them for several weeks.

Logistics and JIT influence quality, productivity and profitability. They establish regular and close relationships between supplier and customer. They must make plans together and connect their systems into a fluid process which requires investment and continuous maintenance and improvements. It becomes a partnership, an alliance, rather than a supplier–customer relationship. The earlier strategy for organizational buyers was to use multiple

---

[32] Delaryd (1989, p. 73ff).
[33] Womack, Jones and Roos (1990).

suppliers and to play them against each other and press prices. The trend has gradually turned in the direction of fewer and closer supplier relationships, with less weight on price and competition and more on collaboration. During the 1990s, Sundstrand in Germany has gone from 550 suppliers to 120, Ford in the USA from 6000 to 2000, and McDonald's from 175 suppliers of beef in the USA to only five. IKEA decided to cut the number of subcontractors in Northern Europe from 400 to 300, demanded cost reductions of 15 per cent from the remaining suppliers, but also offered assistance with the implementation of the reductions. One of the issues was the closing of a central warehouse and introducing JIT deliveries direct from a factory to the furniture stores.

Although JIT is usually discussed for goods delivery, it is equally applicable on services, people and information. As services are partly produced and consumed simultaneously, they must be produced when needed. Extreme examples are emergency services performed by the police and paramedics.

Waiting lines have not been particularly investigated in marketing. From a customer point of view, I would like to propose the following definition: *A waiting line is an inventory of customers waiting to be served.* A waiting line contributes no 'value-added', only 'value-reduced'. A service delivery system stores capacity to perform services, but the services themselves must be delivered JIT; they cannot be stored in a ready-to-use shape.[34]

T50, a huge project run by ABB to reduce cycle time, is an example of time-based management or speed management. T50 meant reducing cycle times by an average of 50 per cent. Some results: an order that took 3 hours to process via telephone or fax now takes 2 minutes; an order for an axis to an electric engine took 4 weeks and cost 200 euros to process but now takes 2 days and costs 30 euros; and a proposal for an electric transformer required 7 man weeks but can now be delivered in 24 hours based on the customer's own design, which required 10 minutes using ABB software.

To have access to a distribution network can be the most critical element of marketing. Distribution networks are often locked by those who have established themselves in the networks. It may be difficult or costly to set up a new network. Although US companies have a competitive advantage on the Japanese market concerning lifestyle and youth products – Coca-Cola is the most popular soda, McDonald's the most popular fast-food chain, Disneyland the most popular theme park – they have difficulties in getting into the Japanese distribution networks.

Remarkably enough, foreign companies have some privileges in the Japanese financial market. But also there, entry into distribution systems can be hard. Citibank, aiming for the private customer market, had difficulties in getting access to a sufficient number of networks of ATMs. Foreign insurance companies are kept out of the distribution network for car

---

[34] Waiting lines are treated in queue theory but primarily from a short-term cost perspective.

insurance, as this is sold through car retailers. The distribution of cars is blocked because most car retailing is owned by the manufacturers and therefore only offers one brand.

Keiretsus have made up impermeable networks, based both on regulations, cross ownership between members of the network, and social and personal relationships. Habits change, however. In the wake of globalization, catalogue sales by Land's End and L.L. Bean direct from the US are gaining market share in Japan. Internet shopping will shake up national, locked distribution networks.

Looking at channels through the relationship eye-glasses, we see networks and partnerships in which processes between manufacturers, service producers, intermediaries and customers are being integrated. This requires trust more than power-based control mechanisms, contracts and formal vertical integration. Although most literature does not particularly stress it, relationship building has been salient in many channels. Negotiations between manufacturers and retail chains often have a strong social content, where personal relationships and trust, joy and enthusiasm are crucial ingredients.

Collaboration in distribution networks is a requisite for success:[35] 'Marketing channels cannot function without sustained cooperation in which each party knows what to expect from his opposite number.' A current example of this is *efficient consumer response* (ECR). Consumer goods manufacturers enter into partnership with retailers. In collaboration they try to reach consumers with the right product line in order to increase revenue and slash cost. This leads on to *category management*, to handle categories of products linked to specific consumer needs and consumption behaviour. One category could be 'breakfast'. Managing this category means arranging products in a retail outlet around the breakfast need, not around the type of product. The breakfast category can consequently include yoghurt, fruit, jam, bread and cereals.

IN BRIEF

By looking at distribution channels and channel management in the light of RM, we are provided with a different focus:

- RM sees distribution as a complex network of interactive relationships rather than a sequential supply chain.
- Distribution should be a value-enhancing service in which goods are just one component. The RM focus should be on the total offering and the customer's combination of components and interaction with providers and others.
- Distribution literature sets the headlights on consumer goods and less on industrial goods, and there is not even a flickering candle to shed light on the distribution of services, people and other living organisms, and information.

---

[35] Alderson (1965, pp. 239–58; quotation from p. 239).

3

Special market relationships

> **INTRODUCTION**
>
> Chapter 2 presented classic marketing issues interpreted through the relationship eye-glasses. This chapter deals with special market relationships. They are all rooted in R1, the parent relationship of marketing. The focus of the relationship eye-glasses allows us to see other aspects of marketing, those which do not stand out well in the general marketing management approach but are of current significance for marketing success (R4–R15).

RELATIONSHIP 4

Relationships via full-time marketers (FTMs) and part-time marketers (PTMs)

Marketing cannot survive in isolation from other functions. This has been pointed out in Chapter 1 and in the treatment of logistics and JIT in R3. Marketing management theory does not specifically address the dependency between functions, although many have over the years pointed to the inadequacy of functional silos. In practice, the marketing function is spread throughout the firm, and the marketing and sales departments may even play a limited role in the total marketing effort. Perhaps there is not even a marketing and sales department. Instead, each and everyone is involved in marketing. This may be perceived as an organizational dilemma, but should be seen as a possibility to enhance marketing resources.

We can identify two types of marketers: *full-time marketers* (FTMs) and *part-time marketers* (PTMs). These are not only found within a company, but also in its environment. They are defined as follows (Figure 3.1):

> **INSIGHT**   Full-time marketers and salespeople (FTMs) are those who are hired for working with marketing and sales tasks. Part-time marketers and salespeople (PTMs) are all others in the company and those in its environment that influence the company's marketing.

FTMs are found in *the marketing and sales departments* and among *external providers of marketing services*. Outsourcing of services has increased in recent years and these services are reinforcements to the marketing function. Distributors offer transportation, wholesaling and retailing services, all strategic and crucial for success in marketing. The marketing function also engages external professionals such as advertising agencies, market research institutes

Resources Role as marketer	Internal	External
Full-time marketer, FTM	Marketing and sales staff	Distributors, advertising agencies, etc.
Part-time marketer, PTM	All those who are not FTMs	Customers, investors, media, etc.

Figure 3.1 Internal and external FTMs and PTMs

and internet consultants (see R29). At the time these providers are engaged, they can be viewed as FTMs for their client company.

Salespeople are professional contact people who build relationships; they are FTMs. But they can never make it on their own. *FTMs cannot be at the right place at the right time with the right customer contact and right knowledge, but the PTMs can!* Unsuccessful marketing is not solely the responsibility of the marketing and sales departments, but also the marketing function as a whole and its lack of integration with other functions.

The distinction between FTMs and PTMs has extensive consequences for the approach to marketing. It makes it legitimate and imperative for everyone to influence customer relationships. CRM, by furnishing the organization with more data, easier access and opportunities to combine data, supports not only the FTMs but facilitates the role of PTMs.

Two cases will be shown, one from manufacturing and one from services. The first concerns the marketing organization of a large manufacturing company which sells primarily to other companies and government agencies (Figure 3.2).

FTMs are found in the marketing and sales departments and in the group of reinforcing specialists, PTMs in the other boxes:

- *Management* spends time on designing marketing strategies, negotiating major contracts and entertaining VIP visitors.
- *Product development*, including R&D, design and engineering departments, has to understand the needs of customers, design quality into the specifications and blueprints, and prepare for the user-friendly operation of the finished equipment.
- *Production*, including operations management and manufacturing, influences customer relationships by fulfilling specifications (production quality) and keeping delivery times.

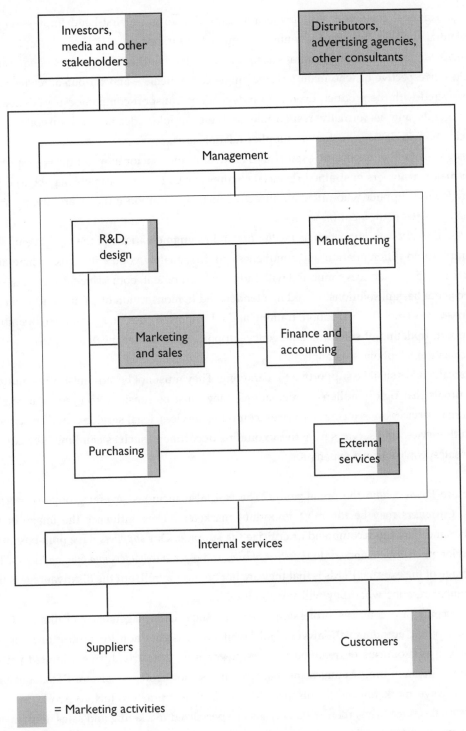

= Marketing activities

Figure 3.2 Principal components of the marketing function of a manufacturer of industrial equipment

Organizational customers visit plants for inspection to get a first-hand impression of a potential supplier, but also for continuous quality assurance.

- *Purchasing* affects customer relations as the end supplier has the responsibility of equipment sold – irrespective of who manufactured single components – and for outsourced services connected with the product. Even if an independent transport company causes damage to the goods and is formally responsible and the supplier declines responsibility, such incidents will damage customer–supplier relationships.

- *Finance* is often an important – sometimes *the* determining factor in major deals – especially for major customers in strained financial circumstances. Those customers may be forced to buy from a supplier who offers an attractive financial solution rather than looking at the quality of the equipment or services.

- *External services* are important as facilitators and as augmentations of the equipment. They contribute to differentiation and uniqueness, and ultimately competitiveness. There are a large number of services connected with industrial equipment, both *before-sales services* (such as custom design, solutions offered in a tender, and demonstration of equipment) and *after-sales services* (such as installation, training and education of customer personnel, operations support, updating of software, emergency support, and maintenance), and *general services* such as the telephone exchange.

- *Internal services* shall be supportive to marketing. They must not be 'administrative routines' or rituals that rigidly adhere to regulations; they must be sensitive to needs. Among the internal services are secretarial services, computer services, legal services, canteen services, health services and services from the accounting department, such as handling invoices and the salespeople's travel expenses.

These are PTMs *within* the organization. The case also includes several groups of *external PTMs*. *Customers* may be the most important marketers. They influence the image of the supplier and they can recommend or criticize the supplier. Our *suppliers* have opinions about us and let others know, and so do *investors, media*, and *other stakeholders and opinion leaders*. The advantage of the external PTMs is that they are not on our payroll, but the disadvantage is that we cannot prescribe what they will say about us.

The second case concerns professional services such as management consultants, CPAs (certified public accountants), lawyers and architects. It is common for professionals to see themselves as producers of qualified services, negotiating contracts during a limited part of their time. In small professional firms, partners and senior professionals are PTMs and they often perceive marketing as a nuisance that steals time from 'productive' work. In large professional service firms, there is usually also a specialized marketing and sales department. This department has to include experienced professionals who have a gut feeling for the service delivery process. In order to get leads and introductions to prospective clients and information about competitors, the department has to draw on the skills and contacts of those professionals and assistants who are carrying out assignments and have inside knowledge from the field. They also have to rely heavily on the professionals creating long-term relationships with clients leading to extended assignments. The marketing and sales departments, if they exist, are populated by FTMs, while other employees are PTMs (Figure 3.3).

Figure 3.3 FTMs and PTMs in a consulting firm

Just as in the case of the manufacturing firms, there are external marketers. Present and former clients are instrumental in enhancing or degrading the image of the professional service firm. But above all, *former employees* become influential PTMs. Consultants who take up positions in existing or potential client companies will buy consulting services in the future. It is therefore essential that 'beautiful exits' are offered so that departing consultants are treated well and leave gracefully, keeping a positive relationship with their former employer. Remarkably enough, many consulting firms behave naively from a marketing point of view, and make it difficult for employees to leave or to start their own business. The employer considers the consultants as owned assets and want to be compensated for damages. Other consulting firms see departures as part of their marketing strategy. The management consulting firm McKinsey, with over 4000 employees in thirty-five countries, is such an example. In their recruitment brochure, they present the opportunities for consultants both to make a career inside and outside the firm. When consultants leave they are offered membership in an alumni association, become subscribers of a newsletter and are invited to various events: 'McKinsey keeps in active contact with its alumni. Wherever they go, there remains a strong bond between McKinsey and its alumni, with most people maintaining close personal and professional relationships for a lifetime.'[1] There are consulting firms who get half or more of their assignments from former employees; they have become the most valuable marketers although they are unpaid PTMs.

The PTM concept dissolves the boundaries for marketing responsibilities to embrace not only the marketing and sales departments (and probably never did in successful companies). The job of creating and maintaining market relationships is being shared between the professional FTMs and the ubiquitous 'amateurs', the PTMs. The network of contacts inside the firm, the formal and the informal, the professional and the social, become part of the marketing function.

> INSIGHT   Everybody is either an FTM or a PTM. Those employees who do not influence the relationships to customers full-time or part-time, directly or indirectly, are redundant.

---

[1] The quotation is from a recruitment brochure for McKinsey (1991, p. 14).

RELATIONSHIP 5 — The service encounter – interaction between customers and service providers

The emerging understanding of the unique properties of services has given new meaning to relationships and interaction. Marketing embraces not only the customers' contacts with sales staff, but all types of contacts with the service provider's personnel and equipment during the production and delivery of the service. We can talk about *interactive marketing* but also about *interactive service development, production* and *delivery. The provider and the customer create value together.* The marketing that takes place during the interaction is often the most important, sometimes the only marketing the service provider does. Although FTMs are central to many service companies, the PTMs account for the major share of customer contact.

The interaction between customer and provider is referred to as the *service encounter*, or in popular management jargon the *moment of truth*.[2] This encounter becomes increasingly more important for all types of enterprises, both those who are habitually called manufacturing companies and those who are called service companies. ABB, IBM and General Electric are examples of large corporations who today like to refer to themselves as being in services.

The following interactive relationships can be defined in the service encounter, as seen from a customer perspective (Figure 3.4):

- *Interaction between the provider's contact personnel (the front line) and the customer.* This can be the contact between the doctor and a patient, an advertising agency's account manager and a marketing manager, or a flight attendant and a passenger. Only if the customer cooperates during the production of the service – the patient takes the prescribed medication, the marketing manager briefs the advertising agency properly or the passenger appears at the gate on time – will the quality of production and delivery be secured. The customer becomes a co-producer and this gives rise to a different type of relationship between customer and service provider than the relationship between a customer and a manufacturer. Most customers, particularly consumers, never participate in the work in a factory, but are labourers in the 'service factory'.
- *Customer-to-customer interaction (C-to-C).* The customers partly produce the service together if the provider offers the right system, environment and personnel. An obvious example is the dance club. In order for its core service – dancing – to be produced, the guests must dance with each other. The provider can only make sure that the arena for interaction is inviting. Customers who wait in line or listen to a concert interact and influence the

---

[2] The service encounter is in the centre of any treatise on services. For a popular version of the success of good moments of truth, see Carlzon (1987); for a scholarly study of the intricacies of even simple service encounters, see Echeverri (1999).

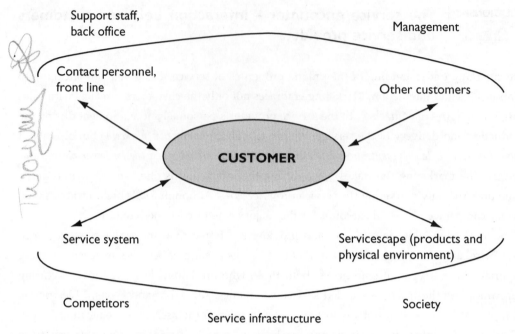

Figure 3.4 Interactive service production and marketing from the customer perspective. Source: revised from Gummesson (1993, pp. 106–8)

production of a service. When a city or country's team win a major championship, streets will be blocked with enthusiastic fans who celebrate the event and this is an essential part of the service quality of the event. Unfortunately, sports games attract hooligans and trigger destructive emotions leading to vandalism; a limited group of customers can ruin the quality of the service for all the other customers.

■ *Interaction in the servicescape,[3] between the customer and the provider's products and physical environment.* One example is the supermarket, where the location of the products, the way in which they are exposed, the layout of the store and the convenience of the parking will affect the customer's behaviour and their relationships to the store. The marketing director of a hamburger chain considered the most important people in his marketing function to be six architects. They designed the physical surroundings – the buildings, signs, tables, colours, music – which all add to the relationships with customers in the service factory of the fast-food restaurant. The staff are scarce and the physical environment, the servicescape, becomes a prominent part of the service.

■ *Interaction between the customer and the provider's service system.* This interaction between human beings and systems is just as important as between people, for example between

---

[3] A term used by Bitner (1990).

man and banking systems (manual service, ATM or Internet bank), or a taxpayer and the tax system. The system should be customer friendly and educational in its construction or the customers will not function well and will perceive their relationship with the provider as less satisfactory. Unfriendly systems scare customers away and even if they do not leave there will be constant hassle and fire-fighting. Through IT, the more intangible system takes over from the tangible servicescape.

In the view of Cova,[4] the northern approaches to RM (Northern Europe, North America) advocate organized and tightly controlled customer interaction in clearly designed systems and servicescapes. The purpose is 'user value', a no-surprise service that complies with customer expectations. In contrast, the Latin School sees products and services as carriers of 'linking value', getting people together in communities where they can express individual needs as well as tribal identity. The service provider, then, should offer 'wilderness servicescapes',[5] which ' ... reintroduce recesses, corners and curves, fuzziness, enabling people to meet, to get together in a part-open and part-closed space that favours community encounters ... ' with opportunites for ' ... micro-events, incidents and happenings ... '. The customer-to-customer interaction becomes especially pivotal, outweighing much of what is commonly referred to as superior service quality, such as short waiting time and predictable delivery.

Four roles for 'personnel' can be discerned which together shape the production and delivery system. Considering their role as co-producers, the customers should be treated as members of the service-providing organization, as part-time employees. *Contact staff (the front line)* consists of those who have the immediate contact with the customer. The *support* or *back-office staff* are found backstage; these employees are not visible to the customer but interact with the front line. Furthermore, there is *management*. By focusing on each of these roles separately it is possible to see the service encounter from different perspectives.[6] The relationships are also influenced by the activities of the *competition*, and by *society in general*, for example, and after the infamous September 11 attacks by tighter security controls at airports. The *service infrastructure* includes such things as roads, hospitals and access to news reports. The most recent infrastructural additions are email, the Internet and mobile telephone systems.

If these roles are strictly assigned to employees and never rotate, a major problem arises. Those who never meet an external customer get no opportunity to confront customer behaviour and

---

[4] Cova (1997; quotation from p. 663).
[5] According to Price, Arnould and Tierney (1996).
[6] For a discussion on different perspectives of relationships in a service organization and the roles of the individual, see Gummesson (1993, pp. 94–112). See also the discussion on contextual matrices in the same source (pp. 108–10).

needs. This lack of experience makes employees hallucinate and develop phantom images of customers. It does not result in empathy. Technology can change the relationship between the provider and the customer with ensuing consequences for marketing. Banks have gradually moved their relationship from face-to-face to a *faceless relationship* via cash machines and Internet banking. Instead of going to the bank to pick up cash we go to ATMs. Bank cards connected to a credit or debit system allow you to withdraw money outside the branch office of another bank than the one where your salary is deposited or where you have your mortgage. Therefore, you may not even notice at what bank you are withdrawing your money. Little personal contact will be left with the bank. The only contact person who can charm you or scare you off is represented by a call centre telephone voice, the one that happens to be available when you telephone. This means that if you need to telephone several times to settle an issue you can be sent off to different people each time. These people are rarely empowered or enabled to complete more than standardized machine-like tasks. The relationship has become mechanically neutral, even sterile. The service encounter has moved from the bank office – the money retail store – to the street, the telephone, the laptop on your kitchen table, and a standardized 'human' voice. The servicescape has entered a new climate zone.

During the service production and delivery, the interaction process offers marketing and sales opportunities – *points-of-marketing*. Good service encounters encourage the customer to speak well of the provider and eventually to become valuable PTMs. These points-of-marketing can occur in all the encounters between the customer and the provider's organization. A viable strategy in services is to establish the points which make an impact on the customers' relationship to the company and decide how to best handle them in order to cement the relationships and improve retention.

If the interaction works well, customer perceived quality will increase. The customer's *style of participation* – behaviour, lifestyle, mood – becomes important. It is particularly important in *the intensive phase*, which embraces the interaction with the customer during the production of the core service.[7] The provider's ability to design and produce the service and its production and delivery system is equally crucial. The job of the customer must be deliberately matched with the job of the provider. This has led to *service design*, manifested in techniques for making drawings and specifications of a service.[8] Considering that services consist of activities, the drawings resemble flow charts over the process during which the service is produced and consumed, and the organizational structure and the systems which are engaged in the process. What is new and differentiates the traditional administrative flow chart from the service drawing is the fact that the customer's behaviour and perception provide the vantage point, not the producer's systems and organizational structure.

---

[7] Participation style and intensive phase are concepts taken from Lehtinen (1985).
[8] See Shostack (1981); and Kingman-Brundage, George and Bowen (1995).

build up customer trust to encourage the customer to submit to the guidance of the Financial Adviser

The relationships between the consumer and the provider can be of different character. The following ten bonds have been found.[9] The first five – legal, financial, technological, geographic and time-based – can be controlled by the provider and it can be difficult for the consumer to leave the relationship. If you have your mortgage with one bank, legal and financial dependencies are there, maybe also geographical. The remaining five bonds – knowledge-based, social, cultural, ideological and psychological – are primarily tied to the personalities of the consumers and their perceptions of the provider.[10]

I once learnt about the doctor–patient model in which the doctor–patient relationship is '... the voluntary and trusting submission of the patient for treatment, and the essentially prescribing role of the doctor'.[11] The doctor establishes the patient's symptoms and prescribes a therapy and the patient follows the doctor's orders. It is a stereotype interpretation that doctors are know-all experts and patients are ignorant amateurs. It is a highly asymmetrical relationship with all the power on the doctor's side. A close look at the roots of the word 'patient' in an encyclopaedia also uncovers a bundle of obsolete, bureaucratic–legal values. A patient is a miserable creature, passively undergoing treatment, suffering, waiting and not complaining. The reverse is also possible in service encounters if the customer bullies the staff.

These types of relationships do not develop quality in its commonly used sense. Quality is the outcome of interaction between equal parties, where each party contributes with his or her knowledge and activities. The doctor represents a competence for setting a diagnosis and recommending a remedy. The patients have knowledge about themselves and motivation to contribute to the right outcome quality, that is, eventually to become well or at least improve their health. By looking at websites and reading about symptoms or about their illness, asking questions and getting tip-offs from others, the patients can be better prepared.

The Ritz-Carlton hotel chain was one of the first to win the Baldrige Quality Award.[12] Its credo is 'We Are Ladies and Gentlemen, Serving Ladies and Gentlemen'. It proposes that the hotel staff and the guests are equals and both have a role in the service production. This is very different from the roles of master and servant or expert and amateur which still prevail in many service encounters, backed by either or both parties.

Service encounters include people with differences in life situation, demands, social status, age, sex, language, and other physical, cultural and social aspects. As contacts are often very

---

[9] Liljander and Strandvik (1995).

[10] Although studies routinely compare differences between male and female views and behaviour, it is only recently that gender has entered research in marketing on a relational and more fundamental level; see Palmer and Bejou (1995).

[11] Cang (1976, p. 4).

[12] The Malcolm Baldrige National Quality Award is the prestigious US quality prize which has become a role model for quality prizes throughout the world (see also R26).

brief, the parties have little opportunity to develop empathy. One example of a delicate and often irritating interaction in the service encounter is tipping. Shamir (1984) claims that the custom of giving gratuities is actually what differentiates services from goods. He asks: How does tipping influence the relationship between service personnel and customers? How does a service firm, which attempts to standardize services in large-scale or multiple operations, handle this tacit, uncontrollable and individualized method of payment? Tipping – which is not dealt with in the services marketing literature, but has a significant effect on pricing of many services – is the outcome of economic, social and psychological elements in the interaction between provider and customer. In the 1933 edition of the *Oxford English Dictionary*, a tip is defined as 'a small present of money given to an inferior, especially to a servant or employee of another, for a service rendered or expected'. Note the word 'inferior'! In some countries, tips were the only 'salary' for the staff. They became related to performance; those who did a good job and were pleasant could earn more. Then, in some countries, a certain percentage gratuity was added automatically to the bill; the customer was forced to pay whether the service was excellent or not. It is not clear for the customer what is included in the price of the service and what is extra service. A subculture develops in which the employees, the provider and a whole service industry make customers feel uneasy. For many who travel between countries, tipping is a constant nuisance. You can pay extra everywhere to get rid of the issue and take the cost as a necessary evil, or you can feel a constant irritation and insecurity. In some service areas and cultures, tipping has degenerated into organized begging. To me it creates a relationship of disrespect between contact personnel and me as customer. Is tipping just accepted out of tradition and not tried for functionality, a sign of the happy slave syndrome? In Europe tipping is declining but is still expected in parts of the United States. Furthermore, where does tipping end and become bribes, for example in the relationship with government officials? Or with 'facilitators' in major international purchasing? (see R17, the criminal relationship).

CASE STUDY   **Australian resorts**

Two Australian resorts can serve as cases of services high up the interaction intensity scale. Lizard Island, a reservation in the Great Barrier Reef, has one hotel with thirty-two rooms. Its strategy is high-quality service and a premium price level. All front-line employees address the guests by name. Meals are served at the tables and the guests take their time; the dinner offers a five-course menu. The days are filled with sports activities, among them snorkelling, diving and boat excursions. The guests interact both with the staff and with each other, but guests who prefer to be on their own are left alone. Camp Eden – a health spa off the Australian Gold Coast – goes even further up the intensity scale. Thirty guests form a group during one week. They all arrive at the same time and in the welcome speech they are informed that there are two options: 'Either you are here and stick to the programme or you are not here.' Apart from health food and physical exercise there is mandatory training in emotional development and group relations. A guest's interaction with staff and other guests is sometimes so intense that conflicts occur; they may even be evoked as part of the service, and there is no chance for a guest to be left alone.

The intensity of relationships and interaction can vary considerably. The front-line staff who have continuous but brief contacts with customers – the cashier in the supermarket, the receptionist, the waiter, the ticket collector in the cinema – can experience emotional strain. At the Disneyland Paris hotel, New York, I found a poster in my room with Disney's 'Ten Standards of Excellence'. Number 3 reads: 'We smile. It's contagious. Remember: we create happiness and memories'. This seems an excellent strategy, but a demanding one. In all intense or frequent interactions with customers, the strain on personnel is high. The natural smile can lose its warmth and turn into just showing your teeth. Many services are concomitant with emotions, insecurity and severe stress for the customer, for example hospitalization, fear of flying, making certain that the craftspeople do a proper job in repairing your house, and engaging a lawyer in a divorce case.[13]

> INSIGHT As all corporations which traditionally classify themselves as manufacturers also deliver services, and increasingly so, studies of the relationships in 'pure' service organizations are of general interest for marketing.

 The many-headed customer and the many-headed supplier

When we leave the simple dyad, we quickly enter into increasingly more complex networks. In B-to-B – including marketing via wholesalers and retailers – both the customer and the supplier can be many-headed. Companies are made up of individuals, and relationships

---

[13] Goodwin (1994).

between companies have to be tied to people in order to become tangible; the company as such is an abstraction (see Chapter 7). A company does not buy and sell, individuals do. IT offers some exceptions and the buying and selling are sometimes delegated to computers; the Procter & Gamble and Wal-Mart examples have already been mentioned. Behind the computers, however, are systems generated and maintained by people.

Models of organizational buying behaviour emerged in the 1960s and 1970s. These models are presented in marketing textbooks and often constitute the ground for the presentation of B-to-B. The models have obvious merits and contribute to RM. However, additional approaches are needed in order to understand the game in which goods and services are invented, designed, produced, marketed and bought.

In the many-headed customer and many-headed supplier relationship, people representing a variety of functions and expertise on both sides participate in the marketing and purchasing process (Figure 3.5).

In order to find one's way in such a network, guidance is needed by concepts, systematic studies, long-term strategies plus stubborn endurance. Knowledge of the network becomes an asset, an investment in marketing.

The complexity of the network increases if the product consists of high-tech equipment and accompanying services, and if the market is global. In this sense, Ericsson is an obvious case. Its products are telephone systems and switches, and during the past decade it has become a global market leader in cellular telephony. Its largest customers are major telecom operators around the globe. Ericsson has 100 000 employees and many of their key customers are of the same size. In those cases both parties, therefore, are large and powerful organizations. A deal

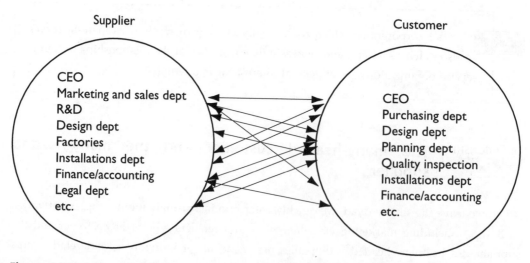

Figure 3.5 Relationships between the many-headed supplier and the many-headed customer

concerning a new telephone system – which often is a matter of several hundred million US dollars – emerges in stages. Several employees are involved both from the supplier and buyer side. The following stages for such relationships have been discerned and the division in stages of the customer–supplier relationship are based on studies of Ericsson:[14]

1 *Establishing contact and credibility.* If the customer is new, the supplier must start by establishing an initial contact with the customer and create credibility. The first objective is to be considered for tendering. Professional and personal relationships need to be established with key personnel in the buying organization, usually on several organizational tiers and in different functions.

2 *Competitive bidding.* During this stage the tender is made and presented to the customer. The idea behind tendering is to 'let the best man win'. As was discussed in R2 on competition, marketing and purchasing are reduced to an allegedly 'objective' and 'unambiguous' presentation of price, technical quality and other clearly measurable requirements which have been specified by the buyer. To advance their competitive position, suppliers circumvent the 'rational' bidding procedure; it simply becomes too burdensome. There can be intermittent contacts for clarification of specifications. Illegal means through facilitating payments may be tried (R17). Mega relationships with lobbying activities can play a role (R19), and so can the formation of alliances (R20).

3 *Evaluation.* Usually the law demands that evaluation of tenders must be made without contact between the bidders and buyers. However, efforts to circumvent the rules of the bidding procedure can become even more elaborate and initiate further manoeuvring than at the bidding stage.

4 *Contract.* This may be preceded by a 'letter of intent', which is a declaration that the customer is inclined to buy from the supplier. The design of the formal contract may require final negotiations and the complete deal can consist of several subcontracts.

5 *Planning, engineering and market adaptation.* Provided the contract is landed, this stage embraces planning the execution of the contract and fitting the equipment to an individual customer's specific technical requirements. It means an ongoing relationship between Ericsson personnel and customer personnel.

6 *Production.* The relationship continues, partly with other people involved. Quality inspectors from the buyer may show up without appointment to check quality levels, to make certain that delivery dates will be kept, and to prevent problems with potential delays before they become acute.

---

[14] The division into stages of the customer–supplier relationship is based on studies of Ericsson (Gummesson, 1984).

7 *Delivery and installation.* Deliveries are made during a long period of time, sometimes several years. There is collaboration between the installation team of Ericsson and the customer's employees to make certain that the equipment and systems function according to requirements. Only when an 'acceptance test' has been completed does the customer take over the responsibility.

8 *After sales.* In this stage the supplier must make sure that the customer is satisfied. If not, problems must be cleared up. These can be technical, but can also concern, for example, payment. This stage is an opportunity for further sales. If relationships are successfully cemented, future business will follow. The next contract goes through the same stages as before but often in a much simplified form. The buyer may not ask for bids from others, and the evaluation of the offering from the supplier is negotiated without direct competition, albeit with the threat of potential competition.

9 *Conclusions and evaluation.* It is desirable to reflect over a completed deal and learn for the future, both what was good and bad. Unexpectedly, and almost in shock, Ericsson lost a prestigious deal with the national telecom of Norway. ITT, a then major competitor, won. In retrospect it was clear that Ericsson neglected to establish credibility on the mega level, among politicians and the general public, while ITT devoted considerable resources for this. ITT had hired a public relations firm and one of its tasks was to design the final bid to communicate properly, and not just become a technical document. Ericsson took for granted that its reputation in Norway was superior to that of other suppliers. An analogous pattern of events had occurred in Mexico a couple of years before, but organizational learning had not taken place as the same individuals were not involved in both deals.

During these stages, Ericsson is represented by individual members of management, sales engineers, designers, operations management staff, educators (to train customer employees to use new equipment), financial officers, lawyers and others. Some of these come from corporate headquarters, others from local subsidiaries. On the customer side, relationships are established with individuals from management, technical departments, planners, financial officers, lawyers, installations people and those who receive education from Ericsson. The marketing and the whole production process become a joint project; the parties are producing value together. Both professional and social interaction is essential on these occasions.

Figure 3.6 shows a case of a complex network of relationships where the key players were Atlas Copco, an allied supplier, and a customer in Ecuador. Atlas sells equipment for drilling to be used in the construction of, for example, tunnels, and its ally represents the building and construction industry. Liljegren[15] has made a thorough analysis of the relationships and interactions in this deal. He speaks about the complex networks of

---

[15] Liljegren (1988, pp. 244 and 250).

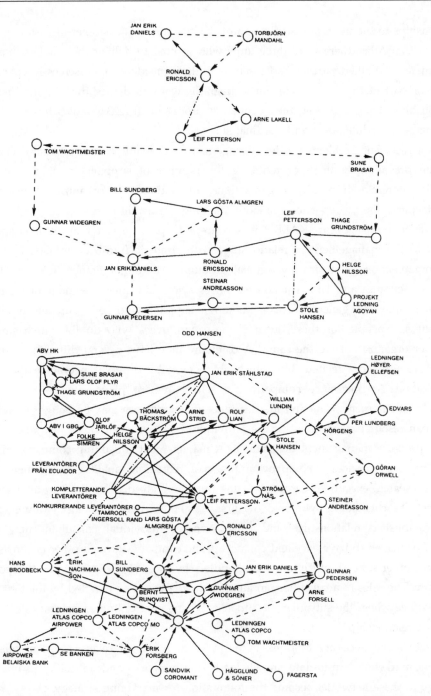

Figure 3.6 Networks of relationships. The figure shows three stages in negotiations between Atlas Copco, an allied partner, and a buyer in Ecuador. The lines denote: ————— regular and active relationships; - - - - existing relationship which is irregular and passive; ------- new relationship. Source: Liljegren (1988, pp. 174, 243 and 255). Reproduced with permission of the author

relationships to the internal organization of the customer as 'customer-in-customer relation-ship'. Within Atlas, there were three units who wanted to deliver the whole or part of the equipment. The allied partner had three units that considered themselves in charge of the whole or part of the deal. Some thirty diagrams were used to show how the network of relationships changed during the negotiation process. Figure 3.6 shows three of these: an early stage, a middle stage and the final stage.

It is a recurrent problem in sales management how many headed a relationship should be. The prevailing strategy of reducing the number of suppliers and integrating their activities more closely requires organizational adaptations. The organization on either side must facilitate the processes of a smooth, ongoing partnership.

Key account management (KAM)[16] is a concept to provide just that, as it is specifically geared to the management of relationships with strategic B-to-B customers. In Ericsson's new organization there are five global accounts: Vodafone, France Telecom, Deutsche Telekom, Telfónica and Tim. The concept raises a series of questions, none of them new or with a simple and general answer. Should a supplier who sells different products use different salespeople for these, even if those employees who do the purchasing in the customer organization are the same? A company may have several different product lines which are somehow related, but which are bought by different people in the customer organization. An insurance company can sell retirement plans, life insurance and fire insurance. Retirement plans and life insurance for employees may be bought by a financial or human resource department or the individual employee, while fire insurance is bought by the property management department. A management consulting company might offer many types of services – company audits, cost reduction, quality management systems, market research, executive search – and the purchases are decentralized to the users of the services. The consultants who sold the first assignment may wish to continue, since they have established relationships and trust. Another individual consultant may consider himself or herself to have excellent contacts in the company through other channels. Selling to a customer's head office may be handled by one of the offices of the consulting company. The sales to a subsidiary in another district could be handled by the first office or by the office where the subsidiary is situated. We are confronting an eternal dilemma: Who 'owns' a relationship?

R6 shows the necessity to think in terms of networks of relationships in business-to-business marketing. Up-to-date knowledge of the networks and an ability to interact and manage in these networks become the foundation for marketing strategy.

---

[16] McDonald, Millman and Rogers (1997).

The relationship to the customer's customer

In B-to-B customers are using received deliveries as input to deliveries to their customers. It can be the same product, which is sold onward, or a delivery that goes into further manufacturing or assembly; it can be equipment or facilitating goods and services such as office supplies or security services.

Every supplier has a relationship to the customer's customer. It is there even if it is indirect and not recognized. Many products pass through several stages before they reach the end user. The stages can represent different companies, more or less related to each other. Iron ore becomes steel and then sheet steel, which become components which are assembled into a car which is then sold to a consumer. In between, there can be different types of distributors. This creates a dilemma: Who is the customer and whose needs and specifications should be satisfied?

The dilemma has been expressed in the following way: 'It is also possible that the properties sought by the customer may not be the same, or may even be at odds with those properties required by the user further downstream. In this respect the injunction to match the product not only to the needs of the immediate client, but also to those of the user further downstream is worth recording even if this is difficult to achieve in practice.'[17] Sometimes a new product may be neutral to the intermediary, but of special value to the end-user. Should a supplier then turn directly to the end-user? This may seem rational but at the same time it means a disturbance in the relationships to the middlemen, who feel that their positions are threatened. The intermediaries in turn may protect their business by withholding information and blocking personal contact between the manufacturer and the user. If the trade is international the distance grows not only physically but also culturally through differences in language and legislation.

The suppliers can choose their mission to be 'helping customers to do business with their customers'. They must then understand the customer's customer. They must understand that if a delivery does not arrive on time, the workers and the machines in the customer's factory will be idle, and the customer's customer is put in the same predicament. Chain reactions occur which may not be obvious to the first supplier in the chain. This was pointed out in R3 in connection with physical distribution, logistics and JIT.

Even if Ericsson delivers systems to telecom operating companies it should understand how telephone subscribers think and feel. The question is what type of relationship they should establish with their customer's customer. Ericsson's long-time strategy was not to interfere with the subscribers' behaviour or problems for fear of disturbing the relationship to the telecoms. Unfortunately, most of these were state monopolies, and several of them did not feel

---

[17] Smith and Laage-Hellman (1992, p. 47).

they should put the subscriber, above all not the household or the small firm, in focus. With deregulation and new technology, smaller and more customer-centric telecom operators have emerged. The cellphone has opened up a new relationship to consumers. With its roots in B-to-C, Nokia had experience of televisions sets, toilet paper and rubber boots, an experience which Ericsson lacked. Sony Ericsson, the new joint venture on the mobile side, needs to understand how the phone itself is used as a lifestyle product where design and a stream of new features are far more important in some age niches than the basic telephone function.

The importance of understanding the customer's customer is also imperative when it comes to consumer goods and retailing. A brewery uses the distinction between customers (wholesalers, retailers, restaurants) and consumers (the beer drinkers). In retail chains, the central buyers for these chains have been endowed with power over the manufacturers. They are intermediaries between manufacturers and consumers, and they are closer to the consumers than the manufacturer is. The manufacturer risks not knowing enough about customer needs and behaviour and how these change. They lose the opportunity for customer interaction. To mitigate the power of the intermediaries, manufacturers take marketing action toward consumers by means of image and brand advertising and sales promotion in stores. Their representatives travel to the stores to inform, deliver promotion material, help to fill shelves and offer samples to consumers. ECR has already been mentioned as a strategy to create a mutually beneficial partnership between manufacturer and retailer.

Today, ordering is increasingly computerized and online with suppliers. Manufacturers also do their own consumer research, for example through consumer panels who meet regularly to discuss tastes, fragrances or new products.

In the previously mentioned study of Atlas Copco,[18] it turned out that changes with the customer's customer influenced the delivery of drilling equipment from Atlas to the construction and building industry. Atlas' customers had local and regional governments as well as factories and estate owners among their customers. Their projects varied over the years from increased production of housing, roads and bridges during the 1970s to more individual homes and large international projects at the end of the 1970s, to repair and maintenance during the 1980s. Atlas had to keep track of these changes and if possible predict them.

Figure 3.7 is a generalized model of customer–supplier relationships as an endless chain. 'Company∞' signifies an undetermined number of relationships embedded in a more complex network. In order to recognize the multiple-chain relationships, two more companies have been added before the consumer, the end-user, is reached.

The relationship between Company∞+1 and Company∞+2 develops between a supplier and a customer, where the customer is an organization which resells a product as is, or after using it in manufacturing. This is business marketing. Company∞+2 must protect the relationship

---

[18] Liljegren (1988, pp. 399–401).

Figure 3.7 Customer–supplier–consumer relationships as a never-ending chain

both to its supplier and the consumer. This is natural if we see companies as members of networks where everything that happens in the network can influence everything else. If not, the contact will be adversarial and the goal of either party becomes that of outsmarting and pushing the other for short-term profit. Companies begin to change this attitude and see suppliers as partners in a win–win relationship. AT&T talks about a 'vendor relationship',[19] Philips about 'co-makership'. The term 'reverse marketing' has been coined for upstream marketing, directed to suppliers, as an addition to the ordinary downstream, customer-directed marketing. The supplier relationship is particularly crucial in times of shortage, for example during a boom.

The relationships between Company∞+2 and the buyer and consumer must also be considered by Company∞+1. The consumer constitutes the terminal point of a supply chain. We are now in the transition phase from business marketing to consumer marketing, characterized by the fact that the customer is the consumer and not a supplier to someone else. The buyer and consumer can be the same person, but in a household they can be different people. If one person buys food which the whole family and the dog eats, there is an in-household supplier–consumer relationship.

In RM, interaction and dialogue in two-way relationships are emphasized, while in mass marketing relationships are primarily one way. Consumers also have an active relationship to suppliers. The notion of the seller being the aggressive party and the buyer the passive party is erroneous. Just as often an organizational buyer or consumer is the active and aggressive party; the initiative can go in both directions. Consumers wish to have pleasant relationships to their retailer, gas station, hairdresser and doctor. In times of ample supply of goods, the relationships can be dependent on a store or gas station having a courteous staff, being located in a good spot and having a system that is known by the customer. With doctors it can be different. Through the

---

[19] This and the following terms are quoted from Payne (1993, p. 34).

relationship it becomes easier to get an appointment; the doctor already knows much about the consumer, who can count on being well taken care of. The consumer's behaviour becomes part of the service production and the interaction determines the quality.

The construction of the distribution channel can be used to differentiate one supplier from the other. Channel management and channel leadership become important parts of the distribution network. The management and leadership of a channel can be located with the manufacturer, the wholesaler or the retailer, or any other type of distributor.[20]

| CASE STUDY | **The customer's customer** |

To a consumer it is not always obvious who the supplier is. A consumer needed a new toilet. A plumber was contacted to deliver and install it. He bought the equipment from a well-known manufacturer. The toilet did not work after installation. It leaked when flushed and the lid could hardly be lifted. When telephoning the plumber, he referred to the manufacturer as the one responsible for the guarantee, but with whom the consumer had not had any contact whatsoever. When contacting the manufacturer – a large, anonymous and disinterested organization – they told the consumer to wait for a fortnight. They considered it only natural that the bathroom was out of order for two weeks! The consumer called a member of his Rotary club – the local club is a network of members with different professions – who was president of one of the major plumbing firms and asked for advice. 'Call the head of the division and refer to me,' he said, 'we are one of their biggest customers.' After several calls – the division manager was not too keen on consumer contact – he finally answered. Just as uninterested he tried to get out of it, but afraid of disturbing his relationship with the consumer's Rotary friend, he promised to fix it. All the same it took two days. The consumer felt he was the customer of the plumber, whereas the plumber felt he was only an intermediary without responsibility and without customers. The manufacturer was not prepared to handle consumer relationships. Needless to say, they both lost one customer for good.

Even if you can see the consumer as the terminal link of the chain, there is reason to point to R3 (the distribution and logistics relationship) and R15 (the green relationship) in which the

---

[20] The importance of distribution channels in a network is treated by Stern, El-Ansary and Coughlan (1996).

fact is considered that production–consumption are increasingly viewed as an ecological cycle. Then there is no terminal point; the manufacturer or distributor becomes liable for closing the circle and recycling the product.

INSIGL It is easy to lose sight of the relationships to the customer's customer or not even make an effort to look one step beyond. The relationship is there whether you care to acknowledge it or not. As our customers live by their customers, it is an intelligent marketing strategy to help our customers help satisfy their customers.

RELATIONSHIP 8 ## The close versus the distant relationship

Both marketing literature and managers can give the impression that market surveys and research techniques, particularly the use of quantification and statistical formulas, provide first-class knowledge about customers and the effect of marketing activities. Closeness to the customer seems to be of little significance.

In my view it is the other way around: *the interaction with customers is the single most important source of marketing knowledge and the cry for more market research is often a sign of failure.* Top management and marketing executives often have such limited contact with customers and the front line that they do not understand what is going on in the minds of customers and competitors. They are forced to hire someone to ask their customers for help and to make historical reconstructions. History is reported in seductive multimedia presentations where the design of coloured graphs, animations and music offer an illusion of knowledge. In reality they drive into the future with a steady glance in a dimmed rear-view mirror.

This was the dark side of market research. It might have sent shock waves through the minds of some readers. Sometimes market research techniques are required as certain data are difficult to access in the daily operations. Statistical and computerized customer satisfaction

Figure 3.8 The physical proximity to the customer versus the distant relationship via market research reports

surveys have been polished since George Gallup's polls in the 1930s. The early focus on attitudes and opinions has been supplemented by more interest in actual behaviour and the link between satisfaction and profitability.[21] CRM with data warehousing and data mining offers new possibilities to use customer data and statistical connections. Despite these developments, my conclusion is as follows:

> Market research, with the use of approved techniques, is a
> supplement to the knowledge which comes naturally through
> customer relationships, interaction and active reflection but it is not
> the prime source of marketing knowledge.

The basic problem is *access* to customers, competitors and others. The relationship to the customer can be *close* or *distant*. The close relationship is *direct* and *personal*. The distant relationship is *indirect* and *impersonal* with market survey reports as intermediaries (Figure 3.8).

The current trend goes in both directions: increased distance knowledge and increased knowledge through proximity to the customer. This is not an oxymoron. It is simply that the interest in the customer has grown dramatically in marketing practice; in the marketing textbooks it has always been there. This is of course commendable. However, market research and the techniques that are used are a consequence of the mass manufacturing and mass marketing of the industrial era. In current and future society, with more customized production and marketing, mass marketing research techniques – in which individual differences are concealed and evened out – should not play the star part.

In search of access, I have found it essential to discriminate between *understanding at first hand* via personal experience and involvement, and *understanding at second hand* via intermediaries.[22] 'Experiencing customers' – through discussion, observation, participation, working at the front line and continuous reflection – renders deeper understanding than can be reached through research performed, reported and interpreted by others. Mass marketing largely builds on second-hand understanding and recommendations based on the interpretations of intermediaries. This is sometimes advantageous, because an outsider to the firm or the industry may see things in a new light. But it can only be supplementary. Despite the fact that techniques for market research are becoming more sophisticated, for example in search of the multiple characteristics of lifestyles, it is difficult to present valid and useful studies of consumers and the cause and effect of behaviour. Proximity, the pulse, the richness

---

[21] Johnson and Gustafsson (2000).

[22] The concepts access, understanding and pre-understanding are treated in Gummesson (2000, pp. 25–54 and 57–72).

of variation – it is all degraded to standardized statements and simplistic conclusions. The customer becomes an average, a number, a percentage and sometimes even a couple of decimals. The personal relationship has turned into a *statistical relationship*.

Certain parts of marketing operations are difficult to review through presence and interaction. Access to the customer or the data is sometimes both physically and mentally barred. If you need certain quantitative data – how much, how many, how often – or macro data, you probably need systematic and statistical research.

The closeness to the customer deteriorates when a company grows and gets thousands or millions of customers. At least, it may seem so. Small companies can get their knowledge about the customer through close relationships, but only if they are sensitive to the knowledge. This is true for stores as well as hotels and factories. R6 defined relationships between many-headed customers and many-headed suppliers. Representatives of both parties have close contact on several levels and build knowledge about one another. Alliances between suppliers and customers are often formed with the purpose of facilitating knowledge transfer (see R21, the knowledge relationship).

In hotel rooms, we find questionnaires asking guests to assess the hotel and its services. They could have a function, provided that the guests fill them out and the hotel uses the responses. Seldom do these forms tell you more than how much the hotel values your views and nothing about what they intend to do with them. I often make a list of things I am not satisfied with, but I rarely tell the hotel management. They do not give the impression that they really want to know and the risk of standing out as an odd grumbler holds me back. Despite the physical proximity that exists between a hotel guest and the staff, the mental proximity is not present and the 'communication' is left to a questionnaire.

Ingvar Kamprad, the founder and owner of IKEA, has 150 giant furniture stores in fifty countries. These receive 120 million visits from shoppers in a year. As long as the stores were few, the management could keep in close touch with customers and personnel. The management of each separate store can uphold this contact, whereas international corporate headquarters in practice cannot. In order to compensate for the relationship difficulty, 'anti-bureaucrat weeks' were introduced. During these weeks, staff from the corporate head office work in the stores. In an interview, Kamprad said that he does not trust statistics or reports; he wants to be directly confronted with reality.

Hyatt Hotels send their bosses to 'In-Touch Days' and on one day per year head office is closed for all, including the CEO. Top managers work as janitors, cleaners and in other hands-on jobs. This is excellent *per se*, but a single day or week is short for the day-to-day reality to get under your skin. As an IKEA executive said: 'You are just a guest to reality.'[23]

---

[23] The data on IKEA are based on documents and a presentation by Pelle Zandén (1992).

The old expression 'all business is local' also concerns today's global society. Joshua Tetley in the UK controls some thousand pubs. In order to strengthen the personal relationship to the consumer, the '100 Club' was established. Eligible for membership were personnel who knew the name and habits of a minimum of 100 guests. A misgiving was expressed that no one would qualify for membership, but the outcome was staggering: 250 employees knew the names of 500 customers or more; fifty could address 1000 customers by name; and the champion could address 2000 customers.[24]

The Italian Benetton family, merchants of branded fashion clothes and accessories, has 6400 franchised shops in some hundred countries. Its founder, Luciano Benetton, travels to the stores to exercise leadership and collect his own impressions, as do 200 of his staff. Furthermore, the Benetton shops are part of an online computer network, which enables global monitoring of current sales. This is both a close and distant relationship, based on personal contact, utilization of state-of-the-art IT and streamlined logistics.

Instead of measuring customer relationships at a distance, a company could engage the customers in interactive improvement and development work. Marriott Hotels collaborated with business travellers in the design of the motel chain Courtyard. When the Swedish Railroads launched the long-distance rapid train service X2000, the introduction was a six-month test period and this was explained in the advertising. Business travellers were offered free tickets to make them test the train as an alternative to flying. The railroads dared not let the train travel at full speed in the beginning as it put high demands on the rail network and safety precautions. A railroad operation is a closed network and all train movements, such as delays, affect all other trains. Personal interviews were made on board the train with a sample of passengers, and questionnaires were distributed to all passengers.

The staff was selected for those with the capacity of listening, observing and suggesting improvements. The train crew convened before departure and after arrival to plan and assess the journey. They also had regular meetings with management. The 'product manager' of this particular train service also travelled on the train several times per week. Taken together, the railway company deployed both the personal face-to-face relationship and systematic, standardized and continuous information as support. Moreover, the interactive research became a way of engaging and influencing the customers – it became an important part of the promotion.

The examples show that it is possible to keep close contact with the front line – both staff and customers – even if the operations are large scale. The real impediment is not size, it is soiled relationship eye-glasses and lack of innovation. Supplementary input from other sources such as the deployment of market research techniques can add to the knowledge.

---

[24] According to Tetley's Personnel Director, Terry Lunn (1990).

Social and psychic distance are key concepts in RM. The further we are apart the greater the risk for misunderstandings. This can be particularly disturbing in international trade, where not only physical distance but also culture and language raise obstacles.[25] If customers are kept at arm's length and are only percentages and anonymous masses, you do not apply the same ethical standards as if you are close to the customer. Anthropological studies have given rise to the hypothesis that honesty in exchange relationships is inversely related to the social distance.[26] Studies of fraud show that staff do not feel as much hesitation to cheat an anonymous customer as they would a person they know and meet. Blumberg sums up his conclusions in the following way: 'The injury done to others is often impersonal . . . People die in automobiles far from those who have designed them. Smokers die quietly far from those who manufacture and advertise cigarettes . . . in a large bureaucratic organization people abandon their role as full moral human beings.'[27]

Management and personnel can hide in large organizations and systems, and rarely have to take direct responsibility for the relationship to the customer. Through size and distance, large scale promotes inferior ethics and inferior relationships. However, the distance can be reduced in many ways and several of the 30Rs concern the reduction of social and mental distances.

| INSIGHT | My conclusion is unequivocal: *You can only understand customers by regularly meeting them, training your empathy, and reflecting over your observations.* |

RELATIONSHIP 9 | The relationship to the dissatisfied customer

When customers are dissatisfied they have the following options:[28]

- *Exit* – The customers leave for a competitor, or stop buying the goods or services temporarily or permanently.
- *Voice* – The customers speak their mind and demand correction.
- *Loyalty* – The customers remain loyal for lack of alternative suppliers or prohibitive switching costs, inertia, ideological reasons and others, at least within limits.

[25] Hallén and Widersheim-Paul (1979).
[26] Czepiel (1990).
[27] Blumberg (1989, pp. 106–9).
[28] According to Hirschman (1970).

All these options are used by customers. The feelings behind them, however, are largely a black box to suppliers. When British Airways commenced its quality improvement programme in the 1980s they were surprised by the reaction from customers: 'Recovery was the term we coined to describe a very frequently repeated concern: if something goes wrong, as it often does, will anybody make a special effort to set it right? Will someone go out of his or her way to make amends to the customer? Does anybody make an effort to offset the negative effects of the screw-up? Does anyone even know how to deliver a simple apology?'[29]

Recovery is more than settling a claim, it is the restoration and strengthening of a long-term relationship. The course of action must be constructive, not just mechanical or routine. *Complaint management* is becoming a discipline of its own.

In the spirit of modern quality management, a zero-defects strategy – always doing it right the first time – should be pursued. Errors will occur despite the strategy, particularly in service production. A positive way of dealing with the error must be designed into the customer relationship. In brief: 'Combine ultra-reliability with excellent recovery.'[30] The conclusion builds on research which says that 'reliability' is the central quality dimension – the product should not break, the train should leave on time, the customer must be able to trust the hotel room reservation.

An often suggested strategy, particularly in the USA and Japan, is 'customer delight', not only meeting customer expectations but giving a little extra. Applied to complaints management it would mean being generous, overcompensating the customer. It is a delicate balancing act between giving just enough and giving too little or too much. To add to the dilemma, customers have individual and changing expectations and demands. A study of Norwegian consumers indicated that it was not necessary to delight customers in order to regain their confidence and loyalty.[31] The requirement was compensation for actual cost, ascertaining that the customer perceived the treatment as fair. The study further showed that single negative experiences – properly settled – did not make customers defect.

Two cases from a study of critical incidents in the relationship between consumers of retail banking may serve as illustrations to alternative treatment of dissatisfaction:[32]

1 A customer wanted to withdraw money from an ATM but only received a fraction of the amount. The customer telephoned the bank who promised to make an instant investigation. Service staff were sent to the ATM and they noted that banknotes were stuck in the machine.

[29] Albrecht and Zemke (1985, p. 34).
[30] Berry (1989, p. 27).
[31] Andreassen (1997, pp. 209–13).
[32] From Olsen (1992, p. 369), who reports 272 critical incidents in his study.

The incident has not impaired the relationship with the bank as the bank took the customer seriously and quickly solved the problem.

2 A man and a woman had standing orders for payments coupled with their accounts. They later opened a new account together and informed the bank that the standing orders now should be charged to their joint account. The woman later received a letter which claimed she had overdrawn on her account and that continued overdrafts would ruin any possibility of future loans. She concluded that the bank had erroneously proceeded to withdraw money from her old account and told the bank so. The bank clerk promised to correct the mistake, but nothing happened. After further contacts with the clerk and with others in the bank no correction was made. The customer lost her trust in the bank and transferred to another bank; she 'didn't want to nag any more'.

In the first case the bank acted correctly although not with any particular generosity. In both cases the banks caused the customer costs, trouble and insecurity, in the second case maybe even sleepless nights and depression. The demonstration of social, mental and physical distance – a tradition of many bank managers and clerks to shield themselves from mismanaged relationships – obstructs the application of RM. From the bank perspective the customer is a free utility. When banks charge for their services, they should naturally pay 'fees' when they cause customers extra work. The production of bank services is an interaction where the customer does most of the job. The gradual transfer to Internet banking which is forced on customers will mean that, in the future, the customer will do most of the work. If the customer has power over the bank by being a major corporation, the customer can influence the conditions and 'voice' compensation. In many places today, the bank culture is so uniformly uncooperative that 'exit' is no actual alternative for consumers or small firms; the grass is seldom greener elsewhere.

The inability to understand the customers' lack of power in a relationship when a bank has failed, when passengers miss their connection, or when a hospital gives a patient the wrong therapy, is no less than tragic. Most of us have encountered situations of this kind. Why do they arise? I have never been able to grasp why the same mistakes must be repeated over and over again, so that eventually you believe that is the way it must be. Nor have I been able to reconcile with it. Is it incompetence, deficient systems, indifference, lack of empathy, arrogance? I am inclined to conclude that all of these explanations have validity.

Usually members of the front-line staff cannot correct mistakes themselves, as these are designed into the goods, services, systems, organization and resources. Therefore, management should promote both vertical interaction between the layers of the hierarchy and horizontal interaction between departments and functions (see also R25). From the quality awards that have been introduced around the world, it is obvious that quality can never be made certain unless the whole organization is geared toward quality. According to one of the

Figure 3.9 Alternative relationships to the dissatisfied customer

best-known quality crusaders, Edwards Deming (1986), the operating staff can only correct a small percentage of defects; the majority are built into the systems and organizational structure.

In the same way as in R8 – the close versus the distant relationship – dissatisfaction can be handled through direct contact with decision-makers or indirectly through middlemen (Figure 3.9). Companies have established customer service departments and call centres to handle customer relationships, concerning service, information and complaints. The ability of a member of a call centre to relate to dissatisfied customers is strongly dependent on personality, but also on the organizational culture. Sometimes call centres are outsourced to telemarketing companies. If their contact staff have been both empowered and enabled to solve complaints when and where they arise, disputes can be settled quickly and smoothly. Unfortunately, at the same customer department you can encounter anything from empathic employees who graciously set things right to hibernating Soviet commissars.

There can be several reasons for establishing call centres.[33] An increasingly more important reason within RM and CRM is to stimulate more customer contact, not least to build individual profiles and learn continuously. Another is to unload people in the organization from continuous disturbances caused by calls, emails or letters from customers. A third is to keep customers at arm's length, a fourth to get away by stalling. At the same time as a call centre is established, a natural access opportunity between customers and managers is abolished. The good intentions of proactive complaint management turns into a vicious circle. Customer service staff can experience difficulties with their internal relationships to support staff, such as middle managers. The experience and knowledge that piles up at customer service may never reach the bosses; if customer service employees become too obtrusive in their efforts to get internal response, they may get into trouble. The messengers of bad news risk getting their career paths blocked.

Baldrige, the American quality award, lists complaint management as a special 'area':[34]

---

[33] See also Fornell and Westbrook (1984); and Fornell and Wernerfelt (1988).
[34] Malcolm Baldrige (1997, Area 3.2, p. 23).

The principal issue is prompt and effective resolution of complaints, including recovery of customer confidence. However, the Area also addresses how the company learns from complaints and ensures that production/delivery process employees receive information needed to eliminate the causes of complaints. Effective elimination of the causes of complaints involves aggregation of complaint information from all sources for evaluation and use throughout the company. The complaint management process might include analysis and priority setting for improvement projects based upon potential cost impact of complaints, taking into account customer retention related to resolution effectiveness.

It is imperative to separate what is right from strictly legal considerations and technicalities, and what is right from a long-term relationship perspective. If a customer has bought machinery and made modifications, which in turn cause disturbances, the supplier is probably not legally responsible to repair the machinery. In Japan and many other countries, the correct relationship strategy is often to offer assistance to the buyer without charge. The production manager who initiated the modifications may be criticized by his superiors. He comes out of this predicament if the supplier takes the blame. As a consequence 'he owes you one', which opens up for future deliveries. It is not a matter of the repair cost, it is a matter of investment in long-term relationships. It is RM investment, not a manufacturing cost.[35]

Being both employees and consumers, many of us have noticed that a customer complaint resolved well creates a solid relationship, sometimes even better than it was before the incident. There are companies that do not take performance too seriously, but are very prone to settle disputes in a generous way. There are even stories about companies which deliberately make mistakes just to be able to show how good they are at correcting them. I am not sure, however, that this is a commendable marketing strategy.

Frequently, the customer does not know whom to talk to. The person who receives the complaint is often badly trained, has low status in the organization and little chance of contacts higher up in the hierarchy. Silly replies and explanations should therefore not in the first place be attributed to front-line staff but to their president and top managers. Furthermore, consumers in many cultures are too timid to ask for recovery. Japanese consumers raise their voices, although politely, and the supplier makes apologies. The important thing is to restore trust, or the Japanese customer will be quick to inform authorities and others.

In her report on trends, Popcorn claims that the 'vigilante consumer' who takes personal action is a new and growing phenomenon in the USA: 'For years, consumers couldn't see the

---

[35] The Japanese example is taken from Delaryd (1989, p. 69).

man at the top of the corporate ladder. Now we want him out front, and held accountable.'[36] In the US, the consumer can also sue companies for damages that are totally out of proportion; this is hardly a reality in other countries (see also R16, the law-based relationship). Apart from directly criminal operations, the worst sinners are found in the government sector. Officials have been able to hide behind locked doors, lawyers and stalling tactics. Whether the situation has improved during the past twenty years is doubtful, despite all the quality programmes, awards and ISO certifications. In a sustaining spirit of beraucratic–legal values a plethora of government agencies have seen the light, but they are often difficult, sometimes next to impossible, to benefit from, for example for a maltreated patient. Consumer organizations have been established on a voluntary basis to support citizens in distress. It is a bizzare situation where the citizens – who own the state – have to establish their own organs to fight the state. It's a lose–lose situation.

Offering a guarantee is a way of preventing customer dissatisfaction. Richard Chase, professor at the University of Southern California, Los Angeles, has introduced a course guarantee. The students who were not satisfied were promised $250 plus reimbursement of course material expenses. During the first years of its existence no student has evoked the guarantee. Guarantees in services, however, are scarce even though they have been more attended to during the past few years. Warranties for goods have been there a long time, even if they often imply extensive extra work for the customer. The fact that there is a guarantee can exert pressure on a company to do a better job, as evoking the guarantee is an indicator of failure.

Unfortunately, it is often inconvenient for customers to use a guarantee. A good guarantee shall fulfil the following requirements:[37]

- be unconditional and free of the fine print in legalese, and not make exceptions for everything of importance;
- in clear and simple terms, state what the customer needs to know;
- focus on customer needs;
- be meaningful both to the customer and the supplier;
- easy to evoke;
- the customer should not have to beg for its implementation.

The customer and the supplier front-line personnel face a particularly loaded moment of truth when a customer is dissatisfied, be it for goods or services. According to one study, a customer

---

[36] Popcorn (1992, p. 69ff).

[37] This is based on Heskett, Sasser and Hart (1990, pp. 89–90). They deal solely with service guarantees, but the same guidelines seem applicable to goods too.

whose complaints have not been solved well will tell ten to twenty people; one who gets well treated will tell only five.[38] This shows the merciless revenge that can be taken by dissatisfied customers in their role of PTMs, and the value of the satisfied PTMs. Furthermore, it is claimed that research shows that few consumers raise their voice when dissatisfied. On the other hand, they punish the supplier by exiting, now or later.

Initially, the options of exit, voice and loyalty were quoted. In the spirit of RM I would like to add a fourth option – *collaboration*. The parties solve a problem together – in interaction – with the purpose of creating joint value out of the current situation. It has already been advocated that collaboration is the most significant contribution from RM to general marketing.

 RELATIONSHIP 10

The monopoly relationship – the customer or supplier as prisoners

This section is about *monopoly* and how monopoly affects the relationship to customers, suppliers and other interacting parties. Economic theory talks about monopoly when there is only one supplier, and *monopsony* when there is only one customer.[39] The term monopoly will be used here to denote any party who has power over another in a relationship; monopoly is accepted jargon for power and power misuse. It is an asymmetrical relationship, where one party has unlimited, or almost unlimited, control over the other party.

The causes for pursuing a monopoly strategy are manifold: lack of empathy between the parties in a network; one party's desire to dominate over the other and misuse power; short-term greed; or simply the adherence to a taken-for-granted tradition.

I would like to introduce the concept of *power organization* for a company or public agency that has power, either as a traditional monopoly, or by being in a relationship where the customer or any other party is in practice imprisoned. Monopolies can, however, be both benevolent and predatory. A series of examples will show different types of monopolies.

We are involved in more monopoly relationships than we are aware of. In several of the 30Rs abuse has been brought to the fore, leading to captivity instead of freedom. Table 3.1 features a sample of these.

A subcontractor can be in the palm of a single customer. The customer demands reports of the subcontractor's costs, and the price is set by the customer. The subcontractor's business becomes customer controlled, most evident in a JIT system. When IKEA demanded a price cut

---

[38] TARP (1986, p. 50).
[39] Monopoly and monopsony come from the Greek *'monos'* (alone), *'polein'* (sell) and *'opsonein'* (buying food).

Table 3.1 Examples of power organization effects on relationships

R9	The relationship to the dissatisfied customer	A product or service fails and the supplier makes it difficult for the consumer to evoke the warranty.
R11	The customer as 'member'	It can be expensive for the customer to change supplier (high switching cost) through negative pricing (penalty for leaving).
R16	The law-based relationship	Legal technicalities are misused; the power organization dictates 'justice'.
R18	Personal and social networks	Can require unwanted social adaptation, but not being in the network can make business impossible.
R20	Alliances	Alliances can create power industries where every supplier behaves uniformly and no genuine alternative remains for the customers.
R22	Mega alliances	Misgivings that the EU will force small member countries to accept rules and activities that impair their economy.

from suppliers by 15 per cent, suppliers had two choices: comply and face a challenge, or go bust. Finding a new large customer in a recession is next to impossible, but the demand from the buyer may be an incentive to cut fat out of the organization and its processes. Power can be used constructively for a symbiotic rather than a parasitic relationship. By being dependent on a big and responsible customer, the small supplier enjoys a certain security and stability. A big customer can also be dependent on continuous delivery. If the switching costs are sizeable, a small supplier has power. This is particularly so if the adaptation process has made the companies structurally dependent after having integrated their systems and product or service development, or if the supplier offers a unique strategic component or service.

'Power corrupts,' says a well-known adage. Corruption in business is usually associated with *financial corruption*, that those in power are paid unofficially or enjoy freebies. The 'nomenklatura' of former communist countries – the upper class of the classless society – was corrupt in this way and a large number of them survive today in the new economies, retaining similar or even better privileges.

There is also *mental corruption* in which you imprison both others and yourself. Morgan's (1997) metaphor of the company as a psychic prison can be transferred to the customer's and supplier's propensity to handcuff themselves. The American auto industry became inmates of its own escape-proof cells built on its historical record of success. When the small car arrived – first the German Volkswagen and later Japanese cars – the auto industry could not absorb the information or adjust to the new competition. It did not understand the small car concept. It did not want to understand the combination of improved quality and lower price of the

Japanese car. When consumerist Ralph Nader suspected General Motors' Chevrolet Corvair to be defectively designed and that this was the cause of hitherto unexplained accidents, the manufacturers did not listen and examine the suspicion. They knew. In industry conventions, the car-makers determined that such accidents were caused by 'driver error', a catch-all concept for unexplained events that was erroneously perceived as an explanation. The design could simply not be deficient.[40]

Public agencies can only plead the prerogative of making authoritarian decisions when such power is called for and adds value to society and its citizens; only then should they be allowed to act as power organizations. Those who travel by air are often imprisoned by airport authorities and sometimes by airlines. An airport authority must have full and undisputed authority in air traffic control. But it should not impose this power on services in general. Authorities embrace bureaucratic–legal values which are in direct confrontation with RM. An airline has a certain market share protection through 'slots'; these are the permits to traffic the airport at certain times. If they have concessions and the attractiveness of the destination is growing – like Brussels because of the EU headquarters – airlines will continue to get more passengers, irrespective of the quality of their services.

If you have installed oil heating in your house, you are forced to buy oil. The installation is so costly that the sacrifice in money, time and trouble provides an insurmountable switching cost. Same thing if you have your mortgage in a bank and a long-term contract, or if you live in a place with no choice of convenience stores. Hotels in Northern Europe usually include a self-service buffet breakfast in the room price. In some countries this is rare; premium prices are asked, the customer has to wait to be seated, wait for service and be expected to enjoy somebody else's idea of a standardized breakfast. The breakfast customer is treated as a prisoner. Remarkably enough a majority of guests succumb to this treatment, probably being under the impression that this is the way it must be.

It is possible to order, for example, theatre tickets by giving your credit card number over the telephone. As no ID and no signature are required, it opens up the possibilities for fraud at the same time as it is convenient for both the theatre and the customer. When credit card companies try to create relationships with customers through the legal system (see also R16) by utilizing force and the customer's lack of power, they become power organizations. They cannot constructively exploit the benefits of RM. Such behaviour is not only unethical, it represents a stupid marketing strategy.

Official monopolies are not the same as real monopolies. Nor is the presence of several suppliers a guarantee for absence of power organizations. If all companies in an industry belong to alliances, social networks and trade associations they become power organizations, even if they seem to compete. Together they constitute *power industries*. From the customer's

---

[40] Nader (1965).

point of view, there is no actual competition when the suppliers are primarily protecting each other. There is no choice, everybody is as good or bad as the other. The relationship between the competitors has then become too collaborative, they have become colleagues instead of rivals. They meet in the industry association to unite against the ugly customers, authorities and other 'threats'.

Many successful upstarts have clashed with the accepted practices of the trade, set up by an established power industry. In its early days, IKEA was perceived as a threat to the traditional furniture stores and as it turned out rightly so. The reaction, however, was less appropriate. Instead of improving themselves, the members of the industry used the hypercompetition strategy to harass manufacturers and threaten to blacklist them if they delivered to IKEA. Eventually, IKEA had to turn to suppliers behind the Iron Curtain, which proved to be a brilliant strategy and still is. Finland managed to keep IKEA out for thirty years through the lobbying of the local retailers. BBBK, a pest control company in the United States, was frowned upon by the industry when it introduced unconditional guarantees. The establishment of the trade had monopolized truth and functionality.

Within some areas of expertise, competition is curbed with reference to 'scientific requirements' and 'scientific evidence'. We can call these *expert monopolies* protected by *expert power*. Within these restrictions, they can do a lot of good in certain areas. It is when they believe that their expertise is the one and only approach, and they begin to fight competition based on rival approaches and new developments, that they become a menace to the free market. Health care is an obvious case. The medical establishment and its perception of what science is puts limitations on the development of medicine. This is sometimes for the benefit of customers and citizens, sometimes not. For example, ordinary patients and practising dentists have observed and suspected that fillings, primarily amalgam based on poisonous mercury, could cause severe disorders. In many countries this is stamped as nonsense by the representatives of dental research and assigned to mental problems; the patients are referred to psychiatrists. The reason is 'lack of scientific evidence', a declaration so devastating that consumers and practising dentists are knocked out. Lack of scientific evidence, however, only means that nothing has been discovered through the application of routine and narrowly delimited research techniques, not that an observation is untrue. More innovative and adequate research techniques could show different results. 'Truth' had become the monopoly of a power industry. Until 1997, with reference to 'science' and legal technicalities, a united power industry claimed that cigarette smoking did not cause lung cancer and was not addictive.

When the Consumer Cooperative was founded in 1844 in Rochdale, England, the customer was truly a prisoner. The factory owners ran the stores, set the prices and let the workers buy on credit. As long as the workers were in debt to factory owners, they could not leave their jobs, they were imprisoned. The co-op released the prisoners.

In the cases where a company has a real monopoly, it can disregard customers. Monopolies therefore become complacent, fat and lazy. There can be exceptions, however, provided that customer-oriented values prevail. In some countries – among them Finland, Norway and Sweden – spirits, wine and strong beer are only sold in state-owned monopoly stores. The purpose is to keep excessive drinking down. The Swedish retail monopoly on alcohol has a demanding mission: lower the consumption of alcohol by promoting sounder drinking habits, develop a taste for wine at the expense of hard liquor, and offer an attractive product line in high-quality and high-productivity stores. How much of the alcohol consumption that goes beside the monopoly is difficult to assess; a monopoly is rarely absolute. Buying alcohol in other countries or at tax-free stores at airports and on ferries are options for the traveller, although these have largely disappeared in Europe through EU regulation; private production may be illegal but is carried out all the same.

If competition grows because of deregulation, the arrival of substitutes or the product loses its flair, the monopoly must either adjust or close down its operation. Public agencies often have a monopoly and react in different ways, sometimes by adjusting to new conditions, sometimes by demanding more protective legislation, sometimes by support from ideologies or politicians.

According to the original bureaucratic–legal values, it is a virtue to be inaccessible. Personal contact is replaced by impersonal 'systems contact'. People should have positions, be easy to substitute, go by the book and handle each case 'objectively'. This, in practice, only works for extremely simple and standardized matters. A more customer-oriented approach has been introduced in some niches of the public sector. After having been a dirty word, marketing has gained acceptance, and has in some cases even become a fashionable buzz-word. Government organizations and authorities have been forced to obtain revenue from sources other than taxes, which requires marketing. Unfortunately, they often mistake marketing for colourful advertisements, glossy brochures and a fancy logo, and do not introduce a changed mode of operations with the customer and citizen in focus.

Organizations also have *internal monopolies*. Forrester expressed this succinctly more than thirty years ago:[41]

> On a national level monopolies are forbidden because of their
> stultifying influence on economic efficiency. Yet within corporations
> monopolies are often created in the name of presumed efficiency and
> are defended as avoiding duplications efforts. For most activities the
> economies of scale are not as great as commonly supposed ... It
> should be a principle ... that every type of ... service must exist in

---

[41] Quoted from Forrester (1993).

multiple. No person is limited to a single source for his needs. No person is dependent on a single user of his output.

A rationale for the decentralized organization is to provide profit centres with the choice between insourcing and outsourcing (see R24).

In conclusion, a power organization and power industry can lock an economy into a permanent marketing disequilibrium. Sometimes, though, monopolies and unrestricted power are required for security and human reasons. In general, however, the market economy works best when there is an ongoing search to balance competition, collaboration and regulations/ institutions.

The customer as 'member'

If you buy a Harley-Davidson, the king of motorcycles, you become a member of Harley Owners' Group (HOG), with 360 000 members, spread around the globe in 1000 local chapters. The club offers insurance, emergency assistance, contests, magazines and, most important, the opportunity to make friends and hit the road with other Harley fans.

HOG is an example of a growing marketing strategy: 'membership' for commercial purposes. Membership usually means being a member of an association for idealistic reasons, personal development, sports and leisure activities. *Genuine membership* is non-commercial or commercial in a cooperative sense; it is not there primarily for a profit reason. We are also 'members' of a nation or a mega alliance such as the NAFTA or EU, but there we are not just customers, we are also *citizens*.

Membership is used commercially to reinforce customer loyalty and to promote long-term relationships. There are combinations of genuine membership and commercial purposes, for example through affinity cards. Affinity credit cards are issued to members and supporters of a special organization and cause, for example the World Wildlife Fund and the protection of endangered species. They require a relationship between a credit card company, an affinity group that gives the issuer access to their membership list for marketing purposes, and the members. In return the issuer makes payments to the affinity group, the size being dependent on the number of cards issued and the frequency with which they are used.[42]

Membership can be demanding or non-demanding. The customer who wants to visit a 'private' nightclub might be able to enlist at the door, maybe only for a single night. Membership of golf clubs may cost thousands of dollars per year, and there are even exclusive clubs that charge US $100 000 or more. The strategy of subscription is close to membership; you

---

[42] See Worthington and Horne (1993).

pay as long as you do not cancel your relationship to the telecom provider, the *Wall Street Journal* or the bank.[43] If everybody can become members with a simple qualification and the relationship is commercial, it is a *pseudo-membership*, not a genuine membership.[44]

The following way of classifying pseudo-membership has been suggested:[45] *full choice* for the customer (the customer can choose to be in or out, but can use the supplier in either case), *price-driven membership* (offers lower prices), *earned membership* (you must spend a certain amount of money to qualify for benefits) and *access membership* (only members get access to the goods or services). If membership is easy to copy, it loses some or all of its impact on the market. The relationship gets thin with little customer commitment.

The idea behind a cooperative is that the members themselves own and run the operations as an economic and democratic association. The consumer cooperative emerged in the nineteenth century because the retailing, banking and housing industries were mismanaged. In the spirit of the original cooperative idea, the consumers shopped in their own stores and were genuine members. This turned into a pseudo-membership when the co-ops grew in size and members became anonymous and lost their individual influence on the stores. The members became just customers and the strong loyalty advantage, which differentiated co-ops from other stores, was lost.

With 150 furniture stores, a growth rate of 5 to 10 stores a year, activities in 50 countries and 1500 suppliers of 12 000 different products, IKEA develops and maintains a complex network of relationships. The most intimate relationships between the customers and IKEA are established when customers visit a store. The relationships, however, must be kept alive from a distance. One activity is the yearly mailing of 60 million catalogues. Another is membership in the IKEA Family, which gives benefits such as discounts and pre-sale invitations. In the early 1990s there were 2 million members in 10 countries. Members buy 30 per cent more than non-members and the contact is upheld with 5 to 6 letters per year. 'Warehouse clubs' have grown quickly in America.[46] The strategy includes:

- low price and strictly for members;
- low cost locations but still accessible;
- concentration on the most popular brands;
- 4000 articles instead of 80 000 in a full service store;
- rapid turnover of goods;
- only cash;

---

[43] See Lovelock's (1983) classification of 'membership relationship' and 'no formal relationship'.
[44] Björn Lindvall has drawn my attention to the risk of commercializing genuine membership by appointing the members 'customers'.
[45] Gruen and Ferguson (1994).
[46] Degan (1992).

- no advertising;
- large packages;
- other cost saving measures.

Frequent flyers' loyalty programmes are the technically most advanced attempts to create long-term individual relationships through membership.[47] The member collects points for travelled mileage and can turn these points into free airline tickets. Membership gives access to special check-in facilities, lounges with free meals and newspapers, and availability of various services like Internet connection and fax. British Airways have gone far in customizing meals. On a long distance flight with British Airways I was offered a choice of seven special meals (apart from the standard offer): 'Asian vegetarian, vegetarian (lacto-ovo), vegetarian (non-dairy), kosher, Hindu, Muslim and seafood'. In addition, there were eleven variants of 'medical meals'.

With its AAdvantage programme, American Airlines were the pioneers in the beginning of the 1980s. Ten years later they had sixteen million members in the United States and the regime had spread to airlines around the world. Today, no major carrier can exist without a loyalty programme.

In the USA there are 30 million members in the airlines loyalty programmes, but an assessment has shown that only 15 per cent make use of the benefits. Many become members of several programmes, but the real pros stick to one or maybe two airlines. One of the best relationship strategies has proved to be the upgrading of members to elite status: silver, gold, platinum cards. This gives extra benefits, for example that every mile is counted as two miles if you carry a gold card. The purpose is to increase share of customer, that is, the ratio of a customer's total purchases of a specific product or service that goes to a specific supplier.

Through the alliances in the airline industry, a member of a bonus club can use the benefits of membership in one club on all allied airlines, including earning mileage points. For example, being a member of SAS Eurobonus and SAS being a member of the Star Alliance, I had access to a network of twenty-nine airlines in the beginning of 2002. Finnair is part of OneWorld, consisting of nineteen airlines and, as a member of the Finnair Plus club, I can benefit from the access to all of these. Membership provides a unique source for efficient CRM. The use of certain data, however, may conflict with laws on privacy. In applying for the SAS EuroBonus membership you have to sign an agreement to the following: 'SAS will register the information you give in this application and use it as a base for marketing communication. SAS will record when you order a ticket. This is necessary in order to calculate the points that give you the EuroBonus benefits.'

Information about individual customers has been used in the practice of marketing long before the advent of IT, but marketing theory has been preoccupied with averages and masses.

---

[47] The data on the frequent flyers' programmes are primarily taken from Rice (1993).

USAA in San Antonio, Texas, was founded on insuring motor vehicles of military officers and their families, but their operations have since been broadened. For USAA it is advantageous to insure a homogeneous group, characterized by an economy in good order. Historical statistics, which are the grounds for insurance, offer reliable predictions. The company takes service quality seriously, for instance by calling the customer after a claim has been processed to make certain that they are satisfied.

Trading stamps or gifts, which have long been used to promote loyalty, give little continuous customer information. The pseudo-membership and the card offer better opportunities. Argos is a card system in which the consumer collects points for purchases, which can later be used in Argos-associated stores. Any retailer can join the system. In the UK, the retail chains Boots and Sainsbury offer the possibility of collecting points for train and airline tickets.

The value of a customer database can easily be overrated, it is not self-organizing. It offers opportunities, which demand active management and innovative and systematic utilization. RM supported by eCRM is likely to develop continuously during the next decade. CRM is often mentioned as the greatest advantage of IT.

There is no doubt that pseudo-membership provides benefits to customers. But it also requires work from the customer. The provider and the customer are co-producers of a win–win relationship, although the many and sometimes intricate membership regulations can make customers behave irrationally. For example, upgrading on flights has proven attractive for business people. Instead of arriving just before check-in and boarding time, surprisingly many come even two hours before to line up for a possible upgrade. The customer may become imprisoned in a rat race for benefits. Furthermore, being a member in too many commercial clubs makes it difficult to keep track of all the cards, codes and offerings.

In summary, membership serves the following purposes for the supplier:

1 It helps increase retention and share of customer.
2 It provides more information about customers, and CRM makes it possible to build a database of any number of customers, thus replacing blunt mass marketing with targeted communication and customized offerings.
3 If the competition offers membership, an individual supplier may have to join in order to stay in the market.

The e-relationship

E-relationships embrace relationships, networks and interaction based on IT. Like eCRM, e-relationships have appeared throughout the text, naturally as they exist in some form in all company, consumer and citizen activities. Under R12, a more comprehensive review will be given, discussing strengths, weaknesses and question marks.

IT introduces a new infrastructure in our economies and offers new opportunities for marketers. To understand what happens in the network society requires a great deal of creativity, reflection and experimentation. IT is presented as the saviour, the pill that combines penicillin, Viagra and Prozac, and is prescribed to every company, government, consumer and citizen. The dotcoms were bestowed upon us as the fast lane to wealth in mushrooming stock with the World Wide Web as its vehicle. But the steering system turned out to be defective.

Whereas the Harry Potter stories are sold as fiction, witchcraft and wizardy, the dotcoms and the Internet were sold as reality. It is inevitable to be influenced by the sensations offered by corporations and the media; they form their own reality however unrealistic it turns out to be. IT companies, finance institutions, consultants, stockbrokers and most of all the media have a self-interest in hyping the information to maximum decibels. The urgency for common sense is nowhere as evident as in IT. There is a Pareto optimality; 10 per cent of what is communciated is useful, 90 per cent is garbage. But the embarrassing question remains: *Which 10 per cent is of value?*

A book on RM can contribute to put the e-relationship into a context and thereby renew marketing theory. Just like in RM, the heart of IT is relationships, networks and interaction. IT reinforces the significance of a new economy and it is most clearly evident in eCRM. We cannot, however, just hook on to extant marketing management. When introducing websites and CRM systems, a company must convert to a true e-business with strategy, organization and systems which take advantage of the new opportunities and let them loose with full power.[48]

To give context and theory to marketing with IT we should give history a chance without regressing to conservatism and nostalgia. Somebody has said that 'the only thing we learn from history is that we do not learn from history'. We find that IT promises rarely become reality, at least not within the same decade as they are proclaimed. Sometimes the news becomes swiftly obsolete and sometimes there is no need in the market. Next to the industry of politics, no industry litters the road with so many unfulfilled promises as the IT industry. Products, services and software are launched on visions, at worst illusions. Personally I have fallen into many of the IT pits, both as consumer and businessman.

IT offers a complement to other networks – roads, railways, canals, airlines, post, telephony, radio, TV – which have long since formed an infrastructure for business and marketing. The networks meant great changes in our ways of communicating and doing business. Some are very old. Printing gave rise to the first mass medium in the fifteenth century.

The predecessors of today's telecom, the telegraph and the telephone, have been there long. Alexander Graham Bell patented the first usable telephone in 1876 and Ericsson celebrated its

---

[48] For current efforts to put IT in a marketing context, see Gabbot (1998); Kalakota and Robinson (1999); and Newell (2000).

125th anniversary in 2001. Electronics and its practical applications have grown with progressive speed during the past forty years. IBM launched mainframe computers in the 1960s, and Apple Macintosh made the personal computer user-friendly during the 1980s. The fax got its breakthrough in the late 1980s. It took over a large part of postal services, but ten years later it had been marginalized by the Internet, email and mobile telephony.

Today's IT integrates the telecom, computer and media industries, all with different histories and cultures. A new wave in communications and relationship building has seen the light of day. The Internet is an electronic network of relationships, and links market, mega and nano relationships. And it is all growing more mobile. In many countries more than half the population is connected to email and the Internet, and in Northern Europe more than 70 per cent have cellphones.

Contrary to the popular talk about faster and faster development and changes, IT is not an instant revolution, it is a slow evolution. Lennstrand puts the philosophical question: 'Why does it move so slowly when it moves fast?' What happened to distance work, e-learning, navigation systems in cars, e-publishing and e-commerce?[49] These questions and their doubts are corroborated by Microsoft's Bill Gates, who says that companies must view the use of the Internet and the Web as long-term investment which demands redefined marketing strategies. The Internet and the Web will not reach their full potential until after ten or twenty years. The profits will not come immediately. Nicolas Negroponte, the MIT Media Lab professor, recently said: 'The only industry that has made any money on the net is the porno industry.'[50]

From having primarily offered *information* – an electronic brochure and a billboard – the Internet and its websites have become a *market* where you buy and sell, and an *arena for experiences and social contact*. All three tasks will remain, but they need to mature and develop further. All have a role in RM and CRM.

The traditional physical *marketplace* is being supplemented with the *e-market, the marketspace*. For example, the spot market for oil was once in Rotterdam, The Netherlands. Today it is an e-network, spread around the clock and the globe. It is everywhere, but yet it is nowhere. 'Any time, any place' is becoming a real marketing strategy with the assistance of the e-relationship.[51] Time and space perceptions are invalidated. The customer and supplier scripts are rewritten. Through the Internet, food can be ordered and Internet banks can process bills when it suits the customer. Call centres can be physically placed anywhere.

The Internet offers a break for C-to-C interaction which is not constrained by the physical marketplace or a phone call between two people. It offers enhanced interaction between people with similar interests and lifestyles; you find new friends on the Web. Electronics build

---

[49] Lennstrand (2001).
[50] At a presentation in Stockholm, Sweden, spring of 2001 (author's notes).
[51] Davis (1987, pp. 12–89).

informal and self-organizing networks, small communities in the large society with little chance for politicians and governments to exert control. Chat groups can exchange views on the quality of goods, services and suppliers. If you are ill you can seek medical information not only in databases, but also from fellow patients around the world. You can be well equipped before the high touch meeting with a doctor.

There is more high-tech news: *the search agent, the artificial customer.* The machine can function as a proxy for the real customer both within B-to-C and B-to-B, searching for information according to customer profiles and needs, and execute purchases. In many cases B-to-B has already turned to M-to-M, machines selling to and buying from machines. The customer gets a butler, available for the ordinary person and not just for the rich and famous. The artifical customer may grow in importance but does not exist in economic theory.[52]

Electronics is not just an aid for mass processing, storing and transportation of data. It is a tool for strategic marketing, which is epitomized by eCRM. It creates new markets which are missing among the type of markets in economics. If the company does not appear in a certain e-network, it is out of the market. If farmers did not appear at the town square – the original physical marketplace – they did not exist in the local networks of those days and could not sell their carrots and eggs. This market, just like that of today's brick-and-mortar grocery store, was physical and tangible. Now there are global market squares where the computer screen is the stand; it has been called click-and-mortar. E-markets will not replace other markets – there are still local markets at the town square – but the proportions between marketplace and marketspace will change.

Although IT is presented as conveying and processing information in a richer and faster way, it offers primarily *media – conduit – and not better content.* A letter does not improve in content because it is written on a computer or sent via the Internet. On the other hand, there is a link between content and media. Even if we do not entirely subscribe to Marshall McLuhan's famous thesis that 'the medium is the message', the chosen medium influences the receiver's perception of the content. It partly offers a new context. Davenport (1997) speaks of information *ecology* instead of information *technology*. Ecology stresses the social context and relationships. To become meaningful, he states, data need to be converted to relationships. Consequently, e-networks should be designed to manage relationships; only then do they offer meaningful information.

IT is high tech that can, under certain circumstances, be a rational tool to make things quicker, cheaper and simpler. The major contribution, however, is that IT creates new markets, new relationships and new roles. IT would not be given a prominent place in RM if it were only a matter of technology and faster data processing. The interactive role of the

---

[52] Gatarski and Lundkvist (1998); Gatarski (2001).

customer, as well as customer power, grows. But IT is a secondary enabler; the real enabler is the human being.[53] IT offers no markets if there is no one to organize them, and consumers and companies must be connected to the networks to explore their potential. 'Making sense of technology' becomes imperative. IT must find its place in the daily life of the consumer, not just in the plans of the bank directors.[54] IT supplements our achievements just like the crane spares our backs and the car speeds up transportation. E-relationships are technically relationships at a distance that sometimes translate into a totally new type of close relationship.

IT has gradually influenced the structures and processes of companies. eCRM can contribute to glue together activities which are taken from different parts of an organization, from different legal units with different owners, and from different geographical locations. IT can mean enhanced ability to act and reduced cost of customer contact. This may only be the overture to a new type of company where the future possibilities of electronics are now being explored: databases with rapid access to customers, rapid networks of communication and standards that allow rapid application of new knowledge.

A reason why IT forecasts and applications have sometimes shot off the target is the inability to combine *high tech* and *high touch*, where high touch represents human contact. We have met eCRM and hCRM already. I encountered high tech–high touch in Naisbitt's book *Megatrends* as early as 1982. Going back to the book twenty years later, I find that the idea is more alive than ever.[55] High tech–high touch builds on the need to balance ' . . . the material wonders of technology with the spiritual demands of our human nature' and Naisbitt's conclusion was: 'The more high technology around us, the more the need for human touch.'

Instead of *substituting* technology for human contact, technology has become an *impetus* for more human contact, partly in new forms, partly in old forms. The urgency of human contact is obvious; for example, the face-to-face contact between the elderly and a nurse.[56] To make care 'efficient' by replacing high touch with alarm systems and TV screens is absurd and irresponsible; technology can at best be a complement.

Downsizing has become a euphemism for firing people. Automation is good in certain applications and for certain individual customers, and can lead to improved service and less work. For other customers it can be a burden, for example for the largest segment in our economy, the senior citizens. To train yourself to take over the job of a bank teller or a travel agency clerk is presented as 'knowledge development', but for many it is just deteriorating service. The customer is expected to invest in a computer, and Internet subscription and

---

[53] Wikström, Lundkvist and Beckérus (1998, p. 17).
[54] Carlell (2001; the quotation is the title of her book on banking and consumers).
[55] Naisbitt has followed up the idea with a recent book called *High Tech/High Touch* (1999). The quotations are from Naisbitt (1982, pp. 42 and 52).
[56] Mattsson and den Haring (1999).

software, learn how to operate the system, and carry the hassle of unintelligible instructions and pig-headed computers, and bad support from the supplier. Customers undertake the larger share of IT development, the correction of faulty programmes and systems that are down. Over the long term this may or may not stand out as rational. The customer is thus a co-developer, co-investor and a co-producer, sometimes voluntary, sometimes through crude force from the companies.

Many observations support the mutual dependency between technology and human action. One example is the Bay Area in California, where two cultures were nurtured: IT with its heartland in Silicon Valley, and the alternative lifestyles of New Age hippies and the gay movement in the neighbouring city of San Francisco. One observation is that there have never been so many international conferences with so many delegates as during the past few years, coinciding with the breakthrough for the Internet and email. Why don't these delegates, in the name of economic rationality, meet in Internet conferences? They do not need to leave their homes of offices, pay airline tickets and hotel nights. Until the setback that occurred after the 11 September 2001 attacks against the World Trade Center and the Pentagon, the growth of travelling has never been so rapid. This has led to congested air space above airports with delays and inferior service quality. The e-relationships have spawned a need to meet in real life, not, as was postulated, a reduced need.

A possible explanation is that faster and simpler communication permits more productive human encounters, both to work more efficiently and to mingle socially, for example, play golf, share adventures like white water rafting, and enjoy a concert. It is a yin and yang relationship where the tension between the extremes and an eternal ever ongoing effort to strike a balance is the vitalizer. If one extreme takes charge, life will come to a standstill. Yin and yang are often quoted but misunderstood concepts. They say that the opposites are dependent on each other, that life is a matter of both – and not of either/or. It is not either IT or human touch, it is not either competition or collaboration, but both. In this sense the opposites are not adversaries but partners.

Parallel to high tech we can see the need for experiences and kicks. We have the dedicated consumer, the experience junkie, relentlessly chasing trends, challenges and adventures. Whereas Amazon.com has grown and broadened its product line, the traditional bookstores have become experience centres. Barnes & Nobel and Chapters keep their store open until 10 or 11 p.m., and offer cafés and restaurants and evenings with authors. The mobile phone has become a social toy where ten-year-olds send SMS messages and play games, and compare features and models rather than talking. As an Italian woman in her mid-thirties said to me when I expressed irritation over her constantly ringing cellphone: 'But Evert, this is my social life.' Perhaps this is the future way of never being physically and mentally at the same place. Presence 'here and now' is replaced by an infinite compulsion to fast-changing experiences.

Even if high tech may be felt as cold, it is not a given that personal contacts are friendly and passionate. The lack of knowledge and social intelligence among front-line service staff is one of the most frequent causes of customer dissatisfaction. As a customer you often have no desire for contact; you want to be left in peace and prefer a machine or self-service. High tech can even add human dimensions that do not exist in the physical world. The computer enables employees to remember and consider the habits and needs of loyal customers. Marriott hotels have a database – today we should say a CRM system – with customer information. It contains such things as credit card number, corporate rate, non-smoker and a room with a street view, all that will facilitate reservation and check-in procedure. This is a practical measure which creates a bond but not an intimate relationship. It does, however, facilitate positive interaction between hotel staff and customer. The disadvantages of impersonal treatment fostered by large-scale operations can be offset by the combined CRM system and personal contact at the local hotel.

E-networks thus build relationships between suppliers and customers and other stakeholders. Here are some examples of applications.

B-to-C[57]

Great expectations have been tied to home shopping, that is, retailing via the Internet; 'retailing' became 'e-tailing'. Instead of visiting a store, the consumer visits a website and gets the goods delivered at home. There are advantages with e-markets: speed, global reach, access to current information and online purchasing with credit card. There is also reason for shopping for daily goods on the Net: less dependence on the hour, price can sometimes be lower, price comparisons may be facilitated, easier to shop globally. It may be a relief to be spared inevitable C-to-C interaction. E-commerce may give rise to new consumption patterns that can, for example, augment the value of bookstore services.

Still, however, most of what websites can offer is bought better and cheaper in shops; groceries may even be more expensive on the net. Home shopping will find its niche but, in the beginning of 2000, the average market share in Europe was 0.2 per cent and in the US 1.2 per cent. Ordering goods is not new, that was more efficiently done sixty years ago. You called the grocer, left a note in the store or just told what you needed. After an hour or so a little sweating errand boy came biking with the goods and was given a few pennies as a gratuity. Internet shopping becomes more expensive today as the distribution work done by the customer must be done by others, but it is not clear if it is more convenient for the customer. There is little sense in being able to send an order via the Internet if the goods are still

---

[57] This section is partly inspired by Frostling-Henningsson (2000).

distributed with traditional logistics: pick the goods from the shelf, pack them and deliver them. There are also other obstacles: technical hassle, impersonal, unsafe payment, and goods missing at delivery. A study of consumer Internet shopping in the UK showed that 40 per cent of the deliveries were late, 17 per cent were not delivered and 5–10 per cent were sent back by the customer.[58]

B-to-B

Of all e-commerce in 2000, B-to-B accounted for almost 90 per cent. In the US this meant $157 billion (against $22 billion for B-to-C) and the (uncertain) prediction for 2003 is $2500 billion, an increase by sixteen times in a few years.[59] Retailers order their goods via portable terminals in the store or online with the manufacturer's factory or warehouse. In R6 (the many-headed customer and the many-headed supplier) it was clarified that it is not companies but individuals who buy and sell. This is no longer the whole truth as M-to-M trading is made possible. The documents and the logistics are programmed for recurrent delivery between firms who have established a long-term relationship, and the effect is reduced cost. One application is simplified public purchasing. The government sector – such as defence and health care – is one of the largest markets in every country. Within the mega alliance of the EU, government purchasing is gargantuan.

Information-based products

Software, financial information and tickets are examples of offerings that are particularly well suited for the Internet. For these, there is no need for physical transportation but the information can be downloaded from the Web to the customer's computer. The Internet should be perfectly suited for e-tickets loaded into your credit card or airline bonus programme. Despite my recurrent efforts with SAS, spread over a year, I have not even, as a gold member, been able to find enough information and instructions within a reasonable time to make a ticket purchase complete. How many hours do providers expect their customers to put in? Research projects have shown that the time-saving promoted by banks and retailers is rarely there; on the contrary, it often takes more time.[60] Either providers do not invest seriously into a functioning website or it is much more complicated to design the site than top management

---

[58] According to a study by UK Trading Standards, reported in the media in 2000.
[59] According to a study by Merrill Lynch, reported by MSI, Marketing Science Institute (2001, p. 1).
[60] Frostling-Henningsson (2000) and Carlell (2001).

can envision. IATA (International Air Transport Association) has decided that, from 1997, e-tickets shall replace the conventional tickets.

Other media products such as books and records can be sold in two ways, either to be downloaded from the Net or to be physically distributed. ABBA exists physically as the nostalgic musical hit 'Mama Mia', but the group has been dissolved for twenty years. Their CDs sell and they exist as a website. Downloading music from controversial sites such as Napster was considered a threat by the music industry. Napster used C-to-C interaction, 'peer-to-peer technique', meaning that the customers swap music files with each other. After legal action was taken, the question remains what the net effect will be: reduced CD sales because of 'bootlegging' or increased interest in music with subsequent sales increases.

Much of e-commerce is mail order, which is now advertised on the Net and ordered there instead of being advertised in magazines and ordered by coupon, phone or fax. The majority of Amazon's 7500 employees are busy picking, packaging and dispatching books, records and their non-media products, just like any mail-order business has been doing for a hundred years.

Money

In the financial sector – banks, insurance, stock exchanges, brokers, finance and accounting departments, consumer transactions – membership of an e-network is a *sine qua non*. The historical date when the London Stock Exchange went electronic (8 March 1987) is referred to as 'the big bang'. The traditional, elderly London City banker and broker, dressed in bowler hat, umbrella and with a Rolls-Royce, was replaced by the computerized yuppy dressed in Italian fashion suits, with credit cards and a Porsche. The old boy network of British gentlemen, held together through their fathers' social relationships, the school tie, the club and title, began to lose its grip. Computer knowledge, youth, action and a stream of financial innovations became the hallmark when the marketplace transformed to marketspace. Difficulties arose for the old broker companies, whose previously stable and impermeable networks became redundant. In buying shares, you no longer become the owner of a tangible certificate on paper, it is an intangible 'electronic share ownership' in a 'certificate-less society'. Today, the broker relationship is on its way to becoming a broken relationship altogether. This is so because customers can open accounts with e-brokerage services and do the trading themselves. It is quicker and cheaper, but it lacks the personal advice and assistance, whatever that is worth. Through its speed, however, it offsets a healthy type of inertia of the traditional system which allowed better control and held back premature reactions.

DIAL, a European insurance company, is an example of efficient administration and marketing through IT. Its insurance for cars and homes is sold via direct mail, telephone or computer, and personal relationships are only required in special cases. Swift is a system between banks in sixty countries with the purpose of handling payments. It is so far unclear what are hyped dreams and what is reality to the consumer. Two of Sweden's largest banks who boast about their IT readiness have difficulties even to send a sum of money to Norway (Handelsbanken needed five days and a large form to fill out for the transfer of 200 euro) or Finland (Nordea could not get the money underway until a tabloid made a feature article and the bank president intervened). Internet banks become more common and the industry has decided to force them on the market. This illustrates the dilemma of the marketing concept: Are companies really customer-centric or are they governed by power and size? Is the customer slow and conservative? Does the bank know best and have to take on an educational task? Or is the bank a victim of its own self-created perceptions and trends – its 'group think' – which is then forced on its private and business customers at all costs?

These are examples of current marketing practices involving electronic relationships. But electronic relationships are not limited to marketing. Henry Ford acquired fame through his declaration that 'everybody can get the colour of the car they want, as long as it is black'. This one-size fits all strategy became a 'truth' in the era of standardization and mass manufacturing, when productivity was maintained through long series of identical products. For many years, we have been able to buy basic car models with options for colour, air-conditioning, automatic or manual gears, among others. It is a *modular design*, which the computer can handle by combining a large number of standardized modules. It has been given the paradoxical label *mass customization*.[61]

Those who did not grow up with the present electronics may have difficulties in utilizing the potential; there are cognitive and emotional walls to knock down. The CEO of Sony Electronic Publishing Co. may be correct in concluding that when people come home and sit down in front of a television they are only open to interaction with the refrigerator.

The technical impediments are stumbling blocks that must be removed and the users need to adjust their behaviour and attitudes. Electrolux and Ericsson started a joint venture to turn the kitchen into the 'brain' of the 'intelligent building'. The refrigerator was supposed to order new orange juice for me before I ran out of it. The president of Electrolux replied to the question why the project was not a smash hit: 'The consumer is more conservative than we thought.'[62] I wonder if the reactions of consumers are not rather signs of common sense. 'Make my day,' Clint Eastwood and Ronald Reagan would have said.

E-markets give rise to a series of questions. Will a new type of social and commercial relationship be established between people who grow up with the Internet? What type of

---

[61] Davis (1987, pp. 138–40).
[62] Interview with Michael Treschow in *Svenska Dagbladet*, 23 September 2001, p. 5 in the business section.

business cultures will IT create? What happens to the high tech–high touch balance? What happens when h-relationships – the close face-to-face or ear-to-ear relationships – are replaced by distant e-relationships? When the bank moves home to the telephone and the PC, the bank will only 'know' its customers as transactions and statistics, not as human beings. How can one company get its customers to its website when it is so easy to surf from one site to another? How do we learn to design customer-friendly sites that really work and where customers do not get fed up by all irrelevant 'information' and demands on filling in time-consuming profiles and forms? How do we make money from websites and how do we make payment safe? And finally, the eternal question for marketers: timing! When is the time ripe to do what? And a question for scholars: When is the time ripe to enter the marketspace and e-relationships into marketing theory, and not just add them as anecdotes? When will the artificial agent become part of buyer behaviour theory?

> INSIGHT Whatever the answers to these questions are, IT will change market, mega and nano relationships.
>
> *E-relationships will create new markets and new ways to run a business.*

Parasocial relationships – relationships to brands and objects

RELATIONSHIP 13

In her bestseller *No Logo*, Naomi Klein directs severe criticism against global brands. She points out that industry now understands that ' . . . successful corporations must primarily produce brands, as opposed to products'.[63] Brands are old, and the core of politics and the church has often been symbols – the crown, the coronation, Buckingham Palace, the White House, the cross, the communion, the Vatican – rather than content, such as a promise or a message. Industry, however, has been more oriented toward manufacturing products and has seen brands as a form of advertising. Increasingly, the brand has become the 'real' output, and manufacturing has become a network of partners and subcontractors.

We usually think of relationships as personal and the 30Rs are primarily relationships between people. But there are also *parasocial relationships*,[64] which involve objects, symbols and

---

[63] Klein (2000; quotation from p. 3).
[64] *'Para'* is Greek and means 'beside'; parasocial relationships then are relationships beside the relationships between individuals. For a discussion of its meaning for RM, see Cowles (1994).

other less tangible phenomena. Our relationships to corporations, their services and products are often impersonal but yet important through the *image* they convey to us. These relationships are manifested in the connotations of company names, brands, trade marks and well-known business leaders or other people who symbolize a business. Just like a person, a product or a company has a soul, a personality and a body language. A limousine and French champagne have a different appeal than a taxi and beer. Russian caviar, oysters and red roses symbolize festivity, romance and wealth.

The established term 'brand' emerges from a product tradition and agriculture; a symbol was burnt into the hide of cattle to mark ownership. It is equally applicable to services, companies, people or other carriers of symbolic values. The brand can be a word, an acronym, a token or a graphic design such as a logotype. It can also be a human being whom you do not meet, or who may not even exist. Companies have signed direct mail with genuine-looking, yet fictitious, names and if a consumer has asked for the name on the phone, someone has answered with this name. Tobacco companies use healthy-looking beauties and tough cowboys on horseback to spread the blessings of smoking. It is embarrassing to the manufacturer, the media, consumers and society in general that some of the best-known models have died of lung cancer. The tobacco companies of course want to limit the dissemination of such information and are quite successful in doing so.

The importance of brands and *brand identity* has become all the more emphasized during the past decade. The value of a company's stock has become its *brand equity*, the capital it represents. It reflects how well known a company is, how satisfied the customers are, customer loyalty and the connotation that it sparks off. A compehensive literature on branding has been published.[65] R13 is not focused on the brand as a general phenomenon but on its role as a relationship-booster, something which is less prominent in the literature.

Goods and services have certain inherent properties, but just as important are the properties we as individuals or groups allocate to them. Companies, goods, services and celebrities become surrounded by myths. 'Reality' can be seen as a social construct in which goods and services are consumed for their symbolic meaning. In a broader social context, consumption not only includes the relationship between the supplier and the customer, between the customer and the product, but also between the supplier and the product.[66] *Positioning* is a strategy for allocating a position – a cell in the consumer's brain – to a product or service in order to make the consumer think of a special brand when a purchase is pending.

According to Linn,[67] the *meta product* is 'the whole of the invisible world of perceptions which we link to a branded product'. He proceeds: 'Every object has its metaphysical

---

[65] Standard references are Kapferer (1992); and Aaker and Joachimsthaler (2000).
[66] See overview by Saren and Tzokas (1994).
[67] Linn (1985; the quotations are compiled from pp. 9, 26 and 28).

properties. It is sufficiently strong in symbols like the Christian cross, the David star or the hammer and the sickle for people to sacrifice their lives ... ' He gives the classic example of the Volkswagen 'Beetle': 'It was so personal that it was almost provocative ... people established a relationship to the car. You had to react, it was hard to be indifferent ... If we want to see the whole in which the marketed product thrives, we must look more to men and their relationship to the products than we do today.' The perceived reality is not constituted by the product and service as independent objects, but by the relationships and interactions between the beholder and the product/service.

DeBono (1992) says that offering *integrated values* is the third stage of a firm's development. It has been preceded by a product-oriented stage when goods were scarce and manufacturing was the overriding issue. In stage two, competition was in focus. Companies are now approaching the third stage, but this stage is still in its infancy.

Taking a closer look at image, brands and quality, it is easy to find examples when the 'reality' is in the customer's eye, heart and brain, and does not exist in an objective sense. In an essay on pop art and restaurants, its author says:[68] 'There is any number of Pizzeria Napoli around the world and often these are more "original" than the "original" in Naples. By the way, is there an original at all? Isn't it so that Pizzeria Napoli rather imitates a popular image of what a pizzeria in Naples should look like? If there is no original, there can't be any copies.'

It is both an opportunity and a risk to use aesthetic gimmicks such as imaginatively designed and animated Powerpoint presentations, fancy logotypes, glossy brochures and beautifully decorated premises to make the market believe that you are something you are not. Rationality – that if you cannot live up to your image, customers will unmask you after some time and exit – should not be taken for granted. One example is the cosmetics industry, which can deliver very little of its promises – youth, beauty, happiness and romance – but the consumer wants to believe it.

In entertainment and culture, mass production is often a goal; the bigger the audience of your show or circulation of your book, the more successful you are. The relationship between the entertainer and the consumer is rarely a personal friendship. Celebrities such as rock groups or sports champions become symbols of lifestyles, beauty, strength and smartness. Sometimes an actor's charisma, star quality, visibility and private life are equally important or much more important to the fans than his or her professional performance. People know them from their appearances but also from news media and gossip columns. The fans can come close to their idols in their imagination. *It is a personal relationship for one party, and a mass relationship for the other; the fans 'know' their stars as individuals, but the stars usually know their fans as anonymous audiences.* The role and the stage personality are perceived as real, and get mixed up

---

[68] Nilsson (1993, p. 27).

with the private person. The fame of the star can be used to add credibility and popularity to products and services, and to boost images.[69]

The strength of the parasocial relationship became blatantly obvious when Diana, Princess of Wales, died in a Paris car accident in 1997. Her beauty, love affairs, and care for the less privileged, combined with her own vulnerability, captured the minds of people around the world. They genuinely mourned her as a close friend. Her relationship with the paparazzi and reporters included mutual dependency, but an inability to turn it into win–win relationships.

A new generation of exotic brands have seen the day on the IT stage: Amazom.com, Yahoo!, eBay. They are often linked to persons with media attraction whose celebrity status can boom quickly, establish itself, but equally quickly be replaced by other heroes. Businessmen Richard Branson in the UK and Donald Trump in the US are celebrities. Music groups in which one or two members are launched as stars have long been given fancy names. Even in the early days of Hollywood, film stars to be launched were given new names and even fake biographies to make them more mysterious and sexy. When Greta Gustafsson, renamed Garbo, died, she had not done a movie in fifty years; her celebrity status was upheld by the fact that she became a recluse and never gave an interview.

For decades Marks & Spencer was the flagship of British retailing, known for high quality and low prices. I used to shop there every time I was in the UK. During 2000, a setback occurred, one reason being that its brand St Michael began to lose its flavour. Whereas Twiggy, trendsetting fashion model of the 1960s and 1970s, willingly posed in St Michael jumpers, this would be unthinklable for Posh Spice of the Spice Girls and other teenage icons; here, the novel and expensive was in vogue, Gap, for example. The relationship is to Posh Spice rather than to the retailer or manufacturer.

Rapp and Collins[70] point to new types of brands, *relationship brands*:

> . . . with the ability to identify prospects and customers by name and
> address, learn more about them, and interact with them in an
> ongoing relationship, a new form of branding is evolving:
> 'relationship branding'. You no longer simply brand or promote what
> you sell. You brand and promote the relationship as well.

In a similar vein, Duncan and Moriarty offer an RM model claiming that 'communication is the primary integrative element in managing brand relationships', with brand equity as the goal

---

[69] See also Rein, Kotler and Stoller (1987).
[70] Rapp and Collins (1995, pp. 197–298); and discussion with Stan Rapp in 1997.

and core category.[71] A relationship brand has a name, a logo, usually offers membership, is advertised and includes continuing involvement.

Harley Owners' Group (HOG) has already been presented as an example of a customer club, established to increase customer retention. But it is more than that, it is also a successful relationship brand. Customers do not only have a relationship to the Harley-Davidson brand and its motorcycles. HOG is in itself a brand that represents a relationship to a community of people, an affinity group. Harley owners rarely used their bikes – it was no fun hitting the road on your own – and consequently did not buy more than one motorcycle in their lifetime. With the HOG clubhouses, strategically located in the dealerships, Harley owners consume their product as part of a community. They have not just bought a product, they have joined a group. They further identify with the group through branded Harley merchandise. And the HOG members are extremely loyal, with a 95 per cent repurchase rate. The parasocial relationship to the Harley-Davidson brand has spawned the HOG social relationship.

Monopoly means that the market is ruled by a single supplier. When there is competition, companies differentiate their offerings. One strategy is to achieve a *value monopoly*.[72] There are many cities, paintings, movie directors, cartoons and awards, but only one Venice, one Mona Lisa, one Ingmar Bergman, one Donald Duck and one Nobel Prize. Patents give a temporary, innovation-based value monopoly. A corporation can dominate its industry, like IBM ruled over the computer industry up until the 1990s. Then Microsoft took over the star role and its president Bill Gates became the symbol for the new and exciting IT future.

The cost of breaking a value monopoly can be so excessive that no competitor will succeed. A handful of such brands are known throughout the world: Coca-Cola, Sony, Mercedes, Kodak, Disney, Nestlé, Toyota, McDonald's, IBM and Pepsi Cola.

Some brands have become so well known that they degenerate as brand names and are identified as synonymous with the generic product. 'To Xerox' now means to take copies even if the brand of machine is Canon, and Caran d'Ache, the Swiss pencil manufacturer, is used as the word for pencil in Russian. When New Zealand growers launched the kiwi fruit on the world market, it became such a success that other countries began to grow the fruit and profit from its formally unprotected name. The kiwi is a local bird which has become a national symbol; New Zealanders are colloquially called Kiwis. In 1997, the New Zealand-grown kiwi was renamed Zespri, a name that research showed to have the desired connotation: fun, energetic, effervescent and nutritious. 'The issue is whether we're going to try and market a superior branded product that captures premium prices and consumer loyalty or trade a generic perishable . . . ' says the chief executive of Zespri International.[73]

---

[71] Duncan and Moriarty (1998, p. 1).
[72] DeBono (1992).
[73] Based on Teutenberg (1997).

An intriguing issue is the ratio between price and the symbolic values of a parasocial relationship. What does it take to break a relationship between a customer and a brand? As it is a commercial relationship, it has a price. In England, the major retail chain Sainsbury introduced a new brand for a cola drink, Classic. The price was set 25 per cent below the price of 'the real thing', Coca-Cola. It soon surpassed the sales of Coca-Cola. In Canada, a similar development occurred when another retailer, Loblaw's, introduced President's Choice.

When Nestlé bought Rowntree-Mackintosh and the brands After Eight, KitKat and Quality Street, the price exceeded the tangible assets by 300 per cent.[74] The price reveals brand equity – the financial value of these brands. It was a purchase of both tangible product values and abstract values. In traditional accounting terms, goodwill is not registered as an asset unless a certain amount of money has been paid for its acquisition. There are also negative connotations of the global brands who may be perceived as the new colonialists who through sheer power threaten national independence and destroy local cultures.[75] Companies choose different strategies in building an image and value monopoly:

- Unilever, one of the world's largest corporations, does not advertise its corporate name to consumers but has invested in strong brand names, such as Cornetto ice-cream, Lipton's tea, Surf and Bio Luvil detergents, Lux soap and Pepsodent toothpaste. All these are well-known convenience goods brands throughout the world.
- BSN, the third largest producer of branded food in Europe after Nestlé and Unilever, used a different strategy. In 1994, it changed its name to Danone.[76] This was its brand for dairy products and after Coca-Cola the largest brand in the food stores. The company chose to invest in corporate image rather than in brand image. The urgency of a name change was felt; BSN was unknown and in Spain there was a bank with the same name, in the US a textile firm, and in Japan a TV channel.

Marketing via symbols can be seductively low-key. I should like to introduce the term *subtle marketing*, as opposed to the usual obtrusiveness of television commercials and other types of promotion. One example is the doctor and the 'health and illness industry'. By creating an air of divine powers – the rulers of health and disease, of life and death – medicine has built an almost invincible image. The connotation of the white coat and the characteristics of the hospital environment have become strong symbols, which govern the relationship to the customer and the interaction process. Through laws and membership to associations the industry has monopolized alleged abilities. According to the American Medical Association,

---

[74] Nilson (1993, p. 154).
[75] Klein (2000).
[76] The example is taken from *The Economist* (1994, p. 7).

only members are allowed to claim that they *cure* disease. If others so claim, they will be taken to court. The expert monopoly becomes a reality, a unique and timeless 'patent' supported by a veil of 'scientific' jargon. As no monopoly is free of leaks, alert patients look for alternative treatment and seem to be doing so increasingly.

The issue of brands and image is not new, but is currently stirring up more interest than ever. By approaching the issue through the relationship eye-glasses, new marketing insights can be generated. We even find relationship brands. There is no doubt that parasocial relationships belong in RM. In the global economy, brands and logos ' . . . by force of ubiquity, have become the closest thing we have to an international language, recognized and understood in many more places than English'.[77]

The non-commercial relationship

Marketing is primarily about the commercial part of our economy. It applies to companies that are run on market conditions with profit as the yardstick of success and survival. Economies are also based on non-profit organizations. The public sector, which is mainly a non-commercial service sector, has gradually begun to understand that marketing – in an adjusted form – is necessary. There are also other huge non-commercial sectors which are poorly described in official statistics, notably the voluntary sector with associations and clubs. And where do households and do-it-yourself fit, although they are fierce competitors in, for example, care and repair services and are gradually taking over service tasks from government by means of the Internet?

The non-commercial sector has some fundamental properties, which separate it from the commercial sector and give rise to relationships of a partly different character. Pricing belongs here. *In public services, pricing and payment are not part of the same system as production and delivery.* It is often not the same person who pays and benefits from the services. Even if it is, payment and delivery do not coincide in time. Payment can be a general insurance cost via the tax bill, for example against illness, or it can be a help to the less privileged, such as unemployed people. The customer – the citizen – does not perceive a tangible connection between price, cost and such public services as health care, education and police services. Payment – the tax – disappears into a black hole; when you benefit from taxes, the money appears as windfalls. The services may easily be perceived as 'free', which from an individual standpoint is true at the time they are needed. This may lead to excess consumption or inability to value the services: 'Those who are offered a free meal do not go to McDonald's, they go to the Ritz'.[78]

---

[77] Klein (2000, p. xx).
[78] Based on Albinsson-Bruhner (1993).

In commercial marketing, payment and performance belong to the same system and are largely simultaneous. But even here it can be difficult to see the connection between price and performance if, for example, daddy pays and kids consume.

R5 dealt with the service encounter and the individual's relationship to a service provider. The notion of the service encounter is also applicable to public sector services. Public agencies, however, offer two types of services. One type is services which could also be private and where both private and public alternatives may exist, for example in education and health care.

The other is the authority that public agencies are allowed to exercise. From the individuals' point of view, there is a positive side when authorities assist them. There is also a negative side to contacts with authorities, a *service collision* rather than a service encounter. Authorities provide both services to the community of all individuals, and to the single individual. Some authorities have the monopoly of using force against the individual for the benefit of the whole of society. Those who get arrested or are forced to pay additional taxes are not inclined to see this as a service; the encounter becomes a collision. There is also a collision when authorities fail because of disinterest, inertia, sloppiness, legal technicalities or red tape. The criminal is let loose and the victim is offered no help; the little guy is harassed while the big crook is left alone. The 'values' of the legal and bureaucratic establishment are often far apart from what citizens perceive as fair.

Figure 3.10 shows one possible pattern of a purchasing procedure for public services, in this case public health care. The service is produced directly between the customer/citizen and the hospital staff. The payment, however, goes via the taxes to a budget for public expense. In this case, hospitals offer their services in competition through bidding, a committee selects the winner and payment follows a contract.

The terms customer and supplier are now being used in non-commercial operations too. It is an effort to change the relationship between, for example, the customer/citizen and the tax authority, and to make the tax authority both an *authority* and a *service organization*, not just an authority. The two roles of authority and service provider have been mixed up when publicly owned organizations behave like an authority in instances when they should be performing ordinary services. This attitude has created an unhappy relationship to the customers/citizens and low quality and productivity. By handling service tasks well, however, it becomes easier to exercise authority. The tax agency must ascertain the revenue from taxes. At the same time, the citizens and the companies perform services when they fill in tax forms and deliver money. Laws and regulations are frequently difficult to understand intellectually. They are sometimes ambiguous and sometimes not even passed before they are supposed to be applied. No wonder that the taxpayer makes mistakes or cheats. A majority of the mistakes can be prevented or smoothly corrected if the authority enters into constructive interaction with the citizen. This requires that the authority informs in a way

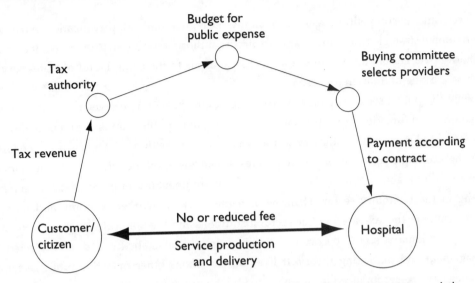

Figure 3.10 The relationship between payment of taxes and public services and the customer/citizen

that is comprehensible to the citizen and is available for consultation. In most countries availability is a major hurdle even if some countries' authorities have realized the need for change of attitude and work procedure. Through websites and email, contact with public authorities can sometimes be facilitated.

Unfortunately, many of those employed by authorities do not realize that they are there for the citizens, but believe that the citizens are there to serve them; the organizational culture inverts the roles. The citizens' perceptions of relationships with authorities have been characterized by the French author Anatole France as 'the State is a surly old man behind a window'. In service research we had predicted that a new generation of officials would emerge, representing relationship and service values, thus replacing the bureaucratic generations. It is sad to have to say it, but even if many changes have taken place, the historically bureaucratic–legal values are still predominant.

It is difficult to draw a line between what types of consumption should be a human right, and what should be the effect of own work and earnings. Much of the political tensions between different economic systems are caused by conflicting opinions about a fair trade-off between rights and own performance.

Public authorities and service agencies increasingly become 'borderline organizations'.[79] They live in a fuzzy zone between public and private, between the non-commercial/tax

---

[79] Winai (1989).

financed and a competitive market economy. Deregulation and privatization have been international strategies for many years. An airport authority may be state operated. It exercises authority over certain aspects of the airport such as air traffic control, and operates services such as parking and tax-free sales.

While the public sector is paid via taxes, the voluntary sector receives its means through donations and unpaid work (to some extent through public funds and taxes though). According to Drucker, the voluntary sector, which he calls the third sector, has been the fastest growing economic sector in the United States; it engages more people than the private and public sectors together.[80] Churches, scouts and environmental groups, such as Greenpeace, belong in the voluntary sector. Their work neither fits the market economy and its price mechanism, nor the tax-based public sector institutions and the political system. In spite of its size, the voluntary sector becomes a residual in official statistics and is neglected by management and marketing theory. It lives on conditions other than the public sector. Its missions have been unnoticed or mismanaged by the private or public sector, or they lack the capacity to handle them. Voluntary work is often pioneering, often scorned and actively opposed by the establishment, one example being environmental protection. The third sector has a long tradition and is used to handle many of the issues which were later transferred, at least in part, to the public sector. We could also add a fourth sector which embraces what we do for ourselves, our family and friends.

The board of directors has a special role in voluntary organizations, namely to be the driver in the collection of funds.[81] This is an additional role from the board in a commercial enterprise or a public agency. An important part is building relationships with donors for fund-raising, or better: *fund development*. The change in terminology is essential for RM. To *develop* funds is more long term and more intimate than to *collect* funds. According to Dudley Hafner, head of the American Heart Association: ' . . . your true potential for growth and development is the donor . . . someone you want to cultivate and bring along in your programme. Not simply someone to collect this year's contribution from.'

The quotation stresses that long-term relationships must be cultivated through a programme, as compared to the transaction, the occasional gift. One strategy is to engage the donor in actual work in the organization. Hafner continues: 'Someone who pays taxes does not think of himself or herself as getting involved in the welfare programme. But if they become involved in a Salvation Army activity or the Visiting Nurses programme, they *are* involved. They are involved spiritually and they are involved monetarily. That makes a difference.' If an organization consists of members – real members and not pseudo-members – these can be both recipients of the organization's offerings and producers for themselves or for others. This way of looking can

---

[80] Drucker (1989).

[81] This and the next paragraph are based on Drucker (1990; quotations from pp. 85 and 88).

be expanded to seeing nations as organizations of 'members', the citizens. To regard members or citizens as customers requires the insight that their role is only partly commercial.

Companies are increasingly developing strategies for their donations by funding long-term projects.[82] This corporate philanthropy aligns self-interest with doing good for society, the companies becoming corporate citizens. Examples of causes are increasing literacy, AIDS prevention, school reforms and environmental programmes. It does not only include cash, but also advice and the use of their technology and human resources.

A large share of the cultural sector is non-commercial. A museum must target its relationships in four directions.[83] One is to *visitors* and, in order to reach them, the museum needs *intermediaries*, like tourism organizations and the media. Then there are those who support the operations through *contributions*, such as corporate sponsors, local governments and grant committees. The fourth is *inward bound*, the organization of the museum and those who propose exhibitions, plan them and implement them. All this is tied together; it is three perspectives of the marketing of a museum.[84]

When I was born, savings banks presented newborn babies with a bank account and a small deposit.[85] When I started school, I received a savings box, which was emptied regularly under the supervision of the teacher, and the money was deposited in the bank. This was seen as community work without a profit motive. The savings banks had an assignment from society, just like the schools had. Saving was a virtue: 'Save First, Buy Later!' The mission of the savings banks was to give the less privileged a chance to improve their financial situation, go to college and acquire their own home, and to let small farmers and firms develop their operations. The savers were members and citizens rather than customers. The now twenty-five-year-old Grameen Bank in Bangladesh has targeted segments which have no attraction for the traditional banks, namely the poor and women. Every loaner buys a share and becomes an owner and there is a 'peer review' when someone applies for a loan: customers assess each other, a type of close C-to-C interaction. The bank now operates in sixty countries and contrary to conventional bank 'wisdom' the bad debts are much lower than in ordinary banks.[86]

The non-commercial relationship is ever so important for the commercial economy and the marketing equilibrium. What cannot be handled through market mechanisms must be handled by the public sector and the political system – including setting up adequate regulations and institutions – and by the voluntary sector. Relationships between customers, suppliers and other stakeholders are important all the same, but are of a somewhat different character.

---

[82] Smith (1994).
[83] Bradford (1991, pp. 93–6).
[84] See also Kotler and Andreasen (1991).
[85] This section is primarily based on Hessling (1990).
[86] Yunus (1992).

The green relationship

> Dear Guest: Try to imagine how many tons of towels from all hotels
> around the world are washed unnecessarily. Think of the enormous
> amount of detergent and water, which thereby contribute to the
> strain on the environment. Please note that if you put the towel on
> the floor it means that you would like it to be replaced. However, if
> you leave it hanging on the rack it means: I can use it again – and
> help protect the environment.

This type of message is increasingly found in hotels. It is an instance of a growing phenomenon – the green relationship. Hotels are trying to establish a relationship with guests through environmental issues. They want interaction and co-production with the customer. They have found that green issues are not just costs and threats, but also offer opportunities for cost reduction and revenue enhancement.

The green relationship concerns the company's way of handling environment and health issues in its offerings and the relationships that are created to specific individuals and communities of individuals. Despite the fact that the environment and health have been in focus for public debate for decades, they are the objects of a new type of relationship to consumers and society.

Companies as well as governments have been reluctant to take action. 'Our company does not cause pollution! It's fad and fashion among confused idealists and will soon pass! It costs too much! There is lack of scientific evidence! The customer does not want to pay for it! We will lose our competitive edge!' Legislation has often not been enforced and companies have been granted temporary exemptions that have turned permanent. Those who have been appointed responsible for environmental issues at corporations often lack power. It has turned out to be difficult to enforce effective agreements on the environment and health with the EU, UN, WTO (World Trade Organization) and other supranational organs.

The green relationship in a broader sense is ethics and good citizenship, which may partly be perceived as contrary to commerical interests. Business is more often than not characterized by resistance to change and has great difficulties in seeing any but short-term bottom-line effects. *Cause-related marketing* has, however, become a term for 'doing good in society', but is primarily part of sponsorship and public relations with the purpose of boosting the public image.

In recent years, interest has grown and more people are beginning to grasp the necessity for action. *Green marketing* is becoming a sub-discipline of marketing.

In the mid-1990s, US consumers spent over US $100 billion on products from companies that they perceive as environmentally and socially progressive.[87] In one study,[88] 84 per cent of all Americans considered pollution a serious problem getting worse, 75 per cent that the air was getting more polluted and that 80 per cent of lakes and rivers were more polluted than twenty years ago. The group of 'green consumers' who take an interest in the environment and health is growing. Previously, protests against environmental destruction were most visible in demonstrations and efforts to boycott companies. Consumers 'vote' by their purchases of goods and services, and a growing share of 'voters' refuse to buy products which are detrimental to health and the environment; 54 per cent of Americans read the labels on packages to find out if the product was environmentally friendly, and 57 per cent looked for products and packaging made from recycled material. The number of green products has grown. In 1985, they accounted for 0.5 per cent of all new products, in 1989 for 4.5 per cent, and in 1991 for 13.4 per cent.

Figure 3.11 shows green market relationships – to individual consumers and middlemen – and relationships on a mega level, to citizens as a group. Companies sell their goods or services to customer segments or individuals who can be more or less environmentally and health conscious. There are communities of people dedicated to green issues. Children have been inclined to accept the messages and have begun to influence their parents' purchasing habits.[89] Producers of daily goods establish closer relationships to the distribution channels in order to solve environmental problems – not least with packaging – and to explore the sales opportunities provided by the increasing green interest. Investment in good relationships with authorities, environmental organizations and the media can be supportive to marketing. During its 150-year history, Church & Dwight in the USA, makers of Arm & Hammer baking soda, have worked with both the product and its package to make it more environmentally friendly. Its representative says: 'Building coalitions with all stakeholders keeps the company abreast of environmental regulations, issues, debates, technology, and attitudes ... [which] results in a dialogue ... '[90]

Companies and consumers alike are in continuous interaction with the environment. The consumer might not notice much of this, as a large share of environmental destruction caused by production and consumption appears with delayed effect and away from the consumer's location. The general environmental destruction, which we cannot do much about as individuals, hits back at us as members of a nation, as citizens. The products we consume have an impact on our individual well-being. This is obvious with food, a choice we can partly

---

[87] Entine (1996, p. 31).
[88] The data in this paragraph are quoted from Ottman (1992, pp. 3, 8 and 13).
[89] Ottman (1992, p. 146).
[90] Ottman (1992, p. 146).

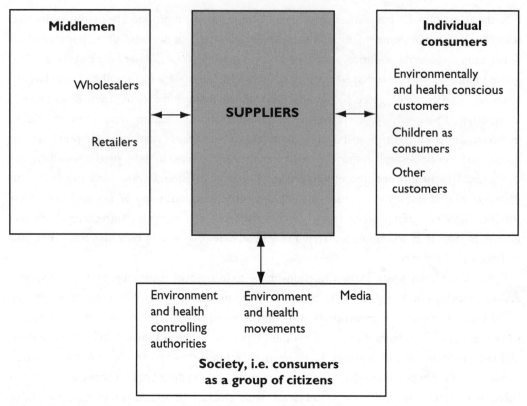

Figure 3.11 The company and its relationships in the green network

control. If wrongly combined, it impairs our general health status and immune defence system and causes disorders. We incur costs both directly as consumers and indirectly as citizens. The bulk of health care cost, which is one of the largest costs for society, is caused by lifestyles, not least through inadequate nutrition. The interest in health food, fruit and vegetables has got a kick forward through BSE ('mad cow disease'), foot and mouth epidemics, and the negative media exposure of animal transports and slaughterhouses. *Functional food* with a focus on health effects is being established.

Marketing as a discipline is primarily dealing with issues of a micro and short-term character. Companies endeavour to maintain long-term profitability and survival, but in practice short-term considerations are given priority. Survival this year is a necessary condition for long-term survival. The consumer is often focused on satisfying momentary needs. In a macro perspective and over the long term, both companies and consumers have a responsibility as citizens which is partly in conflict with the individual's immediate self-interest.

Reasons for a delayed breakthrough for green marketing are therefore found in the conflicts between our responsibility as individual consumers, suppliers and citizens. There are *short-term* and *long-term* effects, as well as *direct* and *indirect* effects.

Individual consumers

In our role as *individual consumers* we can choose to buy certain goods and services. We demonstrate environmental and health awareness through our consumption habits. This requires that the products we want are available at a reasonable price or the green considerations will become too much of a burden of daily life. One obstacle is the lack of infrastructure such as distribution networks based on ecological considerations. If consumers want to buy organically grown food, they usually find that availability is low, both in stores and restaurants. If consumers want to patronize manufacturers that use recycled material, reliable information is difficult to obtain. Much of what we do as individuals has a direct, predictable and short-term impact. Indirect and long-term effects are vague and provide weaker incentives.

Suppliers

In our role as *suppliers*, we can choose to produce goods and services as long as we live within the law – or, more realistically, do not risk to be discovered or punished – and as long as it pays. Today, environmental costs incurred by companies are passed on to others, or society at large, even to other countries via air and water. Even worse, pollution and the consequent destruction of natural resources has a more general consequence. It is stored in molecules, which are then distributed through the ecological cycle. We get 'molecular rubbish', the invisible rubbish which is ten times the amount of the visible rubbish.[91] In the long run, we cannot dodge payment of these anonymous costs; they will hit us as consumers and citizens.

Citizens

As *citizens* – that is *us*, the same people as those mentioned above but in a different role – it is comfortable to hide in the collectivity of society. We may not see ecology as our responsibility,

---

[91] Robèrt (1992).

and as single individuals we may feel we cannot do much as long as authorities do not take action. This is also a neat excuse for doing nothing. Politicians are squeezed between a will to act on issues which have not matured in public opinion and to become popular and attract votes. A more developed collective consciousness is a necessary antecedent for more far-reaching and sustainable change.

GMO, gene manipulated food, was on its way to establishing itself, particularly through the aggressive actions by Monsanto. Consumer and political protests in the United States and most of Europe were lame, probably because Monsanto and other actors used a scientific front to impress the public and assure that GMO had only advantages for the consumer. In contrast, the UK debate went high from 1999 and onwards and many of the sophisticated 'promises' were exposed. The president of Monsanto eventually had to publicly admit that the company could not live up to its claims.[92]

It would be easier if environmental and health hazards could be clearly identified by mainstream scientific research. In many cases there is overwhelming evidence both from science and common-sense observations; no more research is needed. In other cases treating green issues as part of an ecosystem requires new scientific mindsets. With the profits and stakes involved, however, it is tempting to modify green issues to greed issues; changing just

Table 3.2 Drives of companies to deal with environmental and health issues

Law driven firm	Public relations driven firm	Value driven firm
Defensive strategy	Opportunistic strategy	Offensive strategy
Cost to be avoided	Image enhancement	Basis for revenue
Consumers do not really care	Consumers want it to some extent	Consumers demand it
Resistance	Cosmetic add-on, green-washing	Inherent in their business mission
Threat	Faddish	Opportunity for sustaining competitive advantage
Let the court decide what is a good citizen	Efforts to be perceived as a good citizen	Genuine desire to be a good citizen

---

[92] Hertz (2001, pp. 109–12).

one tiny letter changes the whole strategy, just like changing one tiny gene changes a whole organism – and the effects are unknown.

Table 3.2 shows that companies are driven by different motives in their environmental considerations. *Law driven firms* heed environmental issues only when forced to by court orders. They often try to escape the issues through massive use of lawyers and stalling techniques. Lobbying organizations have been formed to discredit environmental efforts and to spread disinformation, even demanding free use of nature for the benefit of short-term business profits. No doubt, environmental enthusiasts have sometimes gone too far, not accepting any kind of human interference with nature. The fifteen-mile bridge between Sweden and Denmark had been the object of environmental studies and controversies for decades before the actual construction could start. This has forced the proponents of the bridge to consider – and reconsider – its effects on the flow of the water and the living conditions for fish and organisms. Any change, however, will have some effect on nature, and the question is how much is acceptable and how the harm can be reduced.

Public relations driven firms seem to constitute the most prevalent species. For them, green issues are trendy and if consumers seem to want them, firms offer them in order to enhance sales and image. They apply a 'green-washing strategy' rather than implementing fundamental changes. This is in line with the values of the 4P approach with promotion, persuading the customer to view the company in a positive light, a matter of 'information'. A study in the USA showed that 87 per cent of consumers thought that less than half of all companies took environmental issues seriously.[93]

Value driven firms – those who understand and believe – are still a minority. Green products are often manufactured and distributed by voluntary organizations based on personal beliefs and values, such as those of anthroposophs and biodynamic farmers. Some of the companies that have seen the business opportunities in environment and health are Ecover in Belgium, Ben & Jerry's Ice Cream in the USA and The Body Shop in the UK. More traditional companies have sometimes spent large sums on green programmes and made certain improvements, but the larger share of their operations continue as before. It is hard to uncover if there is, besides the voluntary and idealistic organizations, any commercial enterprises that fully embrace green values, not only in rhetoric but also in action. We would like to believe their claims and some companies have received extraordinary media coverage for promoting green issues.

Particularly in Europe, where consumer and producer cooperatives have large market shares in the food market, one could have expected leadership in green marketing. The explanation may be simple: management never understood that environment and health could be part of a business mission. A survey of advertisements from the period 1950–1985 indicated that

---

[93] According to *Marketing News* (Schlossberg, 1992).

companies did not reveal any growing awareness of green opportunities, although the arguments for health increased somewhat during the 1980s.[94]

Environmental aspects are embraced by the ISO quality certification system (ISO14000) and by the quality awards that now exist around the world. In the *Baldrige Award* in the USA, societal responsibilities, including environmental improvements, appear in several of the criteria. Reference is made to green technology and green manufacturing, health and safety, emission levels, waste stream reductions, by-product use and recycling.[95] According to former Baldrige chief executive Curt Reimann, the importance of environmental issues for the applicant is weighed against a company's potential impact on the environment. Consequently, a producer of chemicals is judged by tougher standards than, for example, a life insurance company.

CASE STUDY   **The Body Shop**

The Body Shop's products seem to sell themselves through unique perceived qualities and consumers constitute the sales force as voluntary PTMs. The company has never advertised but claims to get 10 000 favourable mentions in the media per year. It was founded in 1976 with one store in Brighton, England, and twenty-five years later there are 2000 stores in fifty countries. The official strategy is to make both the products and the packaging as environmentally friendly as feasible. They are based on natural ingredients and must not be tested on animals. The Body Shop has introduced a rolling five-year rule in its relationship to the suppliers. Twice a year, suppliers must sign a confirmation that the ingredients or the finished product have not been tested on animals during the past five years. Companies that currently practise animal testing but cease to do so can become suppliers to The Body Shop five years later. Bottles are standard plastic bottles used by pharmacies and consumers can get them refilled. Plastic has been a major problem, and the company has worked systematically to recycle the material; this is now beginning to succeed. Every individual store has an environmental programme, a requirement in the franchise contract. The Body Shop establishes relationships with environmental organizations, among them Amnesty International and Greenpeace. From 1984 – when the company went public on the London Stock Exchange – to 1993 the value of the stock increased by 10 944 per cent. The growth, which has

---

[94] Feurst (1991).
[95] Malcolm Baldrige Award Criteria (1997, pp. 5, 27 and 30).

taken place through franchising, is exceptional. Obviously there is no contradiction in marketing green products and running a profitable operation, as has incessantly been claimed by traditional companies.

Its founder and president, Anita Roddick, expresses her business philosophy in the following way:[96]

> ... many trading companies are now fighting to clamber on to the bandwagon and are loudly proclaiming their brand-new, shining green products and policies. I would be happier if I thought they were motivated by real concern for the environment.
>
> ... at first media and the politicians ... categorized environmentalists as brown sandal freaks with a screw loose. They sneered at them.
>
> The Body Shop is, and has always been, an unshamedly green company ... it was a simple expression of our core values and beliefs, values that are constantly policed by our customers and staff ... [97]

The traditional task of companies is production and marketing, the task of consumers is to consume, and it is the task of local governments to dispose of the rubbish. In an ecological perspective, however, the whole must be considered. Rubbish disposal and recycling must be designed into the product and the delivery systems; it must be a natural part of the logistics. A major share of environmental pollution is directly coupled to daily consumption, how the raw material was produced, how the products were manufactured and transported, and how they are taken care of as rubbish; 60–85 per cent of household waste could be recycled or composted.

In the future, producers will be responsible for their products all the way to scrapping and wasting, which means a role after sales and consumption. The supply chain is extended and the network of relationships with consumers, intermediaries and others changes shape. This will require a dramatic redesign of the logistics of the producers. While only 5–10 per cent of packaging is recycled today, 90–95 per cent might be a future goal.

---

[96] Roddick (1991, pp. 220–1).
[97] It has been argued by Entine (1996) that there are flaws in the green Body Shop facade, the image being glossier than the reality.

Car manufacturers have developed systems for recycling. A new model of Mazda was introduced as a cleaner, quieter and safer car: 'Naturally such a lovely car can be recycled. All metal and 80 per cent of all plastic components can be used again.'[98] In the Italian Fiat cars, plastic material is going to be used up to three times. Counting the life expectancy of a car to twenty years, the material will be around for sixty years. Security details such as bumpers are made of new plastic, which will be recycled and used for less critical components. Manufacturers recycle toners for copying machines and printers, and ask the customer to return them to retailers. For the future, the distribution system needs to be as efficient *from* the customer and retailer as it now is *to* the customer and retailer. Recycling requires new systems and processes, in fact a whole new infrastructure. This strategy is 100 per cent different from the 1960s, when throw-away and 'no deposit–no refund' was considered the most efficient production and consumption strategy.

The trends in production and consumption are puzzling and contradictory. The consumption of junk food and alcohol is on the increase; a more liberal view toward drug abuse is being adopted by politicians and the police; illegal drug consumption for kids is being romanticized by the music industry; elite sports are contaminated by drugs; the breeding of animals and the growth of plants are increasingly more artificial; and gene manipulation is sneaked in through the back door to avoid the consumer noticing it. There are also signs that a changed and more constructive view on green marketing is slowly coming forth, even if the degree of awareness varies considerably between consumers, industries and countries. In order to break through among consumers, green products have to be as easily accessible as a can of Coca-Cola. Marketers begin to see opportunities, eloquently epitomized in the following words: 'When the boss got green glasses, the red numbers disappeared.'[99]

The law-based relationship

'When ITT came to the customer for final negotiations and to sign the contract,' an international businessman told me, 'the delegation consisted of nine lawyers and one engineer. When Ericsson came, they were nine engineers and one lawyer.'

This anecdote uncovers two very different relationships. For one company, it is first and foremost a legal relationship with the courts hovering over the negotiations. For another, it is

---

[98] Advertisement in *Svenska Dagbladet*, 18 January 1992.
[99] Karpesjö (1992, p. 9).

a professional and even personal relationship focused on technology, with some provision for legal features.[100]

The formal regulations/institutions of the marketing equilibrium are partly found in the law-based relationship. It involves three objectives:

1 *Quality assurance through prevention.* Law for preventive purposes, during negotiations and in contracts, is used to avoid potential misunderstandings and install a certain protection against a party that does not fulfil its obligations. The work of legislators and lawyers then is quality assurance. As in all quality work, prevention should be maximized. If relationships are good, parties usually solve a dispute without taking it to court. Oral and informal agreements where people trust each other are continuously being made in business and are a necessity for the market to operate smoothly.

2 *Quality inspection and solution of disputes.* Prevention is always more effective than measures taken after the problem has arisen, not least if the goal is long-term relationships. The world is not perfect so legal procedures are also needed for quality inspection and rework, as a ground for settling a dispute and for dealing with outright dishonesty. Misunderstandings can occur, however; if the parties cannot reach an agreement through a benign and constructive effort, they may be forced into a law-based relationship. The outcome of legal procedures can solve a problem, but there are dark sides. Winning a war is not the same as winning the peace; even the winner of a case becomes a loser if the cost of litigation in money, time and psychic effort is substantial. The outcome can also be random or controlled by technicalities, obsolete legislation, ruthless smartness of lawyers, and ignorant courts. Unfortunately, sometimes prevention can be an antecedent to a win–lose relationship; the stronger party makes certain that it is exempt of all responsibility and only has rights.

3 *Manipulation.* Law is also used to deliberately trap another party. Within the marketing mix and the 4Ps, law ought to have its own P for the art of using legal technicalities to exploit and fool another party, thus winning a 'victory' over a customer, supplier, ally or employee. This type of law application is counterproductive to RM and CRM and can only function in transaction marketing and situations where the customer, or other party, has little power; it is also unethical. Notorious examples are fine print in contracts, which cannot be understood without the assistance of lawyers and courts. In hypercompetition though, manipulation of the law is part of the ongoing marketing warfare and win–lose values.

The law-based relationship to the customer is partly an indirect relationship. It goes via a 'repair crew' of law firms, prosecutors, courts, juries and judges. They work as intermediaries

---

[100] For a discussion of contract law and its transactional and relational qualities, see Macneil (1983, 1985); and Paulin, Perrien and Ferguson (1997).

Figure 3.12 The law-based relationship as a substitute for burst social and business relationships

– wholesalers, retailers, agents – who are distributors of decisions about who is right and who is wrong. They also function as the refuse collectors of broken human relationships; they are expected to clean up where others have littered. The fact that legal institutions have to be activated is a sign of relationship failure (Figure 3.12).

Although rarely mentioned in marketing texts, bankruptcy is a natural ingredient of the market economy. It is a way of tidying up in the marketplace, a Darwinian selection, the survival of the fittest. Through periods of snowballing bankruptcies in many countries, they have become a more obtrusive part of the relationship between supplier and buyer. Suppliers are vulnerable in a customer bankruptcy; little is usually left to pay invoices. Tax authorities and sometimes banks can have preferential right to remaining assets. This is remarkable as banks boast about being professional credit assessors, while a supplier seldom has a chance to foresee the failure of a customer company. A failure has a domino effect: a supplier goes bankrupt because his customer did and he cannot pay his debts to his suppliers, and so forth.

Bankruptcy often leads to legal proceedings where fraud and unethical practice are uncovered. Some bankruptcies are a deliberate and systematic abuse of the legal system and a way of making money. Most failures, however, are not deliberately criminal, but formal mistakes are often made in the confusion that precedes the failure. In either case, bankruptcy leads to law-based interaction.

In the airline business there has been a partial switch from a bureaucratic–legal paradigm to a service and relationship paradigm. It has been a well-known secret that airlines overbook. Promises are given but the airlines do not know if they can deliver. It was quite common that they refused to admit overbooking, blamed the passenger, the airports or the weather, and disclaimed all responsibility. Today, serious airlines acknowledge overbooking, or 'denied boarding' as they prefer to call it. The financial necessity to overbook has been explained together with the best techniques to make the overbooked passenger satisfied.[101] Some airlines ask for volunteers to give their seats to a traveller with an urgent need to be on the flight. They promise the volunteer a seat on the next flight and offer a free ticket for a future flight or cash compensation.

The value of a free ticket for a customer usually exceeds by far the cost for the airline. The failure is turned into recovery, a win–win relationship flavoured by customer delight, the little extra, which is often recommended in modern quality management.

From a strict, legal perspective, airlines could probably waive the responsibility or make it burdensome for passengers to claim compensation. Compared to goods transportation, passenger transportation has been neglected by the legislators.[102] Airlines and many others have realized the importance of long-term relationships and understand that legal tricks spoil relationships. Instead, they volunteer to solve problems and the outcome is reinforced relationships.

In 1970, the USA had 355 000 lawyers, in 1984 they had grown to 622 000 and at the turn of the millennium they were close to one million. In the mid-1980s the USA had twice as many lawyers per capita as the UK, five times as many as Germany and twenty-five times as many as Japan. The USA has 5 per cent of the world's population but 26 per cent of its lawyers according to one source, even 70 per cent according to another source.[103]

All these lawyers must find work. One way is to indulge in more fierce and innovative marketing, in hypercompetition. By tradition or formal regulation, lawyers only got jobs through personal relationships and professional networks. In the USA, the marketing of legal services can be extremely aggressive, both through advertising and personal sales. There are 'ambulance chasers', looking for traffic victims, helping to sue as many parties as possible in the vicinity of the accident. They encourage citizens to sue each other. In some countries lawyers take on cases on speculation and the customer does not take a monetary risk; the lawyer's fee may be a third or half of the settlement if they win. It can therefore pay to speculate in law just like in a lottery. *Frivolous suits* in the USA are a speculation on the imperfections of the law, shortcomings of judges and jury members, and the other party's frailties or lack of power. It is not a matter of who *is* right, it is a matter of who *gets* right. Law can both support security and cause insecurity.

Another strategy of securing the future of the legal profession has the character of mega marketing; by making sure that new legislation is continuously passed, the market keeps expanding. A good political support for the future is the fact that 46 per cent of the members

---

[101] See, for example, *The SAS Quality Book* (1987).
[102] See Sisula-Tulokas (1985).
[103] The numbers are compiled from Hartley (1985, p. 179); Ramsey (1991); and Blumberg (1989, pp. 210–11).

of the US congress and 63 per cent of the senate are lawyers. Going to law school is considered a road to a bright future for students.

The threat of litigation, together with the bureaucracy and complicated inter-state regulations in the USA, is a major hurdle experienced by overseas companies. Here are some other examples of legal applications in the US market which show the difficulty for companies used to another type of business culture:[104]

- Electrolux, with 30 per cent of its sales in the USA, had eight lawyers at its American headquarters dealing with some 400 legal cases. At its international headquarters there were four lawyers dealing with the rest of the world, but with no case taken to court for several years.
- Primus-Sievert, makers of camping stoves, terminated its US sales in 1983 after a series of lost cases. Half the premium the company pays for insurance against damages goes to the 4 per cent of its Canadian sales. This is not because the insurance is needed in Canada but because Americans who buy the stove in Canada or receive it as a gift from Canadians can sue the manufacturer in US courts.
- According to US law there is a strict product liability. It is enough if a product is present when an accident occurs – not to have caused the accident – to make the manufacturer potentially liable. A Volvo owner in California filled up with contaminated petrol and after a while the engine stopped. The driver parked the car by the kerb and walked across the street when he was hit by another car and broke a leg. He sued Volvo. The strategy is 'Go for the deep pocket'.
- Two of the most publicized instances of punitive damages in the USA concern a doctor and a granny. The doctor managed to get $2 million in compensation for bad paint on his BMW car. A granny, departing from a McDonald's drive-in, spilt hot coffee and burnt herself. For this inconvenience, which would have gone unnoticed in most countries, she was awarded $2.7 million by a court although the amount was later reduced.

These examples sound like fabrications for a comedy soap opera – and they are funny until you discover they are for real. This type of legal action is far away from common sense. A serious and devastating attack on legal and bureaucratic systems – with the striking title *The Death of Common Sense: How Law is Suffocating America* – is offered by Howard (1994), himself a lawyer. The randomness of the courts' decisions where a jury of lay people are influenced by the sued company being rich, domestic or foreign, and how pitiful the prosecuting party stands out, adds no value to the market or society. They are lawsuit lotteries.

---

[104] The examples from Electrolux, Primus-Sievert and Volvo, as well as some of the background material for this section, are taken from Ramsey (1991).

Mass torts, where a large number of customers simultaneously sue a company, are becoming a special type of litigation. When customers experience that a product has been damaging to their health, they have no other chance than to unite. Injuries caused by a herbicide and asbestos fibres each had a quarter of million claimants; Dow Corning and other manufacturers of breast implants had almost half a million claimants.[105] And in June of 1997, the tobacco industry agreed to set aside funds for the victims of smoking, to the amount of $350 billion, that is, the staggering sum of three hundred and fifty thousand million dollars!

In Japan, contracts are expected to be brief and allow a flexible interpretation. To be forced to go to court is a defeat for all parties. Those who break a business agreement will not be seen as trustworthy in the future and will be excluded from the business community. In US business life it is considered smart to trap counterparts; in Japan a trial has only losers.[106] On the other hand, Japanese business can be ruthless to foreign companies who have to sue them and be persistent to secure, for example, patent rights.

The way legislation has mushroomed in America creates a strained relationship between customers and suppliers, such as between patients and hospitals. Both health insurance and hospital insurance rates rise, in turn burdening the patient's cost. Doctors have to be on guard every moment. There is also a positive side; the insights into the secluded guild of doctors are improved. The USA has gone to a ludicrous extreme and fantasy damages can be awarded to people who are in a legal sense maltreated. In other countries, for example Sweden, you must have robust health in order to survive if you challenge the health and hospital systems; the damages for malpractice are no more than an insult to the consumer.

I can speculate in two explanations for these developments. One is that the bureaucratic–legal values have taken over from common sense and human empathy. The other is that citizens have got so fed up with the treatment they have received as consumers – unfulfilled promises in advertising, low-quality products and services, little or no willingness to settle complaints, monopoly behaviour – that they are now hitting back.

Suing someone is a natural part of marketing in the USA, but it is not mentioned in marketing texts. When *Fortune* magazine reports the alliances in the computer industry, one of the properties of relationships could be labelled 'litigation'. Microsoft has strengthened its alliance with Apple by successfully developing software for Macintosh. This has occurred despite the fact that the two corporations are direct competitors in some areas and that Apple has sued Microsoft for theft in connection with Microsoft's launch of Windows software. This is accepted with the motivation that 'This is business. We're not allied with Apple out of love.'[107]

---

[105] *Fortune* (Nocera, 1995).
[106] The Japanese examples are based on Delaryd (1989, pp. 57–9).
[107] Michels (1992, p. 8).

According to Blumberg:[108] 'It is an elementary sociological fact that as the social fabric of society unravels, shared values and norms that once guided behaviour break down and are replaced by formal codes, regulations, and laws. As the sense of community withers further, social conflict intensifies and litigation proliferates as each person seeks advantage at the expense of others.'

New forms for mitigation are sought, however. In the USA, 95 per cent of all cases are solved in the last minute before a trial. Legal systems – or rather a set of loosely linked components – are extremely closed and tied to rituals. One practical solution is a private American company organized around a network of 2000 retired judges who solve disputes faster and more simply than the courts do.[109]

In a thesis on the significance of contractual law for organizing companies and markets, an article from 1931 by Karl Llewellyn is quoted:[110] ' . . . transactions come in a variety of forms and . . . a highly legalistic approach can sometimes get in the way of the parties instead of contributing to their purposes. This is especially true where continuity of the exchange relation between the parties is highly valued.' The statement is equally applicable today; it shows that RM as a phenomenon is an old common-sense practice. The author further points out that a transaction which is unambiguously defined in a contract and which is then fulfilled in each and every detail is unusual, and that we deceive ourselves by believing otherwise.

In the spirit of RM, it is more realistic to speak about *relationship contracts* which also include judgement calls, negotiations to solve a problem, an assessment of the long-term consequences for future collaboration, and high ethical standards.

The criminal network

Many have asked whether I really consider criminal networks to belong in a book on RM. My questions is rather: How long can marketing textbooks pretend that organized crime and financial criminality do not impact on marketing strategy and daily marketing. Organized crime wipes out the blessings of sound competition and has an effect on customer relationships in many markets. It is growing and it infiltrates governments on all levels as well as legitimate enterprises. Media report that even a financially well-off and sophisticated country like Switzerland has found mafias from one of the least sophisticated countries, Russia, intruding on a large number of Swiss corporations.

Nowhere are the networks more closed and less transparent than in organized crime. The networks are frequently reinforced by ethnicity and are tightly kept within families. Organized

---

[108] Blumberg (1989, p. 209).
[109] Based on Harper (1993, p. 10).
[110] Quotation from an article by Karl Llewellyn and reproduced by Williamson (1981).

crime can consist of a global mafia, but also of a long-term relationship between a local thief and a fence. The presence of criminal networks impacts the relationships between the triad of suppliers, customers and competitors, and impairs the marketing equilibrium. Economic crime disturbs and threatens the functioning of whole economic systems or it can hit single individuals. The networks comprise organizations built on a criminal business mission such as trade in narcotics, fencing and 'protection'. It can also comprise legal trade with goods and services which, behind a respectable facade, is using bribery, murder and threats to get orders. Within legal trade there are also false promises, illegal use of brands, tax fraud and computer crimes.

This section aims to show two things. First, networks of relationships are a condition for sustaining criminal business operations. Second, if the good market forces in certain industries or geographical areas are obstructed, the rules of the competitive game are set aside and the existence for law-abiding businesses is jeopardized.[111]

Obviously the reason for detailing criminal relationships is not to teach unethical and illegal behaviour. The reason is that illegal networks are widespread and that it is important to demonstrate their effect on legal marketing. For the same reason, the University of Buenos Aires introduced courses in the mechanisms of corruption and other illegal procedures.[112]

When monitoring professional journals and news media for organized crime and other illegal acts by companies and governments, I found the subject to be treated daily. It stood out clearly that organized crime and corruption are not limited to a few countries and regions; they are omnipresent, although their 'market share' and influence vary. A report[113] on corruption in the world, based on the experience of business people, puts New Zealand, Northern Europe and Canada at the top of countries where corruption is infrequent, while a number of developing countries are at the bottom of the list. In countries with a low rate of domestic corruption, major cases of corruption were reported to surface from global companies. In their efforts to increase smoking in a situation where countries prohibit cigarette advertising and smoking in buildings, Philip Morris and R. J. Reynolds are accused of organizing large-scale cigarette smuggling. The former Director of Research at one of the large tobacco companies has revealed how ingredients were added to escalate nicotine addiction. His experiences have been exposed in the movie *The Insider*, a drama documentary from 1999 with Al Pacino and Russell Crowe.

Organized crime is reported through official investigations, research institutes, investigative journalism and memoirs, and it is a pet theme in novels and entertainment. Scholarly research on organized crime is limited. It is a matter of surveying closed and protected networks; talk

---

[111] For an overview of economic effects of organized crime, see Fiorentini and Peltzman (1995).
[112] From *Time* (10 May 1993, p. 16).
[113] According to a survey by Transparency International (1998), as reported in the press.

about proprietary information! Even if ongoing criminal activity is publicly known, people are frightened of speaking out or taking action. It is both difficult and dangerous to research the area. It can be done through covert action research where researchers infiltrate an organization under disguise. It can also be done through people who have defected and are willing to talk, and through criminal investigators and courtroom proceedings. The story by Italian judge Falcone about his war on organized crime, told just before he was assassinated, has credibility as a report from the inside.[114]

Organized crime builds its operations on a criminal business mission and the illegal marketing is performed through networks. Except for the godfather, no one is supposed to be able to overview the cells and relationships of the network. A family is often in the core and social ties are strong. Telling on someone produces a clear feedback; you are not fired, you are fired at.

The shadow economy of a country – its unofficial economic sector – consists of the black, illegal economy, and of household and voluntary activities which are not registered in the GNP. All statistics of the shadow economy are uncertain, but assessments of 10–20 per cent of the economies of industrialized countries are often reported in the media. The abandoning of the border checks within the EU and the dissolution of the Soviet empire offer new 'business' opportunities, and so do sales taxes, value added taxes and subsidies which operate within deficient control systems. The turmoil and ignorance of this new situation, and gaps and differences in legislation and institutions between countries, are taken advantage of. The EU and its just introduced common currency, the euro, not only facilitate operations for legitimate businesses, but also facilitate money laundering.

Illegal trade in narcotics, gambling and prostitution was assessed to be 1.1 per cent of the US GNP in the mid-1980s.[115] Revenue from the narcotics trade in Europe was estimated to be between US $200 billion (corresponding to the GNP of The Netherlands) and US $800 billion (the GNP of Italy). The amphetamine exports of The Netherlands are claimed to be bigger today than its well-known trade in tulips and bulbs. Bolivia, Colombia and Peru account for 98 per cent of the world cocaine trade. According to the Italian Mafia prosecutor Caselli, organized crime worldwide had a global revenue of US $700–1000 billion in 1996. The narcotics trade alone was estimated at US $500 billion, which makes it the second largest industry in the world after arms, but before oil. Another source claims that narcotics amount to 8 per cent of world trade. According to a UN investigation in 1999, organized crime had a revenue of US $1500 billion. This is ten times as much as the revenue of the world's largest

---

[114] Falcone and Padovani (1991).
[115] According to *Newsweek* (1986) and *Fortune* (Rowan, 1986). The rest of the paragraph is based on continuous media reports.

corporation, General Motors. It is one sixth of the GNP of the USA and eight times as much as the GNP of Switzerland.[116]

Covert price cartels are another type of illegal network. Representatives of the largest companies in some industries meet once or twice a year to fix world market prices and decide on markets and market share. They meet in an airport hotel, different each time, and leave no written records behind. Bidding cartels – competitors that agree on who is going to give the lowest bid and thereby get the order – kill competition in certain areas of the building and construction sector. These illegal forms of RM also occur in companies where everything else is operated according to laws and regulations.

Money laundering is an important part of illegal trade. Black money which can be traced must be turned into white money. If 70 per cent of black money from the drug trade is laundered, US $15–60 billion of 'dirty money' will be passed through the international financial systems. Parlour offers the following description of the laundering process and the network, which is required to perform the process, follows a certain pattern.[117] First, the money must be deposited (placement). Then the money is separated from its source by a series of confusing and complex financial transactions which make it hard for accountants and police to trace (layering). Eventually, the money is placed in legitimate funds (integration). He forecasts ' . . . further sophistication of money laundering techniques, greater investment of dirty money into established businesses, further internationalization of money laundering networks and intensified involvement of criminal organizations'.

A disquieting but long-term trend is that legitimate and illegitimate practices are woven together into a fabric of relationships. Invisible power organizations – octopuses stretching out their many arms – are created; they are in a double sense imaginary organizations. Organized crime increasingly seems to establish itself behind respectable fronts, investing in companies on the stock exchanges, using IT and sending their staff on executive training programmes. The illegal becomes even more intangible as some of those who are appointed to fight corruption themselves become members of the criminal network.

The establishment of mega relationships in order to involve people in high places is a necessity for organized crime. It cannot thrive without the support of a network of government officials, police and courts, and specialists such as lawyers, accountants, chemists and physicians. Crime becomes embedded in the power centres of society. In the Russian parliament, the douma, it has been estimated that 40 per cent of the members have organized crime connections. A seat in the douma is a strategic investment as its members have immunity from the law and cannot be the object of criminal investigation or prosecution.

---

[116] Lilley (2000, pp. 28–9).

[117] Parlour (1993; quotation from p. 66).

In order to be competitive, organized crime indulges in a series of most effective acts, such as physical threat, bribery, kidnapping, blackmailing, assault, murder and arson, and legal technicalities are used to obstruct justice. These marketing tools are never mentioned in marketing textbooks. It is hard to tell how frequently they are used, but there is no doubt that they are crucial for marketing 'success'. All the same, organized crime can run into financial difficulties. In 1995, an accumulation of events led to red figures for Italian Mafia organizations. Some 4000 bosses, 'employees' and affiliates were in prison; lawyers' fees skyrocketed, as did the monthly salaries guaranteed by the Mafia to its inactive staff; property had been confiscated by the police; and operations in their most lucrative market – bidding for building and construction contracts – had been halted by the authorities.

'Facilitating payments' can be a euphemism for bribes, but the term also comprises the need for support; it may be a condition for certain types of business. Such payments are usually illegal, but appear under various disguises. It is hard to uncover what is behind certain consulting fees and commissions. The borderline between corruption and legal dealings is unclear and each country has its own laws and customs. The arms contract between Bofors and India became a sensitive issue at the end of the 1980s; government members and officials involved in exercising pressure and facilitating payments were suspected. During the 1990s, corruption among Italian politicians and civil servants has been continuously reported. These have been given *'tangenti'* – kickbacks – which means that to make a buying organization accept a supplier's offer, a percentage of the order sum has to be returned as a personal gift to those who handle the purchase. The Milan scandal showed that *tangenti* were a *sine qua non* to getting orders for building, construction and service contracts for the subway, airport, railroad, sports stadium and theatre.[118] In defence of competing suppliers, it was established that there was no realistic way of getting an order without facilitating payments.

Organized crime is a challenge to the 'violence monopoly of the state'. One definition of organized crime is 'violence-based private protection operations in conflict with the state violence monopoly'.[119] The inertia of bureaucracy and its red tape, impossible regulations, and a lack of leadership and institutions open up a market for organized crime. When a state cannot handle the protection of citizens, for example against muggings and shoplifting, criminal groups can provide the protection for a fee and do it efficiently. The boundary between legal regimes and authorities and illegal organizations then becomes subtle. A legal system can be designed in a way that it is next to impossible to do business. Established gangs, *'yakuzas'* in Japan, work more or less overtly. If *yakuzas* are left with their trade – primarily gambling and betting – they help the police to keep other crimes down. They can also be hired for special assignments, such as intimidating competitors or people who refuse to sell a

---

[118] According to the *Wall Street Journal* (Bannon, 1992).
[119] Lappalainen (1993).

company or a house.[120] In some areas of the world, the majority of small stores and restaurants are forced to pay for 'protection' in order not to become victims of violence.

Here are some examples of multinational 'corporations', based on a criminal 'business mission' and organized as networks:

- *Italy.* Organized crime in Italy accounts for 2 per cent of GNP.[121] Eighty per cent comes from strictly illegal operations – drugs, car theft, hijacking of trucks and their loads – and the rest from legal activities carried out with illegal methods. The latter often concerns tenders and public contracts. The Italian statistical bureau ISTAT in 1993 estimated illegal crime revenue to US $18 billion with a staff of 170 000, making it the country's fifth largest corporation. Sixty per cent of the money lands on the official financial market. The three largest 'corporations' are *La Mafia* (Sicily), *'Ndrangheta* (Calabria) and *La Camorra* (Naples), all in the south. In the richer and industrialized northern Italy', says a business person, 'you can still say no to corruption, in the south they shoot you'. According to Lilley[122] ' ... there is increasing evidence that the Italian Mafia are creating strategic alliances with other international organized crime groups, together with successfully exploiting new channels such as Internet stock trading'.

- *Russia.*[123] In the new millennium Russia has taken over Italy's role as the leader of organized crime. As much as 70 per cent of Russia's business is estimated to be criminal, with up to 5800 crime syndicates, of which 1600 have access to top government, industry and financial circles. As organized crime has taken over an estimated 80 per cent of Russian caviar production, quality has gone down dramatically and prices have been dumped. This can mean that Russian caviar is rapidly losing its image and value monopoly.[124] Soviet organized crime was divided among different 'corporations'. The Krasnodar mafia ruled the tourist trade in the Crimea; there was the Uzbekistani cotton mafia and the Azerbaijani petrol mafia. A string of organizations had conquered niches of the market, such as fruit and vegetables, collection of customs tariffs and foreign trade. The political power and organized crime were united in securing privileges for the 'nomenklatura', the communist elite. Today, largely the same people, together with trained members of former 'security' organizations, constitute the core of organized crime. A particularly profitable service industry during the 1990s is based on prostitution, both in domestic and foreign markets. According to statistics from the Russian Ministry of the Interior, prostitution is Russia's third largest industry after

---

[120] According to Rossander (1992).
[121] According to the Italian Institute Census.
[122] Lilley (2000, p. 177).
[123] Based on Waksberg (1992, 1994).
[124] *International Management* (1994).

the weapons and drug trades. The largest threat to the creation of a market economy in Russia is probably organized crime and the lack of adequate institutions and regulations.

Foreign companies that established themselves in Russia and the Baltic states during the 1990s have had to pay special attention to organized crime. In 1994, after its president had been assaulted, Finnish oil giant Neste stopped all investment in Latvia while waiting for the authorities to guarantee the safety of their employees.[125] The gas stations of Statoil, the Norwegian oil corporation, were exposed to car bombs. The objective of Statoil was to open forty stations in the Baltic states by 1998. Two security companies have been hired for twenty-four-hour surveillance of stations, offices and the residences of key staff. The infiltration of organized crime among authorities has not been confirmed but there are strong suspicions about corruption. For example, both Statoil and Electrolux have been victims of brutally executed tax raids.

■ *Hong Kong*, which is now part of China, has been described as a 'supermarket of crime'.[126] It is estimated to have some fifty criminal 'triads' with at least 100 000 members and these are closely related to other triads in China. 'Triad' here stands for the three elements of life – heaven, earth and human being. The organizations consist of 'a network of shady businessmen and friends in high places'. Just the smuggling of people to America gave a revenue of US $2.4 billion in 1992. Those who run and finance criminal operations such as drug trafficking are often business people, politicians and members of the legal system, including the police. For them, it is just one of many types of investment. In Hong Kong it is obviously part of daily business to be exposed to threats unless you pay for 'protection'. Competing triads also collaborate in alliances, for example to facilitate the collection of debts, and outsourcing the heroin distribution in America to the New York mob.

These three countries serve only as examples. Organized crime and corruption are integral parts of every economy. An intriguing fact is that Hong Kong has one of the most flourishing economies in the world, Russia is financially a failure and Italy counts among the wealthy nations. Let us recall Blumberg's (1989) paradox discussed in R2, claiming that the strengths of the market economy – competition and the profit incentive – encourage fraud. In economic theory and its limiting assumptions about market mechanisms, violence is not included. In reality it is different; in some markets violence is the number one marketing tool. Both marketing theory and economics are treating criminal market mechanisms with naivety. Both white collar economic crime and organized violence distort the functionality of the marketplace and obstruct the dynamics of the marketing equilibrium.

---

[125] The example is taken from Paulsen (1994).
[126] From *Time* (Walsh, 1993, pp. 36–41).

IN BRIEF

There is little doubt that criminal networks gain more power and that they gain it through alliances with companies and governments, sometimes through infiltration and pressure, sometimes through bribery. A provocative hypothesis – and not a very agreeable one, but probably true – is that a certain element of illegal action is necessary to make an economy work. Weak governments and inadequate official institutions/regulations open the market for illegal entrepreneurship. RM, however naively, is based on a belief in win–win not only in individual relationships, but also from a societal perspective.

4

Mega relationships

Chapters 2 and 3 dealt with market relationships, the relationships to suppliers, customers, competitors and others who operate in the market. This chapter is about mega relationships, located a step above the market relationships, in society in general. The mega relationships (R18–R23) set conditions for market relationships.

RELATIONSHIP
18

Personal and social networks

In many cultures, business is not conducted with strangers and where business with strangers is accepted, the preference is for people one knows and likes. This is often perceived to be the typical case in Asia and some other areas, but also in Western Europe and the USA, personal and social networks carry weight. Even in the age of the Internet and e-relationships, the h-relationship remains pivotal. Personal and social relationships are the most stable part of business life and can even help to mitigate recessions.[1] The formation and maintenance of social networks are important tasks for top management, marketing and sales. Sometimes social networks may even be more important than professional relationships and a supplier's competence.

As Figure 4.1 shows, personal relationships and social networks have emerged from different areas of life, and they mostly have an origin other than business. It is therefore justified to approach them as mega relationships.

Personal networks – the old boy network, invisible colleges – are locked for non-members. It may be just as appropriate to speak about old girl networks, as those can be strong through family, friendship, ownership and class bonds, and their power is probably underrated.[2] Gender-based networks have attracted growing attention, particularly as women have formed their own networks against the suspected conspiracy of male networks. Rotary, composed of 'prominent representatives' from different trades and professions, used to be open only to men, but since the end of the 1980s it has also been open to women.

It is possible if not always easy to establish new business relationships in the USA, but it is just as easy to break the relationships. In Japan it is difficult to be accepted, but relationships last. 'Keiretsu' is the designation for long-term, personal and financial relationships between companies. The good side is the potential productivity of a stable relationship, the bad side is that others are locked out. In the six largest keiretsus, firms are fifteen times more likely to borrow capital within their own group and three times more likely to trade with members than

---

[1] See McKenna (1985).
[2] Kahn and Yoshihara (1994).

Figure 4.1 Different types of relationships that constitute an individual's social network

with outsiders.[3] The president of the US Chamber of Commerce in Japan claimed that *keiretsus,* bidding cartels and personal networks are formidable obstacles for US firms in Japan, whereas Japanese firms in the US do not encounter similar resistance.[4] At the same time, a study concludes that 94 per cent of large multinational corporations established in Japan are doing very well.[5]

According to Nakane:[6]

> In scope and density of personal relationships and in availability,
> 'school clique' relationships function more effectively than kinship ...
> those educated outside Japan are handicapped in their careers. On
> the other hand, a foreigner who has been educated in Japan is
> accepted in the group and can enjoy and make use of in-group
> feelings ... the sharing of experience during the critical period of the
> teens and twenties has life-long effects.

[3] Gerlach (1992, pp. 121 and 144).
[4] From an interview in *Fortune* (Faltermayer, 1992).
[5] According to Kahn and Yoshihara (1994).
[6] Nakane (1981, p. 134).

In Japan, both presidents of large corporations and government organizations come primarily from the University of Tokyo and some of the other leading universities.[7] Together with corporations, government agencies and politicians, they form a comparatively closed system within which a power elite is produced. Only when there is need to refill the systems are new members let in. It is common that an official of a public agency, at the age of forty to fifty, transfers to industry and becomes a colleague with his fellow students who entered a business career. In the meantime, their sons grow up and enter the system and social alliances are formed through marriage. Clans and dynasties are established. The German word 'Schicksal-verbundenhei' – to be linked through a common destiny – has been adopted by the Japanese language. An example is found in the case study below.

CASE STUDY   **Japanese friendships**

Yoshihiro Inayama and Shigeo Nagano were both graduates from the University of Tokyo, one in 1924, the other in 1927. Nagano began his career at the private steelworks Fuji, and Inayama at the state-owned steelworks Yawata. In 1935, the two corporations merged into Nippon Steel. Nagano became section manager of the purchasing department and Inayama received a position in the sales department. After the Second World War, US general MacArthur broke up the merger for antitrust reasons. Nagano advanced to chief executive of Fuji and Inayama to chief executive of Yawata. In 1963, Nagano was elected chairman of the iron and steel industry organization, and was succeeded by Inayama some years later. The two again merged Fuji and Yawata into a new Nippon Steel with Nagano as chairman of the board and Inayama as CEO. Nagano later became the leader of Nissho, a powerful coalition of chambers of commerce. Ten years later, Inayama became head of Keidanren, another coalition between businesses. The two friends now headed one of the world's largest steelworks and the two mightiest business coalitions in Japan. Taira and Wada conclude that ' . . . the two close friends ruled Japan's business community and indirectly governed Japan itself'. The behaviour of the whole steel market was controlled by the personal relationship between two school friends.

---

[7] This and the following paragraph are based on Taira and Wada (1987); the example of the steel industry is taken from p. 271.

Networks based on friendship and family bonds are highly stable but require the members to adhere to tacit regulations/institutions. The team feeling is highly developed in Japan and it is almost a capital punishment to be excluded from the family, company or university alumni association. It is practically impossible to exist in business if you are out of favour with the group.[8]

The ties to family and friends are grounded in strong feelings and values, not restricted by national boundaries or current domicile. Kotkin (1993) claims that 'the global village' is built of tribes, people with the same ethnic and religious roots. Their bonds outrank national industry policies and traditions. He lists several such networks: Jewish families have, since the Middle Ages, engaged in trade and finance; the Anglo-Saxon tribe consisting of Calvinists who emigrated from the British Isles to America spread their accounting system and trade law, and English as the international business language; Japanese expatriates who left their resource-poor home country see loyalty to their countrymen as the number one priority; Chinese and Indian clans control global networks of finance, and manufacture and market textile products, jewellery and IT products. The swift rise of the Chinese market economy during the 1990s has been made possible through relationships with Chinese expatriates. This 'bamboo network' favours relatives at the expense of Western investors.[9] Western business people getting into China are at a disadvantage as they lack social bonds with key informants and gatekeepers.[10] There is strong distrust toward strangers; they do not get access to information on potential customers, for example on upcoming tenders. The *'guanxi'* network is highly personal; social relationships come first – they are on a mega level – and they can be followed by market relationships and form the basis for new network organizations.

Social relationships and personal networks also play an important role in the American society. In his study of trust, Fukuyama[11] says that:

> ... if Americans were traditionally as individualistic as they think they are, it would be hard to account for the rapid rise of giant corporations in the United States in the nineteenth century ... These supposedly individualistic Americans have also been, historically, hyperactive joiners, creating strong and durable voluntary organizations from Little Leagues and 4H Clubs to the National Rifle Association, the NAACP, and the League of Women Voters.

---

[8] Delaryd (1989, p. 175).
[9] Wiedenbaum and Hughes (1996).
[10] Björkman and Kock (1997).
[11] Fukuyama (1995, pp. 270–2).

Network membership can also fool you. Membership based on position alone is lost if the position is lost. Presidents of important corporations often draw their power solely on their position. I have met a number of ex-chief executives who have been forced to leave their job because of a merger or disagreement with the owners, sometimes also because of failure. They are forced to find a new job, or start their own business, or become consultants. They often claim that they have contacts everywhere, but their 'friendship' was based on their position. When the position is snatched away, the 'friends' quickly leave the sinking vessel.

US ex-presidents are asked for as advisers and board members as well as speakers. Former Secretary of State Henry Kissinger established Kissinger Associates, Inc. The business mission was exploitation of Kissinger's experience and personal network, and the unique knowledge and power that followed. His capital was personal access to government members and other key leaders throughout the world. He sold informed advice on international affairs, access to the powerful elite and the opportunity of hobnobbing with Henry Kissinger.[12] Among his thirty customers have been Coca-Cola, GTE, Volvo and Montedison.

The borderline between social and professional relationships is partly erased; work may become an around-the-clock lifestyle. Membership in professional associations gives an opportunity to meet competitors and have informal discussions, sometimes of great significance. Playing golf has long been considered a key to informal but crucial business decisions.

Friendship is characterized by people speaking to each other, helping each other, trusting each other and spending leisure time together.[13] This can also happen in a commercial relationship which gradually changes character into genuine friendship: 'In communal relationships, members have a special obligation to be responsive to one another's needs, whereas in exchange relationships they do not'.[14] It can, however, result in abuse, and 'the friendly thief' is born.[15] You buy from a friendly person or friend because you feel an obligation and the buying becomes part of the social protocol. Home-party selling thrives on this. The salespeople are often housewives who arrange selling parties with invited neighbours. It can feel awkward to leave the party empty-handed. At the same time the party fulfils a social need which you as friend/customer may value and be willing to pay for.

It is hardly news for marketing practitioners that social networks exert influence. Sometimes they are critical, sometimes of little significance. Their role has not been taken up in the marketing and economics literature, especially not when the focus is directed to anonymous mass marketing, which has characterized marketing management and economic theory during the past decades.

---

[12] *Newsweek* (1990, pp. 34–5).
[13] According to Goodwin (1994).
[14] Clark (1983, p. 282).
[15] Cialdini (1984, p. 163ff).

<table>
<tr><td>RELATIONSHIP
19</td></tr>
</table>

RELATIONSHIP 19

Mega marketing – the real 'customer' is not always found in the marketplace

Apart from the relationships between individuals in the seller's and buyer's organizations and their social networks, there are other relationships that open or close the presence in a market. This requires *mega marketing*.[16] It is marketing above the market proper which addresses public opinion and political power. Without the initial mega decision there is no market to address. This type of marketing seems to be growing in strategic importance.

Often the real battle for the market is not fought in the market. *The real battle is about being in the market at all*. Only after *mega decisions* have been taken in the non-market network – above the market relationships – is it wise to start building market relationships.

Through the lenses of economic theory, markets are seen as intensely competitive and rational. The invisible hand – the ability of the market economy to strive in the direction of equilibrium between supply and demand – is not always an abstract and self-regulating phenomenon. It is also a hands-on intervention by powerful agents whose influence is not visible from the outside.

For example, the market system in Japan is partly out of function through centralized control, disguised to give the impression of competition.[17] Former students from prestigious universities, industrial heads and government representatives make the decisions. If you are not accepted by them, you have little chance of success. It is essential to exploit both the market mechanisms and the central control: 'Successful Japanese businessmen who are adept at utilizing the rules of the marketplace are also generally good at the use of the nonmarket network of kinship and marital ties.'

CASE STUDY **The French government and telecom companies**

In the mid-1980s, the French government decided that the state-controlled manufacturing of telecom equipment should benefit from competition from a second source located in France. Candidates were American AT&T, German Siemens and Swedish Ericsson. Their proposals had been compared by technical experts and all complied with the required specifications, albeit with differences. The final decision rested with politicians. It is rumoured that US president Ronald Reagan gave discreet support to AT&T, German Chancellor Helmut Kohl and the

---

[16] Kotler (1986; definition on pp. 117–18).
[17] The paragraph is based on Taira and Wada (1987; quotation from p. 288).

President of the EU Commission, Jacques Delors, to Siemens. Ericsson negotiated through its chairman and its CEO, who met members of the French government on several occasions. Under French Premier Fabius, a decision was taken to award the contract to AT&T, but this was undone by the new government under Premier Chirac. The new Secretary of Industry and the Secretary of Telecommunications recommended AT&T, whereas the Secretary of Finance recommended Siemens. Ericsson was ultimately awarded the contract, possibly because it could unite the two opinions and was politically harmless.[18]

Mega marketing is often the most important part of marketing for companies producing goods and services of infrastructural character, like telephone systems, military equipment and nuclear power plants, but it can be the concern of any product and market.

The principal idea behind mega relationships is shown in Figure 4.2, which is an extension of Figure 3.5. The figure illustrates B-to-B of a complex offering, but the same notion can be adjusted to B-to-C.

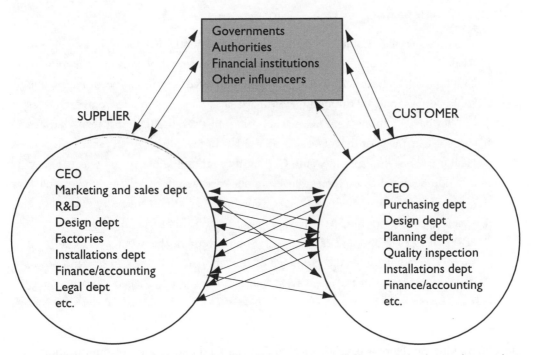

Figure 4.2 The real 'customer' can be found in a non-market network above the market

---

[18] Based on Hallgren (1987).

Mega marketing is by no means new, but has not previously earned its way into marketing theory. One example is the financial wizard Ivar Kreuger, who built an empire during the beginning of the twentieth century. By merging factories in many countries, Kreuger became the world market leader in safety matches and was granted a monopoly in several countries where he offered favourable credits to governments. At most he had an 80 per cent world market share. Despite the financial crisis that followed Kreuger's sudden death in 1932, the foundation was laid for a monopoly-like market status that has partly been sustained. The relationships on the mega level made marketing possible.

There are also general instances of locked networks on the mega level such as the 'military–industrial complex'.[19] Buyers are national military organizations and suppliers are domestic and foreign manufacturers of weapons and defence systems. Within the military–industrial network there is an extreme need for mutual trust. Suppliers design specifications that must not leak to the enemy. The belonging of the seller and buyer countries to defence pacts can determine the outcome of the negotiations.

| CASE STUDY | **Healon** |

Healon is injected into the eye during surgery and gently lifts and stabilizes the eye tissues. The substance dramatically enhanced the quality and productivity of common cataract surgery, but it required a revised surgical procedure. Healon could not be launched through the ordinary sales force, as the sales representatives did not have credibility among eye surgeons. Instead, the ten most respected eye surgeons in the world were selected as the target group. If they converted to Healon, others would follow suit. Getting through to the megastars was not easy, it had to be achieved on a mega level. In one case, an effort was made to establish a relationship with a top Spanish surgeon who refused to meet vendors. A meeting was suggested with the Spanish Minister of Health, an ambassador, the president of Pharmacia-Upjohn and the surgeon. The purpose of the event was to perform surgery together under the guidance of the surgeon – on eyes from dead cows, though. The status of the event was such that the surgeon agreed to participate.

Mega marketing can be of a psychological and social kind and require communication with opinion leaders in the market. In order to reach difficult-to-access personalities, mega

---

[19] See Arndt (1979).

relationships are needed. The launching of a liquid for eye surgery, Healon, by Pharmacia-Upjohn provides such an example (see case study above).[20]

Lobbying is part of mega marketing. The term lobbying comes from the US Congress and its lobby, in which people waited to get an opportunity to speak to congressmen. Lobbying has developed into a profession. It is performed by trade organizations and interest groups as well as by single corporations. When FedEx were about to start, changes in the regulations for postal services were needed, and the company managed to get these thanks to lobbying in Washington, DC. Corporate contributions to presidential campaigns have increasingly been reported. What comes under the eyes of the public is more likely just the tip of the iceberg. More aggressive research, more lawsuits, deeper investigative journalism, clamour for transparency, and citizen movements with demonstrations and open conflicts are making the abuse of lobbying more exposed. According to the media, Washington, DC harboured 15 000 registered lobbyists in 2000 and several tens of thousands who were not registered. Among former members of Congress, 128 worked as lobbyists. A stream of detailed regulations has been introduced – no golf or ski weeks together, legislators can be asked to lunch no more than twice a year, to eat in sombody's home is allowed as long as people are not seated – but innovative loopholes are found continuously.

Currently one of the largest lobbying projects concerns public opinion and political acceptance of gene manipulated food. One important objective was to introduce the new designation 'gene modified organism, GMO', which sounds less menacing than manipulated, and this introduction has been successful. The marketing of GMOs is implemented with the help of consultants; the establishment of networks of 'friends' among politicians, public administrators and scientists, the latter group renumerated indirectly through research grants; by whisking seemingly harmless but mandatory decisions through the EU, WTO and other supranational organs; by planting articles in papers and journals; and through advertising disguised as documentaries. The misgivings of the consumer are belittled or met with silence, and active opponents are labelled eco-terrorists. One strategy is unobtrusiveness and leave the consumer with no choice in the end. Hazardous to the health and the environment or a means to boost health and solve ecological problems, those who run the campaigns are taking on a huge responsibility for the future, one, however, that they do not expect to have to face personally.

The systematic and goal-directed pursuit of an issue by means of lobbying is referred to as 'issues management'. There is a need for industries, companies and others to become involved in political decision processes at an early stage. If they become aware of a decision only through the news media, it is too late. Their knowledge of political decision processes is often superficial and therefore they need help from consultants. Lobbyists must belong to, or be able

---

[20] Based on discussions with the executives in charge of the launching of Healon.

to access, a network of relationships within the environments in which they operate. Presidents have these powerful networks, and ex-presidents relieved of their official duties have been called 'the ultimate lobbyists'.

Close relationships to a certain political group or individual politician can provide a strong marketing edge. If these 'friends' lose power and popularity, however, the intimate relationship can backfire. Business generally tries to be non-political and sell to everyone, irrespective of political colour. The skill of maintaining relationships with many political parties may be the ground for future business. Such a non-political strategy made possible the Iraq rearmament in preparation for the Gulf War in 1990.

In marketing terms, lobbying has been characterized as a decision market, the place (or space) where decisions are bought and sold. There is an evil and a good side of lobbying. In its good sense, lobbying conveys information and persuades politicians and others to consider the issues more carefully, using available knowledge. The need for lobbying is an effect of representative democracy not being, in practice, representative. It its evil sense, powerful economic interests can surpass the interests of society and citizens so that decision-makers dare not act, or are misled. In order to prevent the misuse of lobbying, President Clinton introduced several regulations. For example, top officials and politicians are forbidden to work as lobbyists within five years of leaving office, thereby preventing them from 'selling' their administrative and political networks to external clients. Assignments must be registered in order to reduce the hush-hush surrounding lobbying.

The mega relationships involve customers, suppliers and others more deeply into the societal mega networks, not only in market networks. Approaching the customer with the marketing mix and the 4Ps is meaningless unless the basic conditions for marketing exist. There must be a stage to perform the play. In the examples above, the real 'customers' have been politicians, presidents, government members and famed eye surgeons. None of these were accessible for a sales force. These real decision-makers are not identified in marketing theory as being part of the market.

Marketing seems to be increasingly dependent on mega relationships, as the following example indicates. It concerns complex products of importance for the buying country's infrastructure:[21]

- *1950s* – Direct exports and imports.
- *1960s* – Buyers stipulate that the sellers manufacture a small part of the delivery in the buying country.
- *1970s* – Demands on local manufacturing, national co-ownership and support with financial solutions for the purchase.

---

[21] Based on the author's study of Ericsson.

- *1980s* – Additional demands include: performing part of design and engineering in the buying country; supporting the exports of part of their production; establishing R&D projects together with the supplier; and barter.
- *1990s* – Through deregulation in the industrialized world and the rapid development of technology the buying countries press their demands further. The Swedish defence negotiated the purchase of tanks from American General Dynamics. One stipulation was that the supplier should make sure that ABB would get a major order for rapid trains from Amtrak, the US railroads company. According to US law, a minimum of 50 per cent of the trains had to be manufactured in the USA, which was feasible through ABB's network of subcontractors.
- *2000* – The previous requirements will be even more important.

A study of the relationships within Japanese business and between business and the public sector came to the conclusion that:[22] '. . . business and government in Japan are like two major divisions of a well-run organization – Japan itself . . . the personal networks and contacts of the public officials and private business leaders render the formal structural distinction of government and business almost meaningless in Japan'.

As should be obvious from the examples, *mega marketing requires different skills than those usually existing in marketing and sales departments*. Marketers are not trained to play a political game on a mega level. Top management involvement with the aid of politicians, diplomats, lobbyists and others is required. My contention is that *lobbying and other mega influences will increase in importance and should consequently be explicitly accounted for by marketing theory*. As lobbying builds on networks of relationships within which interaction takes place, it has a central role in RM and CRM.

 ## Alliances change the market mechanisms

Alliance is a designation for organized and agreed relationships between parties, for example between suppliers and customer and competitors. Companies can enter a large variety of dependencies which do not stand out in the traditional classification used in economics, such as monopoly and oligopoly. Alliances are part of corporate strategy and exist above the market relationships and the daily marketing routine.

While competition means that companies oppose each other, alliances mean collaboration. The incentives to enter into alliances vary. Alliances also vary in intensity and duration: they can be one-shot projects; imply limited but continuous collaboration; or take the parties so

---

[22] Taira and Wada (1987, p. 264).

close that they may lead to a merger or acquisition. For Corning, alliances are so central that the corporation now describes itself as 'a network of organizations'.

Five types of actors on the competitive arena have been identified: *present competitors, potential competitors, competitors that offer substitutes, customers* and *suppliers*. Between these, *competitive forces* develop as threats and power to bargain and influence.[23] Interpreted within the spirit of RM, these competitive forces could also be perceived as *relationship forces*, giving birth to alliances.

Alliances appear in many costumes. Ohmae (1985) points to the necessity of global corporations establishing themselves in the triad of the world economy – North America, Western Europe and South East Asia – and how this can be achieved through alliances with competitors. He gives examples from the auto, computer and robotics industries, which have formed alliances based on technology, marketing and finance. In the UK, American Xerox has an alliance with Rank, marketing to Europe, Africa, the former Soviet states and China. In Japan and India, Xerox has joined forces with Fuji and Modi. Thanks to these alliances, Xerox became the global market leader in the copier market. In Salisbury, England, visitors to the cathedral were offered a Pergamon roll as a token of their visit, together with a discount coupon to McDonald's. The hamburger restaurant pays for the roll and gives a contribution to the restoration of the church. Body and soul have entered an alliance supportive to both of them. Disney and McDonald's have announced a promotional alliance; Disney merchandise can be marketed through McDonald's 30 000 restaurants in 120 countries.

CASE STUDY   **Apple and Sony**

Another case is Apple Computer, which established an alliance with Japanese Sony.[24] Apple made drawings and specifications for a new portable computer, the Macintosh PowerBook, which Sony took from the design office to the factory and assembly line in just thirteen months. What were the advantages for the two partners? Apple could not mobilize enough designers to handle all the new products to be launched during 1991. Nor did Apple have experience in miniaturizing products, which Sony had; the PowerBook was to become a four-pound (two-kilo) variant of a sixteen-pound (seven-kilo) Macintosh. Sony wished to learn more about laptops at the same time as it increasingly manufactured for others. It was also a strategic and prestigious assignment. Seven of the best designers were placed at their disposal and the CEO of Sony followed their progress personally.

---

[23] Porter (1985, p. 5).
[24] See *Fortune* (Schlender, 1991).

Collaboration *per se* is not new. It partly occurs in all buying and selling. When relationships are aiming for longevity and continuous development, outsourcing and imaginary organizations emerge, and the relationship comes closer to formal alliances. The 'make or buy' choice has long been an issue in manufacturing, using different strategies. For example, GM manufactures 70 per cent of its components in-house, while Chrysler only manufactures 30 per cent. The rest is outsourced to others who increasingly deliver more composite modules and not just single components. Reebok develops and markets technically advanced and trendy shoes for sports and leisure. It has no factory of its own but outsources the manufacturing to Taiwan, South Korea and other Asian countries. The outsourcing of services is of more recent origin. Among the services that are contracted to other providers are transportation, cleaning, property maintenance, computer services and canteens.

There is yet another link between companies that I have found little observed in the literature. We can call it tacit alliances. These emerge through industry consensus and mean that all industry members behave in the same way. In an industry association, for example, good 'bedside manners' develop. These can grow slowly over a long period. A positive side is that they can instil ethical behaviour; a negative side is that they uphold the past at the expense of the future. Competitors – who have been converted to colleagues – protect each other and assume a hostile attitude to change, or at least pursue a wait-and-see strategy. Innovation then requires revolution, breaking with the tacit alliance.

> INSIGHT   I would like to introduce the concept of the alliance market with the following
> definition: *an alliance market consists of companies which at a certain point in time are*
> *possible partners for an alliance.*

The concept has similarities with a market for matrimony, with the difference that polygamy is allowed, even recommended. The alliance market operates at a corporate strategy level, above the market relationships. The first step is to find partners in the alliance market, the next to address the customer market.

When the major air carriers in Europe began to look for partners, only few attractive partners were available and everybody knew everybody else. Scandinavian Airlines (SAS) is one of the oldest alliances in the world; it has been in operation since 1946. It is made up of three companies from three countries – Denmark, Norway and Sweden – and owned fifty-fifty by the three states and private enterprise. In spite of this long experience of keeping an alliance together, SAS was not successful in extending it to other airlines. Efforts to enrol Belgian Sabena failed; it had a tarnished image of bad service and incompetent and bureaucratic management, but had the growing European 'capital', Brussels, as its hub. Eventually, in 2001,

Sabena was declared bankrupt without being able to adjust to the new economy, despite the most advantageous location in Europe. In the late 1990s, SAS, Lufthansa, United Airlines, Thai, Air Canada and Varig announced the birth of the Star Alliance covering 700 destinations and 95 per cent of all airports with regular passenger traffic. The alliance has since expanded considerably. For the airlines it means cost reduction, for the passenger it means better coordination of timetables and destinations, easier check-in and better use of a bonus club card.

The expected outcome of airline alliances is improved competitiveness, increased sales, increased revenue and lower cost through coordination of destinations, timetables, reservations systems, ticketing and staffing.

In the USA, the number of formal business alliances increased by an average of 27 per cent per annum between 1985 and 1991, and the growth continued in the 1990s. The five US corporations which have most ardently pursued an alliance strategy put some 400 formal alliances together in the beginning of the 1990s: IBM (136 alliances), AT&T (seventy-seven), Hewlett-Packard (sixty-five), Digital Equipment (sixty-three) and Sun Microsystems (forty-five).[25] In addition, these companies form an unknown number of informal alliances.

In a study of the globalization of hotels and restaurants, four groups of formal alliances were defined: strategic alliances, franchising, management contracts and joint ventures.[26] Strategic alliances can vary from a common reservation system to complex networks including not only hotels but travel, holiday packages and conference service. The European reservation system Amadeus and the American Sabre are of this character. Franchising is used by, for example, Holiday Inn, with 1900 hotels offering 360 000 rooms. Those who run a Holiday Inn are independent firms but work strictly according to the concept of the hotel chain. The chain is entitled to a fee based on a percentage of the revenue. Management contract is an undertaking by someone to run a hotel for the owner, by applying skills, knowledge and systems, but also to offer well-known names such as Hyatt or Hilton. SAS's earlier expansion in the hotel market together with Intercontinental Hotels and Saison of Japan, and later with Radisson, is an example of joint ventures.

According to a study by McKinsey, out of forty-nine alliances, one third failed. Short-term alliances to achieve quick results, such as cost reduction through downsizing, did not pay off; alliances should be strategic and long term. Alliances may look good on paper but may not work in practice. Another study showed that 70 per cent of all strategic alliances were discontinued or do not live up to expectations.[27] In an interview, the CEO of Whirlpool said that alliances are trendy but do not work. There follows comments on two issues, values and management, which are frequently reported to cause problems with alliances.[28]

---

[25] See *Forbes* (Gumpert, 1992).
[26] Based on Tse and West (1992, pp. 126–32).
[27] Kanter (1989).
[28] See, for example, Lorange and Roos (1992), and Lowe's (1998) study of a merger.

Values

Making relationships between two corporate cultures work is known to be hazardous. Confrontations between value systems and cultural shocks are the rule rather than the exception. Time and patience are required to build relationships. There must be mutual trust. Trust cannot be assured through contracts, and those who believe that lawyers can prevent the risks and hurdles of collaboration are bound to be disillusioned. As compared to many other cultures, the US business tradition seems to have a weakness in handling the more subtle aspects of relationships. The RM values discussed in Chapter 1 become clearly tangible in alliances. Alliances must be win–win, parties seeing each other as equals, as partners. Otherwise the parties will act covertly, trying to outsmart one another and thus pursuing hypercompetition strategies rather than RM strategies. It is not the formal structures – for example, that each partner owns equal shares of the alliance – which are crucial, but the spirit of the alliance. There are also obstacles in antitrust legislation, patent laws and the right to intellectual property, degradation of the other partner's ability, and the tradition to work alone rather than together.

Management

It is not easier to manage in a network of collaborating individuals and organizations than to manage a traditional hierarchical organization. Doz and Hamel[29] claim that 'Managing the alliance relationship over time is usually more important than crafting the initial formal design.' Management is definitely different, although it offers more opportunities and varieties. If disputes arise, these cannot be settled by an executive in the same way as in the single enterprise. Managing an alliance jointly is not recommended; the risk of coming to a deadlock is pending. You either turn the alliance into a separate corporation which answers to its board, or you let one of the partners run it. The latter is recommended for an alliance where one partner possesses unique expertise which is crucial for future success. Giving the alliance full autonomy can be necessary for several reasons. The alliance must adjust to conditions prevailing in its market and not be drenched by its parent's financial control system and a standardized reporting format unfit for the operations of the alliance.

The advice provided by a marriage counsellor is surprisingly well suited for the advice needed for a company entering an alliance – choose your partner carefully, invest in a win–win relationship, stay attractive to your partner, develop a sound economy, and search for a division of labour that works for all parties. Good vibrations are needed, even if it is not

---

[29] Doz and Hamel (1998, p. xv).

passionate love. Still we know that decisions on cohabitation are taken under uncertainty with no guarantee whatsoever of the outcome.

Alliances lend opportunities for a company to achieve both economies of scale and economies of scope and yet stay lean and flexible; alliances are important elements of an imaginary organization. In order to cut down time to market and become more competitive – to create 'the fifteen minute advantage'[30] – companies can work together in constellations, concurrently performing several operations and, via computer networks, do this in real time. Spellbound by the promises and potential of the e-relationship and eCRM (R12), it may be easy to forget the importance of social relationships (R18) and the closeness to the customer (R8).

Alliances give birth to power networks, which in themselves create partly locked markets. The complex networks of relationships which exist in markets create multifaceted interaction patterns between buyers, sellers and others. These patterns become institutionalized and limit the space for the market mechanisms. Within the spirit of RM and the marketing equilibrium, however, it is equally as important to utilize collaborative forces as it is to utilize competitive forces.

 ## The knowledge relationship

Knowledge can unite and divide. Established knowledge can inject stability and professionalism; if it becomes obsolete it will stifle operations. New knowledge can initiate change, dissolve established industry definitions and create new ones, transcend geographical borders, and create novel technological conditions. Knowledge is often the basis for an alliance. The daily applications of knowledge may be part of the market relationships and the nano relationships, whereas new combinations of knowledge and new ways of commercializing knowledge largely exist on levels above market relationships.

In order to explore the knowledge relationship, we can ask the following question: 'If we look at the corporation from a knowledge perspective, what do we see that is pertinent to RM and CRM?'

Companies need knowledge to develop, produce and market goods and services. Knowledge is progressively perceived as the core driver of competitiveness. In some organizations this is so evident that they are called knowledge-based organizations or intelligent enterprises.[31] Current society is often referred to as the knowledge or information age. We hear more often these days that the future corporation is a learning organization – IBM presents this as one of its most prominent strategies for reorientation – and its most eminent

---

[30] The expression is taken from Skandia.
[31] See Drucker (1988a); Quinn (1992); and Sveiby (1997).

resource is intellectual capital.[32] The marketing of professional services has long been treated in the literature,[33] but a more general interest in knowledge and its meaning to organizations and profitability has been steadily growing. The Internet has added yet another dimension to network-based knowldge.

A company can be viewed as consisting of three knowledge processes:

1 The *generative* process, in which knowledge is created.
2 The *productive* process, transforming knowledge into products and services – or rather value-creating offerings.
3 The *representative* process, handling the relationship to customers.[34]

In terms of traditional corporate functions, the generative process comprises R&D, design and engineering; the productive process production and purchasing; and the representative process marketing and sales. But emphasis is on knowledge, its content and significance. In alignment with modern thinking in product development and the launching of new products – concurrent engineering – the generative, productive and representative processes are synchronous and reciprocal, not sequential steps. These processes embrace internal and external relationships that differ from those of the traditional hierarchical organization. The relationships are not tied to a certain structure or function; they constitute elements of a network organization.

Knowledge can either be *migratory* or *embedded*. This division has relationship consequences.[35]

Migratory knowledge is explicit and portable, it can emigrate and immigrate. In order to succeed in this transfer, the knowledge must be packaged in drawings, specifications, books, videotapes, CD-ROMs or the Internet. Furthermore, migratory knowledge can be a product which performs what an individual cannot; a computer and a crane are such examples. A product can be seen as 'frozen knowledge', and a skilled person can dismantle a machine and learn how it is constructed or make a chemical analysis of a substance. This is 'reverse engineering'; you start with the product and then make the drawing and specification instead of the other way around. Knowledge can also be moved when people leave one job and bring it to the next or start a new business. A necessary condition is that somebody can open the 'knowledge package' and has an incentive to do so. Patents and other methods of protecting inventions are insecure, particularly if the knowledge can easily migrate.[36]

---

[32] See Senge (1990); and Edvinsson and Malone (1997).
[33] See Wilson (1972); Gummesson (1977); and Ahrnell and Nicou (1995).
[34] According to Wikström and Normann (1994).
[35] The following two paragraphs are primarily based on Badaracco (1991, pp. 79–81; quotation from p. 79).
[36] Porter (1980, p. 172).

Embedded knowledge cannot be transported as easily; it is tacit, often non-verbal, and dependent on first-hand experience. It is embedded in ' . . . specialized relationships among individuals and groups and in particular norms, attitudes, information flows, and ways of making decisions . . .'. Embedded knowledge is found in the skills of the master and the master's environment.

By being difficult to transfer, embedded knowledge offers a sustaining competitive advantage. In order to acquire this kind of knowledge, companies must have close access to those systems and relationships in which the knowledge is embedded. In their alliances with banks in the West, Japanese banks have insisted that the Western banks hire Japanese staff who can access the embedded knowledge of their allies. This is reported to have caused an asymmetric relationship. Instead of the mutually beneficial strategy of 'you show me, and I'll show you!', the strategy has become 'you show me, and I'll show my boss!'[37] It has also been pointed out that the ability to make tacit knowledge explicit is a strength with Japanese companies.[38]

Knowledge is not only embedded in an individual, group or corporation, but also in the relationships between companies and – on a mega level – between companies and governments and between nations, and geography. Silicon Valley reached a critical mass of companies and innovative people within IT; knowledge was embedded in the community. In a similar vein, Switzerland acquired fame for clocks and watches and Wall Street for financial knowledge. In an extensive study of the competitiveness of nations, the geographically concentrated networks between companies in the same and supplying industries is emphasized:

> Once a cluster forms, the whole group of industries becomes
> mutually supporting. Benefits flow forward, backward, and
> horizontally . . . Entry from other industries within the cluster spurs
> upgrading by stimulating diversity in R&D approaches and
> providing means for introducing new strategies and skills . . .
> The cluster becomes a vehicle for maintaining diversity and
> overcoming the inward focus, inertia, inflexibility, and
> accommodation among rivals that slows or blocks competitive
> upgrading and new entry.[39]

---

[37] According to Wright and Pauli (1987, p. 63).
[38] Nonaka and Takeuchi (1995, p. 11).
[39] Porter (1990, p. 51).

CASE STUDY | **Stradivari**

An example of embedded knowledge is Stradivari (1644–1737), who built violins with a sound quality and beauty that has not been surpassed since. This is not only explained by the skills of the master in using tools, wood and varnish, but also by his network within which others developed raw material, designed violins, experimented with new strings, invented techniques for treating wood, composed music, bought his instruments and played on them. Stradivari worked in Cremona, Italy, where there was a century-long tradition of building violins, and he was the student of the master Nicolo Amati.

This way of working is not outdated or limited to the crafts and odd products like violins. It applies to all activities that require skills and knowledge, to high-tech activities such as the design of software as well as the performing arts.

Embedded knowledge can be moved by moving its holders and offering them a supporting environment.[40] French cuisine was created by Italian cooks. The technological and cultural development of the USA was partly the work of German intellectuals who fled the political persecutions during the 1930s and 1940s. Creative processes and knowledge advancement require interaction between individuals and professions in tightly knit networks. They need a meeting-place in order to interact. It is inherent in the nature of creativity that planned control in a rigid structure is not feasible and the meeting-places therefore are often informal. In Vienna and Paris people met in cafés, in Silicon Valley in bars, in Manchester, UK, at the Chamber of Commerce, and today the encounter occurs increasingly on the Internet.

Embedded knowledge requires a different strategy than migratory knowledge. It requires extensive relationships and networks. These are influenced by the globalization of knowledge and its fragmented specialization to many individuals in many locations. The concept of learning organizations has been revived in the 1990s. Senge[41] lays stress on five 'disciplines' necessary to succeed in continuous learning: individual learning; guiding concepts and mental frameworks; leadership, shared values and visions; team learning; and finally the ability to see the whole, how everybody's contribution constitutes a system. Team learning makes possible knowledge development that individuals cannot achieve on their own, today like in the age of Stradivari: 'The discipline of team learning starts with "dialogue" . . . To the Greeks, *dia-logos* meant a free flowing of meaning through a group, allowing the group to discover insights not attainable individually . . . Interestingly, the practice of dialogue has been preserved in many

---

[40] This section is based on Törnqvist (1990, pp. 49–51).
[41] Senge (1990; quotation from p. 10).

"primitive" cultures ... but it has been almost completely lost to modern society.' He further says that the requisite for team learning is the ability to interact.

Interpreted within RM, the team is more than the closest colleagues. It becomes a network of relationships which outgrows functional and hierarchical boundaries. It outgrows the organization, and extends to customers, competitors, suppliers, scientists and others. It is a matter of handling the dialogue – the interaction – constructively in order to make the network stay alive. Dialogue means availing oneself of existing knowledge, but also creating new knowledge; Einstein is reputed to have said that 'imagination is more important than knowledge'. Furthermore, you must teach others what you have created and the learning organization therefore has its counterpart in the teaching organization.

Knowledge not only creates and dissolves geographical and organizational borders, but also traditional industry borders. Cars, which are basically mechanical, contain more and more computer technology, and a new type of knowledge intrudes the auto industry. Until the end of the 1960s, offices could purchase purely mechanical calculating machines and these were supplemented with electromechanical machines. At the beginning of the 1970s, these technologies were rapidly made obsolete by electronics, an entirely new concept which caused successful manufacturers to go bankrupt; they could not cope with the transfer from one technology to another.

Alliances between companies used to concern migratory knowledge, but the trend has changed.[42] From having been self-contained citadels, companies developed alliances through product relationships in order to transfer migratory knowledge and these then become knowledge relationships for the transfer of embedded knowledge. Knowledge relationships have four characteristics:

1 Learning and knowledge creation are increasingly the purpose of alliances.
2 Knowledge relationships need to be more intimate than product relationships.
3 Knowledge relationships require complex networks. Product relationships were usually established with competitors, whereas knowledge relationships are also established with universities, consultants, inventors, licensers, educators, customers, suppliers and internally with functional departments.
4 Knowledge relationships have a greater potential, as knowledge is more general than a product, which is one single application of knowledge.

Today, products are designed in minute detail and the design is meticulously documented. Despite this, there is tacit knowledge which has not found its place in the documents and is possessed by the master or a professional team. Lowe prefers the terms 'connoisseurship' and

---

[42] Badaracco (1991).

'finesse', which epitomize the more subtle aspects of knowledge. Those properties belong to the master and are difficult to describe; they must be learnt through experience and socialization.[43] Not even computer programmers succeed in documenting all their knowledge about a piece of software, in spite of the thick manuals and the allegedly rational behaviour of computers. Instructions and signs are often hard to interpret, or are based on a logic which is different from the user's logic. We notice this as consumers when we try to install a VCR, or even worse try to use its timer function; we are brought into a jungle of instructions and industry jargon. Assembling furniture from IKEA can be quite an ordeal, but the customer friendliness of the 'follow me' instructions – written in the international language of pictures – has been continually upgraded.

Gustavsson (2001) goes further below the surface by introducing collective consciousness as the substance of the organization. This is more than knowledge, it is the shared insights and wisdom which are revealed in the mode of operating, it is the activation of the deeper layers of our consciousness. Knowledge in this sense is more holistic and embraces not only the knowledge itself, but also the process of creating the knowledge and the personality of the bearer of the knowledge. It is common sense in its broadest sense: 'common to all senses'.

Innovation networks can be established between suppliers and customers and other parties. The seller is usually described as the active driving force of the market through continuous change and innovation. According to one study,[44] however, innovations sometimes emerged among suppliers, sometimes among the future users and sometimes in other organizations. Scientific instruments were developed in 77 per cent of the cases by customers, 90 per cent of ploughs were developed by suppliers, and of equipment for cable connections 56 per cent was developed by secondary suppliers, 33 per cent by primary suppliers and 11 per cent by customers.

Intellectual capital, of which knowledge is part, is not visible in the balance sheet. It is not measured but exists all the same and may be the most crucial resource of the company. Leif Edvinsson became the first known Corporate Director of Intellectual Capital (Figure 4.3), a new position at Skandia that became a model for companies worldwide. The notion behind his title is expressed in the following way:[45] 'While most companies appoint directors of finance and operations and focus company valuation on finance and operations, they lack a function to deal with hidden values . . . The mission of this function [Director of Intellectual Capital] is to identify and improve the visibility of intangible and non material items, to capture and package these items for transfer to users, to cultivate and develop these items through training

---

[43] According to a lecture by Andy Lowe at Strathclyde University, Glasgow, 1993.
[44] von Hippel (1988).
[45] The quotations in this paragraph are taken from Buck-Lew and Edvinsson (1993). Intellectual capital will be treated further in Chapter 6.

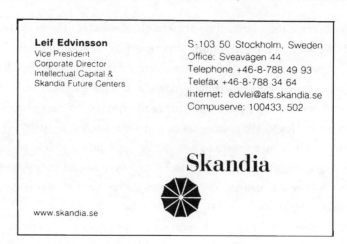

Figure 4.3 Director of intellectual capital

and knowledge networking, and to capitalize and economize on these items through rapid recycling of knowledge and increased commercialization.'

The work is performed in teams in order to secure the representation of all types of knowledge: 'Critical for this development is a federated global organization with competencies and alliances built on intellectual capital, information technology, and leadership around core cultural values.'

To be successful in the future economy, we need network organizations based on knowledge from many contributing sources, and from which tacit and embedded knowledge can be made accessible.

 ## Mega alliances change the basic conditions for marketing

In November 1994, Norway conducted a referendum about future membership of the EU. In front of the TV screens, store owners along the Swedish side of the border watched the outcome with keen interest. It was also a referendum about their future, at that time a matter of some $400 million of consumer money. A yes to the EU would reduce the border trade dramatically, a no – which was also the outcome – meant that Norwegians would continue to cross the border to buy meat, tobacco, wine, liquor, gas and other supplies at attractive prices.

In the previous mega relationships we have met social networks, mega marketing, alliances and knowledge. Mega alliances are alliances above companies, industries and nations. They offer new conditions for business. Mega alliances are established through parliaments, governments and referenda, but also through resolutions taken on a supranational level. They give birth to new relationships and network constellations which become part of marketing.

All the same, the boundaries between corporate alliances and national alliances are partly blurred. Ohmae calls them the cartographic illusion of the interlinked economy. It is meaningless to proceed to view the world as a set of nations:[46] 'Put simply, in terms of real flows of economic activity, nation states have already lost their role as meaningful units of participation in the global economy of today's borderless world.' So it is not only the borders of organizations that become increasingly fuzzier, but also those between states. This is obvious in mega alliances, where the objection often is that the member states lose their independence.

The increasingly larger global corporations are on their way to take charge over nations. Today, fifty-one of the 100 largest economic units in the world are private companies, forty-nine are nations. IBM, BP and Ford are financially bigger than most smaller nations. Wal-Mart's revenue is higher than that of states such as Poland, Slovakia, Ukraine and Hungary.[47] The WTO makes decisions behind closed doors and these decisions are enforced on the member states. Its decisions seem to be more and more in confrontation with the decisions of national parliaments and governments, and in favour of the interests of private corporations. For example, the WTO's resolutions mean limitations in what we can eat and can in turn mean increased health risks.[48]

It is demanding to manage alliances between firms, but to lead mega alliances is impossible; they are such complex networks. Many national governments must come to agreements. Politicians are caught between considerations for national, local, party interests and their own re-election, and international cooperation. One of the dangers with the EU is the growing mammoth-like bureaucracies, another is the abuse of subsidies. According to one assessment, 9 per cent of the EU budget was awarded to fraudulent applications.[49] The many conflicting goals, the bureaucracy and the abuse offset market forces and attempts to reach marketing equilibrium. These difficulties will not disappear. The result is that marketers have to adapt their behaviour accordingly, both accept the EU regulations and apply a certain flexible creativity.

Building mega alliances is a long-term undertaking. The EU springs from the aftermath of the Second World War, when British Prime Minister Winston Churchill proposed a United States of Europe. In 1947, the defence alliance NATO was formed and the US Marshall Plan brought new capital for the resurrection of Europe. In 1951, the Coal and Steel Union was

---

[46] Ohmae (1995, p. 11).
[47] Taken from Hertz (2001, p. 7).
[48] *The Guardian* (1999); and *Fairness and Accuracy in Reporting* (1999).
[49] Based on reports in the *European Times* (1994).

formed with the purpose of preventing new wars. The Rome Treaty in 1957 established the European Economic Community, known as the Common Market, and it contained the seeds to the future mission of the EU: ' . . . to work for a harmonious development of economic activity, continuous and balanced expansion, increased stability, faster increase of living standards, and closer relationships between the member nations.'

The major advantage with mega alliances is free trade. Economists claim that there is overwhelming evidence that free trade leads to increased wealth.[50] Free trade includes 'the four freedoms of the EU', which provide new conditions for marketing: free mobility across borders of goods, services, people and money. Here are some examples of marketing consequences:[51]

- The EU offers opportunities for specialists such as medical doctors, lawyers and engineers to work in member countries without local authorization. Examinations which require at least three years of academic studies will be valid throughout the union, and later shorter specialist education will also be accepted, such as training for nurses. All member countries have not allowed free mobility of labour. In practice, language, nationalism and local regulations for professionals will form barriers for many years.

- Competition for public contracts will change as governments on all levels are no longer allowed to favour domestic suppliers. This market may be worth as much as US $1000 billion, which is more than the GNP of several of the member states. Even if EU legislation takes precedence over national law, it will be difficult to apply unless national governments actively support the implementation.

- A series of IT-based services will simplify national borders for authorities and improve transportation planning, this in turn reducing pollution. SAD, a dismal acronym for Single Administrative Document, replaced some seventy documents needed to drive a truck through Europe. This means that the average speed of twenty miles per hour could be increased considerably.

- A major step was taken on 1 January 2002, when most of the member states – the UK and Sweden were exceptions – replaced their own currencies with the euro (€). It will render the 'bureaux de change' superfluous, as well as the traveller's inconvenience of keeping track of a variety of coins and banknotes.

This all leads to faster distribution, more efficient logistics, simplified inventory, reduced capital employed, cheaper insurance and simpler financial transactions. The cost of goods and services is reduced, marketing is facilitated and competition is intensified.

---

[50] Norberg (2001).

[51] These examples are partially based on Naisbitt and Aburdene (1990, pp. 49–50).

Large multinational manufacturing companies, irrespective of national origin, have for decades been gradually adjusting to the new situation by establishing subsidiaries and alliances inside the EU. Domestic companies and smaller companies, particularly in the formerly protected service sector, are less prepared.

The EU creates mega conditions which determine the rules of the marketplace. As was shown in R19 on mega marketing, companies and industries will try to influence the new conditions through lobbying at EU headquarters. The number of lobbyists has grown from 300 in the early 1990s to over 10 000. It is hard to tell how much the lobbyists can intervene, and how much is just keeping abreast with changes and sending home information for strategic marketing decisions. Close relationships to influential EU politicians and bureaucrats of course mean informal power. There is the misgiving that rich corporations can buy the 'best' professional lobbyists – a full-time lobbyist costs from US $300 000 per annum – while the less rich will be in a constantly inferior position.

The EU demands adaptation in many details, which has provoked consumers in member countries. Local lifestyles are challenged which offer new marketing opportunities and threats. The favourite cigarette of the French, Gauloise, became thinner, to the great dismay of its fans, and French cheese made with non-pasteurized milk ('*lait cru*') was threatened with prohibition. The typical French citizen walking from the local 'boulangerie' with a fresh non-packaged 'baguette' under the arm will be history if unpackaged bread, as suggested, is forbidden.

The North American continent has its corresponding mega alliance between the USA, Canada and Mexico. The North American Free Trade Agreement (NAFTA) was signed in December 1993 and embraces 370 million consumers.[52] Canada, Japan and Mexico are the largest trade partners for the USA, and two of these are now integrated in the mega alliance. Already during the first quarter of 1994, Mexican trade with the USA went up by 17.5 per cent and that with Canada by 30 per cent. There are barriers for European and Asian companies to profit in NAFTA; 62.5 per cent of the components in manufactured products must come from NAFTA countries. This provided an obstacle for Mercedes, who assembled cars in Alabama, USA, but manufactured the components in other countries. A series of non-tariff barriers and 20 000 tariffs will be abolished during a ten- to fifteen-year period, from the Canadian tariff on Mexican tequila of 183 per cent to the US tariffs, which on average amount to 4 per cent. US retailing chains, such JC Penney and Wal-Mart, can open up stores in Mexico, where large-scale retailing has so far been absent. Wal-Mart has entered an alliance with Mexico's largest retailer, Cifra. Alliances are necessary as Mexican consumers have a low per capita income and other lifestyles, but expect more individual service. 'People greeters' wish you welcome to the store and accompany you inside and hand you a trolley; 'the ten-foot rule' states that customer contact must be established within the first ten feet.

---

[52] The text on mega alliances in America and Asia is taken primarily from media reports.

Through the larger market opened up by NAFTA, the possibilities increase for large-scale production and cost reductions on mass-produced goods and services. The bigger markets and deregulation also imply tougher competition. Banks, insurance companies and telecommunications are other industries that see new opportunities. Mexico entered the mega alliance with only eight telephones per 100 inhabitants, while the USA and Canada had over ninety. During the first NAFTA year, Detroit's three largest car manufacturers increased sales from 1000 to 60 000 cars. Through its presence in the USA, NAFTA enabled Skandia to found a subsidiary in Mexico, Skandia Vida.

In 2005, the Free Trade Area of the Americas (FTAA) will be established. It is to include North and South America, with altogether 800 million people and a GNP of US $12 000 billion. Mega alliances are not only permeating business in the US and Europe and changing the marketing conditions and relationships. The same is happening throughout the world.

History shows that mega alliances have always been part of politics, defence and economy. The future value of mega alliances is even harder to evaluate. It is hard to evaluate even in retrospect, as we do not know what would have happened without them. The outcomes of referenda in many countries – where yes or no has won with very small margins – show insecurity and confusion among citizens. It is obvious though that the EU, NAFTA, FTAA and other mega alliances change the rules of the marketing arena and require new relationships and networks. They need to be treated as an integral part of marketing theory in the light of relationships, networks and interaction.

 ## The mass media relationship

Media report events from corporations, governments and markets. Media have an impact on marketing, but exercise their influence primarily on the mega level; they are part of society rather than of the market.

According to one definition, public relations (PR) is 'the management function that identifies, establishes and maintains mutually beneficial relationships between an organization and the various publics on whom its success or failure depends'.[53] PR comprises relationships to stakeholders with the purpose of maximizing image and brand equity of the corporation or industry.

The relationships can embrace society at large, a town, a trade union, the investor market and others. Often PR is primarily a marketing tool. Lobbying, which was treated in R19, can also be part of a PR function and the mass media relationship.

---

[53] Cutlip, Center and Broom (1985, p. 4).

The term public relations is often associated with gimmickry and manoeuvring. Other terms are used to mitigate the negative connotation of PR, such as corporate communications and corporate affairs. Burson-Marsteller, the world's largest public relations consultants, see their work as 'perception management'. Its purpose is to influence perceptions – knowledge, attitudes, values, feelings – of customers and other stakeholders toward a company, a product, a service, new technology or a person.

The media relationship can be split into three types:

1 The relationship between an organization and the media.
2 The relationship between the media and their audiences.
3 The relationship between an organization and the media audience.

There are also intermediaries such as Reuters and United Press (UP) that select and distribute information. They are the wholesalers of the 'news' distribution networks, with television stations, radio stations, newspapers and journals as the retailers. Some of the readers, listeners and watchers are customers or prospective customers (the market relationship), some are politicians, legislators or investors who can exercise influence over a company or industry (the mega relationship), and some are employees (the nano relationship).

The treatment of the media relationship will focus on the first and direct relationship, the one between an organization and the media. They are important to companies and customers whether a company is willing to interact with media or not. Therefore, it is part of a rational and proactive marketing strategy to pay attention to media relationships.

Even if companies and media need each other, there is a goal conflict. Companies want the good news to be published and the bad news to be held back. They want media space as free advertising, with the higher credibility that may be attributed to an editorial text than to a journal advertisement or a television commercial. Media want facts that make news and often preferably news that is sensational and even offer a scandal. The mission of media in democracies is to reflect society and analyse, interpret and report events, and particularly hold misuse of power at bay. Editors and reporters have many incentives, such as passion for the truth, personal integrity, reaching a large audience, fame, esteem among colleagues, vanity and revenge.

Corporations and media nurture a love–hate relationship; they have to stay married for better and for worse. It is essential to strike a balance between the value for both parties, so that both – at least over the longer term – perceive themselves as winners. If the relationship remains asymmetric – one party feeling exploited – the value of the relationship may become continuously negative for both, at the same time as divorce is no solution.

The ability of business leaders to create relationships with media can sometimes be their most important marketing activity, the activity that determines the corporate image. In the

1980s, Lee Iacocca of Chrysler made the headlines worldwide; in the 1990s, Jack Welsh of General Electric, Bill Gates of Microsoft and Richard Branson of Virgin. The host of dotcom whiz-kids in the late 1990s scored high visibility but were largely forgotten a few years later.

CASE STUDY　　**Jan Carlzon and Scandinavian Airlines**

A European example is Jan Carlzon. As president of Scandinavian Airlines (SAS) he became a media pet. Particularly in the beginning, he devoted ample time both to the media and to individual communication with employees on all levels. He skilfully used television to address existing and new groups of passengers as well as employees; much of his internal marketing went via the ordinary television networks. He could explain the role of leadership, the necessity of putting the customer in focus, and the advantages of service and quality. He made new market segments try air travel. He did it in a different and charismatic manner. Friendship with the media is not forever though. When SAS failed to form strategic alliances with European and US major carriers – a necessity for marketing and survival – the media turned against Carlzon with headlines such as 'Are you finished now?' His private life was scrutinized. It all gave free publicity, but it is unclear whether it was beneficial to SAS or not. It certainly kept up the public interest in the company name – and the market needs continuous reminders.

When a critical and unexpected incident occurs, the relationship with the media can determine a company's future. Bergene, Luby's, Ford–Firestone and Hasselblad provide examples:

- *Bergene* – a leading manufacturer of chocolate bars in Norway – followed another strategy. An outbreak of salmonella was located in the raw chocolate used in Bergene bars. The management chose to cooperate closely with media and health authorities and to be totally open. An internal task force, including representatives of the authorities, was appointed and no cost was spared to take necessary action. After an initial drop in sales and a bad year financially, Bergene recaptured its market position.
- *Luby's*, with 145 restaurants in America, had an emergency plan knowing that consumers, media and investors could react randomly and neurotically if a catastrophe or bad publicity occurred. In 1991, twenty-three people were shot down at one of their cafeterias, a killing which had nothing to do with Luby's as such. In one hour the company stopped all trade with its stock. The CEO was at the scene of the crime in two hours, arranging free hotel

rooms for relatives of the victims, setting up a fund and guaranteeing that the employees would keep their jobs if the restaurant closed down.

- It became known that the *Ford Explorer,* a van equipped with Firestone tyres, had met with unexpected accidents caused by tyre explosions. It began in Venezuela and in two years 174 people were killed and 700 injured. It continued in the US. Ford and Firestone tried the cover-up strategy. First, they kept silent and did not alert the Explorer owners. When exposed to the events, they rejected all responsibility, blamed the drivers, each other and poor maintenance of the vans. Their efforts to prevent further accidents were half-hearted. The case is now being tried in US courts and will be there for years, costing fantasy sums. There is no trace of RM values in the behaviour of these two gigantic companies. The bottom line so far: bad publicity and a tarnished image.

- To gain media exposure when new products and services are launched is the dream of all companies. In 1948, *Victor Hasselblad* launched his new camera at a press conference in the USA.[54] He was unknown, but invited twenty reporters from the professional photo press. They hailed the camera as the perfect product. Hasselblad's relationship to this small group of opinion leaders was decisive for the rapid success of the camera. It became the natural choice for the first journey to the moon and fifty years after its introduction the Hasselblad camera holds its position among professional photographers as the king of cameras; it has a 20 per cent global market share in its niche. And it has kept its position as a media pet. In 1995, says a spokesperson for the company, the attention from the professional press was so high that there was no need to advertise the new products.[55]

These cases show different situations of the media relationship and different types of interaction. Bergene was totally unprepared but found an overt and successful strategy, forming a friendly and open alliance with the media. Luby's was well prepared. It is amazing how two such giants as Ford and Firestone, who have the money to engage the best advisors, can fail so completely in their relationship to the market.

Instant and sustaining success through the media like Hasselblad is the dream of every CEO and marketing director. We have seen it happen more recently with dotcoms and some others, but in today's escalated media noise it may not have a long-lasting effect. Today's memory is short. Who remembers what made the headlines in yesterday's newspaper or what CNN reported during the past week? Essential information drowns in the love affairs of presidents and political scandals; red herrings fill much of the information space. 'A weekday edition of *The New York Times* contains more information than the average person was likely to come across in a lifetime in seventeenth-century England,' says Samuel Wurman in his book

---

[54] Based on an article by Hemmungs Wirtén (1992).
[55] Interview with the Hasselblad information director (*Info*, 1996).

Information Anxiety.[56] Even if there is sometimes no response at all, media, including advertising, have a reinforcing role and can activate an interest that is already there. There is no doubt that mass media, not least for establishing and maintaining the parasocial relationship (R13), will remain important even if RM and CRM advocate individualized approaches to both consumers and organizational customers.

An essential distinction must be made between investigative journalists, who are knowledgeable and apply systematic research techniques in long-term fact-finding missions, and the general reporter who is expected to cover any type of event and have an article or newsflash ready in the next few hours. There are reporters and media specialized in certain industries, such as telecom or cars, which they follow continuously. There has even been a special group of reporters and consultants around IBM – the IBM watchers – to focus singularly on IBM reporting and interpreting its decisions and activities.

Media can be approached through a variety of means: formal press conferences, informal meetings, press messages, interviews, etc. It is not just a matter of offering news, but also of a personal and trusting relationship. It requires planning and stamina, just like all types of marketing. The media relationship is part of a total communications process, including internal marketing activities.

Virtual reality is an IT creation. Photos can already be manipulated with fairly ordinary computers; the dinosaurs of the movie *Jurassic Park* came to life through software, and in another movie Forrest Gump shook hands with President Kennedy, who died thirty years before the movie was made. Information and entertainment merge into infotainment.[57] Another unreal reality has long been around, the *pseudo-event* and the pseudo-news. *A pseudo-event is engineered to be reported, it is not reported because it happened naturally.* Examples are the use of celebrities in the launching of a film, book, restaurant, sports game or an art exhibition. Celebrities add glamour to these events; in fact, the events do not receive media coverage for what they are, but for the celebrities. These events build on the marketing of people: actors, authors, chefs, athletes and artists, and also CEOs, scientists and politicians. Media play a major role, maybe even *the* major role in their marketing. Talk shows with celebrities have become everyday programmes of television channels.

---

[56] Wurman (1989, p. 32).
[57] See Postman (1987), who treats the confusion between reality and entertainment which above all television has contributed to.

IN BRIEF

The following lines from a book on 'celebrity marketing' succinctly sum up the importance of the media relationship:[58] 'Because the media make up the most powerful of channels, they are crucial to winning high visibility. Other channels are capable of moving celebrity images out of the warehouse and into the marketplace, but none approaches the cost-effectiveness and audience impact of the mass media.'[59]

---

[58] Rein, Kotler and Stoller (1987, p. 255).
[59] Inspiration for this relationship also comes from Karaszi (1991); and Hadenius and Weibull (1993).

Chapter

5

Nano relationships

INTRODUCTION

The previous chapter discussed relationships above market relationships. This chapter deals with the opposite, relationships below the market proper, that is, inside an organization. These nano relationships (R24–R30) are found in the suppliers' organizational structure, systems and processes. They provide the antecedents for implementation of marketing activities and success with the market and mega relationships. They also provide a basis for handling mega relationships. The nano relationships show that there exists a market economy inside a company and that the boundaries between a company's external and internal work have become increasingly blurred. Companies have become network organizations.

RELATIONSHIP 24 | # Market mechanisms are brought inside the company

Parallel to networks and alliances that curb the free market mechanisms outside the company, there is a long-term trend to install market mechanisms inside the company. The market mechanisms have partly replaced the internal planned economy, and it is not always clear who is the seller, buyer or competitor. The boundaries between 'them' and 'us' become blurred. New marketing strategies are needed to handle the new internal and external market relationships.

In its purest form, a company can be seen as a planned economy where clearly defined activities are coordinated toward clearly defined objectives with the help of a business mission, goals, strategies, production systems, organizational structures, budgets and financial control systems. Planned economies, as we know them from communism, have gigantic problems with productivity, quality and growth. They are known for rigidity, lack of initiative and a general inability to manage their countries. In terms of number of employees, but not necessarily in terms of financial resources, corporations are tiny as compared to nations. Yet companies run into the problems of the planned economy, and have therefore constructed a dynamic internal market economy. This trend has been sustained since the 1960s. It is usually referred to as decentralization, but within the concept of RM, I would prefer to see it as an expression for internal deregulation and re-regulation.[1]

---

[1] An in-depth analysis of decentralization is found in Södergren (1987, 1992). In an anthology, Halal, Geranmayeh and Pourdehead (1993) have focused on the internal markets and their deregulation. They use an approach from organization theory and to some extent from economics. RM adds dimensions to this analysis by including services marketing, the network approach and quality management, together with the concepts of interactive and simultaneous production and consumption, the customer's role, internal marketing, internal and external customers, as well as new accounting theory (intellectual capital, balanced scorecard).

Figure 5.1 Market mechanisms are brought inside the organization

This is pertinent to RM in so far as the relationships inside the organization change in two ways. First, market relationships are brought inside the company, constituting a new base for external market relationships. Second, from having had internal stability (at least in theory) via administrative routines, a market-like relationship is born between the internal supplier and the internal customer.

The introduction of a market economy inside the organization becomes visible in the organizational structure in several ways (Figure 5.1):

- The company is organized in four types of units:

  1 Top management and the board.
  2 Operational units with production and marketing/sales as the core.
  3 Internal service units.
  4 Support or staff units.

- The operative units and service units become profit centres: business areas, division, subsidiaries and smaller profit centres within these. The most important units – strategic business units (SBUs) – are given considerable independence.
- Separating staff units from internal service units is often not easy. Staff units are an extension of management at different organizational tiers. As such, they are treated as cost centres, even if they support and serve profit centres. With the purpose of utilizing the strength of the free-market forces, the strategy is usually to turn as many units as possible into service units. However, going too far in this direction may cause ineffectiveness through internal avoidance of the units, and a stifling and costly internal accounting system.
- The original idea is that profit centres should enjoy autonomy. This means, for example, that a production unit can deliver to a marketing and sales unit, but the marketing and sales unit can use an external supplier if it does not find a brother or sister offering the right conditions. An internal service unit can deliver services together with an external provider and the specialists of an operating unit, but could also sell its services to external companies. The internal business requires an internal pricing system which should be competitive with the prices on the market.

There is no marketing theory treating the internal market mechanisms, despite the fact that decentralization and internal deregulation have gone on for so long. The notion of internal pricing indicates that the market has been let in, although less on market conditions than on accounting conditions.[2] During the 1980s, even the government sector began decentralization with profit centres.

Internal pricing may lead to inertia in relationships. If every cent must be accounted for – you can hardly talk to somebody in another profit centre without receiving an invoice – efficiency is arrested. It is possible for management to use regulations and interfere only when the market mechanisms are not adequate, thereby establishing internal marketing equilibrium. Internal pricing is important for core activities, less so for support functions. If a more rational and cost-effective mode of operations has been established with the assistance of internal pricing and competition during a period, continuous internal charging becomes less important. The practice of internal pricing is, however, an attempt to get away from arbitrary cost-plus pricing, which has the character of internal taxation.

According to transaction cost analysis, the rationale for the existence of organizations is the notion that external information is less accessible and internal information is easily accessible.[3] The analysis assumes that internal relationships are well under control, and therefore the

---

[2] There is a long tradition on internal pricing. The discussion here is partly influenced by an interview with Göran Arvidsson (Wennberg, 1994).

[3] Transaction cost analysis is discussed further in Chapter 7.

internal transactions become more efficient than transactions with external parties. It is consequently easier to operate inside an organization than being dependent on market research techniques and other intelligence for learning about customers, competitors and others, some of them intentionally obstructing access to information. However, the assumptions of transaction cost analysis evaporate if we cannot clearly separate the organization from its environment, if there is interference with the external market mechanisms, and if market mechanisms are introduced inside the organization.

Corporations have been divided into profit centres for decades, but the early efforts created confusion about responsibility and authority. Although relationships between corporate headquarters and divisions are often strained, the ability to manage divisionalized organizations has improved and profit centres are common in all types of organizations.

The internal relationship market may be seen as a triad embracing two profit centres, one being the supplier and the buyer, and a relationship between each of the profit centres and corporate management.[4] The relationships are characterized by collaboration and competition, affinity and conflict. Corporate management enforces a certain amount of regulation. The three units – supplier, buyer and management – are in turn nested in a larger network within which their relationships are affected. In the relationships between supplier and customer, there is exchange between goods, services, money and information. Certain peripheral services can facilitate the relationships, such as computer-based ordering and invoicing systems.

CASE STUDY   **Electrolux, Husqvarna and Mecatronic**

A case study made by Hultbom will serve as an illustration of internal relationships in a profit centre-based organization. The members of the triad are Electrolux corporate headquarters (HQ) and its subsidiaries Husqvarna (selling sewing machines on the external market) and Mecatronic (internally selling components for sewing machines):

In the study of the triad, it is not apparent that the relationship between Husqvarna and Mecatronic was affected by actions from HQ. The two profit centres were left alone. There were no signs that the internal interaction between the two was smoother and the transaction costs lower than if they had been totally independent companies and acted on the external market. Both seller and buyer

---

[4] This is based on Hultbom (1990, p. 101; case study quotation from pp. 136–7).

considered price negotiations cumbersome and information on deliveries was not easily available. Mecatronic found cooperation on R&D and manufacturing issues essential, but Husqvarna employees considered themselves on top of technology and claimed product development was best handled by them. There was an apparent risk for sub-optimization from the point of view of the corporation. The hierarchical power of HQ indirectly affected the selling–buying relationship. Husqvarna, being one of the world leaders on sewing machines, felt secure. Mecatronic, on the other hand, had been through a fundamental restructuring process. It had commenced the manufacturing of a new product which developed rapidly (as viewed from an engineering perspective). It gave rise to insecurity and a protective attitude. HQ demanded a quick return on the investment which could disturb the long-term development of Mecatronic. The cumbersome price negotiations were probably caused by HQ's demand for rapid return. The demand and the internal competition created far less satisfactory information flows in the buyer–seller relationship.

By bringing the market into a company, new types of internal networks materialize. Management will still exercise governance through hierarchical power in the network. In an analogy with the external market, management is a government who can introduce regulations that limit free-market mechanisms:

1 Management monitors the profit centres through financial reports.
2 The acquisition of financial resources is usually centralized, which means there is internal competition for capital. The independence of the operational units in allocating their profits is often limited, for example when new investment and development projects are planned.
3 Top management hire and fire the heads of business areas, subsidiaries and divisions.
4 Everyone is expected to work in alignment with the corporate business mission, goals and strategies.
5 There is informal pressure.
6 The internal units may do business with any supplier or customer outside the corporation if they find this more profitable, but in practice, one cannot be certain that corporate management will support such freedom.

Within this framework, the internal units are allowed to act on market conditions in the relationships with one another. They often belong to different industries. Markets for goods and services exist inside the company and the internal units send invoices to each other. Consequently, the relationships between the employees and functions will be different than in a traditional planned economy hierarchy. The difference between the internal operations of the corporation and the external market becomes less evident.

Internal exchange of information is often filled with conflict, while the exchange can be quite peaceful in external markets. As there is a defined hierarchical structure above the profit centre relationships in combination with market mechanisms, the relationships may even become more complex internally. Market mechanisms require that the interests of different parties are confronted and that goal conflicts are resolved.

The market system involves duplication of work. From an accounting perspective, this is not considered cost effective and is to be avoided through coordination. At the same time, coordination of human activity only works to a limited degree and if driven too far will cause inertia, low productivity and low flexibility.

Critics also claim that the profit centres are just shovelling money around inside the corporation and not adding value. The fact that companies keep decentralizing could be evidence that there are more advantages than disadvantages in the use of profit centres. The dynamics of the shorter and quicker decision routes and the opportunities for profit centres to develop their own relationships and networks outweigh the disadvantages. Inside the organization as well as in the market there is a trade-off between freedom and regulations.

> INSIGHT   In the same way as we need to strive in the direction of marketing equilibrium externally – in the market and society – we must strive for marketing equilibrium inside the organization. This will be explained further in Chapter 7.

Internal customer relationships

Lee Iacocca, who took over as CEO of Chrysler, the third largest car manufacturer in America, described his first impressions in the following way:[5]

> Nobody at Chrysler seemed to understand that interaction among
> different functions in a company is absolutely critical: People in

---

[5] Iacocca (1984, p. 162).

> engineering and manufacturing almost have to be sleeping together.
> These guys were not even flirting . . . The manufacturing guys would
> build cars without even checking with the sales guys. They just built
> them, stuck them in a yard, and then hoped that somebody would
> take them out of there. We ended up with a huge inventory and a
> financial nightmare.

This quotation serves as a perfect introduction to relationships and dependency between different functions in a company, an aspect that is missing or only mentioned in passing in marketing theory. Here, I will borrow two concepts from quality management: the *internal customer* and *process management*.

In Figure 5.2, each ring represents an internal supplier and internal customer, beginning and ending with an external customer. It is a matter of *interfunctional dependency* and *horizontal interaction*, knocking down walls between specialist functions and organizational silos. It is also a matter of *interhierarchical dependency* and *vertical interaction*, as there are also walls between the tiers of the organizational pyramid.

The relationship between operations management – R&D, engineering design, purchasing, manufacturing – and marketing is particularly important. It will be treated as a special case in R26, the reason being that modern quality management, TQM, is specifically addressing the gap between engineers and marketers.

Traditionally, there are conflicts between specialized functions and between organizational tiers. They form subcultures and tribes within the company and tribal warfare is common.[6] But organizations could be perceived as bundles of processes rather than piles of boxes. One such process is visible in Figure 5.2. *Process thinking* is gradually dominating the renewal of corporations. According to Harrington:[7] 'Everything we do today can be done better by concentrating on the process. Management has taken away our employees' ability to produce error-free output by saddling them with obsolete, cumbersome, bureaucracy-laden business processes.' *Business process re-engineering* (BPR)[8] has been promoted as a dramatically new view on management. It requires rethinking the company from scratch without commitment to current structure and to reorganize around processes instead of specialist functions.

The arrows in Figure 5.2 indicate how a process can wriggle its way through a hierarchy. If we mentally erase the hierarchical structure we can visualize the relationships and the process more clearly and surmise a network structure. Principles of process management have been used for many years within manufacturing, but recently they have also been applied to

---

[6] See also Neuhauser (1988).

[7] Harrington (1991, p. x).

[8] Hammer and Champy (1993).

Figure 5.2 Relationships between internal customers, internal suppliers and external customers in a hierarchical structure

internal services and administration. 'If you're not serving the customer, your job is to serve someone who is.'[9] Expressions like 'white collar work', 'office work' and 'administrative routines' are no longer viable; they obscure more than they enlighten.

During the Second World War, the task force of the military became a new mode of operation. In order to reach an objective – beat the enemy at a defined location – a temporary collaboration between different organizational units was established within the allied forces. This way of organizing was introduced in business and it became common to work in projects. Projects were characterized by being temporary and focused on solving a specific task. They used people from various parts of the extant organization, sometimes supplemented with consultants and other external suppliers. With the task completed, the project organization was dissolved. Inside the project there was a certain hierarchy, usually a management group, a reference group and work groups. Today, projects are common in organizations, for example in product development, where they can include people from design, engineering, manufacturing, purchasing and marketing. It is an organized way of achieving interfunctional cooperation.

---

[9] Albrecht and Zemke (1985).

The notion of the internal customer brings customer–supplier relationships into the company. It requires employees to see other employees as customers who receive deliveries of products, services, documents, messages and decisions. The term internal supplier could be added as a companion to internal customer. Usually, an employee fulfils the role of being both a recipient of something as an internal customer and to deliver something in a value-added state to another internal customer. Only when the customers are satisfied – and it is satisfied customers that count whether these are external or internal – a job is completed. Ishikawa, one of the fathers of TQM, used the slogan 'the next process is your customer' back in the 1950s ' . . . to resolve fierce hostility between workers from different production processes of a steel mill . . . [and] still uses it today in his lifelong effort to break through the barriers of sectionalism in business organizations'.[10]

If a company does not consider the links between all functions, there will be 'broken chains', which are one of the 'invisible competitors'; these are more obstructing to success than the visible competitors.[11] One of the messages in the network approach to B-to-B is the interdependency between marketing and all aspects of operations management. This is particularly striking in the manufacture and assembly of complex, customized equipment. In services marketing it has been found that service delivery, production, marketing and service development are largely handled by the same people, thus making interfunctional relationships indispensable.

A process should not be perceived as if there was only one natural sequence of activities. The *value chain*[12] can give the impression that core functions such as R&D, manufacturing and marketing must be performed in that very order. The value constellation (or value star)[13] puts emphasis on the simultaneous rather than the sequential, as well as on the importance of combining functions with regard to needs rather than to follow a uniform procedure. In the value chain, the customer is an external end-user of a firm's output; in the value constellation the customer is part of the process – a co-producer – and not just an end-user.

Like the external networks, the internal networks can be complex. A web is spun between the many-headed internal suppliers and the many-headed internal customers, establishing both formal and informal links between everyone in the organization. Alliances, therefore, are not established only with external partners; there is also an internal alliance market. Purchasing may be handled by a profit centre on its own or through 'pooled purchasing', meaning that a purchasing department might achieve better conditions if buying larger

[10] Quotation from Lu (1985, p. viii).
[11] See also McKenna (1985, pp. 129, 142, 143).
[12] See Porter (1985).
[13] Wikström and Normann (1994).

quantities for several profit centres. 'Sourcing teams' may be used, consisting of members from different functions.[14]

Figure 5.3 shows interaction patterns between different departments in an R&D project. The development took place in an interfunctional project within the spirit of concurrent engineering, but most of the interaction took place within the R&D department. The interaction was also evaluated differently. For example, marketing people valued the interaction with designers higher than vice versa. In another case, the designers were highly negative to the marketers, but appreciated contacts with the buyers.

Complaints that boundaries between departments and tiers are a hindrance against efficient processes date long back. Yet these hindrances are maintained. Within quality management it has become obvious that quality and customer satisfaction cannot be achieved as long as processes are not operating smoothly.

Common sense tells us that the outcome to external customers cannot be satisfactory if the internal customer relationships and collaboration are walking with a limp.

| INSIGHT | By introducing the internal customer–internal supplier concepts, the nano view of an organization becomes a natural part of RM. The organization becomes a network of relationships, processes and projects. |

Quality and customer orientation: the relationship between operations management and marketing

Marketing literature often presents two opposite perspectives, marketing (or customer) orientation and production (or product) orientation. R25 treated interfunctional dependency, and marketing and operations management are two mutually dependent functions. There are reasons to treat their relationship separately. First, they are the core functions of any company, and second, driving them closer together is the most noteworthy contribution of modern quality management.

Quality management is one of the theories that inspired the 30R approach. Modern quality thinking is not only a revolution in quality management, but also a rejuvenation of marketing orientation. In marketing, quality was long used in a general and loose sense. It became a cliché, which was routinely appended to advertising copy, which sales people allowed to litter

---

[14] See Scheuing (1994).

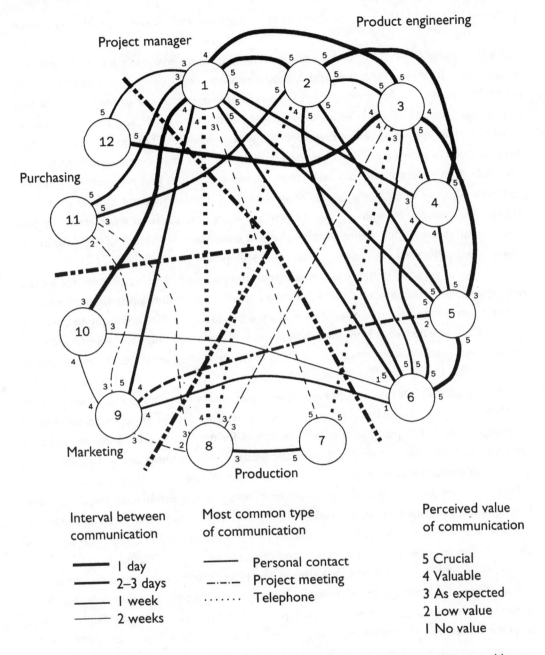

Figure 5.3 The interaction in an interfunctional R&D project. Twelve participants (drawn as circles) are connected through a line and the thickness of the line indicates the frequency of interaction. At the ends of each line, a number shows the participant's evaluation of the interaction (5 is best). The participants include the project leader, and representatives for design, purchasing, manufacturing and marketing. Source: Carlsson and Lundqvist (1992, p. 9). Reproduced with permission

their talk, and which CEOs boasted about at conferences and dinners. Quality became an empty word.

Quality management can be approached externally from the market or internally from the organization. Together, these two approaches constitute total quality management (TQM). Externally oriented quality management is market driven, in contrast to internally oriented quality management, which is technology or systems driven. The drivers in the market are found among a supplier's existing customers, those customers who buy from the competition, future customers who have not yet purchased, and existing and potential competitors.

In order to reinforce marketing orientation, changes in values and personal attitudes are necessary. Values change slowly and the new way of approaching the market must find support in business missions, goals, objectives, strategies, organizational structure and management systems. This in turn requires changed leadership style. Much of the literature on quality today is focused on leadership and the development of employees.

Two frequently quoted definitions of quality emphasize the relationship between the market and operations management. Crosby[15] defines quality as conformance to requirements, meaning that companies must be able to produce a product or service according to drawings and specifications; deviation from these is 'non-quality'. If the drawings and specifications are correct, ideal conditions for quality exist. This is the core of internal quality management, which can also be expressed as 'Do things right!'

A critical question for the marketer is whose requirements the offering shall conform with and how this generates value for the customer as well as for the supplier. In the second definition, Juran (1992) puts the emphasis on fitness for use, which means that the supplier creates value by making certain that the offering is adjusted to customer needs. This is external quality management and its imperative is 'Do the right things!'

Success is not the outcome of an either/or strategy, either production orientation and internal quality management or marketing orientation and external quality management. It is a both/and strategy, a trade-off between the two. We must understand customer needs and be able to design offerings that satisfy needs, and organize for their fulfilment.

To some extent this is still true, but during the 1980s, quality began to dress up in new clothes. Today, the word quality is interpreted as customer perceived quality, meaning that it is marketing-oriented and focused on customer satisfaction. The customer side of quality, however, should not be promoted at the expense of the technology aspect of quality. Prior to the quality revolution during the 1980s, technology aspects were in the driver's seat, and a bias toward customers was called for in order to restore balance. The customer approach to quality management is of course directly pertinent to marketing, although in the long run, I advocate a balanced view.

---

[15] Crosby (1984).

Systematic approaches to quality management grew out of operations management, with limited or no base in marketing until the 1980s. The contributions to service quality became an integral part of service research and practice, and consequently part of services marketing theory.

The quality perspective has successively moved from the shop floor to the management of the whole corporation. This is evident in the now widespread quality awards. The Malcolm Baldrige National Quality Award and later the European Quality Award have become role models for international, national and local quality awards.

Baldrige regulations provide a comprehensive list of criteria which an organization must consider to make quality happen. It is my contention that these awards have given rise to the most comprehensive approach to quality that had hitherto seen the light. It could even deserve to be called a meta theory of quality. The perspective is holistic; the theory consists of quality factors as well as a discussion of links between them.

A brief description of the Baldrige Award will give an idea of the structure of quality prizes.[16] Baldrige offers seven categories of criteria. A total of 1000 points are divided between the following categories:[17]

1 Leadership (110 points).
2 Strategic Planning (80).
3 Customer and Market Focus (80).
4 Information and Analysis (80).
5 Human Resource Development and Management (100).
6 Process Management (100).
7 Business Results (450).

This is nothing less than a list of criteria for a complete company audit! It shows that quality cannot be achieved unless all activities inside a company are directed toward quality; it points to interfunctional and interhierarchical interaction. This does not mean that the quality concept has taken over all management, only that quality development requires contributions from each and everyone. It would of course be surprising if badly managed internal work would end up in quality excellence.

Just over half of the points concern activities and the rest business results. The points cover both internal activities and those directed toward the market and society. In several of the points, the link between quality and relationships is emphasized.

---

[16] Based on the Malcolm Baldrige Regulations (1997) and interviews with former Baldrige executive Curt Reimann.
[17] Malcolm Baldrige (1997, p. 2).

The most important conclusion from the recent unfolding of the quality concept, and which has vast implications for marketing, is the following: Quality management in its modern form fortifies the relationship between operations management and marketing management.

I consider this a hitherto neglected but dramatic change in the management of a business. In Figure 5.4, characteristic features of the internal and external orientations are listed with TQM as the bridge. The quality concept has succeeded in doing what marketing has strived to do for decades, unite production orientation with marketing orientation. From having been based on technical data and 'rational' and 'objective' statistics, quality management has moved to regard customer perceptions and the value for the customer as its touchstone.

Figure 5.4 TQM forging a relationship between marketing functions and technical functions

The external part of TQM starts with customer perceived quality and market needs. The most comprehensive contributions are found in the marketing literature, often expressed in terms of needs, need satisfaction, and satisfied – and today even delighted – customers. Within market research, there is a long tradition of studying consumer satisfaction, consumer behaviour, organizational buying behaviour and customer relationships to brands, but this literature almost exclusively deals with goods, not services. The quality concept from service research is above all externally oriented, toward customers and revenue.

CASE STUDY | **IBM and Apple**

The IBM and Apple approaches to development can serve as an illustration. IBM had a reputation of being marketing oriented (or rather sales oriented), and to balance technical requirements and a tough and systematic salesmanship against an interest for customer needs. IBM has been on top with regard to size, growth and profits, and has been the most admired company, the one university graduates wanted to work for. During the 1980s, IBM's progress slowed down. Former CEO John Akers said in an interview that we ' . . . took the eye off the ball', meaning that IBM lost sight of the customer.[18] He added that he thought IBM ' . . . must become the world's champion in meeting the needs of our customers'. Apple Macintosh, competing with the IBM PC, had taken a different approach to the computer. A Mac should be user-friendly in the sense that anyone should be able to operate it, whereas a PC should be expert-friendly and be used by professionals. Computer experts saw the Mac as a toy; a real computer could not just work that simply! Apple focused on an interactive relationship between the computer and the user. As Apple expressed in an ad: 'Imagine a computer that is not based on the possibilities of technology, but of the possibilities of human beings'.[19]

We now know that the Apple approach won and its software has largely been taken over by Microsoft, IBM, Dell and other PC suppliers, but Apple has not become the world leader. In this sense this is sad considering Apple's efforts to provider customer-friendly solutions. A lesson for marketers is that a good approach is not enough unless you can show muscle on the market.

Three efforts to design models for facilitating the technology–market link will be mentioned here. The first is quality function deployment (QFD). Its purpose is to unite customer requirements with the properties of goods and services. It is also referred to as 'the quality house' after the house-like form of its matrices. What customers want is found out in detail and linked with how the supplier shall achieve this technically in order to design an offering. The connections between the whats and hows are established and analysed, technical conflicts between properties are listed, and finally a specification is established.[20]

The second technique is based on process descriptions of services, already mentioned together with the service encounter in R5. They concentrate on the interaction between the

---

[18] Quotations from *Fortune* (Dreyfuss, 1989, pp. 21 and 23).
[19] Quotation from an advertisement for Apple in *Svenska Dagbladet*, 10 June 1992.
[20] Hauser and Clausing (1988).

customer and the provider's front staff, and the interaction between front staff, support staff and management. The vantage point is the 'customer's path', that is, the customer's way of moving from considering to buy a service and to getting the service produced and delivered.[21]

The third effort consists of the quality awards and certifications which demand integration between technical aspects, internal aspects and customers. The quality standard ISO9000 with its recent and more demanding upgrade ISO9000:2000 requires, among other things, a clear documentation of processes.

Certain services are performed at the customer's site, for example cleaning services. The cleaning company can focus on the customers' need for clean premises, their need for cleaning at a specific time, or on the amount the customer is willing to pay. If the cleaning company can influence the layout of an office before it is built, it can achieve better quality and productivity, which means better value for the customer as well as for the service provider. If a building is difficult to keep clean, efficient techniques and aids can facilitate, but only within the limits of the construction of the building. Improved quality then requires cooperation in an early stage between those who design, construct and maintain the building.

Daily, we interact with deficiently designed and badly manufactured products. Bitner has drawn the following conclusion about the impact of the physical environment on service quality: 'Typically, decisions about employees and the design of physical evidence are not made by marketing managers, but rather by human resource managers, operations managers, and design professionals.'[22] The internal logic then takes over at the expense of the customer logic.

Psychologist Donald Norman has studied the psychopathology of everyday things, their 'mental' shortcomings. Let me end this section with his summary of the designer's dilemma:[23]

> Designing well is not easy. The manufacturer wants something that can be produced economically. The store wants something that will be attractive to its customers. The purchaser has several demands. In the store, the purchaser focuses on price and appearance, and perhaps on prestige value. At home, the same person will pay more attention to functionality and usability. The repair service cares about maintainability: how easy is the device to take apart, diagnose, and service? The needs of those concerned are different and are often in conflict. Nonetheless, the designer may be able to satisfy everyone.

---

[21] See also Gummesson (1993, p. 198ff) and the discussion on contextual matrices (pp. 108–10).
[22] Bitner (1990, p. 79).
[23] Norman (1988, p. 28).

Obviously there are many stakeholders with different needs: designers, suppliers, retail outlets, buyers, users and those who handle the maintenance, plus, eventually, society and the environment. And which of these stakeholders should be considered the customers? For whom should the design be targeted? And how should we build relationships to them and interact with them? We can conclude that – unfortunately – a customer-centric strategy which includes a balanced view of the interaction between producer and user is still not reality.

 ## Internal marketing – relationships with the 'employee market'

So far we have encountered at least two phenomena which could be labelled internal marketing: the marketing between units in the same corporation (R24) and the relationships between internal customers (R25). However, the current marketing terminology reserves internal marketing for a third phenomenon, defined as follows: Internal marketing is the application of marketing knowledge – which was originally developed for external marketing – on the 'internal market', that is, the employees.[24]

Figure 5.5 shows that internal marketing is in-bound and directed to the personnel. External marketing can also have an impact on the internal market, which is shown by the arrow to the right. For example, advertisements for a company sometimes attract the employee's attention more than it attracts the consumer's attention, and if the CEO is interviewed on television the employees watch with particular curiosity.

Internal marketing in the network organizations is much more complex than in the simple hierarchy shown in Figure 5.5: not only must own staff be reached but also other actors in the network. Reasons to apply internal marketing can originate from several sources, and people can belong to several networks. The distinction between internal and external marketing becomes fluid. This stands out clearly as the Internet is usually perceived in marketing as an external relationship builder. It can also be used to establish an intranet which extends to the traditionally internal, the employees, and an extranet for 'specially invited' customers, partners in alliances, own suppliers and others who form a company's network organization. The group of stakeholders with whom you aspire for long-term relationships becomes an 'in-between group', one between the strictly internal and the strictly external. For example, VISA has linked its employees in an intranet which offers a list of the staff, newsletters, lunch menu and more. Its extranet application includes 19 000 allied banks who handle the daily operations

---

[24] Internal marketing appeared as a concept in the late 1970s (see Grönroos, 2000, pp. 330–55). It has been treated by many in somewhat diverse ways. Voima and Grönroos (1999, pp. 747–51) approach internal marketing from a relationship perspective. A comprehensive review of internal marketing is found in a recent anthology edited by Varey and Lewis (2000).

Figure 5.5 The difference between internal and external marketing, and the link between them

of the VISA card. This could also be viewed as an extention of an eCRM system beyond the mere customer focus.

As with the Internet, the technology itself is only of benefit when put to constructive use. The role of managers as well as the tasks of information departments may change, as much information is interactively available on the Net. Despite this, and particularly when internal marketing is used in major changes, personal contact is critical. High tech will never make the need for high touch obsolete.

The objective of internal marketing within RM is to create relationships between management and employees and between functions. The personnel can be viewed as an internal market, and this market must be reached efficiently in order to prepare the personnel for external contacts; efficient internal marketing becomes an antecedent to efficient external marketing. Techniques from external marketing can be applied internally, mainly from the areas of promotion and communications. Internal marketing can be based on personal and interactive relationships, as well as on a certain amount of mass marketing. Traditional activities to reach the employees have often been routinely performed and have built more on bureaucratic principles and wishful thinking than on professional marketing and communications know-how.

To a large extent, internal marketing must be interactive. Traditional ways of internal mass marketing – such as the distribution of formal memos and internal magazines – is insufficient. Social get-togethers are important. My own experience shows that kick-offs have become established as important interactive instruments for management to reach out both with facts and also to shape attitudes and foster a corporate culture. One rapidly growing company in Norway with 250 employees (average age thirty) orchestrated a weekend kick-off which opened with some serious reprimands from the CEO. It continued with presentations by external consultants, one being the coach for the Norwegian national ski-jumping team, proceeded with entertainment by the number one rock star and popular singer, all introduced by the number one TV personality. It ended with a big banquet with awards for best employee performances and dancing. A Swedish global company hired a theatre group from London. Together with the client they set up a three-day interactive kick-off in a large film studio, with both mental, social and physical exercises. The theatre group had done similar jobs for McKinsey, Disney and Dell.

Internal marketing emerged from services marketing. Its purpose was to get the front-line personnel – who have interactive relationships with external customers – to handle the service encounter better and with more independence. It is essential that the contact people are well informed about a company's offerings, but also that they understand the business mission, goals, strategies and organizational processes. It is equally important for support staff to be knowledgeable in order to be able to handle successfully the internal customer relationships.

In two classic articles on 'Mickey Mouse Marketing', the story is told of Disney's successful management of internal marketing (although it was not called so).[25] The staff was either on-stage or off-stage. On-stage, everyone participated in a show whether they were actors in the traditional sense, or sold tickets, served hamburgers or picked litter. Consequently, they should know their part and create satisfied customers. In the 'Ten Standards of Excellence' at Disneyland Paris hotels, 'Commandment no. 8' says: 'We're on stage and we know our role in the show. We're entertainers, we know our "script", we know our standards and we never miss a cue. We consistently give a good show – all the time.'

Even if internal marketing as a concept comes out of services marketing, it seems applicable to all types of organizations. This conclusion is based on the observation that companies in general have taken the concept to their hearts and use it.

CASE STUDY   **Ericsson**

The first example is from Ericsson's unit for components (formerly Rifa). They manufacture electronic components of strategic importance to Ericsson's telephone switches. There is a need for a certain amount of in-house manufacturing to protect

---

[25] Pope (1979a, b).

and develop the core competence, but the company also wanted to exploit its knowledge on the external market. After a long life of internal deliveries without competition, the business area was required to prove its ability to meet the competition from other manufacturers, among them the successful Motorola. A transition to a more business-like and market-oriented culture was called for, and internal marketing is one way of contributing to a new corporate culture. After a survey of possible means of reaching out to the personnel, a publication was made to explain the new situation. It was inspired by the SAS publication Carlzon's Little Red, a much hailed effort to inform the staff.[26] It became an unsophisticated pamphlet with short sentences and simple drawings which presented essential facts and strategies. Two pages from Rifa's pamphlet are shown in Figure 5.6.

In internal marketing, as in everything else, management commitment is crucial. It was important for the head of the business area and his divisional managers to show that they stood behind the message. After discussions and tests it was concluded that the best way would be to appear in person, even if that would take time. How do you do this with 2000 people working in three towns far apart? Fifty-six appearances by the head of the business area and his management team were called for.

Most executives would claim they could not spare the time. Groups of forty employees participated in half-day programmes, which ended with lunch or dinner with management. Considering that many of them worked shifts, several programmes had to be performed at night, ending with coffee and cake. The management team presented ongoing changes and made comments, followed by the participants working in groups around a number of themes with a subsequent plenary discussion. The publication was distributed as documentation when the participants left.

The interaction between employees and external customers can be extensive. This was shown in R5 (the service encounter) and R6 (the many-headed customer and the many-headed supplier). Even if many employees have limited contact with customers, companies are looking – with some desperation – for better ways of preparing employees for changes in business missions and organizational structures. The launching of new offerings, new technologies and new methods requires participation and motivation. There can be a colossal gap between what management wants (and believes is happening) and what actually happens in the minds of employees and external customers. This is frequently observed in service

---

[26] The SAS pamphlet is reproduced in Mårtensson (1984, pp. 118–35).

Everytime a RIFA employee meets a customer, a MOMENT OF TRUTH occurs

negative   or positive
It is the sum of all moments of truth that
determine success or failure

Figure 5.6 Two pages from a pamphlet used in Rifa's internal marketing (Rifa, 1983, pp. 30–1). Drawing by Bengt Mellberg

organizations, and it has come out clearly in problem detection studies (PDS).[27] In a PDS, the researcher makes an inventory of as many problems as possible. Customers are asked about the importance of these problems, and management is asked what they think customers will answer. The match between customer and management responses is invariably low.

CASE STUDY   **Karlshamns**

The second example concerns Karlshamns, a factory making oil-based food products. At Christmas all employees were given a variant of Trivial Pursuit, one of the world's most loved quiz games. The mission of the factory of only supplying consumer cooperative stores had been broadened to include the sales of its products to all types of retailers. A major organizational audit had been performed and the problems of informing everyone were massive. Of the 2000 questions in Trivial Pursuit, 500 were substituted. The new questions were of a local nature, both of general interest such as 'Which year were the first winter Olympics held?' to direct questions regarding the company, for example 'How many small soap bars for hotel rooms does the subsidiary in Stavanger, Norway, produce in one year: 2, 4 or 6 million?' and 'Which are the two most important ingredients in our margarine?'

---

[27] See the gaps model (Zeithaml, Parasuraman and Berry, 1990). The conclusions from PDS are based on my own participation in several studies and discussions with market researchers and their clients.

> The game was a hit. Employees played it over Christmas, in their spare time. That was also the idea; it was handed out during the last hours before the Christmas holiday. This way, its messages also reached family members and friends. Others who did not work in the factory asked for the game after it made the news in the local paper and radio station. So the internal marketing activity reached beyond the staff and had a positive mega communications effect, particularly in the home town of the factory.

At Ericsson the internal marketing was targeted to the traditional, well-defined organization, the nano relationships. In the case of Karlshamn the internal marketing also has a clear effect on market and mega relationships. Internal marketing stresses human resources as key to the development and maintenance of a successful operation. Employees are best motivated to demonstrate service spirit and customer orientation if they are well informed; this effect is best achieved through a marketing approach. It requires both active learning and influence on attitudes.[28] Internal marketing can be a way of knocking down walls between departments and the expertise of employees can be combined in novel ways to challenge the internal activities that need to be changed.[29]

Traditionally, employees stay in the same place at the same time. Flexible working hours have changed this, and so has presence in many locations. More people work from home, not least because of the opportunities offered by IT, but also because of the waste of time on suburban transportation. It may lead to a hollow corporate culture, as working with other people is also a source of inspiration. On the other hand, not all people are happy to work in the same building. Conflicts are common and incidents of sexual harassment are increasingly being noted. Relationships are increasingly upheld via email and the Internet, without those involved ever getting into direct face-to-face contact. The system with lifelong employment facilitates what the Japanese call 'mimikosuri', the ability to 'massage sombody's ears'. The massage facilitates decision-making, smoothes criticism and prevents employees losing face. What did Marshall McLuhan say as his second message: The medium is the massage!

A personal relationship that has been built over decades gives security and support also in the age of the Internet. In contrast, using IT without this personal equity as a foundation can cause problems. Hallowell (1999) points out how increased use of email inside the company can alienate the staff: 'The irony is that this kind of alienation in the work-place derives not from lack of communication but from a surplus of the wrong kind.' High touch knocked out

---

[28] According to Grönroos (2000).
[29] Ballantyne (2000, p. 43).

by high tech when internal e-relationships are taking over from internal h-relationships, and when a distant relationship takes over from a close relationship.

'Management by email' can supersede 'management by walking around'. The fact that the Internet has the potential of interactivity is not enough. There are delayed reactions, and written text – which is deprived of body language – is perceived differently from face-to-face communication and immediate feedback. Steve Balmer, CEO of Microsoft, tells that changes in his company must reach all staff worldwide in twenty-four hours via intranet and quickly be followed by visits from the head office, an effort to combine high tech and high touch.[30]

Finally, some practical advice:

- Profit from the techniques of external marketing on the internal market. By applying an inbound perspective we see things other than if we just stick to the outbound marketing perspective. We are reminded that external marketing is dependent on the success of internal marketing.
- Invest in interactive internal relationships, even if internal mass marketing has a role in the value and network society.
- Apply internal marketing with a network view. Organizations are networks of relationships within which employees interact. Internal marketing can be restricted to employees but there is an equal need to reach the whole network. The market and mega relationships can also be included in a broadened internal network, as the whole network organization must function.

| RELATIONSHIP 28 | **The two-dimensional matrix relationship** |

The word hierarchy comes from the Greek 'hieros' (holy) and 'archein' (order or control). A hierarchical organization is based on clear ranking and absolute obedience. We know today that this holy order is not the best way of getting an organization to perform.

The hierarchy offers a one-dimensional relationship, the matrix organization a two-dimensional relationship and the network organization a multidimensional network. The matrix organization is an effort to get out of the rigid mould of the hierarchy, and a step toward increased network thinking and improved interfunctional and interhierarchical relationships. The matrix has become commonplace and exists in many variants, often in an organization with product managers. It changes the relationships of the hierarchy.

---

[30] Presentation at Svenska Dagbladets Executive Club, December 1999 in Stockholm, Sweden. Author's notes.

Viewed in the light of RM, both the hierarchy and the matrix stand out as crude and naive. The former lives on the dream of unity of command, the latter on the acceptance of the somewhat more realistic – but not too realistic – dual command.

We are unwilling to endorse complexity and tend to see its existence as a failure, not having been able to get reality properly sorted out. The experience of most companies seems to be that the matrix is awkward to manage at the same time as they cannot live without it. On closer inspection behind the neat facade of the matrix, there is a multidimensional, informal, complex and often contradictory network. It is a challenge to find oneself trying to manage such a network characterized by a series of negotiations, unstable balance of power, far-reaching delegation of profits, and a variable structure. But reality provides this dynamic complexity whether we approve of it or not.

The matrix is limited to two dimensions, whereas the number of dimensions in the network is unlimited. We all know from experience that reality is not built on one or two dimensions, but both the hierarchy and the matrix offer appealing mental models of simplicity; we wish them to be true. Studying the matrix, however, may have an educational purpose. It helps us to foresee the complexity inherent in the networks of RM.

The matrix concerns relationships of principal interest to RM. There are many species of matrices:

- Product/service group versus geographical area. This is a combination of products on one side and districts, regions, countries or groups of countries on the other. In the beginning of the 1990s, Ericsson was divided into six product-based business areas, while headquarter sales units and local subsidiaries throughout the world were in charge of sales. Ericsson Telecom, the biggest business area, had divided its geographical market into five country groups: Northern Europe, continental Europe and Australia, the UK, North America, and finally Asia, Africa and Latin America. The areas reflected the importance of the markets.

- Product/service group versus customer segments. A simple matrix in food production consists of product lines on one side and two segments on the other: the retail market and the restaurant market. Sales can be direct or go via wholesalers. The buying behaviour of the two segments is different, and often so is the design of the products and packaging, and the purchased volume, and price.

- Product group/service versus function. I have worked as product manager at a subsidiary of Reader's Digest, an international publishing and direct mail-order operation. As product manager, I was responsible for special books. This included development of the product line, production of the books, marketing, and profit centre responsibility. There were two more product managers, one for its magazine and one for music albums. I cooperated with a series of internal functions: editorial; production of books and promotion material; distribution of direct mail and the books; accounting with budgeting and follow-up of financial results; and some others. I was not in charge of any of these functions and I had to compete for their attention with other product managers. Moreover, in competition with some twenty subsidiaries, I utilized functions at the European headquarters in London and the international headquarters in Pleasantville, New York, for example in market research.

- Geographical area versus function. The geographical representation, for example, of a chain of stores, restaurants or hotels consists of a local unit and its customers. A chain of stores may have a central purchasing department with purchasers for different parts of their product line. The central purchaser of clothing must assess the fashion of the next seasons, prices and expected demand, and the stores are then required to sell the garments.
- Key account management of strategic customers. According to McDonald, Millman and Rogers:[31]

> Key account management (KAM) is ... aimed at building a portfolio
> of loyal key accounts by offering them, on a continuing basis, a
> product/service package tailored to their individual needs. Success
> depends partly on the degree of receptivity demonstrated by the
> customer to a partnership approach ... To coordinate day-to-day
> interaction under the umbrella of a long-term relationship, selling
> companies typically form dedicated teams headed up by a 'key
> account manager'.

KAM was mentioned earlier in R6 (the many-headed customer and the many-headed supplier), pointing to the fact that this is not a new issue. But it is a special case of RM with increasing significance.

- Temporary projects versus the base organization. The matrices that have been described so far are part of the fixed structure of the organization. This matrix variant is an ad hoc organization with projects on one side and a task force of people from different functions on the other. Projects are common in all types of organizations. As organizations change at a faster pace, even the 'fixed' structure becomes a project; it could be called the parent project. If an organization is a bundle of projects, it is already on the way to becoming a network and an imaginary organization.

It is obvious that the crossroads between two types of responsibility can induce constructive dialogue, but also head-on confrontation of strong egos. One product manager competes

---

[31] McDonald, Millman and Rogers (1997, p. 112).

with another for the attention of a functional department. A store manager may feel that central purchasing orders the wrong articles at the wrong prices so that they cannot be sold. At the crossroads there are two views, but a joint decision is called for. Who shall yield? What happens if both drive ahead at full speed? Can we find a form of collaboration that allows both 'vehicles' to cross the junction in accord? The decisions must build on consensus, or the disputes are moved on to the executive level above the crossroads. The exercise in reaching agreements can be educational, or inertia and insecurity can grow. The internal relationships may take up more time than the external ones; they can be demanding on patience, personal maturity and social skills. Even if the matrix in itself carries difficulties, there is an advantage in being able to address the product and the geographic market in combination.

Before its merger with Brown Boveri and the creation of ABB, Asea had an international product/country matrix. An executive vice president, Arne Bennborn, described its intricacies in the following way:

> The international matrix holds a potential for conflicts. We tell
> division and subsidiary managers that they have profit responsibility
> worldwide, and country managers that they are responsible for
> everything inside their country. These are two completely different
> roles, both necessary in a multiproduct/multimarket organization.
> The roles need open-minded managers who can solve a problem
> together. If the matrix managers cannot agree on a solution they can
> come to us for help. If this is repeated time and again, we have to
> replace one or several of them. We need quick decisions in a flat
> organization with frequent interfunctional contacts within an
> overriding philosophy.[32]

Like all other organizational principles, the matrix must be deployed in the right situation. There are those who repudiate matrices as being unmanageable. They claim matrices engender controversies. An alternative interpretation is that they put the spotlight on existing but hidden conflicts.

In many major corporations, matrix designs supersede each other. In order to expose considerations in search of a working matrix organization, the Skandia matrix saga will be told.[33] In 1968, the insurance company was organized as a matrix with certain functions and

---

[32] Arne Bennborn, quoted in Brandes and Brege (1990, p. 131).
[33] The Skandia case is based on Englund (1982) and discussions with Kjell Ängelid, Skandia. The matrices have been put at my disposal by Skandia.

product groups (groups of different kinds of insurance) on one side, and four geographical zones on the other. Two years later, the matrix became more market oriented. Its core became a matrix between zones and insurance to corporations, consumers or groups, or specific applications named motor, sea and air. In addition to the matrix, centralized corporate services were organized. The zones were expanded internationally. Finance was added (which broke the neat logic, as finance is a function) and the two dimensions of the matrix became less distinct. During the 1970s, a gradual transfer took place toward a focus on customers and segmentation. An effort was made to avoid some of the problems with the matrix, particularly duplication of tasks and the abundant number of insurance types. The communications pattern of one of the units is reproduced in Figure 5.7. We can spot a dissolution of the matrix in something that looks like a network, albeit limited to employees and not including customers and other stakeholders.

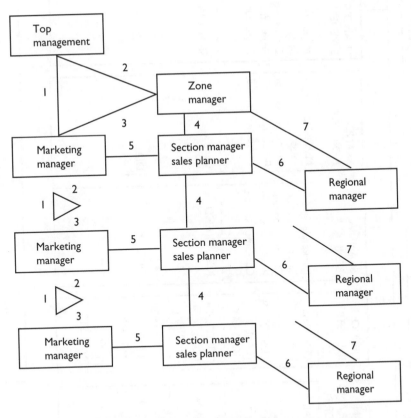

Figure 5.7 The communications pattern at Skandia in 1978. The numbers represent different decisions and types of communication. Channel 5, for example, represents issues on products, markets and damages in everyday operations

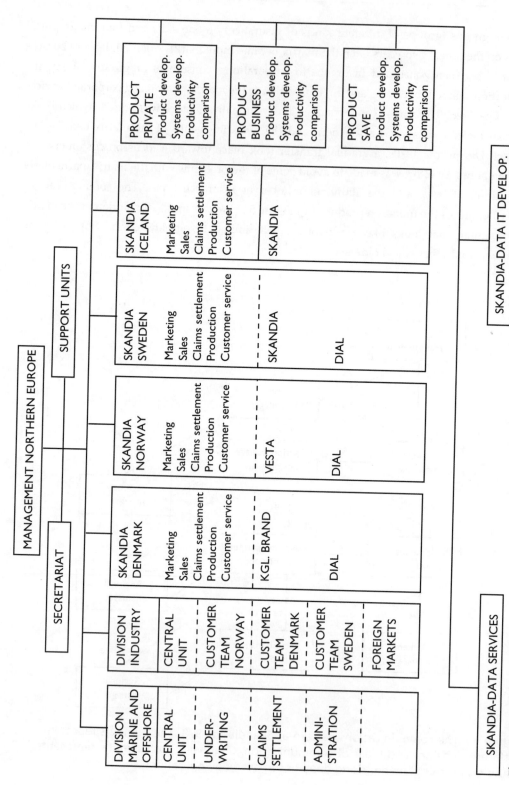

Figure 5.8 The matrix organization for Skandia Northern Europe in 1993

In 1993, the organizational chart shows yet another design; it had been preceded by several others since the 1970s. The insurance market has changed character – changed customer needs, changed competitive situation, deregulation, new types of insurance services – and the group structure of Skandia has also changed. Figure 5.8 shows the matrix for Northern Europe at one point in time. In the new economy the changes are continuous.

In summary, the advantages of the matrix organization are:

- The product managers 'own' the product and can work with all aspects of the product line. They can acquire a complete overview of the product, new technology, customers, competitors, volume, market share, profits and other aspects.
- The geographical area managers 'own' their area and its customers. They have local closeness to the customer. But they also enjoy central support with a product line, advertising and sales promotion, through which experience from many local markets is shared and transferred between markets.
- There is less risk that an issue is abandoned and left in a vacuum. It is particularly important that the customers do not leave the supplier because of obsolete products, vanishing segments or dissatisfied customers. Revenue, cost and profits are monitored both from a product and market view.

The disadvantages are:

- Managers must handle a large number of relationships, both externally and internally. Conflicts easily emerge at the matrix crossroads. For example, a product manager wants to replace a current product for long-term profit growth, while an area manager is first assessed by his or her ability to meet the current budget and prefers to bet on existing products.
- Management does not give enough support to the product managers but is still expecting superior performance. The responsibility placed on product managers is frequently not matched by their authority to make decisions and act. At the matrix crossroads, they run into area managers who are often empowered by a considerably larger organization and budget.

Constructive dialogue, lack of prestige, recognition of different roles, and a holistic view are required human properties in a matrix. Rapid resolution of problems, flexibility and a willingness to change are needed without ending up in diluted compromises.

> But if we cannot manage the simplified two-dimensional network of the matrix, how then can we expect to manage the complex multidimensional networks of RM?

 The relationship to external providers of marketing services

Several marketing tasks are not performed by employees but by external providers. This was conceptualized in R4, with the introduction of the FTMs and the PTMs, the full-time marketers and the part-time marketers. External providers to the marketing function can be viewed as FTMs at the time the buyer pays for them. In these relationships, the providers become part of the customer's marketing and sales organization without belonging to it in the traditional sense. They become part of a network that transcends the organization–market boundaries. The services of the external providers can be split into three groups:

1 Services concerning the physical distribution of goods, such as those offered by haulage firms, wholesalers and retailers. Transportation is one of the major sectors of any economy and has been so for hundreds of years; only now we have more alternatives than before. Physical distribution, logistics and channel (or network) management were discussed in R3.

2 Services primarily concerned with selling and delivering. Wholesaler and retailer services belong in this group. So do agents and brokers, even if they never physically touch a product. So do telemarketing services. In some countries, including the USA and the UK, insurance to individuals is sold by brokers; in some countries they are primarily sold by the insurance companies' own sales organizations. These two approaches generate different market relationships. In both cases the insurance company has to keep up its image and the interest of the consumer. In the broker case, keeping up the spirit of brokers and helping them do good business becomes the number one priority. This can occur through frequent innovations, quality improvements and supportive campaigns.

3 Consulting services of different kinds, such as those performed by advertising agencies, market research institutes, Internet consultants and designers of CRM systems. These providers are primarily advisory – they are knowledge-based organizations – but they can also execute much of the craft, such as the printing of brochures, field interviews, the establishment of websites, and the installation and testing of eCRM systems.

The external providers reinforce and supplement the marketing function. They offer both strategic outsourcing and outsourcing of repetitive routine services. The providers become a hybrid between external firms and internal departments. If the customer interacts closely and continuously with them, in practice they become part of the customer's organization; they may even have permanent office facilities on the customer's premises. The buyer must ask two pivotal questions: 'What shall we do ourselves and what shall the independent provider do?' and 'Is this an occasional transaction or is it going to be a long-term relationship?'

The first two types of external providers connect with the physical distribution (R3), the e-relationship and the distribution of information (R12). The rest of this section will focus on the third type, knowledge-based and advisory consulting services.

Today, all companies use consultants in their marketing function, either on a continuous or ad hoc basis. The consultants provide expertise which is lacking or is in short supply at a specific moment. Several types of consultants are consequential for the success of the marketing function. These will be discussed together with the import of interactive relationships and the ability to obtain maximum support to the marketing function. Consultants to the marketing function are listed below.[34]

Consultants in communications

The advertising agency is the oldest, most ostentatious and most common of all consultants to the marketing function. This is most likely so because marketing is still predominantly directed to mass communication to consumers, and consumer advertising has high public visibility. An ad agency is either hired until further notice and works continuously with its client, or the assignments are tied to specific projects. The agency relationship is constantly under scrutiny, sometimes inspired by the latest invoice. With few exceptions, measurement of advertising effects on revenue is obscure, while fees, price of printed material, and media space are easy to measure. And how do you measure the value of creativity? In-house advertising production exists but is supplemented by agencies; complete in-house agencies are not often found any more. There must, however, be a defined flesh-and-blood client with whom the agency can interact, usually a marketing manager, product manager or advertising manager. Many companies use several agencies and each profit centre has the right to make its own choice. Others request that all their units worldwide use the same advertising agency chain. Advertising brings minds back to mass marketing from traditional marketing management – a subgroup under the third P (promotion) – and not to RM, CRM and e-business, and the snowballing attention given to brands as a ground for constructing parasocial relationships

---

[34] The rest of this chapter is an adaptation from Gummesson (1977).

(R13). Individual and mass marketing will exist in tandem; we accept the paradox of customized mass marketing. Telemarketing companies with their origin in telephone sales have added fund-raising, customer surveys and outsourced call centres to their product line. Internet and website consultants became a rocket that illuminated the sky for a few years, but the rocket has now entered a less spectacular orbit and it glows with a more realistic light. Consultants within public relations, lobbying, sponsoring and event marketing, who all are dependent on networks and individual interaction, are becoming increasingly compelling. To add glamour to events such as company anniversaries, theatre and movie premières, and the opening of new restaurants, another type of consultant seems to be on the increase, the one who sets up the event and makes sure that the right celebs and media are present.

Consultants in marketing management

These can either represent a broad knowledge of marketing-oriented management or a deep expertise in a specific area. Sometimes their strength is the understanding of management and the marketing function, and they work directly under the CEO or marketing director. Their knowledge concerns marketing aspects of areas such as strategy, organization, planning, research, cost reduction and downsizing. Some are specialized in industries, such as retailing or IT. Consultants may also be specialized in a certain technique, such as the layout of stores, or CRM systems. Beginning in the 1980s, quality has become more important to management consultants. Since the current quality concept is strongly customer-centric, the job of the TQM consultant is closely knit to the marketing function. A series of consulting services have followed in the wake of quality awards and ISO certification. In many B-to-B markets today, companies cannot do business without ISO certification and usually assistance from consultants is needed.

Market research institutes

These are specialists in data generation[35] and the application of certain research techniques. They primarily research consumer attitudes to products, services and companies, and compare competitors. They do this at regular or ad hoc intervals, collectively or as separate customized projects. Apart from proficiency in research techniques, their strength is the management of field interviewers and computer systems for the planning, processing, analysis and reporting of a study. Customer satisfaction surveys, in particular, have had a rapid rise.

---

[35] I prefer the term *data generation* to the mainstream term *data collection*. Data in social contexts are usually not there to be collected but are generated through an interpretation process, governed by a preconceived notion of what is essential and what is not, or by total openness and sensitivity to what reality wants to tell the researcher.

To some extent they also draw conclusions and recommend measures. In order to draw conclusions, two types of knowledge are required, but are rarely represented in one individual. One is the technical dexterity to investigate a phenomenon, for example how customers behave and why. The second is institutional knowledge about the industry, the client company, its goods and services, competitive situation, and the more secluded mechanisms that can only be understood by those who live with them continuously: the power game, which decisions are possible to implement and what financial risks are acceptable.

The first type of knowledge is best represented by the research institute, the second best by the client. The quality of the research will be the outcome of interaction between the research institute and the client, and their ability to constructively coalesce their competencies. It is a frequent nuisance that the client does not attach enough weight to the contact with the researcher, but delegates the contact to a staff unit on a middle or lower management level. When the results are presented for decisions, the decision-makers lack in-depth understanding of the quality of the data; those who present it know too little about the whole context of the decision and have no power.

Speakers and educators

These are found among specialists on training and education, university professors, writers, management consultants, and successful business executives. Some have agents, just like actors. They can embrace anything from formal training programmes on general and special aspects of marketing to speaking at kick-offs, business lunches and conferences. The market for these types of services has grown continuously. There is a need to lift the vision from the daily myopic routine and to be inspired by success stories, enthusiastic crusaders and celebrities. Currently, customer in focus themes, such as closer relationships to customers, measuring customer satisfaction, customer loyalty programmes, customer clubs, key account management, brand equity and brand identity, and everything associated with e-business and eCRM, captivate the minds of marketing practitioners, which today also includes public sector representatives. Inviting external speakers is equally often a symbolic event, as it is an event to dissiminate actual knowledge; sometimes it is even close to mere entertainment, especially if the speaker is a celebrity.

Executive search, recruitment and outsourcing of functions and manpower

Executive search and recruitment is handled both by niche firms and management consultants. The recruitment of salespeople is a large business. Recruitment of executives and managers in marketing is handled by head-hunters, who search for individual candidates that fit a specification set up together with the client firm. They do not advertise, but approach candidates through personal contacts. Part of what the client is buying is an entry ticket to their network of relationships. They can approach a person without others knowing that a position is open and can guarantee confidentiality. They have experience in assessing a person's suitability for executive work. The cost of hiring the wrong marketing manager is excessively high, not least through lost opportunities and foregone revenue, so the recruitment procedure should be handled cautiously. Another type is management for hire, where a consultant is placed in an executive position for six months to two years, usually when a company is already in a crisis or to prevent an upcoming crisis, and the outsourcing of manpower, single people or a whole function, such as a sales force.

Some other consultants have already been mentioned. Among them are public relations consultants, specializing in external and internal relationships. They often compete directly with management consultants and ad agencies. Their services as lobbyists have grown, which is obvious in mega marketing (R19) and the mass media relationship (R23). Lawyers everywhere, and in the USA in particular, have become key players in the marketing arena (R16). Others specialize in small but critical niches, for example by helping firms to design and present bids on major contracts. Henry Kissinger was mentioned as advisor on political risks in international markets (R18). Futurists help to discern trends in consumption patterns and lifestyles.

The relationship needs to be interactive in the service encounters. It means a partial co-production between the client and the provider. It is not a matter of giving orders and obeying orders except in certain standardized instances, for example a print order for a brochure. To the ad agency it is a matter of understanding the needs of both their customer and their customer's customer (R7). The strengths of ad agencies include visualization, creative design, and the planning and execution of campaigns. Their knowledge on strategy varies considerably. At some agencies, individuals master a broader field than advertising and those can compete with management consultants.

The planning of an assignment must occur in close relationship between consultant and client. It is imperative that the real decision-makers participate. Intermediaries should be avoided; through them the information – which is often complex and subtle – will be filtered and sometimes distorted. Those who are going to implement the assignment need proper briefings, straight from the client's mouth.

The reinforcement to the marketing function is an example of outsourcing. It is not new, but it has become more significant in today's more complex, fast-changing and network-based economy.

The owner and financier relationship

Not only loyal customers but also loyal owners exert influence on marketing success. A trusting and long-term relationship between owners (and other financiers) and management and the marketing function is a necessary condition for building long-term relationships with customers, suppliers, competitors and others.

The owners' importance for finance is explored in the literature, but its importance for marketing is rarely mentioned. Investors appear in many shapes, with diverse demands on short- and long-term return on capital. They can be active or passive, big or small, known or anonymous. Investors finance the operations of a company at the same time as a company has other financiers, primarily banks and other financial institutions, but also customers, suppliers and governments (through subsidies).

There is an irony that investors have been in the focus of management attention – not customers, not employees – as these have become less and less loyal.[36] However, investor relationships vary considerably between countries. Germany and Japan have had stable long-term owner relationships. Compared to the United States, Japanese stockholding is four times more stable and seven times more likely to be reciprocated.[37] The loyalty of the American investor has been reduced as the turnover of investors has increased from 14 per cent in 1960 to 52 per cent in 1995.[38] This means that today the average investor holds shares for less than two years, albeit with a variation of a few minutes to several decades. Maximum short-term return on capital has taken priority over long-term survival, and shares are bought and sold as transaction goods, much like ice-cream on a hot day on the beach. The relationship between a company and its investors has also become increasingly anonymous; it is sometimes even handled by computers programmed to search for the quickest buck of the day or the minute.

A countermove is the snowballing interest in corporate governance, which stands for active, supportive and responsible ownership.[39]

Demonstrating success through a high and climbing share price can be the most important input to a favourable public image. If the share price is down, customers may feel insecure. This is especially true for cases such as computers and future compatible updates of software, equipment that requires spare parts, and motor vehicles for which the second-hand price is important.

The customers' image of a firm may be affected by the image of its major owner, but most often customers, especially consumers, do not know who owns a company or a brand name.

---

[36] Reichheld (1996).
[37] Gerlach (1992, p. xvii).
[38] Reichheld (1996).
[39] Carlsson (1997).

If you stay at the illustrious Beverly Hills Hotel in California, you are a guest of the Sultan of Brunei, one of the richest men in the world. Of the shares of Disneyland Paris in 1995, 40 per cent were owned by Disney but the next major shareholder was Prince Al Waleed of Saudi Arabia, with close to 24 per cent. The Prince arrived as a saviour in a financial crisis, which was basically caused by deficient customer proximity and excessive pricing, resulting in a cultural clash and too few visitors. In 1996, he agreed to stay on as an owner for another five years, thereby bringing stability to the theme park and instilling belief in its future.

The annual report has been directed to two groups: tax authorities and the stock market; monthly and quarterly reports are directed to the stock market. Indicators of the state and progress of a company primarily offer short-term financial information. In order to educate and inform investors, indicators are needed that show the importance of long-term goals. The balanced scorecard approach offers a framework for a more complete evaluation of a company (see also Chapter 6). I am not, however, a believer in the folklore of measuring everything. Investment decisions are taken out of strategic necessity and estimates of profits are not always possible, for example the change-over from one technology to another or a long-term product development project.

Figure 5.9 Relationships between marketing, ownership/investors and other influencers

Figure 5.9 puts the marketing function in a financier and management context. Ownership affects marketing, and the relationship between general management, marketing management and major owners (who are often on the board of directors) becomes vital. Five types of ownership and financier relationships will be explained below.

Private business run by core owners

The core owners are personally engaged in operating the enterprise; it is part of a lifestyle. This is typical of the small business, like the mom and pop store, the restaurant and the repair shop. The values of the founders and private owners are often strong and consistently applied.

Owner families often continue to run enterprises when they have grown large, and they still know the operations in detail. In retailing there is a series of smashing successes, companies that have expanded through the founder's and owner's vision and perseverance. Examples of strong owner commitment are the Nordstrom department stores, known for superior quality of goods and services, and Feargal Quinn's consumer-focused and profitable supermarkets in Ireland. Another is IKEA. Its founder Ingvar Kamprad has three sons, one daughter, his wife and his brother-in-law by his side. The retailing operation – the 150 IKEA furniture stores and seventy-nine Habitat stores in the UK, France and Spain acquired in 1993 – are owned by a family-controlled foundation in The Netherlands. Inter IKEA consists of the franchise division (comprising IKEA brand equity, copyrights and concepts), the financial division and the real estate division. The Ikano group includes banking, credit cards and insurance. The corporate culture emerging from the founder is extremely strong:[40] ' . . . Ingvar Kamprad is unquestionably "Daddy" . . . For those who have met him it is a great unforgettable moment. And there is a lot of talk about him in the store: " . . . Kamprad would have liked that . . . " or "what would Ingvar have said about that" . . . Especially for the older Ikeans, Ingvar Kamprad represents an important symbol, an example of the true IKEA spirit.'

Even if these private companies should go public, core owners and subtle core values can continue to control the operations. The separation between the role of core owner and the role of manager is common in industrialized nations. A closer look at executives in Europe, however, indicated that they are often directly or indirectly linked to a network of owner families.

The reasons for going public are usually a need for cash flow, but often also to reduce total family control. Family ownership has its hazards, especially when new generations take over. There are also cases when the best strategy should be to go from public back to private, provided that this were financially feasible, which it often is not. A viable strategy is actively

---

[40] Quotation from Salzer (1994, p. 162).

to recruit investors and establish long-term relationships to those who constructively help build the future.

Founders and entrepreneurs are often not easy to please and an employee who does not comply with their leadership had better try another job. They may also be perceived as ruthless in their pursuit of their business mission and survival. The Roddick family, founders and owners of The Body Shop, have recently been accused of driving their franchisees too hard,[41] at the same time as Anita Roddick says: 'I have never been able to separate Body Shop values from my own personal values.'[42]

Single corporations and families can even keep a tight control over total markets and countries. An extreme case is De Beers and its owners, the Oppenheimer family.[43] They control 54 per cent of the stock value on the Johannesburg exchange in South Africa, that is, one quarter of the financial wealth of the nation. De Beers are best known for their control over world sales of non-industrial diamonds; in all, their empire includes 1300 companies in various industries. Companies and countries have tried to break out of the influence of De Beers, but with no apparent success. So the overriding production and marketing strategies of diamonds are globally determined by one owner family.

Long-term investors

The owners see their involvement as long term, but are engaged in different types of industries and do not directly take part in daily operations. The Wallenberg family, which exerts a controlling influence over such diverse multinationals as Atlas-Copco, Electrolux, Ericsson, Saab and SKF, focus their investment on long-term industrial development, internationaliza-tion and stability. There is a commitment, above all in financial and strategic issues, but the knowledge of the daily operations and industry-specific issues is limited.

Long-term ownership may put companies together even though they do not belong together for marketing reasons. It may be right at one time, but not at another. The Saab passenger car operation is now controlled by GM, but the Saab aerospace products and Scania, the world's fifth largest truck maker, have been owned by Saab for twenty-five years. They have the same roots but their products have grown apart. In 1996 they were demerged; there was absolutely no marketing synergy.

Warren Buffett and his company Berkshire Hathaway has been held up as a model of a long-term and extremely successful investment strategy.[44] Buffett invests in a few select companies,

---

[41] Entine (1996).

[42] Roddick (1991, p. 123).

[43] See Kanfer (1996).

[44] Reichheld (1996, pp. 165–6).

retains the investment and says that short-term stock price is not important. This type of owner is the best to make RM become successful. It allows a company to build long-term relationships with customers and others.

Short-term investors

The owners are investors looking for maximum short-term return on investment. Just as customers can be unprofitable even in the long run, investors can be of little support, even be outright parasites. For these investors there is no responsibility, only rights and demands; owning shares is an alternative to gambling in Las Vegas. Institutional investors, such as pension funds, have increased their role on the stock market. They have no sentiments for a specific company, merely for enhancing short-term investor wealth. Investment brokers are paid per transaction, meaning that the more frequently they can encourage big investors to buy and sell, the more they earn. So they are rewarded for transactions and owner promiscuity, not for long-term relationships and loyalty. This, of course, is counter-productive to RM.

It is regrettable when the heart that beats for a product or service – the restaurateur who loves food and ambience, the engineer who enjoys the factory environment, the retailer who understands fresh vegetables and fish – stops beating and is replaced by cash flow analysis, accountants and investment brokers. The publisher who loves books, authors and readers is almost extinct in favour of financial groups who shuffle publishing companies around based on the bottom line and competing investment opportunities in any industry. At the time of writing, Pirelli (tyres) and Benetton (clothes) take power over Italy's telecom operators and in Sweden the Coop Bank is founded by Skandia (financial services), the Consumer Cooperative (retailing) and Telia (the state-owned and former monopoly telecom). There is not much 'heart power' left in these ownerships. Coop Bank may, however, be saluted as an attempt to break up petrified retail banking through competition and thus force better marketing equilibrium.

The 1980s were characterized by changing ownership based on short-term speculation. Corporate raiders made hostile takeovers financed by junk bonds (high risk bonds with no collateral). Their strategy was cost reduction, downsizing and asset-stripping; there was no intention of developing the companies over the long term and no emotional attachment to their products and services. No doubt a shake-up of complacent or inefficient management teams is necessary at times, but then the justification should be long-term survival. Some raiders became unbelievably rich, but many also had severe setbacks and were taken to court, even to jail.

Behind this is the eternal dream of becoming rich quickly and preferably without effort. Greed can never be an acceptable business mission; earnings are just a means. Employees often have no clue who owns the company they are working for, nor do customers know. Infiltration from organized crime is a growing problem. As they say in Palermo, the capital of the mafia, and according to one businessman: 'The mob does not rob banks any more, they own them.'

In order to build a strong marketing function, a certain long-term stability is needed. Reichheld,[45] who puts as much emphasis on loyal investors and loyal employees as on loyal customers, suggests four active strategies for more stable ownership:

1 Educate current investors.
2 Shift to more stable investors.
3 Attract the right type of core owners.
4 Go from public to private.

When instability rules, management attention is directed to things other than the core activities of production and marketing. The top executives risk getting fired any day and it is meaningless for them to make a long-term commitment; on average, a new CEO in a public company in the USA is said to last no more than two years. They are driven to look at short-term results and discard investment in customer loyalty, product development and development of personnel.

The new economy accommodates more rapid change and entrepreneurship than the industrial era did. It has become acceptable, even fashionable, to be an entrepreneur; it is not an emergency exit for misfits and the less talented. Business administration has turned into innovation and leadership. We have especially seen this at the turn of the millennium, with fast-growing Internet consultants and dotcoms. Whereas several have had stable growth both in size and profits, others have just travelled the fast lane of ridiculous stock price increases based on hype from financial analysts and the media. It would of course not be possible if people were not dreaming about sudden fortunes and driven by greed rather than more important values. We see an increasing number of mega mergers. The stated rationale is better products, better service, higher quality, a broader range of offerings and sometimes reduced prices. Some of this may at times be true, but the real motives behind mega mergers are more likely to be the desire to control consumption and reduce competition.

Cooperative ownership

True cooperative ownership has the special commitment that characterizes the successful family firm, but it goes one step further – the owners and the customers are the same people.

---

[45] Reichheld (1996, pp. 160–70).

The customers own the supplying organizations and they do their purchasing in their own stores. Employees are owners and customers as well, and sometimes co-ops are operated by unpaid volunteers. The relationship between co-op members and the personnel in the store is close. This is all very well as long as the co-op is limited in size or split into small independent units. If it grows and functions become centralized and controlled from a distance, it becomes like any other company. The cooperations become corporations and the owners no more feel they are owners than I feel I own Ford, having bought a few Ford shares. The members become just customers and the authenticity of the membership is lost; the owner/customer becomes a pseudo-member, as was pointed out in R11. There are retailer co-ops, and producer co-ops are common in the agricultural sector. There are also voluntary chains such as Best Western Hotels. The co-ops as such have sometimes become so dominant as to imprison suppliers and customers in the way that was described in R10.

Government ownership

In most countries, but to a lesser degree in the USA, the state owns services like the post, telecom, railroads and airlines. The health, education and utilities sectors are often owned by state or local governments. These produce services of infrastructural nature and only in part do these services lend themselves to the forces of the market. Unfortunately, governments have based their management style and values on a bureaucratic–legal paradigm and not on a relationship and service paradigm. This means that these operations have lagged behind, not seeing themselves as a service to the citizens. They have become kingdoms of their own, closed off from the environment. They have been heavily criticized but learnt to accept that as the natural state of affairs. They have spent more time on 'explaining' why things do not work than on making them work. But they are not without competition. For example, FedEx renewed US postal services as a private alternative, operating with service quality and customer-in-focus strategies.

The wave of deregulation and privatization that started in the 1980s has changed the scenery gradually. In the UK, former premier Margaret Thatcher's privatization included the Airport Authority, British Telecom and British Rail. Regional and local governments have increasingly become involved in business-like operations. Governments have both a role as authorities and as service providers, and a long tradition of muddling up the two by covering up for bad service with reference to legal authority. There is a risk that they compete successfully by establishing their own companies, beating private companies with lower bids made possible with taxpayers' money. This has been reported in construction and building, transportation, leisure activities and other markets. There is no doubt that there were unrealistic expectations attached to privatization and deregulation. Some efforts have backfired and even been put to a halt.

The ultimate owners of all government organizations are the citizens, that is, the consumers. In modern terms: They have outsourced certain activities to governments to make the production and delivery of them more efficient. Unfortunately, the owners' prospects of exerting influence through the democratic voting process are appallingly meagre. To influence a state-run mail operation, the citizens are supposed to vote for their candidates at the next election and hope that the right party wins, that the right person is appointed postmaster general, that the right people are recruited to perform to the customers' satisfaction, and that the needs and wants of the citizens are transmitted through leadership, business mission, strategies, organization and systems. This chain of intermediaries is far too long; it is a distance relationship to the customer, so distant that it is pre-empted of all muscle. The direct contact with the post – the citizen in the role of customer – is possible but the citizen has little clout; it is an unusually asymmetric relationship. The relationship between the citizen as an owner of the post and eventual responsibility for its bill via taxes – the same citizen as customer – and the state as administrator is not easily handled from a marketing point of view.

Should the sole goal of the company be to maximize shareholder value, counted in euros and dollars? The short-term investors answer this question with a distinct yes. But could wealth also be to uphold a tradition of a certain industry, like retailing, car manufacturing or film-making, or to operate a business in a specific town, region or country, and be a good corporate citizen? For example, several of the film-making giants in Hollywood are neither owned by Americans nor are the owners knowledgeable about film-making. Metro Goldwyn Mayer was sold to an Italian swindler, backed by the French state-owned bank Credit Lyonnais, which was forced to take over the studio. Columbia was sold to Japanese Sony, Universal to Japanese Matsushita and later to Canadian Seagram, and 20th Century Fox to Australians. Biggest of them all is AOL Time Warner, encompassing film studios, cable television, CNN, books, newpapers, music and the America On Line portal. Both of the recent mega-movies, *Harry Potter* and *The Lord of the Rings*, are AOL Time Warner releases. In 2002, an alliance with American Express was announced. Since this was written, new ownership constellations have emerged; industry scenery keeps changing continuously.

If a company is being quoted on a stock exchange, yet other relationships are born. New demands are put on its financial reporting and this is watched by a number of stakeholders: the big institutional investors as well as the little guy, the stock exchange, financial reporters, analysts and public authorities. Managing investor relations (IR) has become a profession in its own right.[46]

Ownership is an alternative to alliances. In the spirit of the imaginary organization, it is one of a multitude of network formats of the organizational structure. When the Volvo–Renault

---

[46] See Tuominen (1996) for an investor relationship marketing framework.

alliance was preparing for a merger, the meaning of ownership was assessed in the light of Volvo's future prospects. Renault was a French state-owned company for which privatization had been suggested but had not been decided. There was a warranted fear that Volvo would be controlled by the French government. Even if Renault was privatized, Volvo was likely to become powerless in its relationship to the considerably bigger Renault.

Doubts were raised about the purpose of the merger and then about its conditions. The Volvo president called it 'a new model' but it was uncertain how the model would function in a live test. The president was accused of playing a game in order to secure eternal power and that the merger proposal had no direct link to car manufacturing and car sales. Who would decide about new car designs, distribution networks and other marketing strategies? A financial reporter called it 'a multinational monster'. In defence of the merger, cost reductions and coordination advantages were claimed to follow, and furthermore Renault would place large orders with Volvo. The merger collapsed during the autumn of 1993 after protests from owner groups and executives. In 2000, Volvo took over Renault's truck manufacturing and became number two in the world after Mercedes, with a market share in the USA and Europe of 25 per cent. Renault bought 10 per cent of Volvo. And then Ford bought Volvo passenger cars.

A board of directors represents owners, management and other stakeholders. Criticism is often aired against the choice of board members who know little about the company and provide no functional expertise. It is obvious that support from knowledgeable owners and board members, as well as a trusting relationship between them and the corporate and marketing executives, is imperative in order to build a stable position on the market.

IN BRIEF

It is unfortunate if owners are seen by management as a necessary evil which has to be soothed and cajoled. They should be partners. This requires the selection of the right owners, those who not only enhance their wealth through ownership, but also add value to the companies in which they invest. It then becomes a win–win relationship within the RM spirit.

Chapter

6

Do RM and CRM pay?

INTRODUCTION

Chapter 6 deals with return on relationships (ROR), that is, the impact of RM on revenue, cost, capital employed and eventually profits. It ends with a section on strategies for improved ROR, and an RM-inspired marketing plan and audit, introducing the notion of the relationship portfolio.

Return on relationships (ROR)

Someone has said (I think it is Peter Drucker) that 'the language of management is money'. In business life, we want to know the financial impact of our activities; the 'bottom line' is a magic concept. Managers therefore must ask the question of the heading: *Do RM and CRM pay?* It is a matter of making a profit, but short-term profit is not the only indicator of success. Other factors are strategic and qualitative, such as expected growth, long-term research and development, and the establishment of networks; all of these are insurance for the future.

Businesses continuously measure return on financial capital. Is it also possible to gauge the return on relationships, networks and interaction? There have been many efforts to measure marketing costs and the value that is created by marketing in the form of revenue and profit. The best-known effort is probably the *PIMS* (Profit Impact of Market Strategy), a project which started in the early 1960s. Its purpose was to bring law and order to the wild west of marketing by quantifying and defining unambiguously the effect on profit caused by advertising, quality, market share, sales volume and other marketing strategies. In reality it rather measured covariation. Although it probably sorted out a series of factors and their links in marketing, it did not create the hoped for rigour and clarity.

The high claims of *operations research, management science* and *MIS* (management or marketing information systems) promoted around 1970 under the slogan 'eventually management is turned into science' became little more than a red herring. Today, *micro-econometricians* are trying similar conjecture with cross-sectional and time-series data about individuals, households and firms, unfortunately based on poor input and unrealistic assumptions. In my view, they offer what US marketing professor Shelby Hunt has called 'irrelevant elegance'.

The hope that a toilsome wandering through the desert would lead up to the country of milk and honey in the shape of precise metrics and prophecies has not vanished – but perhaps matured somewhat. *Marketing accountability* is a current term for more general efforts to measure marketing's effect on profitability. In one research programme it is named 'the new discipline'. It is new compared to previous efforts in the sense that it is addressing an economy where the Internet, globalization with mega corporations, and new rules of competition within the EU, NAFTA and WTO offer new realities. The programme is asking questions such as: 'How can value be created by marketing and be defined and measured? How can management processes be aligned, with the aim of driving marketing value creation higher and higher? How can traditional financial and purchasing controls be re-engineered, to support marketing value creation? How can employee feedback and learning be improved, to motivate and reward them to maximize marketing value creation? How can IT be applied to measure marketing value and support daily decision-making?'[1] These questions are all of general significance for marketing.

I would like to propose the following definition:

INSIGHT Return on relationships (ROR) is the long-term net financial outcome caused by the establishment and maintenance of an organization's network of relationships.[2]

Some statements pertaining to ROR have already been presented, for example that the lifetime value of an existing Cadillac customer is $332 000, and that it costs five to ten times as much to get a new customer as it costs to keep an existing customer.

The interest in measuring the value of relationships and networks has grown parallel to the rise of RM and CRM. With the above discussion as a general framework, the next section will deal with ongoing efforts to develop marketing metrics and accounting systems to better mirror the realities of the new economy. My stance is that indicators are useful to a degree, but they are supplementary to other types of information. I do not subscribe to the idea that we will eventually generate the universal measurement cure; it is a search for a phantom and will remain science fiction. Attempting to measure quantitatively, one by one, the myriad factors and influences in marketing is a dead end.

Systematic measurement of ROR is in its infancy. The following sections offer a state-of-the-art review, suggest approaches and show examples of applications. The section treats: customer satisfaction, loyalty and ROR; duration, retention and defection; the link between customer interaction and quality, productivity and profitability; intellectual capital and the balanced scorecard; return on the non-measurable; and ROR when a company's whole network is considered.

---

[1] Shaw and McDonald (2000).
[2] Related concepts are *return on quality* (Rust, Zahorik and Keiningham, 1994); Duncan and Moriarty's (1997) *brand equity*, which covers integrated communications and relationships; and Schultz and Walters (1997) measuring return on investment on brand communications.

As was mentioned in Chapter 1, RM and CRM are not fundamentalist religions, even if they offer an improved paradigm of marketing. Sometimes transaction marketing and the zero relationship – the price and convenience extreme on the relationship scale – is the best strategy for the supplier and the best option for the customer. ROR is not pertinent to transaction marketing.

Satisfaction, loyalty and ROR

A common assumption is that an improvement in customer perceived quality will increase customer satisfaction, loyalty and profitability. *The customer relationship life cycle* is based on the belief that the ability of the provider to satisfy needs and fulfil promises determines the chances of retaining the customer. According to *the service profit chain*, the following happens:

good internal quality → satisfied employees → employees stay →
good external quality → satisfied customers → customers stay →
high profitability.[3]

A corollary to these approaches is that vicious circles and failure chains have to be broken.

This logic seems indisputable; when everybody is happy we will do well. But the general validity can be questioned as the market logic sometimes follows other patterns. Doyle[4] has expressed his concern about the role of marketing and the limited power of marketers in the boardroom and on the executive floor. One reason can be lack of credibility. 'Marketers can no longer afford to rely on the untested assumption that increases in customer satisfaction . . . will automatically translate into higher financial performance.'

Although certain studies indicate that customer satisfaction is a predictor of future profits,[5] it is not enough to ascertain that 73 or 86 or even 94 per cent of the customers are satisfied. Volvo, who started a long-term comprehensive RM programme, had previously considered satisfied customers to be loyal. There was considerable leakage though. In the Volvo RM programme, the next step has been taken actively to provide incentives for satisfied customers to remain loyal.

Most of those who leave a supplier say that they are satisfied but they switch for a variety of reasons, such as another supplier's marketing, being persuaded by friends, the desire to test

---

[3] Grönroos (2000); Heskett et al. (1997). These sequences of interdependent events were developed for services, but are also applicable for goods marketing.

[4] Doyle (2000, p. 310).

[5] Fornell (1992); Johnson and Gustafsson (2000).

something new, or mere coincidence. According to the exit-voice-loyalty choice from R9, many dissatisfied customers remain despite the fact that a supplier is charging more or offers lower quality than the competition. They do not switch for lack of time or knowledge or they remain loyal, for example, for nationalistic or ideological reasons. The switching cost can be considerable in the short run. However, retention coupled with dissatisfaction is a ticking bomb.

Some studies reveal that there is a sizeable difference in retention rate between those who say (in a questionnaire) that they are *very satisfied* and those who are just *satisfied*. Pitney Bowes, manufacturers of postage machines, found that 78.2 per cent of very satisfied customers said that they would remain customers in the future, whereas only 20.9 per cent of satisfied customers said they would remain. For Xerox the corresponding figures were 80 per cent and 14 per cent.[6]

A further analysis is found in the *loyalty accounting matrix* (Figure 6.1). The matrix combines the *attractiveness* of a supplier ('brain appeal') and the *strength of the relationship* ('heart appeal'). The most satisfied customers are called ambassadors. They find the supplier highly attractive, have a strong relationship to the supplier, and recommend him to others. The next groups consist of loyal customers who are slightly less enthusiastic than the ambassadors. The diagonal represents risk customers who are easy prey for competitors. The last two groups are those who are actively searching for a new supplier and those who are already lost customers.

A study of one company showed the following pattern: ambassadors 32 per cent, loyal 30 per cent, risk 25 per cent, searching 9 per cent and lost 4 per cent. Ambassadors and loyal customers constituted almost two thirds of the customers, a result that might or might not be satisfactory, depending on the type of business.

Strength of relationship

	Risk	Loyal	Ambassador
Attractiveness	Searching	Risk	Loyal
	Lost	Searching	Risk

Figure 6.1 Loyalty accounting matrix. Source: Johansen and Monthelie (1996, p. 23). Used with permission

---

[6] Quoted from Johansen and Monthelie (1996, p. 17).

It was less comforting to learn that ROR was not well correlated to loyalty. The ambassadors did not make the most profitable customers, those were found among the least loyal groups. There is a paradox that states that the less profitable customers are, the more satisfied they are, while the more profitable customers are, the less satisfied they are. This can be illustrated with the price of the return air fare from New York to continental Europe. An off-season economy class ticket might cost $200, a full business class ticket $2000 and a Concorde ticket $5000–9000. The business traveller is highly profitable and highly demanding. The economy traveller contributes marginally to profits but is grateful for the low price and not as demanding. Value for the business traveller is primarily high quality: punctuality, comfort, the opportunity to work or rest. For the economy traveller, value is primarily low price. The likelihood is high that the business traveller is less satisfied than the economy traveller, although in objective terms the business traveller is offered a better service.

One ROR model further expands the links between satisfaction and profits (Figure 6.2).

Figure 6.2 shows how stages and properties of the relationships between suppliers and customers are linked together.[7] Starting from the left, *perceived value* is defined as the outcome of customer perceived quality and the customer's sacrifice (cost in a wide sense). The perceived value is an antecedent to *customer satisfaction*, which in turn influences customer commitment, bonds to the supplier and *relationship strength*. The higher the relationship

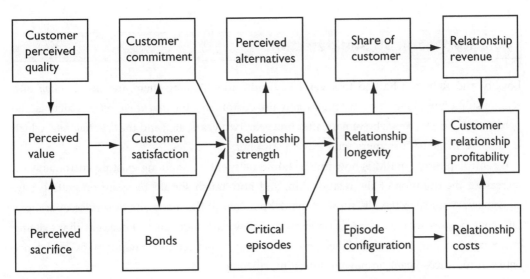

Figure 6.2 A 'relationship profitability model'. Source: Storbacka, Strandvik and Grönroos (1994, p. 23). Reproduced with permission. © MCB University Press

---

[7] Storbacka, Strandvik and Grönroos (1994). The model was originally designed for services, but has been generalized here to embrace all sorts of commercial relationships.

strength and the customer's feeling of loyalty toward the supplier, the fewer the perceived alternatives; when there is a monopoly, however, the customer is a prisoner. The number of alternative suppliers and their attractiveness impact on *relationship longevity*, which is also influenced by the positive, negative or indifferent interaction with the supplier (critical episodes). A long and beneficial relationship may lead to increased concentration of the purchases from a single supplier and share of customer goes up. A single-sourcing strategy pursued by the customer gives the supplier a 100 per cent share and maximum revenue. The length and strength of the relationship also affects the types of interactions that form the relationships (the episode configuration), which in turn determines costs. Finally, relationship revenue minus relationship cost establishes the *customer relationship profitability* or ROR.

Companies may dry out because business has become constant firefighting and eventually there is no water left to throw on the fire. RM promotes long-term thinking, but sometimes today's business has to be saved before the long-term aspects can be addressed. Certain decisions must be taken out of strategic necessity; they are market investments and cannot be financially assessed with simple indicators. They do not belong in the short-term profit and loss statement. You either do it, and stand a chance to survive, or you don't and you will disappear from the market. Declining customer loyalty often builds up in small steps which may not be discernible until it is too late to reverse the vicious circle.

Duration, retention and defection

Loyalty and ROR can be tied to several key indicators. Among them are: the *duration* of a relationship, how long the customers remain customers; the *retention rate*, which is the percentage of customers who remain after one year, two years, etc.; and the *defection rate*, which is the percentage of customers who leave a supplier.

A central question in RM is how much should be spent on retaining existing customers and increasing the duration of the relationship, and how much should be spent on getting new customers. A study in the UK showed that 80 per cent of the managers of service operations felt they spent excessive resources on attracting new customers and 10 per cent that existing customers occupied too much of their resources. Only 10 per cent were happy with the balance between resources spent on new and existing customers.[8]

It is also a matter of adjusting the RM strategy to the buyers' needs and wants. One supplier may badly want a relationship with certain customers, but the customers do not respond simply because they are unwilling or unable to make the commitment. Conversely, suppliers

---

[8] Payne and Rickard (1994).

may pursue a transaction marketing strategy without being empathic to the customers' desires to establish a long-term relationship.[9]

A frequently cited study[10] shows that 68 per cent of customers who defected from a supplier did so because the supplier seemed indifferent and 14 per cent because of unsatisfactory complaints handling. These two failed relationships accounted for 82 per cent of the defection. Only 5 per cent were lost through competitor initiatives and 9 per cent because of lower prices elsewhere.

In an article on 'zero defection', the authors draw the conclusion that a supplier could double net profit if the defection rate is reduced by as little as 5 per cent.[11] They advise companies to make defection analyses. These include interviews with lost customers but should also address the weak signals of a customer entering the risk zone.

Direct Tire Sales specializes in tyres and brakes, and makes three quarters of their sales with regular customers.[12] These customers spend twice as much as the first-time customers who come through advertising ($173 against $90). First-time customers who come through the recommendation of a regular customer spend as much as $224 at the first visit. Credit card company MBNA America did a defection analysis and learned from it.[13] The defection rate went down from 10 per cent to 5 per cent, which was half the industry average, and profitability was dramatically improved. An average cardholder who stays one year causes a loss of $51, one who stays for five years a profit of $55, and one who stays for twenty years a profit of $525. For industry laundry, the profit for Year 1 was $144 and for Year 5 $256; for auto repair, $25 for Year 1 and $88 for Year 5. If defection rates go down from 20 per cent to 10 per cent per annum and then to 5 per cent, the duration will increase from five to ten to twenty years with a consequent increase in profits. If a customer is lost, the whole of the future profit potential goes down the drain. In a comparison between nine industries in which the defection rate was reduced by 5 per cent – among them insurance brokers, computer software and auto repair – profits grew by 25–85 per cent.

Reichheld (1996) presents an elaborate, yet practical, system for assessing ROR. His research has shown that customer loyalty cannot be earned in isolation. It is closely dependent on the loyalty of two other stakeholders: employees and investors. Those who stimulate loyal relationships with customers, employees and investors are amply rewarded. For example, the advertising agency Leo Burnett loses only 2 per cent of its customers per year and its productivity is 15–20 per cent higher than that of its principal competitors. Chick-fil-A, a chain of 600 quick service restaurants, has a turnover of store operators of 4–6 per cent per year,

---

[9] Jackson (1985a).
[10] Research from the 1980s by Miller Business Systems.
[11] Reichheld and Sasser (1990, p. 105).
[12] Johnson (1992, p. 85).
[13] This and the following examples are based on Reichheld and Sasser (1990).

while the industry average is 40–50 per cent. Moreover, its store operators earn 50 per cent more than those of competing restaurant chains. As compared to the industry average, State Farm Insurance agents stay twice as long, have 40 per cent higher productivity and a 95 per cent customer retention rate. Lexus, Toyota's luxury car, has the highest repurchase rate in the premium car bracket; it is 2 per cent of Toyota sales but 33 per cent of its profits.

Market share is a traditional indicator in marketing management, showing the percentage of a total market or market segment that a supplier serves. Fewer and more select customers, each buying more during a longer period, could be a superior way to profits as compared to more customers with a small volume and shorter relationships.[14] *Share of customer* (also called *share of wallet*) is recommended as an alternative ratio to market share. Milliken Company, a leader in textiles and winner of the Baldrige Quality Award, monitors share of customers. A bank can estimate what share of a customer's financial assets and transactions is handled by the bank. Taco Bell is a successful and rapidly growing fast-food chain with Mexican cuisine. The company does not measure market share but 'share of stomach', thereby establishing how much of the customer's intake is delivered by Taco Bell.

The old concept of lifetime value (LTV) has been revived by CRM. It usually refers to the net value of an individual consumer's purchases over his or her lifetime, sometimes widened to the whole family, even to both private and professional consumption. LTV may stand out as fairly clear-cut for consumers, although one has to consider that certain offerings, such as nappies and baby food, are only of interest during a limited (but highly varying) period in a family's lifetime. LTV in B-to-B is somewhat more ambiguous: What is the life-cycle and lifetime of a company? Rust et al.[15] define *customer equity* as 'the total of the discounted lifetime values of all its customers'. Customer equity is the combined outcome of *value equity* (defined as relatively cognitive, objective and rational customer perceptions of quality, price and convenience), *brand equity* (perceptions of a supplier that are relatively emotional, subjective and irrational) and *retention equity* (repeat purchases). According to the authors: 'Customer Equity is the key to the long-term profitability of any firm, and analyzing the key-drivers of Customer Equity provides an overall framework for effectively focusing strategic resources.'

Customer interaction, triplets and tribes

The vantage point of this section is condensed in the statement that: 'Quality, productivity and profits are triplets; separating one from the other creates an unhappy family.'[16]

---

[14] Johnson (1992, p. 79).
[15] Rust, Zeithaml and Lemon (2000; quotations from pp. 4–8 and 12).
[16] Gummesson (1991, p. 6); Gummesson (1998a).

The triplets are all concerned with the same issue: 'How well is the company doing?' But the focus between the three is different and represented by different tribes within the organization. We have the *marketing tribe* and the *accounting tribe*, the *quality tribe* and the *productivity tribe*. They embrace different traditions, vocations and cultures; each tribe's awareness of the total welfare of the company is limited.

Quality tribe members are devoted to revenue issues, they think of customers and revenue, and are closest to the marketing tribe. Members of the productivity tribe are obsessed by costs; in practice, a productivity increase usually means cost reduction and downsizing. The accounting tribe must produce periodic reports with balance sheets and profit and loss statements; its behaviour is largely controlled by legislation. The tribes do not mingle well, although they play in the same orchestra and should be playing the same symphony. They all contribute valuable expertise, but in order to get the best from each, top management must be conductors and lead them in the right direction.

With time, the old and accepted ways of accounting become senile but live on despite the fact that organizations become networks and RM has devised a new ground for marketing. A particularly critical question is: How shall the role of the customer as an influencer of value creation, productivity and quality be assessed? Both customers and suppliers have relationship costs. If the customer is a consumer, costs are incurred in the consumer's spare time and are not part of the GDP. Grönroos[17] examines relationship costs and profitability in service operations and their connection to inferior quality. He makes a distinction between three types of costs that hit both consumer and companies. A consumer pays a certain price for a service, but in addition there are costs to correct mistakes caused by the consumer (direct costs), costs caused by the provider (indirect costs), and mental and social discomfort caused by the correction procedure (psychological costs). If the relationship between the customer and provider is perfect, these costs disappear. In conclusion, relationship costs and quality go in opposite directions – high service quality causes low relationship costs, and low service quality causes high relationship costs.

Our research has brought to the fore the complications of defining the customer's role in service operations and the network organization. In service production and delivery, quality and productivity emerge from five sources:

- the service provider as independent actor;
- the customer as independent actor;
- the interaction between the provider and the customer;
- the interaction between customers (C-to-C); and
- service-supporting infrastructure.

---

[17] Grönroos (1992, pp. 129–40). See also further elaboration of the financial dimensions of relationship quality, based on both service management and the network approach, in Holmlund (1997).

Traditionally, quality and productivity are treated as the sole outcome of the first, the provider's independent work. Neither customer input nor the contribution from the provider–customer interaction are taken into account. Service research has shown that the customer–supplier relationship may be a prime source of quality and productivity. Service production is interactive, as was pointed out in R5, and the inputs from provider personnel and customers are partly substitutes. Furthermore, C-to-C interaction contributes both to quality and productivity. As an independent actor, the customer has several value-adding roles:

- As *consumer*. This is the traditional way of seeing the customer and is the only role that is generally treated in theory.
- As *producer*. Here both services marketing and B-to-B have made it evident that the customer is a co-producer.
- As *marketer*. R4 covered the role of customer as part-time marketer.
- As *manager*. Often the customer both in B-to-C and B-to-B works as the coordinator of production, delivery and sales. This is necessary, especially if the supplier is weak and is not able to keep the whole process together.
- As *supplier of knowledge*. The customer contributes with specifications, statements of needs and other input which the supplier lacks.

In the network approach of B-to-B, relationship costs have been classified as the sum of *activity costs* (activities in a network) and *structural costs* (network investment and maintenance costs).[18] Furthermore, cost in a relationship is a matter of both static utilization of extant resources and dynamic development of the potential of new combinations that the resources of the network hold.[19] Changes in business networks occur every day. The network organization is an expression of this dynamic aspect, the continuous resourcing in an enhanced 'opportunity space'.

The well-known *value chain*[20] is composed of nine elementary internal activities. Primary activities are in-bound logistics (incoming raw material), operations, out-bound logistics (distribution of finished products), marketing and sales, and service. Support activities are procurement, technology development (both technical and systems development), human resource management and firm infrastructure (organization, systems). The value chain attempts to isolate individual activities and see their added value and costs. The chain is essentially sequential and each function is well delimited. To some extent it deals with interfunctional interaction, parallel activities and alliances, which means that there is a slight

---

[18] Eriksson and Åsberg (1994).
[19] According to Håkansson and Snehota (1995).
[20] Porter (1985, pp. 36–43).

affinity to RM. But even if value for the customer is given as a goal, the customer remains a lost soul and a passive recipient of the provider's output.

The *value constellation* (or *value star*)[21] has already been mentioned as an alternative to the value chain. It represents the same phenomena as RM and the network organization, but expresses them somewhat differently. In the value constellation, the relationships and interaction with the customer are viewed as part of a shared value-creating process. Supplier and customer are co-producers, co-managers and even co-developers of a product or service. For the customer, the value contributed by a specific provider is only one of a plethora of values that form his or her value constellation. Joint production through the service encounter is the key element of services marketing and management, but it is also being generalized to include the manufacturing sector. The value chain becomes a special case which is primarily valid in mass manufacturing. The value constellation highlights the integration between functions and concurrent activities, including customer contributions.

According to the value chain, marketing becomes the distribution of value to the consumer, who is a 'value destroyer'. The value constellation, on the other hand, recognizes that value is created through the concerted efforts of functions inside an organization, outsourced functions and the customers. Making a product is one type of value creation, consuming it for a purpose is another or maybe the most important value creation.

If both the customer and the supplier are part of the same value-creating process, the role of price is altered: 'This means that both profits and losses . . . should be shared between supplier and customer. Instead of price-setting, it becomes a question of remuneration for participation in the creation of value. This kind of remuneration must be discussed in very open-minded negotiations between the two parties.'[22]

ROR can be enhanced by changing the balance between revenue, cost and capital employed. Cost and capital employed can be increased in order to increase revenue even more. A revenue reduction – for example, eliminating unprofitable customers – can reduce cost even more. By myopic concentration on cost, the attractiveness of a company is reduced and customer relationships are jeopardized.

Intellectual capital and the balanced scorecard

As numbers from accounting exert a significant influence on decisions and practices, supportive accounting is an antecedent to sound RM and CRM applications. Marketers all too

[21] Wikström and Normann (1994).
[22] Wikström and Normann (1994, p. 62).

often find accounting rigid, traditional and bound by legal restrictions, seldom giving support to essential marketing strategies.

Employees represent different specialities. We have already met the accounting tribe that does not mingle so well with the marketing tribe, there is even the risk of civil war. But in recent years, a revolution has started. New accounting theories and practices, most notably the *balanced scorecard*, register indicators of other types of capital other than financial capital. Among them are indicators concerning the customer base and retention. The original balanced scorecard contains indicators in four groups of capital:[23] *financial, customer, internal business process*, and *learning and growth*.

It has long been popular for executives to say that 'people are our most valuable resource'. The statement alludes to employees, not customers, investors or vendors, even if most of these are human too and provide resources. In the spirit of RM, each and everyone who has an impact on the success of a company should be included, meaning each party in a network of relationships, not least the customers. It is only recently that the *customer capital* – the existing customer base and customer relationships – has been seriously approached.

Traditionally, the balance sheet consists of tangible, hard assets, above all money, inventory, machines and buildings. The human being is worthless, while the chair on which they sit represents a value only to be slowly depreciated according to some accounting principle. The customer represents no official value. However, when a company is sold or its stock is traded on an exchange, buyers pay for intangible assets like goodwill, brands and expected future earnings.

Accounting systems do not catch the value of customer relationships, although building relationships is an investment in marketing. The accounting tribe has often been suspicious of intangible, soft values, and sometimes for good reasons. When profits are down, it is tempting for management to misuse soft values, and claim that book values are not telling the whole truth and that the situation is not all that precarious. These values have therefore acquired a bad reputation. However, the interest in human resource accounting, social audits and the financial aspects of personnel is on the increase. More often these days we encounter such concepts as customer capital, relationship capital, human capital, knowledge capital and social capital.

The traditional balance sheet is not particularly informative about service companies and knowledge-intensive companies. Efforts have been made to find procedures for presenting a more realistic value of these companies. As all companies – including manufacturing operations – to an increasing extent comprise services and knowledge, the issue is of general concern.

---

[23] Kaplan and Norton (1996).

In new and broader accounting systems, the concept of *intellectual capital* is challenging the supremacy of short-term *financial capital*.[24] Financial capital must of course exist in every organization, and in the balanced scorecard financial capital is assessed together with intellectual capital. When capital is defined as 'something of value' – a resource – we realize that money and other hard assets are not the only capital.

Intellectual capital is defined as follows: *Intellectual capital is the total value of a company – the price of its shares – minus its book value.* It means *all assets except those in the balance sheet.*

A company's survival and growth are eventually determined by its financial outcome. The issue is to recognize the long-term importance of intellectual capital for the generation of financial capital, and to gradually convert intellectual capital into financial capital.

Intellectual capital can be divided into two major types: *human* (or *individual*) *capital* and *structural capital.*

Human capital consists of employees and their qualities. It includes the individuals' knowledge, behaviour and motivation, and also the individuals' network of relationships. This network consists of personal relationships which have been cultivated over a long period, and the trust and confidence that an employee has established among customers and others. The power and prestige of individual capital is evident for an advertising agency, or a partnership of lawyers who thrive on their personal interaction with clients. But it is also important for a retail store, a bank branch office, a car repair shop or a manufacturing operation. This was pointed out in the service encounter (R5) and the many-headed customer and supplier relationship (R6).

There is also capital built into an employee who can quickly gain a customer's confidence, a quality which is particularly essential in a salesperson. In R1, the story was told about the top performing Electrolux door-to-door salesman. He said that knocking on doors gives him twenty seconds to gain the confidence of the consumer.

If an employee leaves a company, the individual capital vanishes. You cannot own human beings, that would be slavery. The company borrows them 'from 9 to 5', a concept made classic by Dolly Parton in a movie and a song.

In the knowledge relationship (R21), knowledge was presented as a prime reason for alliances. Two types of knowledge were discussed: migratory knowledge, which is portable, and embedded knowledge, which is inseparable from its environment. Embedded knowledge is part of the *structural capital*. It does not disappear if an employee leaves; it is owned by the company. In an RM sense, structural capital consists of relationships which have been established with a company as such, and are tied to culture, systems, contracts, image and the network to which a company belongs. The more successfully a company ties relationships to its structure, the less dependent it is on individual employees.

---

[24] Edvinsson and Malone (1997); Sveiby (1997); Stewart (1997).

CRM is a means to convert human capital into structural capital. eCRM is primarily structural capital. The customer information which was previously stored in the heads of one or a few people can now be stored in data warehouses and be exposed to data mining. The information stays even if the employee leaves. However, keeping the data warehouse in shape is the overshadowing challenge which the computer cannot manage on its own; it is primarily an hCRM task.

As all companies and marketing situations are unique in at least some aspects, applications must be adapted to each specific situation. ABB is currently in a change and improvement process which has more focus on soft investment: software and services have replaced locomotives and nuclear plants. This requires new accounting approaches. Electrolux and SKF are companies that test new ways of measuring performance.[25] Three cases which show the application of the balanced scorecard and intellectual capital and their significance for RM will be presented below.

CASE STUDY   **Skandia**

For many years, Skandia has been an international leader of designing and implementing the balanced scorecard and intellectual capital indicators.[26]

Skandia developed a list of 111 indicators and a reserve of another fifty-five. This is certainly no short list and it may scare off any executive as being too much and too complicated to report, let alone act upon. Of the total number of indicators, twenty have a financial focus and the others an intellectual capital focus. The following indicators have apparent relevance to RM:[27]

■ With the focus on customers: annual sales/customers, customers lost, average duration of customer relationships, rate of repeat customers, average customer purchases/year, average contacts by customer/year, points of sale, customer visits to company, days spent visiting customers, and a satisfied customer index.

■ With the focus on employees, but with consequences for customer relationships: motivation index, empowerment index, employee turnover, and average years of service with company.

---

[25] Olve, Roy and Wetter (1999).
[26] See Buck-Lew and Edvinsson (1993); and the Skandia Annual Report Supplements (1995–1999).
[27] Edvinsson and Malone (1997, pp. 151–8).

- With particular focus on customers and the electronic relationship: IT investment/customer, IT investment/service and support level, number of internal IT customers, number of external IT customers, and IT literacy of customers.

It takes time to make these indicators operational and practical, and to select a manageable few that uncover useful information. It takes years before time-series are established and trends can be discerned.

CASE STUDY **TurnIT**

Another case shows how a successful and fast-growing Swedish company, TurnIT (2000), has customized the scorecard and intellectual capital to its needs. TurnIT offers IT support to businesses in supplies, software, communication, consulting and outsourcing. Its sales in the year 2000 were $160 million (in 1996: $5 million) and the number of employees was 1300 (in 1996: 16). The scorecard includes four types of intellectual capital: *business formula, human capital, organization-based structural capital* and *relationship-based structural capital*. Within the last category there are three subcategories: *network* (the strengths of relationships to partners, suppliers, intermediaries and others), *brand* (brand equity in various target groups) and *customers* (size and breadth of customer base, loyalty, potential and so forth). Assessments of the indicators are made on scales through internal and external interviews and accounted for in the annual report, together with financial data. The assessments are made in three dimensions to grasp the dynamics of the present and the future rather than history: *current position, efforts to improve* and *risks of deteriorating*.

CASE STUDY **Banks**

The Banks case will illustrate the critique that Johnson and Kaplan (1987) have pronounced against the lost relevance of accounting. It essentially concerns arbitrary distribution of cost. The way costs are distributed on products, services and departments is reminiscent of Russian roulette; the lucky one survives but you cannot influence the outcome. In a later book, Johnson (1992) revised and further developed the critique by blaming the problem on top-down management and remote control via ratios. Ratios offer simplistic and delayed information. They do not heed quality, neither the degree of customer satisfaction, nor the degree of employee motivation. They disregard the living processes of a company.

Activity-based costing (ABC) offers certain new opportunities to assess cost. It is focused on activities and processes. This is particularly important for services which consist of activities, partly performed together with customers. Like most cost and revenue assessments, however, ABC has indulged in cost, but not in revenue, and consequently not paid attention to the contributions of marketing. Despite its strengths, there is criticism claiming that ABC preserves industrial society features: mass manufacturing, top-down management, remote control and preoccupation with cost. ABC needs to be expanded into D and E, 'demand' and 'effectiveness'.[28] In RM jargon it means that customers and quality need to get a place in the accounts.

Cooper and Kaplan (1991) consider ABC to give rise to better assessments than Pareto optimality or the 20/80 rule (stating that 20 per cent of customers or products account for 80 per cent of profits). They introduced the 20/225 rule, which claims that 20 per cent account for 225 per cent; consequently, the majority of customers or products are unprofitable!

Storbacka's comparison between banks underscores this conclusion.[29] His 'Stobachoff curve' shows the distribution of profits from different customers. According to his bank study, profits can be a maximum of 100 per cent, which was reached with the help of 10 per cent of the most profitable customers. Twenty per cent of customers contributed 140 per cent of profits, but 60–80 per cent of profits were erased by the remaining and unprofitable customers.

In making such assessments, one problem is the hidden links between the services offered by banks. These links imply that seemingly unprofitable services may be necessary requisites for cash cows and customer retention. Furthermore, the unprofitable services/customers carry allocated overheads. By abolishing these services/customers, the base for the overheads is narrowed, and currently profitable services/customers will become unprofitable.

Profit estimates have traditionally been tied to organizational units or products. Data are arranged to calculate the profits on a single transaction and are thus counter-productive to RM; in fact, the accounting system does not allow an RM

---

[28] Frenckner (1993).
[29] These data and the treatment of the Banks case are based on Storbacka (1994).

strategy. Data on ROR of customers as consumer, family member, or a combination of consumer and small business owners, are currently not retrievable from bank databases, and LTV needs to be part of their CRM systems.

ATMs, which handle bank transactions, are considered cost-effective. Studies claim that it costs three to four times as much to deliver the service via a person than via an ATM. It is, however, necessary to know how these estimates have been made and if all costs are included. Since ATMs were introduced, the number of transactions is reputed to have increased, therefore the estimates may be deficient. But it is evident that customer relationships are affected. Relationships to bank managers or clerks are personal and, especially in small branch offices, customers and staff know each other; it is a moderately high touch relationship. Relationships to ATMs, telephone banking and Internet banking are electronic, mechanical and impersonal; they are high tech. How this transition in relationships will affect customer loyalty and retention, we do not know.

Return on the non-measurable

Particularly in the USA we hear: 'what gets measured, gets done'. There is a truth in this, but also a danger. Indicators are often selected because of tradition and because they are easy to measure, not because they are useful. For example, it is easier to quantify short-term profits than the long-term profits lost because of mismanaged relationships.

It may come as a shock to some, but the word 'measurement' is derived from the Sanskrit word *'maya'*, which means *illusion* or *witchcraft*. But it can also mean *image*. Measurements should be images of reality, whereas in practice they are often illusions or witchcraft.

Obsession with measurement means handing over the future of a company to the accounting tribe, abolishing vision and leadership. Many 'leaders' never become leaders, just grossly overpaid accountants.

There are marketers who suffer from measurement fright. They can neither count nor analyse numbers. But there are also measurement fetishists and security seeking CEOs, accountants and marketers. They cherish the illusions of measurement. Their fetishes[30] are the bottom line and short-term profit ratios, which are often devastating to long-term stable development. When indicators are used to pinpoint certain phenomena with reasonable

---

[30] Fetishes are objects – strangely shaped stones, animal teeth, claws, feathers – which are reputed to bring strength and success to their owners, who are usually medicine men, magicians and shamans.

accuracy and validity, there is no problem. When indicators pinpoint the wrong things, employees will go for the indicators that promote their careers and not go for the real thing. Measurement becomes self-deception even if the tables and graphs look impressive.

| CASE STUDY | **Feargal Quinn** |

Certain things must be measured in terms of money, others should never be associated with numbers. Feargal Quinn will serve as an example of the importance of the non-measurable. He is founder and president of Superquinn, a prosperous Irish chain of supermarkets. Quinn expresses his philosophy in the following way:[31] 'Most businesses focus on maximizing the profit from current sales. Of course they are "interested" in repeat business – who isn't? – but often they see it as a bonus rather than the main pay-off. And so they tend to concentrate on what they see as the main pay-off, with the lesser part of the energy devoted to creating a bonus.'

According to Quinn, we should do it the other way around: 'If you look after getting the repeat business, the profit now will largely look after itself.' This is completely in line with RM; short-term profits are an outcome of long-term investment in relationships and consequently one should prioritize the long term.

Quinn found it difficult to prove long-term profit effects to his accounting tribe; confidence in his own judgement and gut feeling was necessary. He says that leadership is not making all decisions based on numbers, but instead to make qualitative evaluations. Leadership is risk-taking, action and vision; it is consciousness about the situation, common sense and intuition. Numbers and accounting can be of assistance within leadership, but they cannot replace leadership. Johnson (1992) says very distinctly in his assessment of activity-based costing that it can improve accounting, but it is no substitute for marketing decisions. Quinn offers the following examples.

- Example 1 – Superquinn stores introduced playrooms for children so that the mothers would be free to do purchasing. If the children enjoy the playroom, mothers were likely to stay longer, buy more and return. But it is not possible to measure the profitability of this investment in hard short-term figures.

---

[31] This section is based on a book and an article by Quinn (1990, 1994); the quotations are from the article.

- Example 2 – Sweets at the cash registers stimulate impulse buying, which gives easily measurable short-term income. While waiting to pay, children are tempted by the sweets and their parents get under fire. Irritation occurs, parents feel uneasy and may prefer to patronize another outlet. This effect cannot be figured out in accounting terms; it must be observed and the decision must feel right.

- Example 3 – When the Irish Post was restructured, it wanted the public to notice the change. The idea was suggested that the old postage cost from the last century, one penny for a letter, should apply during the day of celebration. It was agreed that this would be a costly campaign. To their great astonishment, the campaign paid off in a couple of weeks. People who used to write letters took the opportunity to write more and the number of letters increased dramatically during the cheap day. But return on investment came by return of mail, as the recipients of letters replied and then at full postage. It was the ideal campaign; the payback was instant and the Irish Post reached the public with its message.

In all these examples, the activities are chosen to enhance revenue more than cost, and to achieve long-term and sustainable effects. Correct short-term costs are easy to forecast, whereas long-term revenue can only be assessed strategically and qualitatively.

If the supplier is handling relationships well, the customer comes back. Quinn sums up his philosophy in the *boomerang principle*: 'One of the beauties with the boomerang principle . . . is that you and the customer end up on the same side . . . So the relationship with your customer is not an adversarial one, it is a partnership.'

Feargal Quinn is a prominent spokesman for common sense and so is Stew Leonard, a retailer in Connecticut. Rod, a manager at a Stew Leonard's fresh food store, expressed this very distinctly to us in explaining the three origins of success: 'The first is attitude! The second is attitude! And the third is ATTITUDE!' The attitudes, perceptions and paradigms – our way of facing reality and identifying problems and opportunities – are more essential than IT and sophisticated measurement techniques. Zohar and Marshall express it in this way: 'For the physicist, *measurement* is a way of looking at the situation . . . *Attitude* . . . is the human equivalent of measurement.'[32] Within these human frames, ROR may hopefully thrive and contribute.

---

[32] Zohar and Marshall (1993, p. 100).

ROR and the whole network

The review of the 30Rs showed that RM is not only about customer–supplier relationships, although they are the focal point for CRM. Even if we primarily think of the relationship to our immediate buyer, customer–supplier relationships also include intermediaries, end-users and our own suppliers. Furthermore, market relationships include relationships to competitors and their many faces, being first and foremost rivals, but often being customers, suppliers and partners as well.

Return on non-market relationships – the mega and nano relationships – is not as obvious, especially in the short term. They are antecedents to successful market relationships. Mega relationships are often strategic and structural necessities; without them the supplier will be out of business. Nano relationships offer internal and necessary conditions for external relationships.

Håkansson and Snehota[33] summarize three levels of cost and revenue effects in B-to-B networks. First, business relationships generate revenue from customers and the costs are incurred by suppliers; these revenues and costs are traceable. Second, other costs and benefits of relationships are less obvious and less measurable. These are the costs/revenues of maintaining networks and the quality/productivity emerging from operating in networks. Third, there are the costs and revenue effects that will only become apparent in the future. Although the current outcome of a network is essential, the potential benefits of harvesting, securing survival and perhaps growing may be even more important.

The authors stress the network dependency: ' . . . every business enterprise is a product of its context as much as a force shaping the context.' And they proceed: 'What makes the economy of relationships so special is indeed that a relationship has functions (has economic consequences) for several actors and thus that the outcomes of different relationships are interdependent . . . Thus it is not enough for any actor to be concerned just about itself in order to be successful, as is suggested in all recommendations based on market theory.' We can't just ask 'What's in it for me and my company?', we also have to ask 'What's in it for the other members of the network?' and 'How can we help to improve the competitiveness of the network as a whole?'

'Tomorrow's company will understand and measure the value from all its relationships,' says a British report by an organization with the impressive name of *The Royal Society for the Encouragement of Arts, Manufacture & Commerce* (1994).

---

[33] Håkansson and Snehota (1995, pp. 382–97); the following quotations are from pp. 396 and 284–5.

Strategies for improved ROR

A series of approaches to ROR have been presented. They help us understand aspects of RM, but none of them offers the complete and ultimate solution.

The following paragraphs will summarize consequences and strategies that are essential for improving ROR.

Customer–supplier relationships

- Marketing costs go down when retention goes up; you do not have to recruit as many new customers as before. New customers often have to be acquired with special offers and discounts that make them initially unprofitable. Such campaigns are often successful, but they also attract 'junk customers' with little profit potential. Customers frequently have several suppliers and especially new customers may be low users. If the relationships work out well, they are likely to favour fewer sources and the share of customers increases. Suppliers and customers become better partners, co-producers and even co-developers if they interact more frequently. As a consequence, quality, productivity and profitability improve. Good relationships mean less hassle, for example, if delays occur and faulty goods or services are delivered. It is easier to sort out problems between 'friends' who trust each other. Suppliers get to know their customers better. They can build more useful CRM systems to make them more sensitive to customer needs and wants, and to target their offerings better. The parties should find a balance between their roles as customer and supplier, what each should do independently, and what they should do in interaction.
- Satisfied customers are not necessarily profitable. Watch out for unprofitable customers who hide among the profitable ones. When customers are unprofitable it could be that they are and will remain just that. It could also be that the supplier has not been able to appreciate the actual needs of the buyer and is offering the wrong product at the wrong price. It could further be that senile accounting systems and indicators, which are geared to the mass manufacturing of the industrial era, are used. They are not suitable maps in the value and network society. Therefore, develop sound indicators that consider the impact of relationships on profit. Consider the customer's profitability over a lifetime, LTV, and the profitability links between different products, services and customers.
- Measure what impacts ROR – if it is measurable. Do not fall into the trap of thinking the non-measurable – such as culture, leadership, vision and long-term network building – is unimportant just because it can't be replicated in numbers. Numbers must be linked to common sense, sound judgement, wisdom, vision and endurance.

- Whenever possible, make sure that relationships become part of the structural capital, as the human capital is transient and less controllable. However, caring for the human capital is also imperative. To a degree computers can take over the buying and selling process within B-to-B and also actively search for information. M-to-M gives rise to a new type of RM which we know too little about.

- Appointing relationship managers, CRM managers and key account managers can be successful organizational solutions for supporting the transfer to an RM-oriented approach. RM values and strategies, however, must permeate the whole organization and become part of the corporate culture and daily operations.

- Good relationships make customers better part-time marketers (PTMs), who add marketing muscle without burdening marketing and sales budgets. The PTMs spread positive word of mouth, give referrals, and nourish your image and brand.

- Loyal customers become less price sensitive – within limits – as they also value trust, commitment, convenience, easy access, and social and parasocial relationships. Remember though that customers have to be continuously encouraged to remain loyal.

- Satisfaction indicators must be interpreted; 'satisfied' in a survey can be far away from 'very satisfied'. 'Satisfied customers' may just be 'happy slaves' who think this is the way it must be. A competitor may change all this. Sometimes the customer finds no option, which gives the supplier a real or a perceived monopoly, but the customer may feel imprisoned.

  Dissatisfied customers do not necessarily defect. They do not often complain openly and even if they do the supplier may not be ready to listen and understand.

Competitor relationships

- Competitors have a tougher time when retention and loyalty increase; they are not served new customers on a plate.

- Relationships between competitors are multidimensional. Competitors are often also customers and partners. By collaborating with competitors in certain areas, both suppliers and customers gain advantages through, for example, cost reduction and joint development of products and services.

- Through associations competitors can help each other improve conditions for an industry as a whole and enhance its image, a task where lobbying, public relations and media contacts are frequently used.

- In the network society, individual companies are rarely competing with individual companies – as the conventional wisdom from economics claims – but networks compete with networks.

Non-market relationships

- Return on mega relationships is obvious when, for example, a lobbying campaign is successful or an alliance brings valuable knowledge to a product development project. Nano relationships are partly internal market relationships, such as the supplier–customer relationship between profit centres. ROR can then be measured in the same way as external market relationships. Other nano relationships are sometimes more difficult to assess, such as the value of cooperation between operations management and marketing through quality.
- Analyse the roles of the parties in a network, such as the supplier role and the customer role. Who should do what and what should be done in interaction?

An RM-inspired marketing plan and audit

If we ask companies today how they practise RM, they are most likely referring to the installation of eCRM systems, loyalty and satisfaction indicators, and efforts to increase the interactive skills of their staff. Other bits and pieces of RM are embedded in their marketing, but they are not clearly discernible and they are called something else. In fact, companies are doing a lot of RM, but for lack of concepts, models, a common language, and marketing planning and auditing tradition, the relationship activities are often not openly acknowledged and put to use in a systematic and conscious manner.

It is particularly important to take a fresh look at the planning and evaluation of marketing efforts as RM and CRM offer new conditions. This should be done in two areas of marketing, the marketing plan and the marketing audit.

The RM plan and the relationship portfolio

To carry weight, RM and CRM aspects must be introduced in the marketing planning process. Marketing in the light of relationships, networks and interaction becomes *marketing-oriented management*, and therefore the marketing plan must be an integral part of the *company's overall business plan*.

There is little research available on marketing planning in networks of relationships. One of the exceptions is Benndorf (1987), who studied relationships and networks in B-to-B and their meaning for the marketing planning process. He concluded that companies in a network become dependent on each other's plans. Their resources and activities should ideally be co-planned with regard to network dependencies. Such co-planning is not easy in practice, however.

We know too little about how RM should best be integrated into the planning of a company. The only ways to find out are through trial and error in our companies and through research. For lack of experience of RM planning, it seems reasonable to start by adding RM and CRM dimensions to the marketing plan in use, retaining its basic format.[34] A marketing plan which is focused on the opportunities offered by RM can include the relationships and networks that need to be built, maintained or abandoned.

Activity planning is a normal part of a marketing plan, and activities and interactions in relationships should also be the object of planning. Traditional goals of the marketing plan, such as sales volume and market share, must in part be substituted or supplemented by ROR goals, such as customer retention and share of customer, in the spirit of intellectual capital and the balanced scorecard.

Activities in marketing are usually described as a marketing mix – the 4 or more Ps – including price, sales calls, physical distribution, and other activities and strategies. These are not replaced by the 30Rs, but the way RM has been presented here, the relationships are the vantage point – what we see through the relationship eye-glasses – and the Ps and other activities can be supportive to the relationships. The relationships broaden the interplay between marketing and other functions, such as production and internal services.

Instead of starting with mixing Ps, a company needs to define and review its *relationship portfolio*. I have chosen the word portfolio rather than mix to accentuate a novel perspective and novel values, a paradigm shift. A portfolio is a collection of components and their total benefits should be greater than the sum of the parts; there should be synergy effects. The term financial portfolio is used for a combination of investments that fulfil chosen goals such as balanced risk, maximum short-term yield or maximum long-term growth. In strategic management, portfolio is used for the choice of products to offer on the market (product portfolio) and the choice of customers to target (customer portfolio). The relationship portfolio is a combination of RM activities to be performed during the planning period.

In summary, the following tasks should be integrated with the RM- and CRM-oriented marketing plan:

1 *Select a relationship portfolio!* Analyse the currently interesting relationships and networks, and assess your ability to interact in these. Do this as an active part of the marketing planning and business planning processes. Use the 30Rs as a checklist. Each relationship must be defined to fit a specific company and its specific situation. Select relationships of particular importance which are currently not handled well enough but are gauged to have development potential. Acknowledge that sometimes the zero relationships, transaction marketing, is the best strategy.

---

[34] For a review of systematic marketing planning procedures in use, see McDonald (1995).

2 *Set goals, measure results and monitor implementation!* Goals are an important part of the marketing plan, not only quantitative, short-term goals, but also qualitative, long-term and strategic goals. The implementation processes must be monitored and the outcome compared to the goals. Make certain that implementation is systematic and committed. I have previously claimed that ' ... the ability and strength to execute a decision is more crucial for success than the underlying analysis'.[35]

3 *Assess RM consequences for organization, processes, systems and procedures!* RM and CRM put new demands on the organization and its processes, methods and procedures. This is particularly essential to consider in a company's overall business plan. RM and CRM cannot be isolated to marketing and sales departments and the marketing plan. In the next chapter, the importance of organizational structure and processes for RM and CRM are discussed further.

The RM audit

Marketing is reviewed continuously during the working day and it is reviewed as part of the marketing planning process at least once a year. Marketing is also reviewed in management and board meetings; in meetings with others in a company's network; in special projects for new products, services and marketing channels, and for assessing changes in the marketplace; in troubleshooting missions by task forces; and at kick-offs and marketing and sales conferences. It may be reviewed by our partners in networks. It may even be reviewed by the media. So what is really the use of a marketing audit?

The following definition of marketing audit has been suggested:[36] 'A marketing audit is a comprehensive, systematic, independent, and periodic examination of a company's – or business unit's – marketing environment, objectives, strategies, and activities with a view to determining problem areas and opportunities and recommending a plan of action to improve the company's marketing performance.'

A marketing audit is closely connected to marketing and business plans and reporting systems. The corporate business planning and marketing planning processes are recurrent events, but they primarily produce documents to guide the next planning period. Usually they do not include a systematic evaluation challenging fundamental strategic issues. According to McDonald:[37]

---

[35] Gummesson (1998b, p. 242).
[36] Kotler, Gregor and Rodgers (1989).
[37] McDonald (1995, pp. 28–9).

> Often the need for an audit does not manifest itself until things start
> to go wrong for a company, such as declining sales, falling margins,
> lost market share, underutilized production capacity, and so on. At
> times like these, management often attempts to treat the wrong
> symptoms . . . introducing new products or dropping products,
> reorganizing the sales force, reducing prices, and cutting costs . . .
> But such measures are unlikely to be effective if there are more
> fundamental problems which have not been identified.

This is where the marketing audit enters. It goes a step further than the marketing plan to analyse fundamental marketing issues. In contrast to the aforementioned review activities, the audit must also fulfil the four criteria of the definition. The audit should be:

1 *Comprehensive*, thus covering all marketing aspects.
2 *Systematic*, by using an orderly method.
3 *Independent*, by being conducted by a person or team who do not have a stake in the company's marketing.
4 *Periodic*, that is, be conducted regularly and not just on an ad hoc basis.

RM adds an extra and revolutionary dimension to marketing planning and the marketing audit. In viewing marketing as part of the interaction and events in a network of relationships, we have to broaden the marketing function beyond marketing and sales departments and company boundaries.

Companies and consultants have developed various formats for marketing audits. Even if a company starts out with a general marketing audit checklist, it should adjust it to its specific needs as experience is gained with its application.[38]

---

[38] See marketing audit checklists in McDonald (1995, pp. 30–2); and Kotler (1997, pp. 777–84).

IN BRIEF

Although the checklists may cover certain aspects of RM and CRM, they do not have an RM focus; they are not based on observations made through the relationship eye-glasses. We are not yet ready to suggest a general RM checklist; the empirical base is too thin. In order to be practical, I will settle for suggesting RM additions to existing audit checklists. Therefore, look at each of the 30Rs and their parts and answer the following questions:

- Is the composition of our relationship portfolio satisfactory?
- How well are we handling specific relationships and their parts?
- Are specific relationships or parts of them crucial for success?
- Could specific relationships add to our performance if we improve them?
- Should certain relationships be terminated?
- Do we measure ROR in the best possible way?

Chapter

7

RM, the network organization and the network society

INTRODUCTION

The network organization and its connection with RM and CRM has been examined throughout the text. This chapter deals with this intriguing issue at more length both from the perspective of the corporation and the market economy.

Introducing the new organization

In working with RM, marketing and organization began to stand out as two expressions of the same thing. My conclusion became that *RM is a marketing perspective on the network organization and the network society*. RM requires organizations to change and not least the experiences from installing CRM systems show that changes in both organizational structure and culture are inevitable.

The reason for treating organization separately and more at length is to give the marketer a better understanding of its significance in the new economy and the network society. RM lives in three environments: *the market, society and the organization*. The RM approach means that these three are woven together into a network. The nano relationships show the importance of the internal environment. The notion of network organizations has been used in the book as an umbrella for new organizational thinking. I find that the network structure and its tie to RM and CRM with interaction inside the network constitutes the core of contemporary organizations. But it stretches beyond that to a whole network society, as was pointed out in Chapter 1 with reference to Castells' (1996) comprehensive work. The term virtual organization is also frequently used.[1] According to one definition, the virtual (also called 'imaginary') organization[2] is 'a system in which assets, processes, and actors critical to the "focal" enterprise exist and function both inside and outside the limits of the enterprise's conventional "landscape" formed by its legal structure, its accounting, its organigrams, and the language otherwise used to describe the enterprise'. The idea behind this type of organization is to make the invisible visible and to acquire new frames of reference, to 'imaginize'. The organization is looked at through new lenses, and a new business logic for entrepreneurship and renovation of existing companies emerges. The organization consists of: an own base, which in turn consists of a leader company and an 'imaginator' (the leader, the entrepreneur) and their strategic map; a customer base which is tied to the leader company

---

[1] Davidow and Malone (1992).
[2] Hedberg et al. (1997, p. 13).

through systems for production, delivery, market communications and payment; and partnering companies and others that contribute resources.[3]

The network organization is larger than it seems from the organizational chart. Its most important resource – apart from financial capital – is intellectual capital, which is not found in the conventional balance sheet. Customers are involved in co-production and thus joint value creation and become part of the network. There is a business mission that mentally keeps the network of internal and external relationships together and the organization develops its own unique culture.

The Internet supports the construction of network organizations. By exploiting the Internet infrastructure, the core of the organization can be small but still the company can operate globally, grow quickly and be a market leader in its niche. Amazon.com is not one of the large retailers in conventional terms – its workforce is just 1 per cent of that of Wal-Mart – but has become the world's largest global bookstore. Even if Amazon still primarily sells books (a choice, by the way, that was accidental), the company is not first and foremost product-based but network-based. Its capital is its network of relationships, not only the customer base, but also the relationship to publishers, distributors, authors, and not least investors and the media. It went for growth and not initially for profitability with the idea that a critical mass of customers is required to be able to sell a diverse range of products. Its value on the stock exchange has had little to do with its assets and profits; it is a matter of expectations and the ability to cash in on the network.

Organizational and network properties have emerged in the 30Rs. My guess is that network organizations, just like RM, have been there a long time, perhaps always. Our way of approaching marketing and organization in the textbooks and education leads us astray. The textbooks begin to look like nostalgic albums with black and white picture postcards from a bygone industrial society: factories with smoking chimneys, mass manufacturing, huge companies, hierarchies, clearly defined roles and positions, and blue collar workers as opposed to white collar workers. We have come to a point where the new – or rather the old but newly uncovered – is starting to be visible and is developing with more zest. It is the outcome of a new type of economy which I have classified as a value society (accentuating that the customer buys and co-produces some kind of value) and the network society (the resources and structures that contribute to value creation).

---

[3] New organizational thinking offers a rich fauna of concepts and terms. Among them are: Handy's federative organization (1990, p. 117ff) and 'Triple I' organization – 'intelligence, information, ideas' (p. 141ff); Quinn's (1992, p. 120ff) 'spider's web organization', which is a network, and 'starburst organization' (p. 148), which is a continuously budding organization; Mills' (1991, p. 31) cluster organization consisting of clusters of teams; and Tjosvold's (1993) 'team-based organization'; see also Johnson's (1995) discourse on networks replacing the hierarchical organization. Although they will not be referred to further in the text, I like to give recognition to them here as they all have affinity with the network organization.

In the next sections, my personal interpretation of network organizations will be unfolded in the light of RM and CRM.

Nobody has seen a corporation!

The heading may seem absurd, but when we talk about a corporation we refer to something abstract, although it has certain tangible features. When the CEO is interviewed on TV or when the new model of a car is shown, we catch a glimpse of the being of the corporation. We cannot take a photograph of a business, but we can produce pictures of its elements: a photograph of a building or a group of employees, an organizational chart, a logotype. The goods and services of a company are tangible evidence of its existence. We see the tracks of the elusive animal in the snow, we surmise its presence, we may even catch a quick glimpse before it slips away.

Morgan (1997) approaches the organization with a series of metaphors. The organization is looked upon as if it were a machine, biological organism, brain, culture, political system, psychic prison, flow and change, and finally a tool to dominate society. Metaphors draw our attention to certain qualities of an organism, but they only provide fragments, not the whole. They should not be stretched too far; if they do, they lose their value.

'Objectification' happens when we compare an organization to something tangible, and 'reification' when we mistake the phenomenon for its tangible representation.[4] This may lead to myopia and imprisonment in existing concepts and definitions. Our perceptions about organizations take over, and we become their slaves instead of making them our servants. Inferior quality, disinterest in the customer, erroneous decisions and inertia are blamed on the organization and the system: 'I'm sorry, I can't do anything about it.' This has been called 'learnt helplessness'. Such a state of mind makes lousy marketing and lousy customer relationships. It can be found among companies, but above all among those government organizations which have become a 'reality' separated from us – the impersonal system, the authority, the computer, the state, society, public opinion – and which we ultimately cannot or dare not affect. The map takes over and the landscape gets lost. The renowned painting of a smoking pipe by Belgian artist Magritte, with the inscription 'Ceci n'est pas une pipe' (This is not a pipe), is named 'La trahison des images' (The treachery of images). The artist makes us understand how easily we can mistake an image of an object for the object itself.

---

[4] Gustavsson (1992, 2001).

According to Weick,[5] organizations are relationships and interaction:

> Most 'things' in organizations are actually relationships, variables
> tied together in a systematic fashion. Events, therefore, depend on
> the strength of these ties, the direction of influence, the time it takes
> for information in the form of differences to move around circuits.
> The word organization is a noun, and it is also a myth. If you look
> for an organization you won't find it. What you will find is that there
> are events, linked together, that transpire within concrete walls and
> these sequences, their pathways, and their timing are the forms we
> erroneously make a substance when we talk about an organization.

Whereas Weick's interest is directed to nano relationships, Badaracco[6] describes the transition from the closed and well-defined firm, the citadel, to a market and mega network: 'Firms were ... islands of managerial coordination in a sea of market relationships. But this is an outdated view. Companies are now breaking down barriers which, like the Berlin Wall, have endured for decades. Their managers are now working in a world that consists not simply of markets and firms, but of complex relationships with a variety of other organizations.'

Consequently, management cannot take for granted that the boundaries of their corporation are clear. They are expected to defend a moving fortress which continuously changes character and has different boundaries depending on whose vantage point is prevalent, that of the owners, the customers, the authorities, production or whatever.

Catching the soul of a corporation through relationships, networks and interaction can also become a limiting reification, if it is overdone or misinterpreted. The relationship eye-glasses just offer a language and a metaphor to help us imagine what is happening.

The company and the market: two phenomena, or two perspectives on the same phenomenon?

It has already been said that company boundaries are fuzzy. This dilemma will be further explained in this section by means of systems theory and transaction cost analysis, both with the aspiration of establishing boundaries.

---

[5] Weick (1979, p. 88).
[6] Badaracco (1991; quotation from p. ix).

CASE STUDY   **Volvo and Procordia**

When a deal between Volvo and Procordia was announced, there was reason to ask what the corporations and the market really were. Volvo already owned 43.5 per cent of Procordia stock. Procordia was going to buy Volvo, but the new corporation was going to be called Volvo. Procordia produced tobacco, lozenges and hamburgers, Volvo passenger cars, trucks, buses and aircraft engines. There was no product synergy in sight. The smoker could not care less if the plants were owned by Volvo and some 100 000 anonymous stockholders who change from day to day. The relationship existed between the consumer, the brand and the store where the cigarettes were bought. Moreover, the two companies owned stock in other companies. There was partial ownership between Volvo and Renault, although Volvo was primarily owned by private investors and Renault primarily by the State of France. A large number of subcontractors were tied to their customer Volvo, and from an operations viewpoint they were part of the Volvo empire. Where actually were the boundaries between these two companies, their markets and society?

Applied to the company and the market, *systems theory* assumes that the system (the organization) can be delimited from the *environment* (the market and society), and that it comprises *subsystems* and *components* (the inner functions of the organization). This approach helps to recognize the whole and its parts. In a network, however, boundaries are many and ever-changing. The difference between the company and its market, as well as its functions, is a matter of grade, transitions and difference in species. If decisions are the outcome of negotiations, consensus or power through interaction in a network, clear systems boundaries cannot be upheld. The traditional image of the atomistic market, populated by a large number of independent companies who act against relatively passive buyers, is still promoted in the textbooks, however.

The dichotomy of *open* and *closed* systems from systems theory is eluded by the properties of the network organization. A network is a more open system than the corporation in its classic 'citadel' sense. Networks, however, can also be closed, with openness inside the network, but closeness toward those who do not belong to the network.

The company as an open system means that it interacts with the environment. Today, it may be more appropriate to describe the company *as both interacting with the environment and being integrated with it*. The customer also becomes part of the company, which has stood out most clearly in services marketing. One example of both interaction and integration is Ernst & Young, one of the world's largest firms of accountants. Their office in Chicago was transformed into a 'virtual office' for 500 of its 1360 employees. The accountants work in the clients' offices and conference rooms, in hotel rooms, at airports and in airplanes, in their cars and at home. If they plan to work in their office they call in and book a room the day before ('hotelling') and a room is prepared for them with their telephone connection. From a daily, operative view, the boundaries between the accounting firm and the client do not stand out as particularly important.

Transaction cost analysis[7] claims to be able to guide the establishment of boundaries between a company and its market. The analysis has received extensive exposure as a synthesis between economics, organizational theory and contract theory from law. Unfortunately, the analysis is based on simplified assumptions about the industrial society and manufacturing, and does not pay attention to the service-based economy. It is limited to the 'pure' company and does not treat hybrids such as franchising and alliances. General marketing management has not been included, nor services marketing and the ideas of RM. The assumptions, therefore, seem obsolete and simplistic.

Its basic tenets, however, embrace some elements that can shed light on the differences between RM and the traditional perceptions of organizations and marketing. In neoclassical economic theory there are no transaction costs, so transaction cost analysis, in spite of its shortcomings, adds a new element of realism. The analysis sets the business deal – the transaction – in focus, and postulates that companies strive to minimize transaction costs. These concern the costs of performing business transactions, meaning in practice marketing and purchasing costs. It is cost effective to perform certain activities inside the own organization, and to handle others via the supply–demand mechanism of the market economy by purchasing from external suppliers. According to transaction cost analysis, the cost comparison between own production and purchasing explains the boundaries of the company.

Transaction cost analysis is based on three assumptions about the emergence of a company:

1 By organizing a company under the same owner and management, they can plan the work so that dual tasks and sub-optimization are avoided.
2 As an organization consists of a number of coordinated units under one management, it is easier to solve problems and disputes than it is in a market with a number of independent actors.
3 Inside their own organization, access to information is better.

These, however, are a theoretical conjecture and are not based on real world data.

---

[7] Transaction cost analysis is treated by Coase (1937, 1991); and Williamson (1975, 1985, 1990). In Johanson and Mattsson (1987), there is a comparison between transaction cost analysis and the network approach to B-to-B.

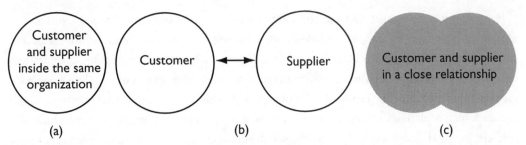

Figure 7.1 Three cases of transaction costs. Cases (a) and (b) are treated by transaction cost analysis. Case (c) is becoming more frequent, and is characteristic of RM and imaginary organizations

So there are two possibilities to handle transaction costs: inside the organization if that is the more cost effective (Figure 7.1a) or in the market if that is cheaper (Figure 7.1b). RM, however, offers a third option which is a combination of the first two, namely to handle transaction costs through a deeper relationship with an outside supplier (Figure 7.1c). In this way, a company can reduce its transaction costs without increasing its size or ownership.

According to transaction cost analysis it is difficult to analyse and measure relationship aspects, and therefore they are disregarded. The analysis does acknowledge two hazards, though: the *bounded rationality* of human beings, and *opportunistic behaviour*. To put it more simply: stupidity, selfishness, greed and dishonesty are such important components of human nature that they affect the applicability of transaction costs analysis.

Every company must have both a strategic core and supporting, ancillary activities. The core is the remainder of the citadel. Transaction cost analysis talks about *asset specificity,* the specific resources which constitute the core. Part of the core must be kept intact to preserve the unique competence of the firm. In the industrial era this was usually manufacturing. In today's economy it may equally well be finance or the maintenance of a brand. Other activities can be handled through outsourcing and partnering, the reason being that external resources can be better equipped to add value, provided transaction costs are not prohibitive.

According to Quinn,[8] ancillary activities are not the only objects of outsourcing, which is often claimed, but so are certain core activities. He recommends that own production be focused on a very select number of internal resources based on knowledge and services where the company has muscle to maintain a sustaining competitive edge. The company must, however, protect its core competency by building moats around the remainders of the citadel. This is argued by the proponents of hypercompetition, who claim that the core competency must be continuously remodelled; you do not survive and prosper by protecting the extant regime, you do it by continuous disruptions of the status quo.

---

[8] Quinn (1992, pp. 47 and 53).

In economics the market and the company are seen as two clearly delimited entities. The market is governed by supply and demand, with the help of price and competition. The corporation is an anonymous black box to the economist, who studies aggregates of companies in industries, regions and nations, unfortunately often based on poor statistics. In a basic book on management from the 1950s, the following definition was found: 'a company is a unit within which a planned economy rules', the ideal model being all employees marching like soldiers in good order toward a clearly set destination. In R24 – market mechanisms are brought inside the company – it was shown that this model is false and furthermore that the external deregulation of markets has its internal consequences. Decentralization and the split-up of companies into subsidiaries, business areas and other profit centres have expedited the dissolution of the internal planned economy.

Which boundaries we choose depends on the purpose of the boundaries. A company thus becomes many different organizations. The desire to draw generally valid boundaries is not possible to fulfil if we require the boundaries to be sharp; generally, companies are fuzzy sets. Several boundaries co-exist:

- Law based, concerning the establishment of a specific corporate format, taxes and annual reporting.
- Financial, concerning the procurement of money.
- Operative, concerning the daily work with partners, customers, suppliers and others.

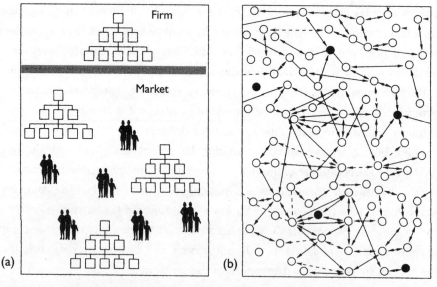

Figure 7.2 The traditional image of the firm and the market in systems theory, transaction cost analysis and economics (a) versus the complex network reality (b)

- Strategic, such as a joint development project with competitors, research institutes and consultants.

- Ecological, concerning the environmental impact of the operations. Customers are found both outside and inside the organization, depending on how the boundaries are drawn.

Looking at business as relationships, networks and interaction makes it difficult to pinpoint the beginning and the end of a company. We need new concepts and models in order to obtain mental access to reality. Figure 7.2a shows the traditional terminology, the company as a clearly defined, hierarchical structure and the market consisting of distinctly identifiable customers, both other organizations and consumers. In Figure 7.2b, we see a network of relationships which contains all types of actors. In this network, we can more or less distinctly delimit clusters of relationships and call them organizations for a specific purpose. The black dots represent core competencies.

We move from the *exclusive* organizational structure – one that excludes and delimits – to the *inclusive* structure – one that includes and unites.

Paradoxes of organizations

A paradox is a seemingly absurd or contradictory statement; it need not necessarily be absurd or contradictory if you dive under the surface. Naisbitt (1994) has defined a number of global paradoxes. One of these claims that the more integrated the world economy becomes, the more important become the small actors. In other words, the larger the global corporations, the more important the small local firms. If this paradox is valid, the atomistic division of companies in either/or – either large or small or maybe medium – becomes meaningless. It may be acceptable in colloquial language, but does not apply in financial assessments and statistical classifications, or in forecasts.[9]

Companies today strive to unify things that we have learnt to be contradictions. They try to be both *local* and *global*, both *small* and *big*, both *centralized* and *decentralized*, both *stable* and *dynamic*. They want to *become bigger without growing*. They want to *offer standardized mass manufacturing, customized mass manufacturing, and individually designed goods and services simultaneously*. These are oxymorons in the mechanically and sequentially formatted brains of Western civilization, but within the logic of RM and the network organization they provide realism.

---

[9] For a discussion on the increasingly more inadequate division of companies into small, medium-sized and large, see Gummesson (2002); see also Hult et al. (2000) and their discussion about the 'solo company'.

In an advertisment, German corporate giant Siemens describes its telecom business with the words 'Local Presence – Global Player' and the headline of the ad is 'Connecting the Global Village'.[10] It is an example of trying to be both local and global, or 'glocal'. It does not mean that you can necessarily sell the same product or run a company with standardized techniques throughout the world. In some cases this is feasible – American soap operas and McDonald's are the same everywhere – while in other cases it does not work as well. It did not work for Disneyland Paris. IKEA sticks to its core concept but makes local adjustments. Sensitivity is needed to exploit the same offering, and sensitivity is needed to make amendments. Standardization and customization unite.

ABB has tried to combine the best of the alleged opposites. The corporation was formed through a merger of Swedish Asea and Swiss Brown Boveri. In the early 1990s, ABB had 215 000 employees, and was divided into eight major segments, sixty-five business areas, 1300 subsidiaries, 5000 profit centres and innumerable teams. The management at headquarters was kept down. The head of operative units and their assistant staff units should, according to former ABB CEO Percy Barnevik ' . . . function on a self co-ordinating basis . . . in a continuing process of contact, information exchange, priority setting and correction cycles'. According to an executive at the competitor General Electric, employees must have ' . . . networking skills, and be able to work in a boundaryless organization'.[11] The desire is to unite the best of the big corporation with the best of the small firm.

The giants of the business world have borrowed their muscle from size and they have also become bigger through the recent wave of mega mergers. In the same way as the dinosaurs, extinct sixty-five million years ago, they risk becoming too clumsy to proact, act and react swiftly and efficiently. The planned economy of the totally integrated company is replaced by

ORGANIZATION	BODY	BRAIN
Dinosaur organization	Big	Small
The network organization	Small	Big

Figure 7.3 The 'dino organization' versus the network organization

---

[10] Advertisement in *International Management* (July/August 1993, pp. 20–1).
[11] Quotations from interviews in *International Management* (Lester, 1992).

a modular company, which preserves a few core competencies inside and buy goods and services from other suppliers.

The new network organization could be contrasted against an old dinosaur organization (Figure 7.3). The 'dino organization' has a big body but a small brain, the network organization has a small body but a big brain. The dino organization is a reflection of the industrial society when a company was composed of a few skilled and powerful people who ruled over hordes of blue and white collar workers.

The human ratio: internal and external 'employees'

In the network organization it is not so evident who is employed and who is otherwise engaged. Skandia AFS describes its organization as consisting of 1.5 million customers, alliances with 95 000 active and independent insurance brokers and banks, 3500 employees, and a core management group of ninety.[12]

The network organization can be described with the human resource ratio, the I/E ratio.[13] It stresses the fact that more human resources (people involved, I) are available for the company than the people employed (E). In AFS the ratio is high: 98 590/3590 = 27. If we classify customers as people involved, the ratio will grow to 445.

'The shamrock organization' has been proposed as a metaphor for the different roles in a company.[14] A shamrock normally has three leaves. These symbolize three types of human resources. The first leaf is the employees, those who work with the core activities of the company. The second leaf is the suppliers who supplement the corporation with resources. The third leaf is the part-time employees and temporary workers. But a special shamrock may have four leaves, the fourth leaf being the customers. In service management, customers have long been treated as part-time employees during the service production, delivery and marketing process. The customers can be seen as the professional representatives of the need and use of the service without whom a service often cannot be produced. The customer base is also increasingly accepted as the most crucial resource of a company.

Although suppliers are not employees, the boundary between suppliers and own employees is fuzzy. 'Cottage industries' in manufacturing have a long history, particularly in textile production. The workers provide flexibility, add resources when sales peak, but cost nothing

---

[12] According to the Skandia Annual Report for 1999.
[13] Hedberg et al. (1997, pp. 124–8).
[14] Handy (1990, p. 87ff).

when sales go down. The 'knowledge industry' employs intellectuals who need to be organized, but is strategically dependent on free intellectuals such as poets, authors and reviewers. The former are officially part of the organization, the latter are part of the external network. The search for the organization of the knowledge-based company partly concerns the form of affiliation for those who generate revenue: employment, full- or part-time work, ownership or shared ownership, and legal design. Financial and tax considerations may influence the structure of the organization. Self-employed freelance workers are common in, for example, journalism and the performing arts. A one-man firm can grow through partnering or from hiring employees. This is typical for most consultants and craftsmen. Companies who arrange for temporary secretaries or other staff, for example through International Manpower, are growing rapidly as a consequence of increasing outsourcing of internal services. Computer consulting firms have often earned the major share of their revenue from renting programmers on long-term contracts. When visiting a corporation today, we may be met at the reception desk by personnel provided by a security company. Building projects have always been network organizations, set up for a specific job and limited in time. Some projects are small, others are huge and last for decades, such as the construction of the Eurotunnel under the English Channel and the bridge between Denmark and Sweden.

Finally, an interesting observation and paradox is that while relationships between suppliers and customers are becoming closer, relationships between employers and employees are becoming looser and more flexible.[15] This is further evidence of the network properties of an organization, and that the distinction between the company and the market is being blurred.

From delimited structures to boundaryless processes

Hierarchy means 'holy management', a designation that may fit the egos of many executives. Its next of kin is *bureaucracy*, which means 'management from the desk', totally impersonal. The dawn of the dissolution of hierarchy is found in the establishment of profit centres and the introduction of the market mechanism inside the company (R24). *Heterarchy* (multi-dimensional management) and *adhocracy* (management to fit a temporary state of affairs) are better designations for today's organization and management.

Bureaucracy and adhocracy are extremes; the demand for rule-based governance is confronted with the demands for flexibility and adaptability to individual situations. The

---

[15] Root (1994).

project organization – which was dealt with in R25, in connection with the internal customer and interfunctional and interhierarchical dependency – used to be a temporary supplement to a relatively fixed hierarchical base organization. Today, the base organization is increasingly dynamic and becomes more of a parent project for a series of subsidiary projects.[16] Perhaps the network organization can be characterized as a sophisticated and timely version of the project organization.

The variability of adhocracy is also part of culture and lifestyle. Adhocracy is characterized by sensitivity for the unexpected, quick action, high degree of freedom, support from management and colleagues, generosity, accepted and necessary messiness, and only the sky is the limit. Bureaucracy stands for the planned and repressive, where the rule and ritual are given priority to the actual issue and the outcome. Bureaucracy in the government sector, industrial companies and consulting firms has a proven record of suffocating adhocratic tendencies.

In its extreme application adhocracy leads to chaos. Again, paradoxically, a great deal of discipline is required to make adhocracy work. The knowledge-based organization therefore needs a dash of bureaucracy. In the language of Tao, *yin* is the adhocratic property and *yang* the bureaucratic. The dynamism is in the tension and oscillation between yin and yang. If yang is given too much rope, the organization is petrified. If yin takes over, chaos and destruction follow. The extremes are companions, not adversaries. The combined outcome is *dynamic stability.*

Chaos and ambiguity are central concepts in Peters and Watermans' classic book *In Search of Excellence* (1982), and later in Peters' books *Thriving on Chaos* (1985) and *Liberation Management* (1992). Ehrlemark (1978) said that 'to consciously keep the firm unmanaged and unmanageable to such an extent that its stability and development is created out of disturbances and disorder is perhaps the true skill in management'. Stacey (1996), in *Strategic Management and Organisational Dynamics*, takes chaos research from physics as his vantage point. The concept *dissipative structures* was used by Nobel laureate and chaos scientist Ilya Prigogene. Dissipative structures are spawned in volatile processes in systems which are in disequilibrium:[17] ' . . . most of reality, instead of being orderly, stable and equilibrial, is seething and bubbling with change, disorder, and process.' Disorder and order coexist and become conditions for each other. Chaos theory in its popular form has become known for the 'butterfly effect': 'When a butterfly flaps its wings in Beijing it affects the weather in New York.' Teeny-weeny episodes have an impact in the spirit of the adage 'the straw that broke the camel's back'. When networks become complex and interactions are countless, a small episode can propagate in the network with an unpredictable and significant impact.

---

[16] Compare the dichotomy parent company–subsidiary which applies to stable base organizations related to each other through formal and legally obliging decisions.

[17] Prirogene and Stengers (1985).

The staff of a knowledge-based organization consists largely of intellectuals and professionals. Independence and opportunities to develop are conditional for their performance. Managing intellectuals is 'institutionalized anarchy', it is managing the unmanageable: 'Managing them is a craft or trade, maybe even an art. It is definitely not a science.'[18] Or in Drucker's terms:[19] 'As the business organization is restructuring itself around knowledge and information, it will increasingly come to resemble nonbusiness – the hospital, the university, or the opera – rather than the manufacturing company of 1920, in which there were a few generalists called "managers" and a great many unskilled and unknowing "hands" doing as they were told.'

The mechanical mode of operation from manufacturing which contaminated – and still contaminates – life in many organizations is obsolete even for its original application. But hospitals, universities and operas also face gargantuan hardships and are searching for new structures. Health care in most countries is in a state of flux and transition, and university bureaucracies are notorious.

The need to flatten organizations has been pointed out by several authors. Former SAS president Jan Carlzon originally entitled his book *Knock Down the Pyramids*.[20] Zuboff (1988) calls hierarchies obsolete and dysfunctional in an era when real power is IT-based knowledge. But there are also proponents for hierarchies, and hierarchies are common in practice. Jaques claims that ' . . . 35 years of research have convinced me that managerial hierarchy is the most efficient, the hardiest, and in fact the most natural structure ever devised for large organizations'.[21]

Peters and Waterman (1982) provided an expressive epithet for an informal phenomenon: skunk works. In R&D and engineering, skunk works are guerrilla operations; they are the outlaws of the formal organization. The skunks are passionate technicians and hackers obsessed with an idea. They hide their work from management who may be too remote from the pulse of the market and new technology. Some of the most successful innovations were skunk products in a period of their development. Among them are the Saab Turbo, the first commercially successful application of the turbo engine on a passenger car, and Losec, an ulcer medication, which has made Astra one of the world's richest pharmaceutical companies. We do not know how many excellent ideas have been systematic victims of abortion. One should not forget, however, that many of the skunk products fail in the market even if the technology is supreme.

Skunks are adhocrats but illegitimate adhocrats. They can be punished and rejected. They can be tacitly tolerated, thus giving innovative minds and entrepreneurs opportunities to

---

[18] Donovan (1989).
[19] Drucker (1988a, p. 3).
[20] The book was published in English under the title *Moments of Truth* (1987).
[21] Jaques (1990, p. 127).

realize ideas with support of company resources, without being burdened by internal red tape; they become intrapreneurs. A passive skunk tolerance seems to be quite common. The global corporation 3M – best known to consumers for Scotch tape – allows its R&D people to set aside 15 per cent of their time for own projects. There are also extrapreneurs who leave as employees but continue to collaborate with the 'parent' or take over some of its customers.[22]

The network organization has affinity to the transcendent organization. It is an organizational format which exists deep in the consciousness of the members of the organization; its base is collective consciousness. It goes deeper than the observable signs and activities of a corporate culture, its formal and informal structures and dos and don'ts. It is manifested in our intuitive and spontaneous reactions.[23] Zohar and Marshall, who talk about the quantum society, an approach inspired by the quantum theory of physics, say:[24] 'Persons are not quite the same as solitary individuals, nor are they a crowd. Persons are living networks of biology and emotions and memories and relationships. Each is unique, but none can flourish alone. Each in some way contains others, and is contained by others, without his or her personal truth ever being wholly isolated or exhausted.' This is a fitting description of the Russian relationship doll, which was used to demonstrate the existence of intertwined market, mega and nano relationships in Chapter 1.

A daring metaphor is provided by quantum physics in approaching reality as either particles or waves. 'The wave aspect is associated with our unstructured potential, with our spreading out across the boundaries of space, time, choice and identity. The particle aspect gives us our structured reality, our boundaries, our clearly defined selves, our ordered thoughts, our social roles and conventions, our rules and patterns,' say Zohar and Marshall. They say that atomism rejects relationships and gives rise to confrontation, whereas we need 'relational holism'. This holistic view of society is akin to both RM and network organizations, and the statement from Chapter 1 that society is a network of relationships. We can let the particles be the well defined, the individual, the formal organization, the buildings, the equipment, that is, everything visible and tangible. The waves then represent the relationships, the collective consciousness and the organizational culture, the coherent processes and the dynamics.

In conclusion, dynamic processes receive a progressively larger role and fixed hierarchies play a diminishing role. This does not mean that well-structured hierarchies become meaningless, rather that processes are given the lead part, as is shown in Figure 7.4. The understanding of processes expands, which was pointed out in R25. The whole company can be regarded as a coherent business process and not as insulated activities which occur in

---

[22] Johnsson and Hägg (1987, pp. 64–74).
[23] See Gustavsson (2001); and Harung (1996, 1999).
[24] Zohar and Marshall (1993; quotation from p. 64; subsequent quotations from pp. 82, 6 and 85).

Figure 7.4 Shifting from structure in focus supported by processes, to processes in focus supported by structure

functional compartments and hierarchical tiers. The processes extend beyond the corporation and unite it with the market. The network is boundaryless and inside the network there is interaction. The sequential has lost in importance and the simultaneous has gained, as has been shown in concurrent engineering and the value constellation.

Our need for security

In Chapter 1, the rationale for RM was defined as:

- enhanced retention and duration in order to improve financial performance;
- a way of creating better conditions for efficient marketing and management.

In the most militant of cases – hypercompetition – competitors turn into lethal adversaries and marketing warfare breaks loose. In the most benevolent case, competitors turn into colleagues and buddies. Or maybe they try to be a bit of both: 'Businessmen and industrialists who on the one hand fight for radical freedom of the *laissez-faire* market none the less find themselves clubbing into lobbies and cartels.'[25] History also shows that relationships and collaboration have always been in the centre of business activity. Why is this so? Let me venture an explanation.

Both consumers and companies need a basic level of security. Security is associated with words such as promises, honesty, trust, reliability, predictability, stability, fear of being swindled or let down, and reduction of uncertainty and risk.

---

[25] Zohar and Marshall (1993, pp. 73–4).

Promise is a core concept in all relationships.[26] Only in exceptional cases are promises legal promises – contracts, which can be forcibly honoured with the help of courts. Most promises are made without written contracts, they are moral and ethical promises to perform a service, deliver goods or collaborate in a development project. The qualities of certain suppliers and their offerings are easy to assess in advance (search qualities), whereas others must be tried (experience qualities). For customers it may often be difficult to assess what they got even after the purchase; they are left to trust the promises of the supplier (credence qualities).[27]

The market – customers, suppliers, intermediaries, competitors – as well as society in general offer so much insecurity and risk that only what is by nature unpredictable should be left pending. What can be planned should be planned. What cannot be planned can best be handled through preparedness for the unexpected. Companies must make certain that promises are fulfilled, both in their role of suppliers and customers. The supplier must be reliable and deliver the right thing at the right time to the right place; JIT (just in time) is the most advanced manifestation of those requirements. The customer should be reliable and not cancel an order or dodge payment. Companies need predictability so that, for example, production can be planned and performed with high productivity and quality.

If society offers a weak infrastructure, companies cannot work efficiently. Frequent electricity failures, unreliable airlines and airports, and a corrupt and unpredictable government sector make it difficult to compete with more reliable societies. When US Mail could not promise delivery, a market was opened for FedEx, DHL and others, who took responsibility for delivery promises. Also, the internal market must be reliable and predictable. There is the story about a New York company that sent internal letters and parcels, addressed to people in the very same building, via Federal Express. The mail first went to the Federal Express hub in Memphis, Tennessee, and then back to the building in New York. Delivery within twenty-four hours was guaranteed, whereas the internal mail needed a couple of days and offered no guarantee. Having experienced the internal mail of large corporations, this anecdote could very well be true. Companies can obtain security through several sources:

1 *Relationships* can create security. People trust each other and plan to make future business with each other. The relationships open up for a plus sum game, for win–win. This is what the whole book is about; it is the soul of RM.
2 Security may also be created through *laws and other formal regulations as well as institutions* that secure compliance. Its unique properties and consequences were discussed in R16 and R17, the law-based relationship and the criminal network. But law is no automatic source of

---

[26] The promise concept is little treated in marketing literature: see Levitt (1983); and Calonius (1987).
[27] 'Search qualities' and 'experience qualities' are terms borrowed from Nelson (1970), and 'credence qualities' from Darby and Karni (1973).

security: 'Formal contracts are often ineffective in taking care of the uncertainties, conflicts and crises that a business relationship is bound to go through over time.'[28]

3 *Knowledge* as a relationship driver was treated in R21. If the customers' knowledge is high, they can rest securely in their knowledge. For most consumers it is a problem to buy medical services or a used car; consumers rarely possess the expertise to assess their quality. The used car trade seems to remain an industry where customer ignorance is a natural part of its business mission. In today's society – which is frequently referred to as the knowledge-based society – knowledge is fragmented. We are dependent on more and more products and service systems, which we only understand to a limited degree. We may be able to use them, but we do not know what is underneath the surface. We become dependent on intermediaries – brokers in knowledge and insecurity[29] – to help us, especially if something goes wrong. Even if we gain more knowledge in absolute terms, the need for knowledge grows faster and we become increasingly ignorant in relative terms. We are left to base our decisions on symbols such as corporate identities and brand names, and what we believe they represent. The image and the parasocial relationships from R13 become important substitutes for knowledge.

4 *Business culture and ethics* – the informal regulations/institutions – can also contribute to security. The culture can be very distinct, with clear rules and a clear ethical code telling us what is right and wrong. It can work like the parlour game where the rules are not negotiable; if the dice shows five dots, you move five steps. The culture can comprise clear rewards and punishments, and those who misbehave are excluded from the business community. If it is a commercial predatory culture as in Russia today, insecurity rules. As is emphasized by transaction cost analysis, the rational behaviour of organizations is impeded by human opportunism.

The four ways of achieving security are not mutually exclusive. Even strong relationships and excellent knowledge may need a dash of formal law. A strong business culture includes social relationships and personal proximity. The USA is an example of a culture with legal dominance and weaker relationships with Japan as its opposite. Even inside a country there may be differences in cultures between industries and places. Global competition and mass markets create anonymity and insecurity about the rules of the game, which can explain a growing need for trust. Con artists are successful in business life through their ability to instil trust and confidence.

My conclusion is that long-term and close relationships best satisfy the need for security, albeit with some support from the other sources. The ratio between the importance of the four sources can

---

[28] Håkansson and Snehota (1995, p. 8).
[29] Giarini and Stahel (1998).

vary. If you are highly knowledgeable in one field, this may be enough to instil security. If the business culture is strong and no one breaks the rules and the law, security also becomes high.

Synthesis 1: from exclusive hierarchies to inclusive networks and processes

The theme for the last twenty pages or so has been RM and the network organization as reflections of one another. With a certain amount of graphic playfulness, the treatment of this theme can be summarized in five images of the corporation (Figure 7.5). The first image (a) is the fortress, the *clearly delimited hierarchical structure*. The second (b) is the *matrix organization* that was treated in R28 as an expansion of the hierarchy and a rudimentary network. Both are traditional images, even if the matrix signals the dissolution of the hierarchy. The third image (c) shows *a multidimensional network*. Its core, the unique competency which empowers the organization, is marked in black. We recognize the characteristic features of RM, the network of relationships within which the parties interact. We surmise the network organization in which actors other than employees are let in, among them customers. The fourth image (d) accentuates the *boundaryless and amorphous amoeba* features of the network organization, the corporation as a fuzzy set. The last image (e) takes a full step toward the *process organization*, a series of harmonious waves and completely concerted processes.

The new is often presented as an extreme alternative, an opposite to old. The network organization as the completely flexible organization with low transaction costs and rapid adjustment to new conditions is an idealized and absurdly simplistic image. The same can be said for RM, which may seem too benign and harmonious to gain credibility in a greedy and imperfect business environment where hypercompetition is lurking around the corner. The new images may appear as mirages in the wilderness; perhaps they can even erect a new mental prison. We may be conned into 'seeing' something in the same way as we 'see' the magician sawing someone in half. RM and the network organization are rather directions and intentions, emphasizing properties in marketing and organization which have been neglected and must now be given more prominence.

In Figure 7.6, the hierarchy, the matrix, the network, the amoeba and the processes have been superimposed on each other into one single image, but without merging their structures. All these structures coexist in various proportions. But the proportions are being re-examined; the role of the hierarchy is reduced in favour of dynamic changes and processes. As the figure shows, it is hard to visualize all of this at the same time; we risk seeing nothing at all, or we just see a mess.

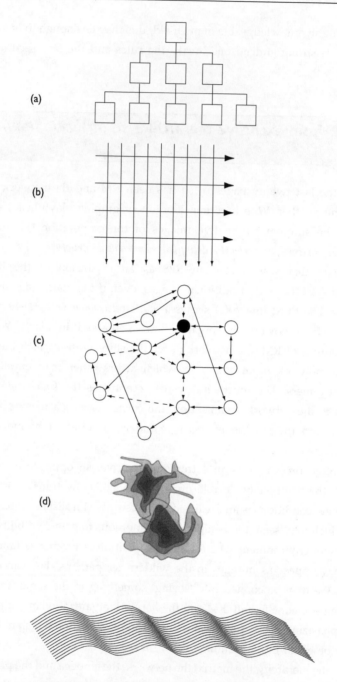

Figure 7.5 Organizational structure transitions: (a) the hierarchy with clear boundaries; (b) the matrix, the two-dimensional network; the imaginary organization first reproduced as a network (c), then as an amoeba with fuzzy boundaries which dissolve from a core competency (d); and finally, the process organization (e), the corporation as a series of processes or waves

Figure 7.6 The corporation as many images at the same time: hierarchy, matrix, network, amoeba and processes

In summary, these are the characteristics of the link between RM and network organizations:

■ RM lives in the market, society and organization. The network organization adds dimensions, which enhance our understanding for the evolution and functions of RM.

■ The organization exists, but not in a physical and tangible body. Its most important resources – its intellectual capital and core competency – do not show in the balance sheet; they show in the network. This in turn leads to a conclusion which has been stated in previous chapters: companies do not compete with companies but networks compete with networks.

■ The network organization is an inclusive organization as compared to the exclusive hierarchy that puts up boundaries. The boundaries between the company and its markets are fuzzy and people engaged are not the same as people employed. A large part of those engaged, sometimes the larger part, are found outside the organization. The customer is integrated with the organization and the customer base is a central resource, sometimes the most important resource. In this way, the roles of supplier and customer become less obvious; value is created through their interaction.

■ Increasingly ubiquitous, mobile and flexible IT offers new opportunities for RM and the network organization to develop. The e-relationship must, however, be balanced against social and human relationships. High tech needs high touch; eCRM needs hCRM.

- The company becomes a parent project and what is traditionally known as a project becomes a subsidiary project. The organization becomes a series of dynamic and coherent processes rather than a stable, compartmentalized hierarchy.

Synthesis 2: from partial to complete marketing equilibrium

A conclusion from R2 (the customer–supplier–competitor relationship) was that the market is governed by competition, collaboration and regulations/institutions. Together, these three forces strive for balance – marketing equilibrium – without ever reaching this heavenly state though. The tension creates a dynamic state as long as no single force becomes excessively dominant.

This conclusion will be carried further in this section by integrating it with the network organization. Marketing equilibrium concerns the state of the external market, whereas the same notion can also be applied to the internal market of a company. Each of these two instances will subsequently be referred to as a partial equilibrium.

The circle that showed the three forces of partial marketing equilibrium in Figure 2.1 is equally needed as a balancing force inside an organization. The corporation is regulated by its control systems, both hard and soft ones. Among the hard ones are the financial

	COMPETITION	COLLABORATION	REGULATIONS & INSTITUTIONS
Traditional perception of a firm's internal operations	No	Yes	Yes
Traditional perception of the operations of the market	Yes	No	No
New perception of the firm and the market	Yes	Yes	Yes

Figure 7.7 Today, the company and the market are controlled by the same forces

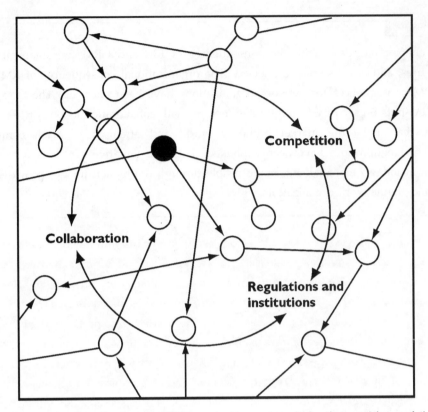

Figure 7.8 Complete marketing equilibrium in the network, both 'outside' and 'inside' the organization

control system, production planning and marketing planning; among the soft ones are business missions, values and collective consciousness. These control systems correspond to regulations/institutions. Competition and the price mechanism have been brought inside the company according to R24, and many of the other Rs support that notion.

The market and the company are thus governed by the same three mechanisms: competition, collaboration and regulations/institutions (Figure 7.7). The proportions between the forces as well as their content can vary between markets and companies, between companies, and within markets. Each specific marketing situation – both inside and outside the company – struggles to reach its own specific marketing equilibrium.

Figure 7.8 combines *partial marketing equilibrium* from R2 (Figure 2.1) with the image of the complex network reality from Figure 7.2, where the clear boundary between the company and the environment has been dissolved. We can then speak about *complete marketing equilibrium*.

IN BRIEF

This chapter has dealt with the consequences of RM and CRM for organizational structures, and also its effect on society. The organizational consequences of RM and the RM consequences for network organizations have been analysed. The emphasis that RM puts on security through relationships, with collaboration as one of the three forces that make the market economy work, and attempts to reach complete marketing equilibrium have been explained. This is a tentative synthesis of several trends in today's management, made visible through the mental images provided by RM and the network organization.

8

The genesis of RM and CRM

INTRODUCTION

This chapter is about the evolution of RM and CRM, and its theoretical and practical foundation. The synthesis toward a more general theory of marketing is presented, contained in the notion of total relationship marketing.

Theoretical contributions to RM

The word *theory* comes from Greek and has the same roots as *theatre*. Both theory and theatre present mental images or scenes, which – if they are good – can show something of interest to an audience.

It is considered an old truth that nothing is so practical as a good theory. The quality pioneer W. Edwards Deming has said that 'experience tells nothing unless it is related to theory'.[1] Robert Pirsig, in his philosophical novel *Lila*, says that 'Data without generalization is just gossip.'[2]

These statements imply that data are of no value unless they can be structured and organized in a category, model or theory, which can later be applied in more than a single case. Theory is a tool to derive meaning out of interviews, observations, statistics, advice and ideas, thus helping to generate usable knowledge. The most burdensome task is not to collect – or rather generate – more data, but to interpret and combine what is already there and make some sense out of it. Theory provides a context, a map that offers guidance.

This requires theory to be good theory. In an applied discipline like marketing, good theory must be grounded in the real world. The maps must be well drawn, or they will lead us in the wrong direction and lure us into morasses or make us drive straight into a rock.

If the marketing that is presented in textbooks and seminars built only on the fragmented contributions from scholarly research, it would be lightweight. It is necessary to fill the gaps with the best available knowledge, namely the knowledge from 'those who were there when it happened'. It is not evident what should be counted as theoretical contributions and what are contributions from practitioners. In scholarly research, theory is accompanied by empirical data. Empirical comes from the Greek *empeiria*, meaning *experience*. In the language of science, empirical refers to real world data generated with certain methods and techniques. Note that the language of many business schools has been impoverished by limiting the term empirical to quantitative data and statistical processing.[3] It is therefore imperative to add the knowledge

---

[1] Quoted at the Ninth World Productivity Congress, Istanbul, June 1995.
[2] Pirsig (1992, p. 70).
[3] For a discourse on the limitations of methodology in research in marketing, see Gummesson (2001b).

and experience of *the reflective man*. Going back to Chapter 1, this guy appeared in many shapes: *the reflective practitioner, reflective customer, reflective researcher*.

It was mentioned in Chapter 1 that RM is inspired by many sources. The imprints of these sources are found in the description of the 30Rs. To remind the reader, the specific marketing sources are: traditional marketing management, marketing mix and the 4Ps; services marketing and service management; the network approach to B-to-B; and current RM and CRM literature. A summary of my views on these marketing sources is presented in the next four sections. The other sources from various areas of management have been specifically covered in the text already: total quality management (TQM) in R26; new accounting theory represented by the balanced scorecard and intellectual capital in Chapter 6; theories of network organizations in Chapter 7; and the recent developments in IT in R12.

Marketing management, marketing mix and the 4Ps

Textbooks and teaching in marketing management are primarily structured around the marketing mix theory.[4] The core of this theory is the use of various means to influence the market. The best-known variant is based on four parameters which all start with a P: product, price, promotion, place. It is popularly known as the 4Ps.

The definition of marketing suggested by the *American Marketing Association* (1985) – and which tends to become official and authoritarian – is based on marketing mix thinking: 'Marketing is the process of planning and executing the conception, pricing, promotion, and distribution of ideas, goods, and services to create exchanges that satisfy individual and organizational objectives.'

Suppliers are perceived as independent units in the market. Using various means, the supplier exercises an impact on the market. This may occur under conditions which are more or less uncontrollable by a single firm, such as consumer tastes, the general economic situation, and legislation. How much of these conditions the supplier can influence depends on its size, power, creativity, persistence and not least coincidence. Even if there is a desire to keep one's customers, marketing management theory and education are mainly about transaction marketing.

In Chapter 1 the marketing concept, which puts customer needs and customer satisfaction in focus, was described. The thinking behind the marketing mix is that marketing, by handling a series of activities, should persuade the consumer to buy a product. If a supplier feels capable

---

[4] Those who wish to study the marketing mix theory can turn to any book with 'marketing management' in the title. See also the critical discussions in Brownlie and Saren (1992); Grönroos (1997); and Gummesson (2002).

of satisfying a need, the supplier must go for it and make sure that the consumer buys its products.

In practice, however, the 4P approach has led to a manipulative attitude to people.[5] If we just select the right measures in the right combination and with the right intensity, the consumer will buy; it is a matter of putting pressure on the consumer. The consumer is a locked black box, maybe with a tiny peep-hole. We often know little of what is in the mind of consumers, how they think and feel, and what their motives are. It is more of a stimulus–response model, similar to the fisherman's relationship to fish. If we improve the bait, the fish will bite and it is hooked. How the fish feels about it has been less considered. The supplier and its salespeople are the active party. Sometimes the consumer is pig-headed and rejects an offering. Conclusion: we used the wrong bait. To face such a challenge – 'Never take no for an answer!' – and turning it to our advantage is part and parcel of an aggressive sales culture.

Instead of being customer oriented, I will contest that marketing management in practice is *supplier oriented*. There is ample experience behind the use of the marketing mix and it is often functional as seen from the supplier's perspective. The marketing mix contains problems, however. One is how to mix the activities. What will be the effect of a certain mix and what happens to the other measures if the value of one of them is altered? What will happen if we reduce the price by 10 per cent? If we invest more in advertising? If we launch a new product for a new segment?

The marketer tries to find an *optimal mix* – or more realistically a *satisfying mix* – which gets a superior response on the market and at the same time creates profits. Because of the complexity in the interaction between different factors and the uncertainty in a competitive market, the mix will be the outcome of the availability of data, analytic rationality, experience, opinions, emotions, intuition and visions.

In Chapter 6 we mentioned the preference for clear guidelines about the rights and the wrongs in marketing. We would prefer strict, scientifically proven links between what we do and the outcome. Failure to establish such links was mentioned in Chapter 6.

The marketing mix theory is founded on studies of the marketing of consumer goods, not of services, not of B-to-B. The literature usually zooms in on the narrower concept of consumer and shows less interest in the generic concept of customer. However, a large share of the studies concern distribution channels, thereby including a part of both services and B-to-B, namely wholesalers and retailers. The channel companies are service producers, but they are treated from a goods perspective.

Marketing mix concerns mass marketing and standardized consumer goods. Such goods are usually packaged and piled on shelves in self-service stores. The interaction between the

---

[5] Anthony Cunningham, Ireland's first marketing professor, has pointed out to me that consumer manipulation was not the intent when marketing thinkers began to teach need orientation and the 4Ps. In practice, however, it may have turned out otherwise.

personnel of the store and the consumer is minimal and left to brief encounters at the cash register. The stores are 'service factories' and the service consists of: convenient location and opening hours; goods available on the shelves; packaging and signs that display information about product and price; several checkout points; and aids such as trolleys, baskets and bags. Consumer goods also include capital goods such as freezers and DVD players. The sales through independent small stores and stores with manual service are frugally treated in the literature. They rely more heavily on personal contact, whereas supermarkets require more of an impersonal mass marketing approach.

The 4Ps have been widely exposed after their introduction in a textbook by McCarthy, first published in 1960. The 4Ps structure is a role model for globally circulated textbooks, all with very similar content. The Ps have also been expanded into more Ps in order to cover the marketing domain more completely.[6]

Even if the 4Ps form the hard core of the marketing mix theory they are incomplete and therefore many other areas have been added in marketing management textbooks. These include: marketing strategy and its link to business mission, goals, objectives and corporate strategies; market segmentation; market research techniques; marketing planning procedures; and the design of the marketing and sales organization. At the same time, the marketing mix theory excludes or treats marginally such things as complaints handling, invoicing, design and production. The 4Ps approach is narrowly limited to functions and it is not an integral part of the total management process. It is marketing management, but not marketing-oriented management.

The marketing mix theory is a child of the standardized mass production of the industrial society and its dissociation from the individual consumer. The contemporary value society and network society clamour for another type of production. Even if mass production and mass

	Dominating production	Dominating marketing
Industrial society	Mass production	Mass marketing
Value society	Customized (mass) production	Customized (mass) marketing

Figure 8.1 Marketing and production in the industrial and value societies

---

[6] See, for example, Booms and Bitner (1982); Kotler (1986); Judd (1987); and Baumgartner (1991).

marketing will always play a significant role in economic life, it should not be the reigning godfather. Instead, the centre of attention should be customization of offerings and a more individualized marketing, often in a combination expressed by the paradoxical concept of *customized mass marketing*.

Marketing management and marketing mix theory particularly treat four phenomena connected to relationships, networks and interaction:

1 The zero relationship (R0). The main focus on transactions has influenced the definition of the zero relationship. Price, being one of the 4Ps and the core variable in economics to explain the functioning of the market economy, is part of the zero relationship together with convenience.

2 The relationship between the supplier and the customer (R1). In the marketing mix theory, this is 'personal selling', a subcategory to the third P, promotion. It deals with the face-to-face encounters between a salesperson and a customer with the purpose of persuading the customer to buy.

3 The treatment of competition, which is comprehensive in both marketing management and specific competition literature and economics. Here it is defined as the relationship between the buyer, the current supplier and the competitors (R2), and efforts to find marketing equilibrium.

4 Physical distribution of goods is found under the fourth P, place, presented as networks of distribution channels far beyond the physical goods (R3).

Within the marketing mix theory, image and brands are treated, but not with a relationship angle. I still do not considered it a classic area for marketing, especially as the views on brands – with brand equity, brand identity, brand architechture and the far-reaching suggestion that brands are the core business rather than the product – are children of the 1990s. They have contributed to the parasocial relationships (R13).

Services marketing and service management

At the beginning of the 1960s, the service sector share of GDP and employment got ahead of the industrial sector. The reactions to this have been slow and it took until the second half of the 1970s for services marketing and management to gain attention. Services marketing had been treated by occasional writers during the 1960s, but obviously 'the time was not ripe' (whatever that means). During the 1980s, services marketing became the fastest growing field of marketing and, together with RM, CRM and IT, it will probably continue to be so. Contributions came from researchers in many countries, above all from the USA, UK, France and the countries in Northern Europe, initially mainly from Sweden and Finland and today referred to as the *Nordic School*.[7]

In the early days of service research, much of the effort was devoted to show differences between goods and services, and to prove that services need their own type of marketing. Still, however, nobody has in a more fundamental and generic way been able to understand what goods and services are and how they relate to each other. Usually, four properties are mentioned in the literature in order to show the differences:

1 Services are *intangible*, whereas goods are *tangible*.
2 Services are *less standardized than goods*.
3 Services *cannot be stored*.
4 Finally, *simultaneity and inseparability*, meaning that the production and consumption of services are partly simultaneous and that customers partly participate in the production process.

I mention these alleged differences as they are continuously repeated in the literature as the rationale for separating goods marketing and services marketing. The properties may seem attractive at first glance – they have face validity – but what are their operational consequences? The first three can easily be dismissed. Let me explain by presenting a few examples.

Airlines are classified as service companies. But the aircraft, the food, the drinks and the staff are very tangible. The airports and the view from the aircraft window and the feeling when there is turbulence are tangible, and if you are fortunate to fly by Concorde you feel the vibrations when the speedometer on the wall says '1 mach' and the aircraft breaks through the sound barrier. If I am operated on at the hospital I am myself the 'machine', the object of 'repair and maintenance'. It is unpleasant, it may hurt. I can get better, worse or die. Can it be more tangible?

Services and goods alike can be standardized and be produced in factories but yet include customized elements. The pizzeria and the retail bank offer highly standardized services, while knowledge-intensive services from management consultants, lawyers and architects are highly customized (although they contain standardized modules).

---

[7] For further discussion on the Nordic School, see Grönroos and Gummesson (1985). The international importance of the Nordic School has been covered in Berry and Parasuraman (1993); Fisk, Brown and Bitner (1993); and Fisk, Grove and John (2000). For general overviews of services marketing with somewhat varying perspectives, see Lovelock, Patterson and Walker (1998); Lovelock, Vandermerwe and Lewis (1999); Grönroos (2000); and Zeithaml and Bitner (2000). The contributions from the Nordic School to RM are discussed in Gummesson, Lehtinen and Grönroos (1997).

The claim that services cannot be stored is nonsense. Services are stored in systems, buildings, machines, knowledge and people. The ATM is a store of standardized cash withdrawals. The emergency clinic is a store of skilled people, equipment and procedures. The hotel is a store of rooms. Fresh bread, milk, fruit, fish and meat are quickly perishable, not to mention an oyster and an opened bottle of Mumm's Cordon Vert. But food can be treated to last longer, some treatments keeping the quality well, whereas others are just preserving cosmetic dimensions, or jeopardizing the health of the consumer by adding chemicals, radiation and gene manipulation with unknown effects.

The last of the four properties is different. The simultaneous production and consumption process, the presence of the customer, and the customer's role as co-producer form the pivotal distinguishing properties between goods and services. These are also salient features of RM and they require interaction in a customer–provider relationship, sometimes also in a customer–customer relationship. The interaction can be face-to-face but it can also take place via IT and other equipment.

Services have more impact on a nation's economy than was previously recognized. The classifications used in statistics, for example the manufacturing industry, with such subgroups as the auto or electronics industries, are production and product oriented and say little of interest to marketing. In the future, less then 10 per cent of the working population of a mature industrialized nation will work on the shop floor.

To make a total offering to customers' competitive and value adding, both goods and services must comply with the requirements of the customers. Services are also used as a means to differentiate an offering and are thereby allotted a strategic marketing role. Moreover, work in an office is now being seen as internal services, not as administrative routines or white collar bureaucracy. Internal services are broken up and given their own identity and profit centres are instituted. The data processing department becomes a computer consulting company, the real estate is taken over by a maintenance company, and a financial company manages cash flow, credits and pension funds. The services then must be marketed and sold internally, and they become support to external marketing.

The need to understand services more in-depth, as we have realized their importance for today's economy, requires more explicit and transparent service design and service development procedures.[8]

Prompted by dissatisfaction with services, much of the development of services marketing has focused on service quality in the sense of customer perceived quality, customer satisfaction and value for the customer. A large number of service quality models have been designed. Lists of quality dimensions – essential properties of a service with which customers are satisfied or dissatisfied – have been established. The dimensions could also be interpreted as

---

[8] See Shostack (1981); Sundbo (1998); and Edvardsson et al. (2000).

factors which enhance or reduce the likelihood of customer loyalty. The most quoted dimensions are:

- *reliability*, the ability to correctly perform a service according to promises;
- *responsiveness*, willingness to serve customers;
- *assurance*, the ability and credibility of service provider staff;
- *empathy*, sensitive understanding and personal care for every customer;
- *tangibility*, the goods and people that are part of the service delivery.[9]

There are also other compositions of general dimensions.[10] At the end of the day all organizations have to pinpoint the dimensions that are of prime urgency for their specific situation; the general dimensions can only be advisory and an eye-opener. There is no doubt that both academics and practitioners have misused the general dimensions and superimposed them on specific situations in, for example, health care, thus missing essential quality issues.

Even if many have tried the same quality dimensions on e-services as they have tried on traditional services, both common sense and research show that IT offers a new situation, at least in part. As additional, specific e-service dimensions, the following have been found in one project: *access to a website, ease of navigation, security and privacy, site aesthetics*, and *customization/personalization*.[11]

Among the core variables – relationships, interaction and networks – *interaction* in particular has stood out as a central concept in services marketing and management, and it also stands out in its contributions to RM:

- Most literature on services marketing is focused on the *service encounter*, the interaction between the customer and the service provider (R5). The fact that marketing and production must work hand in hand is at the core of services theory and so is quality.
- As many services consist of data processing and transmission, the e-relationship (R12) is of primary importance for service companies.
- The concepts of the service encounter and service quality support the effort of modern quality management to bridge the gap between marketing and technical functions (R26).

---

[9] The five dimensions are suggested by Zeithaml, Parasuraman and Berry (1990). Many others have suggested general service quality dimensions, e.g. Grönroos (2000); see also an overview and an integration between goods quality, service quality and computer software quality dimensions in Gummesson (1992, pp. 51–9).

[10] See Gummesson (1993), who compares quality dimensions for services, goods and software; and Reynoso and Moores (1996), who studied the difference between external and internal service quality dimensions.

[11] See Zeithaml, Parasuraman and Malhotra (2000).

■ Services marketing is the mother of internal marketing (R27), which subsequently has earned the status of being generally applicable.

Services marketing has added emphasis to several other relationships. Among these are:

■ the notion that marketing is performed by each and everyone, not only by the full-time marketers but also by part-time marketers (R4);
■ the need for being close to the customer (R8);
■ the relationship to dissatisfied customers and how recovery should be handled (R9);
■ the non-commercial relationship, which is usually about services (R14);
■ the introduction of the market economy inside the organization, among other things the internal trade of services (R24); and
■ the interaction between internal customers and the transcendence of traditional functional and hierarchical boundaries (R25).

The network approach to B-to-B

B-to-B is marketing to other organizations (in contrast to B-to-C, which is marketing to individuals and households), whether this is goods or services or the buyer is a manufacturer, a distributor or the government sector. The previously used term industrial marketing has a limiting connotation; it leads the thought to manufacturing industries selling to each other.

The network approach[12] is a designation for developments in marketing thought from the IMP Group (International/Industrial Marketing and Purchasing Group). The 'group' or rather research tradition has its roots at Uppsala University, Sweden, but has spread to include major universities throughout the world. Beginning in the 1970s, comprehensive studies, which are reported in numerous articles and books, have been conducted. Its work is a reaction against the marketing mix theory, a reaction documented in a book by Håkansson and Snehota in 1976.

A similar approach to B-to-B was taken by Jackson in the late 1970s and early 1980s in the USA. Her findings are close to those of IMP, but she used a different language (relationship marketing versus transaction marketing), and her theoretical and empirical foundation was different. IMP research gave birth to a school of thought and their members have continuously grown in number. Curiously enough, in the era of globalization, Jackson had not encountered IMP research until 1996, when I told her about it.

---

[12] For presentations of the network approach and its research programmes, see anthologies edited by Ford (1990), Iacobucci (1996), and Möller and Wilson (1996); and books by Håkansson and Snehota (1995), and Ford et al. (1998). For a critical discussion on the appropriateness of RM in industrial marketing, see Blois (1996).

According to the basic beliefs of the network approach, a company:

> ... can be viewed as a node in an ever-widening pattern of
> interactions, in some of which it is a direct participant, some of
> which affect it indirectly and some of which occur independently of
> it. This web of interactions is so complex and multifarious as to deny
> full description or analysis. Indeed, the interaction between a single
> buyer and selling company can be complex enough ... [13]

The network approach sees B-to-B as interaction in a network of relationships. Even if the research has been primarily directed to dyadic relationships, it has successively broadened its scope to more complex networks. In addition to networks and interaction, its core variables are activities, resources and actors, as was mentioned in Chapter 1.

The character of relationships varies between companies. They are influenced by product type, degree of standardization, complexity, frequency and technological conditions. Sometimes business aspects prevail, sometimes technological aspects. The relationships between two companies are subsystems of larger networks. The larger networks are inhabited by the customers' customers, the suppliers' suppliers, intermediaries and various other collaborating parties. National relationships are usually more extensive, informal and intimate than international relationships. Many of the general relationship properties that were listed in Chapter 1 are partially inspired by IMP work, such as: longevity and stability of relationships; importance of collaboration as a means to an efficient market economy; importance of active participation of the parties; and importance of power and knowledge. Other important findings are linked to transaction costs and switching costs, and the importance of harmonizing technology, procurement and logistics with marketing strategy.

The network approach is based on case studies of B-to-B and therefore the theory only qualifies for selling and purchasing between organizations, unless further studies widen its field of application. By comparing its results with other theories and data, I see three indications of generality:

1 Its emphasis is on market-oriented management rather than marketing management. Just like in service research, it has been found that marketing cannot be isolated as an independent function but is rather an attitude to management.
2 Its results give food for rethinking both consumer goods marketing and services marketing.

---

[13] Ford, Håkansson and Johanson (1986, pp. 26–7).

3 Marketing situations are seldom clear-cut. Almost all companies sell both to consumers and
  organizations, and offer both goods and services.

The Nordic School of Services in particular has benefited from the network approach, and I
wrote about the integration and mutual benefits of the IMP approach and services marketing
as early as 1983. Representatives of the network approach to a lesser degree have exploited the
results of service research. Although IMP members are increasingly presenting at RM
conferences and are being quoted in RM texts, many have not found RM to be an extension of
or a possible partner to the network approach: ' . . . it is futile to say what comes after [the
network approach], if there is anything.'[14] Some prominent IMP representatives are dismissing
the broader RM concept by claiming that: RM deals with B-to-C; does not heed networks but
rather multiple dyads; ignores actors outside the dyad; and even that RM does not make the
existence of the relationship phenomenon credible.[15] I can concur with one of these points:
networks have been neglected in the RM and CRM literature, a shortcoming that the 30R
approach is trying to make up for.

   This, however, should not dishearten others from making their interpretations and using
IMP research as an input to RM. In my opinion, the network approach offers a unique
contribution to marketing thought which has received international acclaim, even if it plays a
humble role in so-called 'general' marketing textbooks. No other salient theory of B-to-B has
come forth during the past twenty years. The network approach is also influenced by
interorganizational theory, transaction cost analysis and other theories, but above all it is the
outcome of the network researchers' own empirical studies. Its contribution to RM has
received more attention during the 1990s. There is also a reaction that the network approach
has cocooned itself into its historical track record, keeps producing more of the same, and is
unable or unwilling to recognize RM and CRM and relate to a new situation.

   I have made my own interpretation of the network approach and I see it in the light of its
contributions to RM. This interpretation does not necessarily comply with everybody else's
interpretation, but on the other hand there are also several perceptions of the approach among
IMP researchers.

   The network approach is using interaction in networks of relationships as the vantage point,
just like the 30R approach. It has contributed to many of the 30Rs:

- by showing that the customer and the seller are many-headed (R6);
- by showing that social and professional networks are important (R18);
- seeing that relationships above the seller and buyer are influential (R19);

---

[14] Johanson (1994, p. 9).
[15] Easton and Håkansson (1996, pp. 411–12).

- by showing the influence of alliances on the market mechanisms (R20);
- stressing the need for knowledge (R21);
- by showing that marketing is dependent on other functions and has thus contributed to the interfunctional and interhierarchical dependency and the relationships between internal customers and suppliers (R25); and
- although the concept of quality is not in focus in network research, the network approach has put the spotlight on the need to bridge the gap between technology, purchasing and marketing (R26).

Current RM and CRM literature: a comparison with the 30R approach

The review of the three marketing theories, as well as the discussion on the new accounting and the network organization in Chapters 6 and 7, and the continuous reference to quality and IT, has revealed the major antecedents of the 30R approach. None of these theories use relationship marketing (or RM) as their key term, although the term was introduced both in services and B-to-B during the 1980s.

Throughout the book, ample references have been made to those who have furnished inspiration and illustrations. To review everything being presented on RM and CRM in the expanding number of publications and websites is simply not feasible, not even if we limit ourselves to the English language. It is especially difficult to separate the chaff from the wheat when listening to CRM consultants, survey results presented at academic conferences, company success stories, and the news media.

RM and CRM are given different meanings by different authors. The influx and vitality of the current research and debate about RM, although mostly fragmented and addressing special issues in terms of traditional marketing management theory, has become an extra impetus to the evolution of my approach. These sources have modified and broadened my understanding. The 30R approach has received both praise and criticism. It has not been seriously challanged, although some show indifference and some have expressed a negative opinion, unfortunately without any tangible ideas on how to advance the field or make improvements. My conviction to stick to the path laid out by the 30R approach has rather been reinforced.

This section first points to the distinction between the *term* relationship marketing and the relationship marketing *phenomenon*, a greatly misunderstood issue. It proceeds to compare a selection of RM and CRM definitions and multi-relationship approaches.

The term and the phenomenon

There is an unfortunate mix-up between the *term* RM and the understanding of the actual *phenomenon*, a mix-up that should be ducked by scholars in particular but unfortunately is not. A *term* is only a label of the *phenomenon*, it is not the *phenomenon* as such (recall the discussion on objectification, reification and Magritte's pipe in Chapter 7). In order to avoid an intellectual Titanic disaster, scholars are expected to consider the whole iceberg (*the phenomenon*), not just its tip (*the term*). *RM and CRM are new terms, but represent an old phenomenon.*

The *phenomenon* of RM is as old as trade itself, but it has gone unnoticed by most marketing professors, economists, marketing textbook writers and business school educators. Since the 1970s, many *terms* have been used to catch the *phenomenon*, among them the network approach and the interaction approach; long-term interactive relationships and a new concept of marketing; customer loyalty; and interactive marketing. Other *terms* are database marketing, direct marketing, niche marketing, one-to-one marketing, wrap-around marketing, dialogue marketing, and client management.

The *term* relationship marketing was used by Barbara Bund Jackson in her project on B-to-B in the early 1980s, and published in a seminal book and a *Harvard Business Review* article, both in 1985. She used the *term* as an opposite to transaction marketing. The *term* was used by Len Berry in a conference paper in 1983, but exclusively for services. In other words, the *term* appeared simultaneously in B-to-B and services marketing. During the 1990s, the *term* became a general marketing term – accompanied by CRM – although most of the seminal writings on the *phenomenon* before that had used other terms. Considering its long history in the practice of marketing, and the diversity of *terms* used to pinpoint the *phenomenon* in theory and literature, it is pointless to ascribe the 'discovery' of the *phenomenon* of RM to a specific date or individual. The *phenomenon* was part of indigenous knowledge in business cultures around the world. It is beyond my comprehension that marketing and management as disciplines did not conceptualize this phenomenon until recently, and that the discipline of economics still has not made even a note of it.

Many have contributed to make the phenomenon of RM visible, which is evident from the description of the various theories earlier in this chapter. In a number of books, researchers and consultants have developed their own approaches to RM, CRM and 1to1. Some have used these terms in the title.[16] For others the term RM is central in their text, although it is not in the titles of their books.[17] Most of the authors have not used the term RM, but are zooming in on

---

[16] Christopher, Payne and Ballantyne (1991); Peppers and Rogers (1993, 1999); Cram (1994); Payne et al. (1995); Buttle (1996); Halinen (1997); Peck et al. (1999); PricewaterhouseCoopers (1999); Hennig-Thurau and Hansen (2000).

[17] Jackson (1985a); Berry and Parasuraman (1991).

customized marketing and relationships in an innovative and informed way.[18] Similar books have been published in many languages in many countries. Most likely, the phenomenon of RM has also been treated in now forgotten texts. An upsurge in RM articles and conference papers present different ways of approaching RM. Some of these references have been used in this book. Others are found in overviews, which show that different roads lead to RM.[19]

Definitions

The majority of books and articles on RM and CRM do not offer definitions, which makes it difficult for the reader. Short definitions are never complete or unambiguous, but they can hint at the core of a phenomenon and thus provide initial guidance. A selection of RM and CRM definitions is listed in Table 8.1.

The table shows that the definitions vary in scope and emphasis. The Gummesson definition is founded on three core variables – relationships, networks, interaction – that have emerged out of research. The variables are common to goods/services, B-to-C and B-to-B. Whereas the other definitions list activities or properties, this definition provides core variables as vehicles for thought and action. The definition is based on a relationship perspective, hence the notion of the relationship eye-glasses. It is the only definition that includes the concepts of networks and interaction.

Berry's definition is developed within services marketing. He explains his concern to be customer retention and the allocation of resources to keep customers and strengthen relationships, and not just attract new customers. Jackson's definition involves B-to-B customers and individual accounts as compared to mass markets and segments. Her concern is to make the B-to-B supplier choose whichever is the best strategy for each individual customer in each specific situation, either RM or transaction marketing. The messages of the two definitions are similar, but they are grounded in two different types of marketing, services marketing and B-to-B.

Grönroos' definition aspires to be a general marketing definition. It proposes that RM is more adequate as a general marketing theory than traditional marketing management, marketing mix and the 4Ps. He has gradually broadened the definition to encompass relationships to many stakeholders and not exclude not-for-profit government and voluntary sectors. He also points to the need to divest in relationships. Morgan and Hunt as well as Ballantyne offer broad definitions. Together with Grönroos, Porter[20] and Ballantyne stress

---

[18] Sewell (1990); Rapp and Collins (1990, 1995); Scheuing (1995); Reichheld (1996); Newell (2000).

[19] Webster (1992); Morgan and Hunt (1994); Sheth and Parvatiyar (2000) – all with a US perspective – and Gummesson, Lehtinen and Grönroos (1997) with a Nordic School perspective.

[20] Clive Porter is an Australian consultant.

Table 8.1 Selected definitions which emphasize different aspects of RM and CRM

Source	Definition
Gummesson (see Chapter 1)	'Relationship marketing is marketing based on interaction within networks of relationships.'
Berry (1983, p. 25)	'Relationship marketing is attracting, maintaining and – in multi-service organizations – enhancing customer relationships.'
Jackson (1985a, p. 165)	'Relationship marketing is marketing to win, build and maintain strong lasting relationships with industrial customers.'
Grönroos (2000, pp. 242–3)	'The purpose of marketing is to identify and establish, maintain and enhance, and when necessary terminate relationships with customers (and other parties) so that the objectives regarding economic and other variables of all parties are met. This is achieved through a mutual exchange and fulfillment of promises.'
Ballantyne (1994, p. 3)	'An emergent disciplinary framework for creating, developing and sustaining exchanges of value, between the parties involved, whereby exchange relationships evolve to provide continuous and stable links in the supply chain.'
Morgan and Hunt (1994, p. 22)	'Relationship marketing refers to all marketing activities directed to establishing, developing, and maintaining successful relational exchanges.'
Porter (1993, p. 14)	'Relationship marketing is the process whereby both parties – the buyer and provider – establish an effective, efficient, enjoyable, enthusiastic and ethical relationship: one that is personally, professionally and profitably rewarding to both parties.'
Gummesson (see Chapter 1)	'CRM is the values and strategies of relationship marketing – with particular emphasis on customer relationships – turned into practical application.'
PricewaterhouseCoopers (1999, p. 12)	'CRM is a business strategy – an attitude to employees and customers – that is supported by certain processes and systems. The goal is to build long-term relationships by understanding individual needs and preferences – and in this way add value to the enterprise and the customer.'
Eggert and Fassot (2001, p. 5)	'eCRM embraces the analysis, planning and management of customer relationships with the aid of electronic media, especially the Internet, with the goal of the enterprise to focus on select customers.'

win–win aspects (fulfilment of promises, rewarding both parties, value exchange) and, in alignment with Jackson, include the long-term aspect (continuous and stable, lasting). Seven of the ten RM and CRM definitions use terms such as creating and maintaining relationships.

Ballantyne claims that RM is an emerging school of thought. This rings true with reference to the *term*, but not with reference to the *phenomenon*. Relationships not only go far back in the history of business practice, but they are in the core of both services marketing and the network approach, even if the term RM was not used.

Porter adds important social elements. Relationships should not only be efficient and effective, but also enjoyable, enthusiastic, ethical, and personally and professionally reward-ing. Marketing theory seems to forget the importance of social interaction and personality dimensions in a commercial relationship: business is fun! Furthermore, ethical aspects are at the core of RM, which is reflected in the importance that many authors place in trust, for example Morgan and Hunt.

Table 8.1 lists three CRM definitions. Gummesson puts emphasis on CRM as a practical application of RM philosophy and strategy, whereas consultants PricewaterhouseCoopers equate CRM and RM with the addition that CRM is supported by processes and systems. This addition stands out even more in Eggert and Fassot's definition of eCRM, where the Internet has the lead role. They also stress the conscious selection and targeting of individual customers, which data warehousing and data mining should make possible.

Multi-relationship and network approaches

Most RM and CRM definitions limit themselves to the supplier–customer dyad, while some include several parties or stakeholders. In Table 8.2, the 30R approach is compared to three other approaches which go beyond suppliers and customers and see marketing relationships as embedded in a network of multi-relationships.

Christopher, Payne and Ballantyne propose a 'six markets' model, which 'the Cranfield school' has kept in later publications.[21] The six markets consist of: *customer markets* (existing and prospective customers) surrounded by *supporting markets* which are *referral markets* (satisfied customers who recommend the supplier to others); *supplier markets* (to be a partner rather than an adversary to their suppliers); *employee markets* (making certain that the right employees are recruited and promoted); *influence markets* (such as financial analysts, journalists and governments); and *internal markets* (the organization and its staff).

---

[21] Christopher, Payne and Ballantyne (1991, pp. 21–30). The Cranfield school is used here as a designation for researchers from the Cranfield School of Management, a leading business school in the UK, where research on RM and CRM is active; see Peck et al. (1999).

Table 8.2 Comparison between categories in multi-relationship approaches (the number of relationships included in each subcategory is shown in parentheses)

Source	Categories	Subcategories
Christopher, Payne and Ballantyne (1991)	6 markets	Customer markets (1) Supporting markets (5)
Kotler (1992)	10 players	Immediate environment (4) Macro-environment (6)
Morgan and Hunt (1994)	10 partnerships	Buyer partnerships (2) Supplier partnerships (2) Lateral partnerships (3) Internal partnerships (3)
Gummesson (1994)	30 relationships	Market relationships: ■ Classic (3) ■ Special (14) Non-market relationships: ■ Mega relationships (6) ■ Nano relationships (7)

Kotler has not been willing to accept a paradigm shift to RM. In his concept 'total marketing', however, he comes closer to a relationship and network view, albeit as a supplement to traditional marketing management: ' . . . there are at least ten critical players in a company's environment, of which the immediate customer and the ultimate customer are only two'.[22] He makes a distinction between four players in the *immediate environment* of the firm – *suppliers, distributors, end-users* and *employees* – and six in the firm's *macro-environment* – *financial firms, governments, media, allies, competitors* and *the general public*.

Morgan and Hunt[23] suggest ten relationship exchanges with four partnership groups: *buyer partnerships* (ultimate customers, intermediate customers); *supplier partnerships* (goods suppliers, service providers); *lateral partnerships* (competitors, non-profit organizations, governments); and *internal partnerships* (functional departments, employees, business units).

The fourth classification, the 30Rs, has been presented in the previous chapters. It goes further than the others and involves not only parties, but also certain properties of relationships. In that respect it is less consistent than the other classifications, but it is more comprehensive. Generic relationship properties that were listed in Chapter 1 are inherent in

---

[22] Kotler (1992, p. 4).
[23] Morgan and Hunt (1994, p. 21).

the relationships, and other properties have been added to form their own Rs. Some are based on content, such as the green relationship, the law-based relationship and the criminal relationship; others on form, such as alliances; and on conduit, such as the electronic relationship.

In a comparative analysis it became evident that the relationships of all four approaches can be classified as market or non-market relationships and can further be subgrouped into both mega and nano relationships. There is a good match between the approaches, although the emphasis and scope vary. There are no obvious contradictions or conflicts.[24]

Concluding comment

This presentation of a selection of RM and CRM definitions shows that there is a rich literature searching for an identity for these concepts. The growth rate is currently exponential. The approaches have varied in emphasis and scope, all the way from market relationships based on a consumer–seller dyad to a series of supportive, non-market relationships. Some limit RM and CRM to specific applications, such as services marketing or a technique such as the use of databases and the Internet. The 30R approach is the broadest, also aiming to reach a high degree of generality.

Synthesis of theories and experiences to a more general marketing theory

The theories which have been presented above are *substantive* or *specific theories*; they concern a specific area, such as services. The next step in theory generation is to extend these theories in the direction of *formal* or *general theories* which cover a greater domain, if possible all marketing.[25] But this is an ultimate goal which will never be reached. It is not scientifically acceptable to generalize one substantive theory to other substantive areas. Empirical data and empirically grounded theories from each substantive area must be 'heard'. Unfortunately, this very mistake has been made in marketing, most noticeably in the nomination of marketing mix theory to the status of a general marketing management theory.

---

[24] There are also other efforts to consider the integrated aspect of dealing with all stakeholders, instil consistent behaviour in the organization, and communicate a consistent image of a brand or company. One such tradition pertinent to RM is using communication as the key variable. See Duncan and Moriarty (1998, p. 9); Gronstedt (2000); and Schultz and Kitchen (2000).

[25] For a discussion on substantive and formal theories, see Glaser and Strauss (1967) and their grounded theory.

RM becomes a vehicle for generalization in two respects:

1 Generalizing above the traditional dichotomies of goods/services and B-to-C/B-to-B. On this higher level, *the total offering and its value to the customers, suppliers and society are in focus.*
2 Generalizing to a management theory with a marketing perspective, meaning that *marketing management, marketing mix and the 4Ps* are converted into *marketing-oriented management.*

My road to generalization will be laid out below. It is not claimed to be the only road, just the road I travelled.[26]

Figure 8.2 shows that modern marketing in its *first stage* was developed for consumer goods. Marketing management, the marketing mix and the 4Ps emerged to be applied on the mass marketing of standardized consumer goods. This is specific theory.

In the *second stage*, this thinking – in a deductive way and with a weak empirical base – was superimposed on services and B-to-B (Figure 8.3). Thereby, marketing mix theory invaded services marketing and B-to-B. When the theory was confronted with real world data and

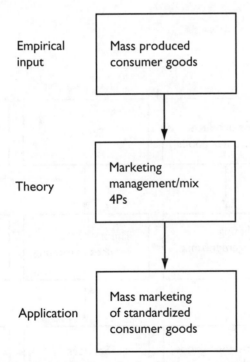

Figure 8.2 The marketing management and mix theory

---

[26] This is a further development from Gummesson (1983, 1987b).

Figure 8.3 The forced transition of the marketing management and mix theory to other types of marketing

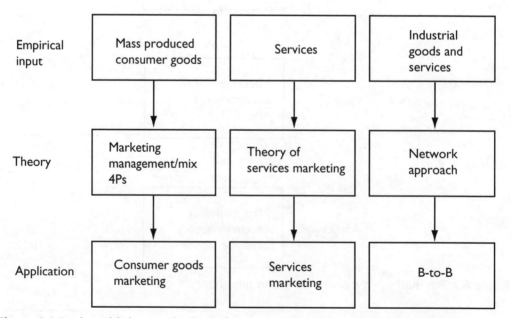

Figure 8.4 Real world data as the basis for three substantive marketing theories

Relationship to / Product	Consumers B-to-C	Organizational buyers B-to-B
Goods	Marketing management/mix 4Ps	Network theory
Services	Services marketing and management	

Figure 8.5 The substantive domains of the marketing theories

practice, anomalies occurred. These were explained away on purely theoretical and deductive grounds. More Ps and tools were added which enhanced the value of the marketing mix theory, but only temporarily. It became a patchwork, and the theory became increasingly strained. To use a term from telecommunications, it became a spaghetti system; it was full of cables and nodes, and finally so entangled that no one could use it. Marketing management also became procrustean science,[27] meaning that reality was forced into boxes where it did not fit. If a box was not filled the theory was stretched; if the box was flooded, overflowing material was cut out.

In the *third stage*, service marketing and B-to-B were studied on their own terms in their own environment. Two theories emerged from inductive, empirical studies of services marketing and B-to-B. The foundation was no longer marketing mix but reality was allowed to shape its own concepts and connections (Figure 8.4). The procrustean science was replaced by sensitivity for what reality tried to tell us – if we were willing to listen to its story.

The three marketing theories presented above can be classified by type of product (goods or services) and type of relationship (consumer or organization). How the theories match marketing situations can be seen in Figure 8.5. None of the situations is clear-cut and completely logical; the classification can rather be used to put emphasis on a certain perspective and not as mutually excluding categories.

In the *fourth stage*, the foundation was reinforced from two directions. First, beside the three marketing theories, contributions came from quality management, organization theory, accounting theory and IT. Second, we enter practical experience and common sense from our

---

[27] Named after the Greek robber Procrusteus, who had the kindness to offer accommodation for travellers, but demanded that they fit the bed size exactly. If they were too short, they were stretched on a rack; if they were too tall, their feet were cut off.

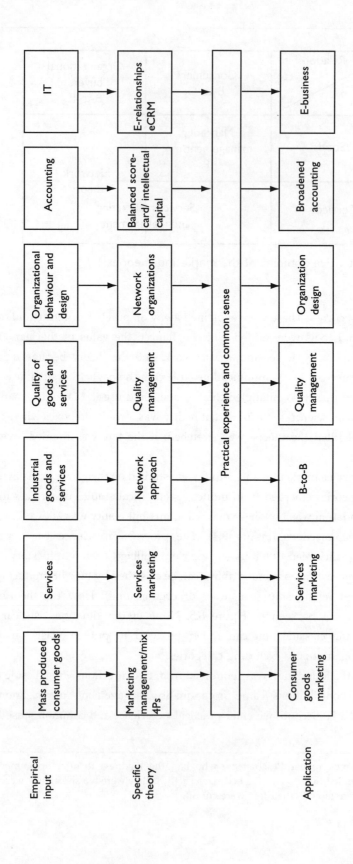

Figure 8.6 Contributions to RM from marketing theories, other theories and practical experience

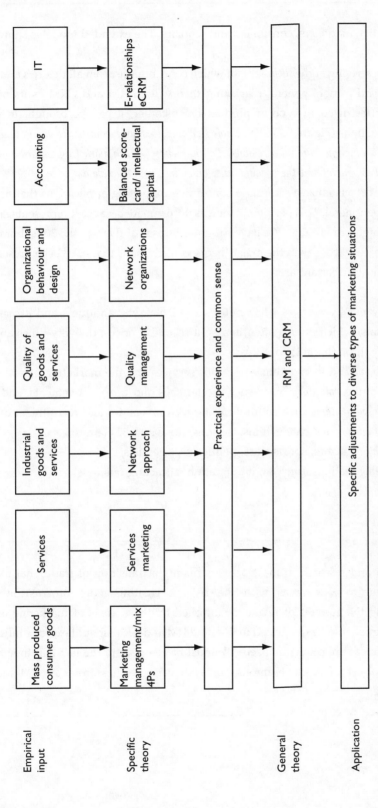

Figure 8.7 Synthesis of specific theories and experiences into a more general marketing theory

roles as reflective marketers, consumers and scholars. The extended model is shown in Figure 8.6.

We are now arriving at the *fifth stage*, in which contributions from all theories and experience converge toward a more general marketing theory, with RM and CRM as its nucleus. The theory is not restricted to type of product or customer; it can be brought to bear on all marketing situations (Figure 8.7). *Please note that this does not mean that it should be applied in the same way to all companies and all occasions; the uniqueness of each marketing situation must be taken into account. The general and the specific must enter into constructive dialogue.*

I can, however, visualize a *sixth stage* concerning marketing applications that have hitherto been seen as peripheral. This peripheral view is unfortunate because it represents large sectors, some with a high growth rate. We have caught glimpses of them in the 30Rs, but they have a less solid theoretical base than the major theory contributions that have been presented above. Among the most important are:

- markets created by *auctions* (distributor's food markets, antiques) and *exchanges* (stock, bonds, metals) which offer – often in a split second – prices, delivery times and payment increasingly through e-relationships;
- the *public sector* and its marketing of public services and the marketing of authorities;
- marketing of the *voluntary sector* such as churches and peace movements, and other *non-commercial organizations* such as fund-raising for universities and recruitment of students;
- *marketing of culture and events*: films, theatres, the Olympic Games;
- *people marketing*: actors, sports stars, politicians, scientists;
- *place marketing*: nations, tourism, immigration, attracting business.

IN BRIEF

The theory and research in these areas is mainly a transition of traditional marketing management to new areas with the risk of creating more procrustean science. Considering the amount of revenue controlled by these areas of marketing and their growth, they should be integrated in RM, and RM and CRM should exercise influence on how these areas are conceptualized. We must be sensitive to the fact that they have not been the object of a great amount of systematic studies from an RM and CRM perspective.

Chapter

9

In conclusion – RM and CRM provide a paradigm shift!

INTRODUCTION

This final chapter sums up the message of the book. It claims that RM and CRM provide a paradigm shift, a new way of approaching marketing. In a sense we have come to the end. In another sense we are only starting out on an adventurous tour into the consequences of a new marketing paradigm in a new economy.

A paradigm shift in marketing

A paradigm shift implies that a science or discipline is given a new foundation, with new values, new assumptions or new methods. The accepted and established must be set aside. It either disappears completely, succumbs to the new, or takes the role of one of several coexisting paradigms. An established paradigm can be a springboard, but it can also be a mental prison.

The American automotive industry is a case in point. When the small car came from Europe and Japan it was not taken seriously by US manufacturers, but it was taken seriously by the consumers. Morgan offers an explanation: 'American auto industry in the early 1970s was a prisoner of its early success. And numerous firms in other industries have shared a similar experience, declining and decaying as a result of policies that made them world leaders in earlier stages of development.'[1]

Organizations get caught in mental traps, 'knowing' how everything is and erecting monuments over their prejudices. 'Group think' is hubris linked with the security in the power group, such as a corporate or marketing management group. No one dares openly challenge the conditions for decisions and action. Snug in 'The Yesmen Choir', the singers are sheltered by the perceptions that might have once been realistic, but in a changed market are nothing but shared illusions.[2]

Some claim that RM and CRM are just marginal add-ons to established marketing management. With such a view, RM is brutally forced into the old and will never be allowed to display its qualities. Paradigm shifts break existing patterns. A small car is not a shrunk limousine, a tanker is not a blown-up rowing-boat. They are based on different concepts and obey different laws. In the same spirit, I see RM and CRM as a paradigm shift in marketing.

The book has shown that RM in many ways offers a fresh view on marketing. Table 9.1 sums up RM and CRM, and their contribution to a paradigm shift and the beginnings of a new theory of marketing.

---

[1] Morgan (1997, p. 201).
[2] For a discussion on the yesman, see Ortmark (2000).

Table 9.1 The characteristics of my RM and CRM concept and their contribution to a paradigm shift in marketing

Definitions	RM is marketing based on interaction in networks of relationships. CRM is the values and strategies of RM – with particular emphasis on customer relationships – turned into practical application.
Making RM tangible	Specification of thirty relationships, the 30Rs, both operational market relationships, and mega and nano non-market relationships.
Relationship portfolio	Selection of the relationships that a company will focus on in its marketing.
Values	Collaboration is in focus; the parties in a network are co-producers of value; more win–win and less win–lose; more equal parties; all parties carry responsibility; long-term relationships; each customer is an individual or a member of a community of like-minded people.
Theoretical and practical foundation	Built on a synthesis between traditional marketing management, marketing mix and the 4Ps; services marketing; the network approach to B-to-B; quality management; network organizations; new accounting principles; IT; and the experience of the reflective practitioner.
Links to management	RM and CRM represent marketing-oriented management – an aspect of the total management of the firm – and are not limited to marketing or sales departments; the marketing plan becomes part of the business plan.
Links to accounting	The balanced scorecard and intellectual capital provide tools for measuring return on relationships (ROR).
Links to organization	RM is the marketing manifestation of the network organization.
Advantages to the firm	Increased customer retention and duration; increased marketing productivity and thus increased profitability; and increased stability and certainty.
Advantages to the market economy	RM adds collaboration to competition and regulations/institutions; the symbiosis of these three contribute to a dynamic marketing equilibrium.
Advantages to society, citizens and customers	RM is the marketing of the value and network society with increased focus on customized production and marketing to the individual, and reduced focus on standardized mass production and mass marketing.
Validity	By focusing on relationships, networks and interaction, RM offers a more realistic approach to the marketing management in the new economy than is currently prevailing in marketing education. In practice, marketing works through a network of relationships.
Generalizability	RM and CRM can be applied to all types of organizations and offerings, but the relationship portfolio and the application are always specific to a given situation.

The paradigm shift has partially taken place in the real world of marketing, but the shift is not properly echoed in theories, textbooks and education. Students bring theoretical knowledge – marketing maps – to their current and future jobs. This knowledge must be usable knowledge, representing the terrain. This year's marketing reality cannot be tackled with previous years' theories.

New concepts

New thinking requires new concepts – reconceptualization – so that the new will be allowed to live on its own terms.

Several new concepts have been introduced in this book or they are developments of concepts I have used before. I believe I have innovated some of them or used them with a novel touch; if I am mistaken I would appreciate being corrected.[3]

Among these concepts are: the relationship eye-glasses; mega and nano relationships; faceless relationships; alliance markets; decision markets; service collision; horizontal and vertical interaction; power company and power industry; the pseudo-personal relationship and pseudo-membership; the value and network society; the bureaucratic–legal paradigm; return on relationships; relationship portfolio; and not least the marketing equilibrium.

Several of the relationships are under-represented in current 'general' marketing literature, such as: the full-time and part-time marketers, the FTMs and PTMs (R4); the many-headed customer and the many-headed supplier (R6); the customer or supplier as prisoner (R10); the e-relationship (R12); the parasocial relationships (R13); the green relationship (R15); the law-based relationship (R16); the criminal network (R17); the knowledge relationship (R21); mega alliances (R22); quality management sponsoring the relationship between marketing and technology (R26); and the owner and financier relationship (R30).

Other concepts and terms are other people's innovations, such as mega marketing, internal marketing, internal customer, the service encounter, network organizations, the knowledge-based organization, and migratory and embedded knowledge. But the concepts have been given a more central role here than in other general marketing presentations and they have been looked at through the relationship eye-glasses.

The new language of RM and CRM accommodates a dilemma. One purpose is to show that the boundaries in a network of relationships – both from a marketing and an organization perspective – are blurred. The boundaries change depending on what they are used for; they

---

[3] As has been pointed out before, it is vital to make a distinction between a phenomenon and the term used to catch the phenomenon. I have not invented any of the phenomena, I have conceptualized some of them and given them names.

are always fuzzy and changeable and they are transcended. At the same time I feel forced to use terms such as internal/external and company/market for want of better. Close friends and colleagues can communicate without words. Reading Marlo Morgan's book (1994) on a walkabout with Australian aborigines through the outback made me envious. These 'primitive' people had a collective consciousness that allowed tacit communication and understanding with an effectiveness that was almost instantly validated in action and results.

RM, CRM and the 4Ps

If RM and CRM take the place of traditional marketing management and marketing mix theory as an overriding structure for marketing thinking, the question comes up: Are the 4Ps (5Ps, 6Ps, etc.) dead? The answer is – No! Product, price, promotion, place and the other Ps will always be important – and they have their role in RM and CRM – but their role changes. In short, I see it this way.

I would like to dissolve the 4Ps and just talk about Ps as symbols for supplier-controlled activities for managing customers and persuading them to buy. A certain element of persuasion and influence will always be needed in marketing. But the role of the Ps should be a supporting role instead of a leading role; a focus shift should take place (Figure 9.1). In practice, the Ps became too manipulative – even if this was not the original intention – and this has damaged the credibility and functionality of the marketing discipline. The Ps are also directed to mass marketing, which is becoming less dominant, but will always be part of marketing. Goods and services will be treated as a way of creating value, together with individual customers, and the customer's role in the production will be more important.

Figure 9.1 A shift from the 4Ps to relationships, networks and interaction

The value society and the network society, modernism and post-modernism

Concepts such as the post-industrial society, the service economy, the knowledge era or the information age try to spot the key changes which have also been labelled the new economy. As has been said already, I advocate the use of two dimensions. One is the *value society* that epitomizes value creation as the desired outcome of economic activity; the other is the *network society*, which describes the structure of organizations and society.

Two additional concepts – modernism and post-modernism – keep intriguing me. Even if they are nebulous, they tease our brains. They attempt to uncover essentials in a long-term passage from certain governing values and behaviour to others. Modernism coincides with the logic of the industrial society, post-modernism with the value and network society.[4]

These represent mega paradigms, a term that may cause cardiac arrest for those who are already at war with the terms of paradigm and post-modernism.

Modernism is characterized by a belief in progress and unbounded trust in science, the rational and the expert; by our ability to take charge over nature and social behaviour; by finding universal laws and absolute truths. Everything is measurable, and if it is not, it does not exist. Common sense and experience are degraded to superstition and opinions to be replaced by facts and objective knowledge. Society will become neatly ordered by means of social engineering, and social equality is infused through planning, regulations and institutions. If we only have enough data we can control and predict society.

Post-modernism turns these tenets upside down. We live in an age of uncertainty.[5] The expert becomes 'a broker of uncertainty', not the sage and assured expert who knows 'how it is' with reference to 'scientific proof'. The volatility of stock exchanges has become hysterical and there is no way of forecasting the price of shares even for a short period. We have seen that the organization, the supplier, the customer and the competitor are ambiguous phenomena. Companies can be suppliers, customers and competitors, and they can own one another. The supplier and the customer are recognized as co-producers of services, and increasingly as co-producers also of goods and eventually of experiences and value. Service customers become temporary workers in the provider's service factory. The physical marketplace is challenged by the marketspace of Internet technology. Personal and organizational relationships, which contain both technical rationality and emotions, are central to marketing. It is accepted that we deal with fuzzy phenomena with a unique core, but with blurred boundaries, perspectives that are multiple and overlapping, and knowledge that is incomplete and variable.

---

[4] The discussion on post-modernism is primarily inspired by Brown (1995, 1998); and Firat, Dahlokia and Venkatesh (1995).

[5] Giarini and Stahel (1998).

The network organization is post-modern, it flows and changes. Complexity, ambiguity and change are natural, not inconvenient and nerve-racking. Chaos is part of everyday marketing, but even if chaos cannot be managed we can learn to manage in chaos. There is lack of equilibrium, but there is an aspiration to reach a balance which will never be reached. Trends are not continuous and many trends appear simultaneously and move in different directions; they carry the hallmark of the paradox but not of the oxymoron. The profound transformation – the discontinuity, the quantum leap, the paradigm shift – can be released suddenly, like the oil crisis in the 1970s; the Soviet perestroika and the fall of the Berlin Wall in the 1980s; the Internet carnival in the 1990s; the entry of the new millennium with dotcom collapse; and the attacks against the World Trade Center and the Pentagon, symbols of the capitalist market economy and power. Technical innovations such as the Internet, the mobile phone and gene manipulation, and social innovations such as deregulation and privatization, shake society.

To a large extent, successful marketing has always been post-modern – without recognizing it. Innovation and entrepreneurship are always unpredictable and create commotion. But the issue is not being either post-modern or modern, viewing society as either a value society or a network society. The issue is where to place the emphasis. RM is an attitude and CRM is a tool; neither represent a fundamentalist religion. RM does not exclude transaction marketing or anonymous mass marketing when those are justified. RM does not throw the 4Ps overboard, just changes their position.

Epilogue: approaching the end of the book – or the beginning?

Peter Drucker has said that ' . . . we are prone, both in academia and in management, to . . . mistake the surface gloss of brilliance for the essence of performance. But it is so easy to fall for sophistry – to mistake clever techniques for understanding, footnotes for scholarship, and fashions for truth . . . '[6] This needs to be observed both by those who appear as attorneys for the defence of the established and those who advocate the new.

Heeding current issues is not the same as being faddish. The phenomena of RM and later CRM caught my interest because I believe they are here to stay. When my attention was first drawn to relationships back in 1968, I had no idea what I was getting into. It took until the script of this book was ready to realize that I had opened the lid to a deep well – and could not see its bottom. RM became a black hole theory, it seemed endless; eCRM is still unproven and perhaps only a passage to a better balance between high tech and high touch. Although stars are glistening here and there, a lot is darkness.

---

[6] Drucker (1988b).

My original reason for treating RM and later CRM was to contribute to a more realistic understanding of marketing through the generation of a new and more general theory. In search of this theory, relationships, networks and interaction have stood out as the core concepts, the foundation. These concepts have stood the test over many decades now and their generality has been underscored by the developments in IT. My most important criterion in selecting and defining the 30Rs has been the pinpointing of phenomena which are of prime importance to practitioners and scholars alike. Observations of current issues in companies, and the study of literature and research, together with interpretations of these sources, have given birth to RM. But 'current' can be deceptive; it can easily be a trap of ephemeral fashion and hype. The issues that have been included here are those that I believe have a future. This is based on judgement calls, however, as no one has but a subjective understanding of what is to come.

As the Rs emerged – without my having a clue how many there would be – I tried to find a unifying logic. The failure to find that logic felt embarrassing until I realized I was misguided. It is unjustified to demand that the relationships in some rationalistic mode should yield to established patterns and a simplistic logic. Eventually, the Rs formed a pattern of classic and special market relationships, and mega and nano non-market relationships.

In Chapter 1, I mentioned a strong influence from inductive research, and especially from grounded theory as developed by Glaser and Strauss. It puts relentless demands on sensitivity, openness and an absence of preconceived notions. Finding categories and core variables is a continuous process of creatively comparing data and phenomena, letting categories and core variables emerge without forcing. In an inductive approach the data are sperms and eggs, and their interaction determines the birth of new life. The final outcome in a grounded theory study is a core category which contains the whole of a phenomenon. Here, the core category became RM, later assisted by CRM.

IN BRIEF

This book has come to an end, but it is meant to be a springboard for something better. I possess boxes of material which I have not yet been able to benefit from and which have not been given a fair chance in this text. Some of this material – if it stays in the archives for a year or two – will have lost its significance; changes are occurring rapidly. Better RM and CRM approaches will hopefully advance our understanding of marketing. Personal and scholarly reflections, and a constructive dialogue around RM, CRM and the 30Rs – and I consider reflection and dialogue the most viable scientific principles – are respectfully invited.

References

Aaker, David A. and Joachimsthaler, Erich, *Brand Leadership*. New York: The Free Press, 2000.

Ahrnell, Britt-Marie and Nicou, Monica, *Kunskapsföretagets marknadsföring*. Malmö: Liber, 2nd revised edition, 1995.

Albinsson-Bruhner, Göran, 'Den rationella välfärdsstatens kollaps'. *Svenska Dagbladet*, 4 September 1993.

Albrecht, Karl and Zemke, Ron, *Service America!* Homewood, IL: Dow Jones-Irwin, 1985.

Alderson, Wroe, *Dynamic Marketing Behavior*. Homewood, IL: Irwin, 1965.

American Marketing Association, 'Board Approves New Marketing Definition'. *Marketing News*, 1 March 1985.

Anderson, James C. and Narus, James A., 'Partnering as a Focused Market Strategy'. *California Management Review*, **33**, Spring 1991, pp. 95–113.

Andreassen, Tor Wallin, *Dissatisfaction with Services*. Stockholm: Stockholm University, 1997.

Arndt, Johan, 'Toward a Concept of Domesticated Markets'. *Journal of Marketing*, **43**, Fall, 1979, pp. 69–75.

Arndt, Johan, 'The Political Economy Paradigm: Foundation for Theory Building in Marketing'. *Journal of Marketing*, **47**, Fall 1983, pp. 44–54.

Axelsson, Björn and Easton, Geoffrey (eds.), *Industrial Networks*. London: Routledge, 1992.

Badaracco, Joseph L. Jr., *The Knowledge Link: How Firms Compete through Strategic Alliances*. Boston, MA: Harvard Business School Press, 1991.

Baker, Michael J., 'Evolution of the Marketing Concept'. In Baker, Michael J. (ed.), *Marketing: Theory and Practice*. London: Macmillan, 1976.

Baker, Michael J., 'Marketing – Philosophy or Function?' In Baker, Michael J. (ed.), *The IEBM Encyclopedia of Marketing*. London: Thomson, 1999a.

Baker, Michael J., 'The Future of Marketing'. In Baker, Michael J. (ed.), *The IEBM Encyclopedia of Marketing*. London: Thomson, 1999b.

Ballantyne, David, 'Marketing at the Crossroads'. Editorial, *Asia-Australia Marketing Journal*, **2**(1), August 1994, pp. 1–7.

Ballantyne, David, 'The Strengths and Weaknesses of Internal Marketing'. In Varey, Richard J. and Lewis, Barbara R. (eds.), *Internal Marketing*. London: Routledge, 2000.

Bannon, Lisa, 'Latin Outrage. A Milan Investigator Opens Pandora's Box of Italian Corruption'. *The Wall Street Journal Europe*, 12–13 June 1992, pp. 1 and 24.

Baumgartner, Jim, 'Nonmarketing Professionals Need More Than 4Ps'. *Marketing News*, 22 July 1991, p. 28.

Benndorf, Hans, *Marknadsföringsplanering och samordning mellan företag i industriella system*. Stockholm: MTC/EFI, 1987.

Berry, Leonard L., 'Relationship Marketing'. In Berry, L. L., Shostack, G. L. and Upah, G. D. (eds.), *Emerging Perspectives in Services Marketing*. Chicago: AMA, 1983.

Berry, Leonard L., 'The Service Quality Agenda for the 1990s'. *Distinguished Papers*, no. DP 89F-2. New York: St John's University, December 1989.

Berry, Leonard L., 'Relationship Marketing of Services – Growing Interest, Emerging Perspectives'. *Journal of the Academy of Marketing Science*, **23**(4), Fall 1995, pp. 236–45.

Berry, Leonard L. and Parasuraman, A., *Marketing Services*. New York: The Free Press, 1991.

Berry, Leonard L. and Parasuraman, A., 'Building a New Academic Field – The Case of Services Marketing'. *Journal of Retailing*, **69**(1), Spring 1993, pp. 13–60.

Bitner, Mary Jo, 'Evaluating Service Encounters: The Effects of Physical Surroundings and Employee Responses'. *Journal of Marketing*, April 1990, pp. 69–82.

Björkman, Ingmar and Kock, Sören, 'Social Relationships and Business Networks: The Case of Western Companies in China'. *International Business Review*, **4**(4), 1997, pp. 519–35.

Bliemel, Friedhelm W. and Eggert, Andreas, *Relationship Marketing under Fire*. Kaiserslauten, Germany: University of Kaiserslauten, Schriftenreihe Marketing, Heft 4/97, 1997.

Blois, Keith, 'Relationship Marketing in Organizational Markets: When is it Appropriate?' *Journal of Marketing Management*, **12**, 1996, pp. 161–73.

Blomqvist, Ralf, Dahl, Johan and Haeger, Tomas, *Relationsmarknadsföring: strategi och metod i servicekonkurrens*. Gothenburg: IHM, 1993.

Blumberg, Paul, *The Predatory Society*. New York: Oxford University Press, 1989.

Boissevain, Jeremy, *Friends of Friends*. Oxford: Basil Blackwell, 1976.

Booms, Bernhard H. and Bitner, Mary Jo, 'Marketing Strategies and Organization Structures for Service Firms'. In Donnelly, James and George, William R. (eds.), *Marketing of Services*. Chicago: American Marketing Association, 1982.

Bradford, Hugh, 'A New Framework for Museum Marketing'. In Kavanagh, Gaynor (ed.), *The Museums Profession: Internal and External Relations*. Leicester, UK: Leicester University Press, 1991.

Brandenburger, Adam M. and Nalebuff, Barry J., *Co-opetition*. Boston, MA: Harvard Business School Press, 1996.

Brandes, Ove and Brege, Staffan, *Marknadsledarskap*. Malmö: Liber, 1990.

Brodie, Roderick J., Coviello, Nicole E., Brookes, Richard W. and Little, Victoria, 'Towards a Paradigm Shift in Marketing? An Examination of Current Marketing Practices'. *Journal of Marketing Management*, **13**, 1997, pp. 383–406.

Brown, Stephen, *Postmodern Marketing*. London: Routledge, 1995.

Brown, Stephen, *Postmodern Marketing Two*. London: Thomson, 1998.

Brown, Stephen, 'The Three Rs of Relationship Marketing: Retroactive, Retrospective, Retrogressive'. In Hennig-Thurau, Thorsten and Hansen, Ursula (eds.), *Relationship Marketing*. Berlin: Springer-Verlag, 2000, pp. 393–413.

Brownlie, Douglas and Saren, Michael, 'The Four Ps of the Marketing Concept: Prescriptive, Polemical, Permanent and Problematical'. *European Journal of Marketing*, **26**(4), 1992, pp. 34–47.

Buck-Lew, M. and Edvinsson, L., *Intellectual Capital at Skandia*. Stockholm: Skandia, 1993.

Bunnell, David and Luecke, Richard A., *The eBay Phenomenon*. New York: Wiley, 2000.

Buttle, Francis (ed.), *Relationship Marketing: Theory and Practice*. London: Paul Chapman, 1996.

Calonius, Henrik, *The Promise Concept*. Helsinki: Swedish School of Economics and Business Administration, 1987.

Cang, Stephen, 'Organisational Change and the Doctor–Patient Relationship as the Model for Client–Consultant Relationships'. Paper presented at *The Seminar on Client–Consultant Relationships*. Groningen: University of Groningen, The Netherlands, November 1976.

Carlell, Camilla, *Technology in Everyday Life*. Stockholm: Stockholm University, 2001.

Carlsson, Rolf H., *Ägarstyrning*. Stockholm: Ekerlids Förlag, 1997.

Carlsson, Matts and Lundqvist, Mats, *Work with and Implementation of New Concepts for Management of Product Development – Some Emperical Findings*. Gothenburg: Chalmers, 1992.

Carlzon, Jan, *Moments of Truth*. Cambridge, MA: Ballinger, 1987.

Carnegie, Dale, *How to Win Friends and Influence People*. Sydney: HarperBusiness, 2000 (1936).

Castells, Manuel, *The Rise of the Network Society*. Oxford: Blackwell, 1996.

Christopher, Martin, Payne, Adrian and Ballantyne, David, *Relationship Marketing*. Oxford: Butterworth-Heinemann, 1991.

Cialdini, Robert B., *Influence*. New York: Quill, 1984.

Clark, Margaret S., 'Reactions to Aid in Communal and Exchange Relationships'. In *New Directions in Helping*. New York: Academic Press, 1983, Vol. 1, Chapter 11, pp. 281–304.

Coase, Ronald H., 'The Nature of the Firm'. *Economica*, 1937, pp. 387–405.

Coase, Ronald H., 'The Institutional Structure of Production'. Stockholm: The Nobel Foundation, *Prize Lecture in Economic Science in Memory of Alfred Nobel*, 9 December 1991.

Cooper, Robin and Kaplan, Robert S., 'Profit Priorities from Activity-Based Costing'. *Harvard Business Review*, May–June 1991, pp. 130–5.

Cova, Bernard, 'Relationship Marketing: A View from the South'. In Meenaghan, Tony (ed.), *New and Evolving Paradigms: The Emerging Future of Marketing, Conference Proceedings*. Chicago, IL: American Marketing Association and University College Dublin, 1997, pp. 657–72.

Cowles, Deborah L., 'Relationship Marketing for Transaction Marketing Firms: Viable Strategy via Command Performance'. In Sheth, Jagdish N. and Parvatiyar, Atul (eds.), *Relationship Marketing: Theory, Methods and Applications. 1994 Research Conference Proceedings*. Atlanta, GA: Center for Relationship Marketing, Emory University, 1994.

Cram, Tony, *The Power of Relationship Marketing*. London: Pitman, 1994.

Crosby, Lawrence, Evans, Kenneth and Cowles, Deborah, 'Relationship Quality in Services Selling: An Interpersonal Influence Perspective.' *Journal of Marketing*, **54**, July 1990, pp. 68–81.

Crosby, Philip, *Quality Is Free*. New York: McGraw-Hill, 1984.

Cutlip, S. M., Center, A. H. and Broom, G. M., *Effective Public Relations*. Englewood Cliffs, NJ: Prentice-Hall, 1985.

Czepiel, John A., 'Managing Relationships with Customers: A Differentiating Philosophy of Marketing'. In Bowen, D., Chase, R. and Cummings, T. (eds.), *Service Management Effectiveness*. San Francisco: Jossey-Bass, 1990, pp. 299–323.

Darby, M. R. and Karni, E., 'Free Competition and the Optimal Amount of Fraud'. *Journal of Law and Economics*, April 1973, pp. 67–86.

D'Aveni, Richard A., *Hypercompetition*. New York: The Free Press, 1994.

Davenport, Thomas H., *Information Ecology: Mastering the Information and Knowledge Environment*. New York: Oxford University Press, 1997.

Davidow, William H. and Malone, Michael S., *The Virtual Corporation*. New York: Edward Burlingame Books/HarperBusiness, 1992.

Davis, Stanley M., *Future Perfect*. Reading, MA: Addison-Wesley, 1987.

DeBono, Edward, *Sur/Petition: Going Beyond Monopolies*. London: Fontana, 1992.

Degan, James M., 'Warehouse clubs move from revolution to evolution'. *Marketing News*, 3 August 1992, p. 8.

Delaryd, Bengt, *I Japan är kunden kung*. Stockholm: Svenska Dagbladet, 1989.

Deming, W. Edwards, *Out of the Crisis*. Cambridge, MA: MIT, 1986.

Donovan, Hedley, 'Managing Your Intellectuals'. *Fortune*, 23 October 1989, pp. 103–6.

Doyle, Peter, 'Value-based Marketing'. *Journal of Strategic Marketing*, **8**(4), December 2000, pp. 299–311.

Doz, Yves L. and Hamel, Gary, *Alliance Advantage*. Boston, MA: Harvard Business School Press, 1998.

Dreyfuss, Joel, 'Reinventing IBM'. *Fortune*, 14 August 1989, pp. 20–7.

Drucker, Peter F., *The Practice of Management*. New York: Harper & Row, 1954.

Drucker, Peter F., 'The Coming of the New Organization'. *Harvard Business Review*, January–February, 1988a, pp. 45–53.

Drucker, Peter F., 'Teaching the Work of Management'. *New Management Magazine*, **6**(2), Fall 1988b.

Drucker, Peter F., *The New Realities*. Oxford: Heinemann, 1989.

Drucker, Peter F., *Managing the Nonprofit Organization*. New York: HarperCollins, 1990.

Duncan, Tom and Moriarty, Sandra, *Driving Brand Value*. New York: McGraw-Hill, 1997.

Duncan, Tom and Moriarty, Sandra E., 'A Communication-Based Marketing Model for Managing Relationships'. *Journal of Marketing*, **62**, April 1998, pp. 1–13.

Dwyer, F. Robert, Shurr, Paul H. and Oh, Sejo, 'Developing Buyer and Seller Relationships'. *Journal of Marketing*, **51**, April 1987, pp. 11–27.

Easton, Geoff and Håkansson, Håkan, 'Markets as Networks: Editorial Introduction'. *International Journal of Research in Marketing*, **13**(5), 1996, pp. 407–13.

Echeverri, Per, *Servicemötets kommunikation*. Karlstad: Gothenburg and Karlstad Universities, 1999.

The Economist, 'BSN Who?' 14 May 1994, p. 7.

Edfeldt, Åke W., *Påverkan*. Stockholm: Proprius, 1992.

Edvardsson, Bo and Gustafsson, Anders (eds.), *The Nordic School of Quality Management*. Lund: Studentlitteratur, 1999.

Edvardsson, Bo, Gustafsson, Anders, Johnson, Michael D. and Sandén, Bodil, *New Service Development and Innovation in the New Economy*. Lund: Studentlitteratur, 2000.

Edvinsson, Leif and Malone, Michael S., *Intellectual Capital*. New York: Harper Collins, 1997.

Eggert, Andreas and Fassot, Georg, 'Begriffsabgrenzung und Anspruchspektrum des eCRM'. In Eggert, Andreas and Fassot, Georg (eds.), *eCRM: Electronic Customer Relationship Management*. Stuttgart: Schäffer-Poeschel Verlag, 2001.

Ehrlemark, Gunnar, *OTOM Paper*, 7 November 1978 (as quoted in *The ForeSight Entrepreneur*, no. 3, 1989).

Englund, Karl, *Försäkring och fusioner*. Stockholm: Skandia, 1982.

Entine, Jon, 'Let Them Eat Brazil Nuts'. *Dollar and Sense*, March–April 1996, pp. 30–5.

Eriksson, Ann-Kristin and Åsberg, Maria, *Kostnadseffekter av affärsrelationer*. Uppsala: Uppsala University, Department of Business Studies, 1994.

Fairness and Accuracy in Reporting (FAIR), 'Media Advisory: Initial Reports from Seattle Gloss Over WTO Issues'. 1 December 1999.

Falcone, Giovanni and Padovani, Marcelle, *Cosa Nostra: Domarens kamp mot maffian*. Stockholm: Forum, 1991.

Faltermayer, Edmund, 'Does Japan Play Fair?' *Fortune*, 7 September 1992, pp. 22–9.

Feurst, Ola, *Kost och hälsa i marknadsföringen*. Stockholm: Stockholm University, School of Business, 1991.

Fiorentini, Gianluca and Peltzman, Sam (eds.), *The Economics of Organized Crime*. Cambridge, UK: Cambridge University Press, 1995.

Firat, Fuat A, Dahlakia, N. and Venkatesh, Aladi, 'Marketing in a Post-Modern World'. *European Journal of Marketing*, **29**(1), 1995, pp. 40–56.

Fisk, Raymond P., Brown, Stephen W. and Bitner, Mary J., 'Tracking the Evolution of Services Marketing Literature'. *Journal of Retailing*, **69**(1), Spring 1993, pp. 61–103.

Fisk, Raymond, P., Grove, Stephen, J. and John, Joby (eds.), *Services Marketing Self-Portraits*. Chicago, IL: American Marketing Association, 2000.

Ford, David (ed.), *Understanding Business Markets: Interaction, Relationships and Networks*. London: Academic Press, 1990.

Ford, D., Håkansson, H. and Johansson, J., 'How Do Companies Interact?' *Industrial Marketing & Purchasing*, **1**(1), 1986.

Ford, David et al., *Managing Business Relationships*. Chichester, UK: Wiley, 1998.

Fornell, Claes, 'A National Customer Satisfaction Barometer: The Swedish Experience'. *Journal of Marketing*, **56**, January 1992, pp. 6–21.

Fornell, Claes and Wernerfelt, B., 'Model for Customer Complaint Management'. *Marketing Science*, no. 7, Summer 1988, pp. 271–86.

Fornell, Claes and Westbrook, R. A., 'The Vicious Circle of Consumer Complaints'. *Journal of Marketing*, no. 48, Summer 1984, pp. 68–78.

Forrester, Jay W., 'A New Corporate Design'. In Halal, William E., Geranmayeh, Ali and Pourdehead, John (eds.), *Internal Markets*. New York: Wiley, 1993.

Fournier, Susan, Dobscha, Susan and Mick, David Glen, 'Preventing the Mature Death of Relationship Marketing'. *Harvard Business Review*, January–February 1998.

Frankelius, Per, *Kirurgisk Marknadsföring*. Malmö: Liber, 1997.

Frenckner, Paulsson, 'ABC-kalkylen: vad behövs mer?' *Ekonomi & Styrning*, no. 2, 1993, pp. 26–9.

Frostling-Henningsson, Maria, *Dägligvaruhandel över nätet . . . vad innebär det?* Stockholm: Stockholm University, 2000.

Fukuyama, Francis, *Trust*. New York: The Free Press, 1995.

Gabbot, Mark, 'Relationship Marketing and IT'. Paper presented at *The 6th Colloquium of Relationship Marketing*. Auckland: University of Auckland, December 1998.

Gadde, Lars-Erik, 'Developments in Distribution Channels for Industrial Goods'. In Baker, Michael (ed.), *Perspectives on Marketing Management*. Chichester: Wiley, 1994, Vol. 4.

Gatarski, Richard, *Artificial Market Actors: Explorations of Automated Business Interactions*. Stockholm: Stockholm University, 2001.

Gatarski, Richard and Lundkvist, Anders, 'Interactive Media Face Artificial Consumers and Must Re-Think'. *Journal of Marketing Communications*, no. 4, 1998, pp. 45–59.

Gerlach, Michael L., *Alliance Capitalism: The Social Organization of Japanese Business*. Berkeley, CA: University of California Press, 1992.

Giarini, O. and Stahel W. R., *The Limits of Certainty*. Dordrecht: Kluwer, 1998.

Glaser, Barney G., *Basics of Grounded Theory Analysis*. Mill Valley, CA: Sociology Press, 1992.

Glaser, Barney G., *The Grounded Theory Perspective: Conceptualization Contrasted with Description*. Mill Valley, CA: Sociology Press, 2001.

Glaser, Barney G. and Strauss, Anselm L., *The Discovery of Grounded Theory – Strategies for Qualitative Research*. New York: Aldine, 1967.

Godin, Seth, *Permission Marketing*. New York: Simon & Schuster, 1999.

Goldman, Heinz, *Att vinna kunder*. Stockholm: Svenska Dagbladet, 1994 (original title: *How to Win Customers*, 1958).

Goleman, Daniel, *Emotional Intelligence*. New York: Bantam Books, 1995.

Goodwin, Cathy, 'Private Roles in Public Encounter: Communal Relationships in Service Exchanges'. In *Proceedings from the 3rd International Research Seminar in Service Management*. Aix-en-Provence: Institut d'Administration des Entreprises, Université d'Aix-Marseille, May 1994, pp. 312–32.

Granovetter, Mark, 'The Strength of Weak Ties. A Network Theory Revisited.' *American Journal of Sociology*, **78**(3), 1973, pp. 3–30.

Granovetter, Mark, 'Economic Action and Social Structure. The Problem of Embeddedness'. *American Journal of Sociology*, **91**(3), 1985, pp. 481–510.

Gray, Barbara, *Collaborating*. San Francisco, CA: Jossey-Bass, 1989.

Grönroos, Christian, 'Facing the Challenge of Service Competition: The Economies of Service'. In Kunst, Paul and Lemmik, Jos (eds.), *Quality Management in Services*. Assen/Maastricht: Van Gorcum, 1992.

Grönroos, Christian, 'Quo Vadis, Marketing? Toward a Relationship Marketing Paradigm'. *Journal of Marketing Management*, **10**, 1994, pp. 347–60.

Grönroos, Christian, 'Relationship Marketing Logic'. *Asia-Australia Marketing Journal*, **4**, 1996.

Grönroos, Christian, 'From Marketing Mix to Relationship Marketing: Towards a Paradigm Shift in Marketing'. *Management Decision*, **35**(4), 1997, pp. 322–39.

Grönroos, Christian, *Service Management and Marketing*. Chichester, UK: Wiley, 2000.

Grönroos, Christian and Gummesson, Evert (eds.), *Service Marketing – Nordic School Perspectives*. Stockholm: Stockholm University, School of Business, Research Report R, 1985:2.

Gronstedt, Anders, *The Customer Century*. New York: Routledge, 2000.

Gruen, Thomas W. and Ferguson, Jeffery M., 'Using Memberships as a Marketing Tool: Issues and Applications'. In Sheth, Jagdish N. and Parvatiyar, Atul (eds.), *Relationship Marketing: Theory, Methods and Applications, Proceedings from the Second Research Conference on Relationship Marketing*. Atlanta, GA: Center for Relationship Marketing, Emory University, June 1994.

The Guardian, 'Feeding Mammon – World Trade Organization: Special Report'. 30 November 1999.

Gummesson, Evert, *Marknadsföring och inköp av konsulttjänster*. Stockholm: Akademilitteratur/ MTC/University of Stockholm, 1977.

Gummesson, Evert, 'A New Concept of Marketing'. *Proceedings from the European Marketing Academy (EMAC) Annual Conference*, Institut d'Etudes Commerciales de Grenoble, France, April 1983.

Gummesson, Evert, *Marketing of Public Telecommunications*. Stockholm: Ericsson, 1984.

Gummesson, Evert, 'Using Internal Marketing to Develop a New Corporate Culture: The Case of Ericsson Quality'. In Congram, Carole A., Czepiel, Johan A. and Shanahan, James B. (eds.), *Services Marketing: Integrating the Competitive Advantage*. Chicago, IL: American Marketing Association, 1987a; also in *Journal of Business and Industrial Marketing*, no. 2, Fall 1987a.

Gummesson, Evert, *Quality – The Ericsson Approach*. Stockholm: Ericsson, 1987b.

Gummesson, Evert, 'The New Marketing: Developing Long-term Interactive Relationships'. *Long Range Planning*, **20**(4), 1987c, pp. 10–20.

Gummesson, Evert, 'Service Quality: A Holistic View'. In Brown, S. W., Gummesson, E., Edvardsson, B. and Gustavsson, B. (eds.), *Service Quality*. Lexington, MA: Lexington Books, 1991, pp. 3–22.

Gummesson, Evert, 'Quality Dimensions: What to Measure in Service Organizations'. In Swartz, Teresa A., Bowen, David E. and Brown, Stephen W. (eds.), *Advances in Services Marketing and Management*. Greenwich, CT: JAI Press, 1992.

Gummesson, Evert, *Quality Management in Service Organizations*. New York: ISQA, 1993.

Gummesson, Evert, 'Making Relationship Marketing Operational'. *Service Industry Management*, **5**(5), 1994, pp. 5–20.

Gummesson, Evert, 'Productivity, Quality and Relationship Marketing in Service Operations'. *International Journal of Contemporary Hospitality Management*, **10**(1), 1998a, pp. 4–15.

Gummesson, E., 'Implementation Requires a Relationship Marketing Paradigm'. *Journal of the Academy of Marketing Science*, **26**(3), July 1998b, pp. 242–9.

Gummesson, Evert, *Qualitative Methods in Management Research*. Newbury Park: Sage, revised edition, 2000.

Gummesson, Evert, 'eCRM and hCRM: Martial Rivalry or Marital Bliss'. In Eggert, Andreas and Fassot, Georg (eds.), *eCRM: Electronic Customer Relationship Management*. Stuttgart: Schäffer-Poeschel, 2001a.

Gummesson, Evert, 'Are Research Approaches in Marketing Leading Us Astray?' *Marketing Theory*, **1**(1), September 2001b.

Gummesson, Evert, 'Practical Value of Adequate Marketing Management Theory'. *European Journal of Marketing*, **36**(3), 2002.

Gummesson, Evert, Lehtinen, Uolevi and Grönroos, Christian, 'Comment on Nordic Perspectives on Relationship Marketing'. *European Journal of Marketing*, **31**(1–2), 1997, pp. 10–16.

Gumpert, David E., 'Big Company, Small Company: The New American Partnership'. *Forbes*, 20 July 1992, pp. 225–40.

Gustavsson, Bengt, *The Transcendent Organization*. Stockholm: Stockholm University, 1992.

Gustavsson, Bengt, 'Towards a Transcendent Epistemology of Organizations'. *Journal of Organizational Change Management*, **13**(4), 2001.

Hadenius, Stig and Weibull, Lennart, *Massmedier*. Stockholm: Bonnier Alba, 1993.

Håkansson, Håkan and Snehota, Ivan, *Marknadsplanering – Ett sätt att skapa nya problem?* Lund, Sweden: Studentlitteratur, 1976.

Håkansson, Håkan and Snehota, Ivan, *Developing Relationships in Business Marketing*. London: Routledge, 1995.

Halal, William E., Geranmayeh, Ali and Pourdehead, John (eds.), *Internal Markets*. New York: Wiley, 1993.

Halinen, Aino, *Relationship Marketing in Professional Services*. London: Routledge, 1997.

Hallén, Lars and Widersheim-Paul, Finn, 'Psychic Distance and Buyer–Seller Interaction'. *Organisation, Marked og Samfunn*, **16**(5), 1979, pp. 308–24.

Hallén, Lars, Johanson, Jan and Seyed-Mohamed, Naseem, 'Dyadic Business Relationships and Customer Technologies'. *Journal of Business-to-Business Marketing*, **1**(4), 1993, pp. 63–90.

Hallgren, Mats, 'Spelet kring en order'. *Veckans Affärer*, no. 20, 14 May 1987.

Hallowell, Edward M., 'The Human Moment at Work'. *Harvard Business Review*, January–February 1999.

Hamel, Gary and Prahalad, C. K., *Competing for the Future*. Boston, MA: Harvard Business School Press, 1994.

Hammer, Michael and Champy, James, *Reengineering the Corporation*. New York: HarperBusiness, 1993.

Handy, Charles, *The Age of Unreason*. Boston, MA: Harvard Business School Press, 1990.

Harper, Ross, 'Hunt for the Holy Grail of Dispute Mediation'. *Scottish Gazette*, 20 October 1993, p. 10.

Harrington, James H., *Business Process Improvement*. New York: McGraw-Hill, 1991.

Hart, Christopher W. L. and Bogan, Christopher E., *The Baldrige*. New York: McGraw-Hill, 1992.

Hartley, Robert F., *Marketing Successes*. New York: Wiley, 1985.

Harung, Harald S., 'A World-Leading, Learning Organization: A Case Study of Tomra Systems'. *The Learning Organization*, **3**(4), 1996, pp. 22–34.

Harung, Harald S., *Invincible Leadership: Building Peak Perfomance Organizations by Harnessing the Unlimited Power of Consciousness*. Fairfield, IA: MUM Press, 1999.

Hauser, J. R. and Clausing, D., 'The House of Quality'. *Harvard Business Review*, no. 3, May–June 1988.

Hawkins, Leonard S., *How to Succeed in Network Marketing*. London: Piatkus, 1991.

Hedberg, B., Dahlgren, G., Hansson, J. and Olve, N.-G., *Virtual Organizations and Beyond: Discover Imaginary Systems*. London: Wiley, 1997.

Heidenry, John, *Theirs Was the Kingdom*. New York: W. W. Norton, 1993.

Hemmungs Wirtén, Eva, 'Mannen som var en kamera'. *Tur & Retur*, no. 3, 1992, pp. 42–7.

Hennig-Thurau, Thorsten and Hansen, Ursula (eds.), *Relationship Marketing*. Berlin: Springer, 2000.

Hertz, Noreena, *The Silent Takeover*. London: William Heinemann, 2001.

Heskett, James L., Sasser, W. Earl and Hart, Christopher W. L., *Service Breakthroughs*. New York: The Free Press, 1990.

Heskett, James L., Sasser, W. Earl Jr. and Schlesinger, Leonard A., *The Service Profit Chain*. New York: The Free Press, 1997.

Hessling, Torbjörn, *Att spara eller inte spara – vilken fråga!* Stockholm: Sparfrämjandet, 1990.

Hirschman, Albert O., *Exit, Voice and Loyalty*. Cambridge, MA: Harvard University Press, 1970.

Holmlund, Maria, *Perceived Quality in Business Relationships*. Helsinki: Swedish School of Economics and Business Administration, 1997.

Howard, Philip, *The Death of Common Sense: How Law is Suffocating America*. New York: Random House, 1994.

Hult, E.-B., Liljeberg, U., Lundström, A. and Ramström, Dick, *Soloföretag*. Örebro: Forum för småföretagsforskning, 2000.

Hultbom, Christina, *Intern handel: köpar/säljarrelationer inom stora företag*. Uppsala: Uppsala University, Department of Business, 1990.

Hunt, Shelby D. *A General Theory of Competition: Resources, Competencies, Productivity, Economic Growth*. Thousand Oaks, CA: Sage, 2000.

Hunt, Shelby D. and Morgan, Robert M., 'The Comparative Advantage Theory of Competition'. *Journal of Marketing*, **59**, April 1995, pp. 1–15.

Iacobucci, Dawn (ed.), *Networks in Marketing*. Thousand Oaks, CA: Sage, 1996.

Iacocca, Lee (with Novak, W.), *Iacocca*. USA: Bantam Books, 1984.

Info, 'Hon har kameran i fokus', 1996, p. 53.

International Management, Advertisement for Siemens. July–August 1993, pp. 20–1.

International Management, 'Black market turns importer to Iran for caviar'. June 1994, pp. 12–13.

Jackson, Barbara Bund, *Winning and Keeping Industrial Customers*. Lexington, MA: Lexington Books, 1985a.

Jackson, Barbara Bund, 'Build Customer Relationships That Last'. *Harvard Business Review*, November–December 1985b, pp. 120–8.

Jaques, Elliott, 'In Praise of Hierarchy'. *Harvard Business Review*, no. 1, January–February 1990.

Johansen, Jon Ivar, *Kunden som kapital*. Oslo: InfoNet Scandinavia, 1996.

Johansen, Jon Ivar and Monthelie, Caroline, *Lojalitetsredovisning*. Gothenburg: InfoNet Scandinavia, 1996.

Johanson, Jan, 'Marknadsnätverkens uppväxtår och framtid'. *MTC-Kontakten*, 1994.

Johanson, Jan and Mattsson, Lars-Gunnar, 'Interorganizational Relations in Industrial Systems: A Network Approach Compared with the Transaction Cost Approach'. *International Studies of Management and Organization*, **XVII**(1), Spring 1987, pp. 34–48.

Johnson, Anders, *Hierarkiernas harakiri – leve nätverken!* Stockholm: Ekerlids Förlag, 1995.

Johnson, Michael D. and Gustafsson, Anders, *Improving Customer Satisfaction, Loyalty, and Profit*. San Francisco, CA: Jossey-Bass, 2000.

Johnson, Thomas H., *Relevance Regained*. New York: The Free Press, 1992.

Johnson, Thomas H. and Kaplan, Robert S., *Relevance Lost: The Rise and Fall of Management Acounting*. Boston, MA: Harvard Business School Press, 1987.

Johnsson, Thomas and Hägg, Ingemund, 'Extrapreneurs – Between Markets and Hierarchies'. *International Studies of Management and Organisation*, **XVII**(1), 1987, pp. 64–74.

Jones Yang, Dori and Warner, Joan, 'Hear the Muzak, Buy the Ketchup'. *Business Week*, 28 June 1993, pp. 40–2.

Judd, V. C., 'Differentiate with the 5th P: People'. *Industrial Marketing Management*, November 1987.

Juran, J. M., *Juran on Quality by Design*. New York: The Free Press, 1992.

Kahn, Sikander and Yoshihara, Hideki, *Strategy and Performance of Foreign Companies in Japan*. Westport, CT: Quorom Books, 1994.

Kaikati, Jack G., quoted in *Strategic Direction*, December 1993, pp. 20–2.

Kalakota, Ravi and Robinson, Marcia, *e-Business*. Reading, MA: Addison-Wesley, 1999.

Kanfer, Stefan, *The Last Empire: De Beers, Diamonds of the World*. New York: Farrar Straus Giroux, 1996.

Kanter, Rosabeth Moss, *When Giants Learn to Dance*. New York: Simon & Schuster, 1989.

Kapferer, J. N., *Strategic Brand Management*. London: Kogan Page, 1996.

Kaplan, Robert S. and Norton, David P., *The Balanced Scorecard*. Boston, MA: Harvard Business School Press, 1996.

Karaszi, Peter, *Använd pressen*. Stockholm: PK FinInformation, 1991.

Karpesjö, Anders, *Miljöprofilering*. Malmö: Liber Ekonomi, 1992.

Kingman-Brundage, Jane, George, William R. and Bowen, David E., 'Service Logic: Achieving Service System Integration'. *International Journal of Service Industry Management*, 6(4), 1995, pp. 20–39.

Kirkpatrick, David, 'Breaking up IBM'. *Fortune*, 27 July 1992, p. 120.

Klein, Naomi, *No Logo*. London: Flamingo, 2000.

Kotkin, Joel, *Tribes*. New York: Random House, 1993.

Kotler, Philip, 'Megamarketing'. *Harvard Business Review*, March–April 1986, pp. 117–24.

Kotler, Philip, 'Total Marketing'. *Business Week Advance*, Executive Brief, 2, 1992.

Kotler, Philip, *Marketing Management*. Englewood Cliffs, NJ: Prentice-Hall, 9th edition, 1997.

Kotler, Philip and Andreasen, Alan R., *Strategic Marketing for Non-Profit Institutions*. Englewood Cliffs, NJ: Prentice-Hall, 1991.

Kotler, Philip, Gregor, William and Rodgers, William, 'The Marketing Audit Comes of Age'. *Sloan Management Review*, Winter 1989, pp. 49–62.

Lappalainen, Tomas, *Maffian*. Stockholm: Forum, 1993.

Laurelli, Rolf, *TOTAL-säljaren*. Lund: Studentlitteratur, 1979.

Lehtinen, Jarmo R., 'Improving Service Quality by Analysing the Service Production Process'. In Grönroos, C. and Gummesson, E. (eds.), *Service Marketing – Nordic School Perspectives*. Stockholm: Stockholm University, School of Business, Research Report R 1985:2, pp. 110–19.

Lehtinen, Uolevi, Hankimaa, Anna and Mittilä, Tuula, 'On Measuring the Intensity in Relationship Marketing'. In Sheth, J. N. and Parvatiyar, A. (eds.), *Relationship Marketing: Theory, Methods and Applications*, 1994 Research Conference Proceedings. Atlanta, GA: Center for Relationship Marketing, Emory University, 1994.

Lennstrand, Bo, 'Diffusion of Information and Communication Technology to Households: How Come it Goes so Slowly when it Goes Fast'. Paper presented at the *Twelfth Biennial ITS Conference*, Stockholm, 1998. Also in Lennstrand, Bo, *Hype IT*. Stockholm: Stockholm University, 2001.

Lester, Tom, 'The Rise of the Network'. *International Management*, June 1992, pp. 72–3.

Levitt, Theodore, *The Marketing Imagination*. New York: The Free Press, 1983.

Liljander, Veronika and Strandvik, Tore, 'The Nature of Customer Relationships in Services'. In Swartz, Teresa A., Bowen, David E. and Brown, Stephen W. (eds.), *Advances in Services Marketing and Management*. Greenwich, CT: JAI Press, 1995, Vol. 4.

Liljegren, Göran, *Interdependens och dynamik i långsiktiga relationer*. Stockholm: MTC/EFI, 1988.

Lilley, Peter, *Dirty Dealing: The Untold Truth About Dirty Money Laundering*. London: Kogan Page, 2000.

Linn, Carl Eric, *Metaprodukten och marknaden*. Malmö: Liber, 1985.

Lorange, Peter and Roos, Johan, *Strategic Alliances*. Oxford, UK: Blackwell, 1992.

Lovelock, Christopher H., 'Classifying Services to Gain Strategic Advantage'. *Journal of Marketing*, **47**, Summer 1983, pp. 9–20.

Lovelock, Christopher H., Patterson, Paul G. and Walker, Rhett H., *Services Marketing: Australia and New Zealand*. Sydney: Prentice-Hall, 1998.

Lovelock, Christopher, Vandermerwe, Sandra and Lewis, Barbara, *Services Marketing: A European Perspective*. London: Prentice-Hall Europe, 1999.

Lowe, Andy, 'Small Hotel Survival: An Inductive Approach'. *The International Journal of Hospitality Management*, **7**(3), 1988, pp. 197–223.

Lowe, Andy, 'Managing the Post-merger Aftermath by Default Remodelling'. *Management Decision*, **36**(3), 1998, pp. 102–10.

Lu, David J., 'Translator's Introduction'. In Ishikawa, K. (ed.), *What Is Total Quality Control? The Japanese Way*. Englewood Cliffs, NJ: Prentice-Hall, 1985.

Lunn, Terry, 'Customer Service: The Joshua Tetley Experience'. Dublin: *Third National Conference of the NSAI*, 1990.

Macneil, I. R., 'Relational Contract: What We Do and Do Not Know'. *Northwestern University Law Review*, **78**, 1983, pp. 340–418.

Macneil, I. R., 'Values in Contract'. *Winsconsin Law Review*, 1985, pp. 483–525.

Malcolm Baldrige National Quality Award, *1997 Criteria for Performance Excellence*. Gaithersburg, MD: United States Department of Commerce, 1997.

Mårtensson, Rita, *Marknadskommunikation*. Lund, Sweden: Studentlitteratur, 1984.

Martin, Michael H., 'Why the Web is Still a No-Shop Zone'. *Fortune*, 5 February 1996, pp. 67–8.

Mattsson, Jan and den Haring, Maarten J., 'Communication Dynamics in Therapy: A Linguistic Study from a Nursing Home for Elderly'. *International Journal of Social Welfare*, no. 8, 1999, pp. 120–30.

Mattsson, Lars-Gunnar, 'Relationship Marketing and the Markets-as-Networks Approach'. *Journal of Marketing Management*, **13**(5), July 1997, pp. 447–62.

Mattsson, Lars-Gunnar and Lundgren, Anders, 'En paradox? – konkurrens i industriella nätverk'. *MTC-kontakten*, no. 22, 1992–93, pp. 8–9.

McCarthy, Jerome E., *Basic Marketing: A Managerial Approach*. Homewood, IL: Richard D. Irwin, 1994 (1960).

McDonald, Malcolm, *Marketing Plans*. Oxford, UK: Butterworth-Heinemann, 1995.

McDonald, Malcolm, Millman, Tony and Rogers, Beth, 'Key Account Management: Theory, Practice and Challenges'. *Journal of Marketing Management*, no. 13, 1997, pp. 737–57.

McKenna, Regis, *The Regis Touch*. USA: Addison-Wesley, 1985.

McKinsey, *A Career with McKinsey & Company*, 1991.

Michels, Antony J., 'Customers Drive Company Tie-Ups'. *Fortune*, 27 January 1992, p. 8.

Mills, D. Q., *Rebirth of the Corporation*. New York: Wiley, 1991.

Mittilä, Tuula, *Relation Trine*. Tampere, Finland: University of Tampere, 2000.

Möller, Kristian and Halinen, Aino, 'Relationship Marketing Theory: Its Roots and Direction'. *Journal of Marketing Management*, **16**(1–3), 2000, pp. 29–54.

Möller, Kristian and Wilson, David (eds.), *Business Marketing: Interaction and Network Approach*. Boston, MA: Kluwer, 1996.

Moore, James F., *The Death of Competition*. Chichester, UK: Wiley, 1996.

Morgan, Gareth, *Images of Organization*. Newbury Park: Sage, revised edition, 1997.

Morgan, Marlo, *Budskap från andra sidan*. Stockholm: Strömbergs, 1994.

Morgan, R. M. and Hunt, Shelby D., 'The Commitment-Trust Theory of Relationship Marketing'. *Journal of Marketing*, no. 58, July 1994, pp. 20–38.

MSI, Marketing Science Institute, *Conference Announcement on B2B e-Commerce*. Cambridge, MA, 2001.

Nader, Ralph, *Unsafe at Any Speed*. New York: Grossman, 1965.

Naisbitt, John, *Megatrends*. New York: Warner Books, 1982.

Naisbitt, John, *Global Paradox*. New York: William Morrow, 1994.

Naisbitt, John, *High Tech/High Touch*. London: Nicholas Brealey, 1999.

Naisbitt, John and Aburdene, Patricia, *Megatrends 2000*. New York: William Morrow, 1990.

Nakane, Chie, *Japanese Society*. New York: Penguin, 1981.

Nelson, Philip, 'Advertising as Information'. *Journal of Political Economy*, July–August 1970, pp. 729–54.

Neuhauser, Peg C., *Tribal Warfare in Organizations*. Cambridge, MA: Ballinger, 1988.

Newell, Frederick, *loyalty.com*. New York: McGraw-Hill, 2000.

Newsweek, 'The Black Economy'. 30 June 1986, pp. 20–6.

Newsweek, 'The Kissinger Clique'. 27 March 1990, pp. 34–5.

Newsweek, 'Eyes on the Future'. 31 May 1993, p. 35ff.

Nilson, Torsten H., *Värdeladdad marknadsföring*. Malmö: Liber-Hermods, 1993.

Nilsson, John Peter, 'Disney à go-go'. *Nobis Nyheter*, no. 3, 1993, pp. 25–8, 40.

Nocera, Joseph, 'Fatal Litigation'. *Fortune*, 16 October 1995, pp. 40–57.

Nonaka, Ikujiro and Takeuchi, Hirotaka, *The Knowledge-Creating Company*. New York: Oxford University Press, 1995.

Norberg, Johan, *Till världskapitalismens försvar*. Stockholm: Timbro, 2001.

Norman, Donald A., *The Psychology of Everyday Things*. New York: Basic Books, 1988.

Normann, Richard and Ramírez, Rafael, 'From Value Chain to Value Constellation'. *Harvard Business Review*, July–August 1993, pp. 65–77.

North, Douglass C., 'Economic Performance Through Time'. Stockholm: The Nobel Foundation, *Prize Lecture in Economic Science in Memory of Alfred Nobel*, Stockholm, 9 December 1993.

Ohlson, Johan, 'Interview with Ove Sjögren'. *Upp&Ner*, no. 6, 1994, pp. 6–9.

Ohmae, Kenichi, *Triad Power – The Coming Shape of Global Competition*. New York: The Free Press, 1985.

Ohmae, Kenichi, *The End of the Nation State*. New York: The Free Press, 1995.

Olsen, Morten, *Kvalitet i banktjänster*. Stockholm: Stockholm University/CTF, 1992.

Olve, Nils-Göran, Roy, Jan and Wetter, Magnus, *Balanced Scorecard i svensk praktik*. Malmö: Liber, 1999.

Ortmark, Åke, *Ja-sägarna*. Stockholm: Wahlström & Widstrand, 2000.

Ottman, Jacquelyn A., *Green Marketing*. Lincolnwood, IL: NTC Business Books, 1992.

Palmer, Adrian and Bejou, David, 'The Effects on Gender on the Development of Relationships between Clients and Financial Advisers'. *Bank Marketing*, **13**(3), 1995.

Parlour, Richard, 'Europe's Fight Against Dirty Money'. *European Business Report*, 3rd Quarter, 1993, pp. 63–6.

Patton, Michael Quinn, *Qualitative Evaluation and Research Methods*. Newbury Park, CA: Sage, 1990.

Paulin, Michèle, Perrien, Jean and Ferguson, Ronald, 'Relational Contract Norms and the Effectiveness of Commercial Banking Relationships'. *Service Industry Management*, **8**(5), 1997, pp. 435–52.

Paulsen, Mats, 'Statoil rustar mot maffian'. *Dagens Industri*, 3 November 1994, p. 15.

Payne, Adrian, *The Essence of Services Marketing*. London: Prentice-Hall, 1993.

Payne, Adrian and Rickard, John, *Relationship Marketing, Customer Retention and Service Firm Profitability*. Cranfield: Cranfield School of Management, 1994.

Payne, Adrian, Christopher, Martin, Clark, Moira and Peck, Helen, *Relationship Marketing for Competitive Advantage*. Oxford: Butterworth-Heinemann, 1995.

Peck, Helen, Payne, Adrian, Christopher, Martin and Clark, Moira, *Relationship Marketing: Strategy and Implementation*. Oxford: Butterworth-Heinemann, 1999.

Pelton, Lou E., Strutton, David and Lumpkin, James R., *Marketing Channels: A Relationship Management Approach*. Chicago, IL: Irwin, 1997.

Peppers, Don and Rogers, Martha, *The One to One Future*. New York: Currency/Doubleday, 1993.

Peppers, Don and Rogers, Martha, *The One to One Manager*. New York: Currency/Doubleday, 1999.

Peppers, Don, Rogers, Martha and Dorf, Bob, *The One to One Fieldbook*. New York: Currency/Doubleday, 1998.

Peters, Tom, *Thriving on Chaos*. New York: Macmillan, 1985.

Peters, Tom, *Liberation Management*. New York: Alfred A. Knopf, 1992.

Peters, Tom and Waterman, Robert J. Jr., *In Search of Excellence*. New York: Harper & Row, 1982.

Pirsig, Robert M., *Lila: An Inquiry Into Morals*. London: Corgi Books, 1992.

Polanyi, Michael, *Personal Knowledge*. London: Routledge & Kegan Paul, 1962.

Popcorn, Faith, *The Popcorn Report*. London: Century Business, 1992.

Pope, N. W., 'Mickey Mouse Marketing'. *American Banker*, 25 July 1979a.

Pope, N. W., 'More Mickey Mouse Marketing'. *American Banker*, 12 September 1979b.

Porter, Clive, quoted in *The Marketing Strategy Letter*, May 1993, p. 14.

Porter, Michael E., *Competitive Strategy*. New York: The Free Press, 1980.

Porter, Michael E., *Competitive Advantage*. New York: The Free Press, 1985.

Porter, Michael E., *The Competitive Advantage of Nations*. New York: Macmillan, 1990.

Postman, Neil, *Amusing Ourselves to Death*. New York: Penguin Books, 1987.

Price, Linda, Arnould, Eric and Tierney, P., 'The Wilderness Servicescape'. In *Proceedings of the 4th International Research Seminar in Service Management*. La Londe, France: Université Aix-Marseille, 1996.

PricewaterhouseCoopers, *The CRM Handbook*. Hellerup, Denmark, 1999.

Prigogene, Ilya and Stengers, Isabelle, *Order out of Chaos*. London: Fontana/Flamingo, 1985.

Quinn, Bill, *How Wal-Mart Is Destroying America (and the World)*. Berkeley, CA: The Speed Press, 2000 (revised edition).

Quinn, Feargal, *Crowning the Customer*. Dublin: O'Brien Press, 1990.

Quinn, Feargal, 'The Boomerang Principle'. *European Business Report*, Spring 1994, pp. 36–9.

Quinn, James Brian, *The Intelligent Enterprise*. New York: The Free Press, 1992.

Ramsey, Richard David, '"It's Absurd": Swedish Managers' Views of America's Litigious Society'. *Scandinavian Journal of Management*, 6(1), 1991, pp. 31–44.

Rapp, Stan and Collins, Tom, *The Great Marketing Turnaround*. Englewood Cliffs, NJ: Prentice-Hall, 1990.

Rapp, Stan and Collins, Tom, *The New MaxiMarketing*. New York: McGraw-Hill, 1995.

Reichheld, Frederick F., *The Loyalty Effect*. Boston, MA: Harvard Business School Press, 1996.

Reichheld, Frederick F. and Sasser, W. E. Jr., 'Zero Defections: Quality Comes to Services'. *Harvard Business Review*, September–October 1990.

Rein, Irving J., Kotler, Philip and Stoller, Martin, R., *High Visibility*. London: Heinemann, 1987.

Reynoso, Javier F. and Moores, Brian, 'Internal Relationships'. In Buttle, Francis (ed.), *Relationship Marketing: Theory and Practice*. London: Paul Chapman, 1996.

Rice, Faye, 'Be a Smarter Frequent Flyer'. *Fortune*, 22 February 1993, pp. 56–60.

Rifa, *Vi skapar framtidens Rifa*. Stockholm, 1983.

Robèrt, Karl-Henrik, *Det nödvändiga steget*. Stockholm: Affärsförlaget Mediautveckling, 1992.

Roddick, Anita, *Body and Soul*. New York: Crown, 1991.

Rogers, Martha, 'Foreword' to Newell, Frederick, *loyalty.com*. New York: McGraw-Hill, 2000, pp. xii–xv.

Root, Paul H., 'Relationship Marketing in the Age of Paradox: What Do We Know? What Do We Need to Know?' Presentation at the *14th American Marketing Association Faculty Consortium*, Emory Business School, Atlanta, GA, June 1994.

Rossander, Olle, *Japanskt ledarskap*. Stockholm: Svenska Dagbladet/Affärsvärlden, 1992.

Rowan, Roy, 'The 50 Biggest Mafia Bosses'. *Fortune*, 10 November 1986, pp. 20–32.

The Royal Society for the Encouragement of Arts, Manufacture & Commerce, *Tomorrow's Company: The Role of Business in a Changing World*. London, 1994.

Russell, Bertrand, *The Problems of Philosophy*. London: Oxford University Press, 1948 (1912).

Rust, Roland T., Zahorik, Anthony J. and Keiningham, Timothy L., *Return on Quality*. Chicago, IL: Probus, 1994.

Rust, Roland T., Zeithaml, Valerie A. and Lemon, Katherine N., *Driving Customer Equity*. New York: The Free Press, 2000.

Ryals, Lynette and Payne, Adrian, 'Customer Relationship Management in Financial Services: Towards Information-Enabled Relationship Marketing'. *Journal of Strategic Marketing*, no. 9, 2001, pp. 3–27.

Salzer, Miriam, *Identity Across Borders: A Study in the IKEA-World*. Linköping: University of Linköping, 1994.

Saren, Mike J. and Tzokas, Nikos X., 'The Nature of the Product in Market Relationships'. In Bloemer, J., Lemmik, J. and Kasper, H. (eds.), *Marketing: Its Dynamics and Challenges, Proceedings from the 23rd EMAC Conference*. Maastricht: European Marketing Academy, May 1994.

SAS, *The Quality Book*. Stockholm: SAS, 1987.

Scheuing, Eberhard E., *The Power of Partnering*. New York: Amacom, 1994.

Scheuing, Eberhard E., *Creating Customers for Life*. Portland, OR: Productivity Press, 1995.

Schlender, Brenton R., 'Apple's Japanese Ally'. *Fortune*, 4 November 1991, pp. 95–6.

Schlossberg, Howard, 'Frequent Mileage Club Sends Consumers Running to Shoe Stores'. *Marketing News*, 3 August 1992, p. 12.

Schneider, Benjamin, 'HRM – A Service Perspective'. *Service Industry Management*, 5(1), 1994, pp. 64–76.

Schön, Donald A., *The Reflective Practitioner – How Professionals Think in Action*. New York: Basic Books, 1983.

Schultz, Don E. and Kitchen, Philip J., *Communicating Globally*. Lincolnwood, IL: NTC Business Books, 2000.

Schultz, Don E. and Walters, Jeffrey S., *Measuring Brand Communication ROI*. New York: Association of National Advertisers, 1997.

Scott, John, *Social Network Analysis*. London: Sage, 1991.

Senge, Peter M., *The Fifth Discipline*. New York: Currency/Doubleday, 1990.

Sewell, Carl, *Customers for Life*. New York: Doubleday, 1990.

Shamir, Boas, 'Between Gratitude and Gratuity'. *Annals of Tourism Research*, **11**, 1984, pp. 59–78.

Shaw, R. and McDonald, Malcolm, *Marketing Accountability: The New Discipline*. Cranfield, UK: Cranfield School of Management, 2000.

Sheth, Jagdish N. and Parvatiyar, Atul (eds.), *Handbook of Relationship Marketing*. Thousand Oaks, CA: Sage, 2000.

Shostack, G. Lynn, 'How to Design a Service'. In Donnelly, J. H. and George, W. R. (eds.), *Marketing of Services*. Chicago, IL: American Marketing Association, 1981.

Sisula-Tulokas, Lena, *Dröjmålsskador vid passagerartransport*. Helsingfors: Finlands Juristförbund, 1985.

Skandia Annual Report Supplements. Stockholm: Skandia, 1994–1999.

Smith, Craig, 'The New Corporate Philanthropy'. *Harvard Business Review*, May–June 1994, pp. 105–16.

Smith, P. G. and Laage-Hellman, J., 'Small Group Analysis of Industrial Networks'. In Axelsson, Björn and Easton, Geoffrey (eds.), *Industrial Networks*. London: Routledge, 1992.

Snehota, Ivan and Söderlund, Magnus, 'Relationship Marketing – What Does It Promise and What Does It Deliver?' In Andersson, Per (ed.), *Proceedings from the 27th EMAC Conference, Track 1, Market Relationships*. Stockholm: EMAC, May 1998.

Södergren, Birgitta, *När pyramiderna rivits*. Stockholm: Timbro/Affärsledaren, 1987.

Södergren, Birgitta, *Decentralisering: Förändring i företag och arbetsliv*. Stockholm: EFI, 1992.

Söderlund, Magnus, *Den nöjda kunden*. Malmö: Liber, 1997.

Solomon, Robert C., *Ethics and Excellence*. Oxford: Oxford University Press, 1992.

Stacey, Ralph D., *Strategic Management and Organisational Dynamics*. London: Pitman, 2nd edition, 1996.

Stenbacka, Caroline, *Brand Visibility*. Helsingfors: Hanken Svenska Handelshögskolan, 1998.

Stern, Louis W. and Reve, Torger, 'Distribution Channels as Political Economies: A Framework for Comparative Analysis'. *Journal of Marketing*, **44**, Summer 1980, pp. 52–64.

Stern, Louis W., El-Ansary, Adel I. and Coughlan, Anne T., *Marketing Channels*. Upper Saddle River, NJ: Prentice-Hall, 1996.

Stewart, Thomas A., *Intellectual Capital*. New York: Currency/Doubleday, 1997.

Storbacka, Kaj, *The Nature of Customer Relationship Profitability*. Helsinki: Swedish School of Economics and Business Administration, 1994.

Storbacka, Kaj, Strandvik, Tore and Grönroos, Christian, 'Managing Customer Relationships for Profit: The Dynamics of Relationship Quality'. *Service Industry Management*, **5**(5), 1994, pp. 21–38.

Strandvik, Tore and Törnroos, Jan-Åke, 'Discovering Relationscapes – Extending the Horizon of Relationship Strategies in Marketing'. In Meenaghan, Tony (ed.), *New and Evolving Paradigms: The Emerging Future of Marketing, Conference Proceedings*. Chicago, IL: American Marketing Association and University College Dublin, 1997.

Sundbo, Jon, *The Organization and Innovation in Services*. Roskilde: Roskilde University Press, 1998.

Sveiby, Karl Erik, *The New Organizational Wealth*. San Francisco, CA: Berret-Koehler, 1997.

Taira, Koji and Wada, Teiichi, 'Business–Government Relations in Modern Japan: A Todai-Yakkai-Zaikai complex?' In Mizruchi, Mark S. and Schwartz, Michael (eds.), *Intercorporate Relations*. Cambridge: Cambridge University Press, 1987.

TARP, *Consumer Complaint Handling in America: An Update Study*. Part II, assigned by US Office of Consumer Affairs, 1 April 1986, p. 50.

Teutenberg, Penny, 'Renaming the Kiwi'. *New Zealand Marketing Magazine*, April 1997, pp. 28–34.

Thorelli, Hans B., 'Networks: Between Markets and Hierarchies'. *Strategic Management Journal*, no. 7, 1986, pp. 37–51.

Time, 'Corruption 101'. 10 May 1993, p. 16.

Tjosvold, Dean, *Teamwork for Customers*. San Francisco, CA: Jossey-Bass, 1993.

Törnqvist, Gunnar, 'Det upplösta rummet – begrepp och teoretiska ansatser inom geografin'. In Karlqvist, Anders (ed.), *Nätverk*. Stockholm: Gidlunds/Institutet för framtidsstudier, 1990.

Tse, Eliza C. and West, Joseph, 'Development Strategies for International Hospitality Markets'. In Teare, Richard and Olsen, Michael (eds.), *International Hospitality Management*. London: Pitman, 1992.

Tuominen, Pekka, 'Investor Relationship Marketing'. In Tuominen, Pekka (ed.), *Emerging Perspectives in Marketing*. Turku, Finland: Turku School of Economics and Business Administration, 1996, pp. 185–210.

TurnIT, *Annual Report*. Stockholm, 2000.

Vandermerwe, Sandra, *From Tin Soldiers to Russian Dolls: Creating Added Value Through Services*. Oxford: Butterworth-Heinemann, 1993.

Varey, Richard J. and Lewis, Barbara R. (eds.), *Internal Marketing*. London: Routledge, 2000.

Verbeke, Willem and Peelen, Ed, 'Redefining the New Selling Practices in an Era of Hyper Competition'. Paper presented at the workshop *Relationship Marketing in an Era of Hypercompetition*. Erasmus University and EIASM, Rotterdam, May 1996.

Voima, Päivi and Grönroos, Christian, 'Internal Marketing: A Relationship Perspective'. In Baker, Michael J. (ed.), *Companion Encyclopedia of Marketing*. London: Routledge, 1999.

von Friedrichs-Grängsjö, Yvonne, *Destinationsmarknadsföring*. Stockholm: Stockholm University, 2001.

von Hippel, E., *The Sources of Innovation*. Oxford: Oxford University Press, 1988.

Waksberg, Arkadij, *Sovjetmaffian*. Stockholm: Norstedts, 1992.

Waksberg, Arkadij, 'Rysk prostitution går över alla gränser'. *Svenska Dagbladet*, 13 June 1994.

Walsh, James, 'The Triads Go Global'. Cover Story, *Time*, 1 February 1993, pp. 36–41.

Ward, Tony, Frew, Edwina and Caldow, Debra, 'An Extended List of the Dimensions of "Relationship" in Consumer Service Product Marketing: A Pilot Study'. In Meenaghan, Tony (ed.), *New and Evolving Paradigms: The Emerging Future of Marketing, Conference Proceedings*. Chicago, IL: American Marketing Association and University College Dublin, 1997.

Webster, Frederick E., 'The Changing Role of Marketing in the Corporation'. *Journal of Marketing*, no. 56, October 1992, pp. 1–17.

Weick, Karl E., *The Social Psychology of Organizing*. Reading, MA: Addison-Wesley, 1979.

Weitz, Barton A. and Jap, Sandy D., 'Relationship Marketing and Distribution Channels'. *Journal of the Academy of Marketing Science*, **23**(4), Fall 1995, pp. 305–20.

Wennberg, Inge, interview with Göran Arvidsson, 'Internpriser behövs'. *Ekonomi & Styrning*, no. 2, 1994, pp. 18–20.

Whiting, Rick, 'Dangerous Liaisons'. *Software Magazine*, no. 18, April 1998, pp. 20–6.

Wiedenbaum, Murray and Hughes, Samuel, *The Bamboo Network*. New York: The Free Press, 1996.

Wikström, Solveig and Normann, Richard, *Knowledge and Value*. London: Routledge, 1994.

Wikström, Solveig, Lundkvist, Anders and Beckérus, Åke, *Det interaktiva företaget*. Stockholm: Svenska Förlaget, 1998.

Wilkinson, Ian F. and Young, Louise C., 'Business Dancing – Understanding and Managing Interfirm Relations'. *Asia-Australia Marketing Journal*, **2**(1), 1994, pp. 67–79.

Williamson, Oliver E., *Markets and Hierarchies: Analysis and Antitrust Implications*. New York: The Free Press, 1975.

Williamson, Oliver E., 'The Economics of Organization: The Transaction Cost Approach'. *American Journal of Sociology*, **87**(3), 1981, pp. 548–77.

Williamson, Oliver E., *The Economic Institutions of Capitalism*. New York: The Free Press, 1985.

Williamson, Oliver E., 'The Firm as a Nexus of Treaties: an Introduction'. In Aoki, Masahiko, Gustafsson, Bo and Williamson, Oliver E. (eds.), *The Firm as a Nexus of Treaties*. London: Sage, 1990.

Wilson, Aubrey, *The Marketing of Professional Services*. London: McGraw-Hill, 1972.

Winai, Peter, *Gränsorganisationer*. Malmö: Liber, 1989.

Womack, James P., Jones, Daniel T. and Roos, Daniel, *The Machine that Changed the World*. New York: Macmillan, 1990.

Woodruffe, Helen, *Services Marketing*. London: Pitman, 1995.

Worthington, S. and Horne S., 'Charity Affinity Credit Cards – Marketing Synergy for Both Issuers and Charities?' *Journal of Marketing Management*, **9**, 1993, pp. 301–13.

Wright, Richard W. and Pauli, Gunter A., *The Second Wave*. London: Waterlow, 1987.

Wurman, Richard Samuel, *Information Anxiety*. New York: Doubleday, 1989.

Yunus, Muhammad, *Grameen Bank: Experiences and Reflections*. Bangladesh: Grameen Bank, 1992.

Zeithaml, Valerie A. and Bitner, Mary Jo, *Services Marketing*. New York: Irwin McGraw-Hill, 2000.

Zeithaml, Valerie A., Parasuraman, A. and Berry, Leonard L., *Delivering Quality Service*. New York: The Free Press, 1990.

Zeithaml, Valerie A., Parasuraman, A. and Malhotra, Arvind, *A Conceptual Framework for Understanding e-Service Quality*. Boston, MA: Marketing Science Institute (MSI), 2000.

Zohar, Danah and Marshall, Ian, *The Quantum Society*. London: Bloomsbury 1993.

Zuboff, Shoshana, *In the Age of the Smart Machine*. New York: Basic Books, 1988.

Index

Marketing titles from Butterworth-Heinemann

Student List

Creating Powerful Brands (second edition), Leslie de Chernatony and Malcolm McDonald
Direct Marketing in Practice, Brian Thomas and Matthew Housden
eMarketing eXcellence, PR Smith and Dave Chaffey
Fashion Marketing, Margaret Bruce and Tony Hines
Innovation in Marketing, Peter Doyle and Susan Bridgewater
Internal Marketing, Pervaiz Ahmed and Mohammed Rafiq
International Marketing (third edition), Stanley J. Paliwoda and Michael J. Thomas
Integrated Marketing Communications, Tony Yeshin
Key Customers, Malcolm McDonald, Beth Rogers, Diana Woodburn
Marketing Briefs, Sally Dibb and Lyndon Simkin
Marketing in Travel and Tourism (third edition), Victor T. C. Middleton with Jackie R. Clarke
Marketing Plans (fifth edition), Malcolm McDonald
Marketing: the One Semester Introduction, Geoff Lancaster and Paul Reynolds
Market-Led Strategic Change (third edition), Nigel F. Piercy
Relationship Marketing for Competitive Advantage, Adrian Payne, Martin Christopher,
    Moira Clark and Helen Peck
The New Marketing, Malcolm McDonald and Hugh Wilson
Relationship Marketing: Strategy & Implementation, Helen Peck, Adrian Payne,
    Martin Christopher and Moira Clark
Strategic Marketing Management (second edition), Richard M. S. Wilson and Colin Gilligan
Strategic Marketing: Planning and Control (second edition), Graeme Drummond and John Ensor
Successful Marketing Communications, Cathy Ace
Tales from the Market Place, Nigel F. Piercy
The CIM Handbook of Export Marketing, Chris Noonan
The Fundamentals of Advertising (second edition), John Wilmshurst, Adrian Mackay
Total Relationship Marketing (second edition), Evert Gummesson

Forthcoming

Marketing Logistics (second edition), Martin Christopher, Helen Peck
Marketing Research for Managers (third edition), Sunny Crouch and Matthew Housden
Marketing Strategy (third edition), Paul Fifield
Political Marketing, Phil Harris and Dominic Wring
Relationship Marketing (second edition), Martin Christopher, Adrian Payne and
    David Ballantyne
The Fundamentals and Practice of Marketing (fourth edition), John Wilmshurst and
    Adrian Mackay
The Marketing Book (fifth edition), Michael J. Baker (ed.)

Professional list

Cause Related Marketing, Sue Adkins
Creating Value, Shiv S. Mathur, Alfred Kenyon
Cybermarketing (second edition), Pauline Bickerton and Matthew Bickerton
Cyberstrategy, Pauline Bickerton, Matthew Bickerton and Kate Simpson-Holley
Direct Marketing in Practice, Brian Thomas and Matthew Housden
e-Business, J. A. Matthewson
Effective Promotional Practice for eBusiness, Cathy Ace
Excellence in Advertising (second edition), Leslie Butterfield
Fashion Marketing, Margaret Bruce and Tony Hines
Financial Services and the Multimedia Revolution, Paul Lucas, Rachel Kinniburgh, Donna Terp
From Brand Vision to Brand Evaluation, Leslie de Chernatony
Go-to-Market Strategy, Lawrence Friedman
Internal Marketing, Pervaiz Ahmed and Mohammed Rafiq
Marketing Made Simple, Geoff Lancaster and Paul Reynolds
Marketing Professional Services, Michael Roe
Marketing Strategy (second edition), Paul Fifield
Market-Led Strategic Change (third edition), Nigel F. Piercy
The New Marketing, Malcolm McDonald and Hugh Wilson
The Channel Advantage, Lawrence Friedman, Tim Furey
The CIM Handbook of Export Marketing, Chris Noonan
The Committed Enterprise, Hugh Davidson
The Fundamentals of Corporate Communications, Richard Dolphin
The Marketing Plan in Colour, Malcolm McDonald, Peter Morris

Forthcoming

Essential Law for Marketers, Ardi Kolah
Marketing Logistics (second edition), Martin Christopher, Helen Peck
Marketing Research for Managers (third edition), Sunny Crouch and Matthew Housden
Marketing Strategy (third edition), Paul Fifield
Political Marketing, Phil Harris and Dominic Wring

For more information on all these titles, as well as the ability to buy online, please visit
www.bh.com/marketing

Learning Resources
Centre